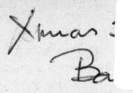

Praise for *The Real Life of Anthony Burgess*

'Clearly a subject so protean, loquacious and self-contradictory requires a biographer prepared to stand back and regard him with a detached and quizzical eye. Biswell succeeds admirably, adopting just the right posture throughout'
Gordon Bowker, *Independent*

'Andrew Biswell's new biography, which generously allows Burgess's friends and enemies to speak in their own voices, [. . .] presents Burgess's life with a sobriety and care that are admirable'
Colin Burrow, *London Review of Books*

'Balanced, lucid, good-humoured, packed full of information and written in an engaging style, this biography is easily the best place to start to get to grips with Burgess'
Hal Jensen, *Times Literary Supplement*

'Biswell's sensitivity to how events can become distorted does not mean the book becomes hagiographic. For all Burgess's grandstanding and pontificating, he emerges as a conflicted, uncertain and unhappy individual'
Stuart Kelly, *Scotland on Sunday*

'Andrew Biswell's magnificent and meticulously researched life of Anthony Burgess is a reminder of just what riches are lost if we ignore those creative individuals who actually write the literature [. . .] This is a wonderful book. Biswell made me want to go and read Burgess. You cannot ask more of a biography than that'
Gary Day, *Times Higher Educational Supplement*

'What Andrew Biswell has done in this truly excellent biography is to show that almost everything to do with Burgess was a more or less disastrous, more or less brilliant muddle [. . .] He didn't just make himself up as he went along; he made up a fair bit of his past as well. Consequently, his life became a chaotic docu-drama to which the judicious Biswell brings order of a sort – though, our biographer being a wise and discerning fellow, not too much'
George Walden, *New Statesman*

'Andrew Biswell was determined to set the record straight, as his title suggests [. . .] The artist who emerges from this portrait is lavishly gifted, and not so much a liar as a fabulator – the novelist, after all, spends his time making up plausible lives, so is it any wonder that he might be driven to invent a past for himself?'
John Banville, *Irish Times*

THE REAL LIFE OF ANTHONY BURGESS

Andrew Biswell has been researching and publishing articles on Anthony Burgess since 1995. He is a lecturer in the English department at Manchester Metropolitan University, and has previously worked as a fiction critic for the *Times Literary Supplement*, *Daily Telegraph*, *Guardian*, *Boston Globe* and *Scotland on Sunday*. He lives in Manchester and Aberdeenshire.

THE REAL LIFE OF
ANTHONY BURGESS

Andrew Biswell

PICADOR

First published 2005 by Picador

First published in paperback 2006 by Picador
an imprint of Pan Macmillan Ltd
Pan Macmillan, 20 New Wharf Road, London N1 9RR
Basingstoke and Oxford
Associated companies throughout the world
www.panmacmillan.com

ISBN-13: 978-0-330-48171-7
ISBN-10: 0-330-48171-1

1 3 5 7 9 8 6 4 2

A CIP catalogue record for this book is available from
the British Library.

Typeset by SetSystems Ltd, Saffron Walden, Essex
Printed and bound in Great Britain by
Mackays of Chatham plc, Chatham, Kent

To Jane Stevenson and Peter Davidson,
who took me to the magnetic North.

What is there to look at? and of the leopard, spotted
underneath and on its toes:

Leopards are not spotted underneath, but in old
illuminations they are, and on Indian printed
muslins, and I like the idea that they are.

Marianne Moore, letter to Ezra Pound, 9 January 1919

Contents

1

Manchester

John Burgess Wilson was born in Manchester at midday on Sunday, 25 February 1917, just after the pubs had opened. His mother, Elizabeth Burgess Wilson, gave birth to this, her second child, at 91 Carisbrook Street in Harpurhey – a small, rented house in a working-class district of north Manchester, famous at that time for its back-to-back slum housing and bad plumbing.

If Burgess's ancestral line is difficult to reconstruct, this is partly because he engaged in a good deal of public and private fantasizing about who he was descended from, laying down an alarming number of false trails in interviews and autobiographical writings. Without troubling to consult the official records of births, deaths and marriages, he drew up a version of his family tree in or around 1985, as he prepared to write the first volume of his 'confessions', *Little Wilson and Big God*.* The story as Burgess tells it begins in 1746, the year of the battle of Culloden, when Prince Charles Edward Stuart, the grandson of King James II, is said to have fathered an illegitimate child in Manchester. This boy, John Stuart, was supposedly adopted by the Wilson family and took their

---

* This family tree is preserved in the archive of his unpublished papers (box 100, folder 1) acquired after his death by the Harry Ransom Center at the University of Texas at Austin.

surname. John's son, Joseph Samuel Wilson, a soldier by profession, was born in 1778. Joseph begot another Joseph Wilson, born in 1800. He, too, became a soldier before returning to Manchester, the city of his birth, where he seems to have gone into business, running a herbalist's shop.

The first of the female Wilsons to emerge is Anthony Burgess's paternal grandmother, Mary Ann Finnegan, born about 1846. Her family, originally from Tipperary, is said to have been wholly Irish and wholly illiterate. She married the herbalist's son, another John Wilson, who was born in or around 1843. This John, known to the family as Jack, boasted that he had once met the Duke of Wellington, and spoke of the Prussians as 'the Prooshians'. He kept a pub in Manchester which Burgess calls the Derby Inn – probably the Derby Arms, which still exists on Cheetham Hill Road, about a mile to the west of Harpurhey. John Wilson's marriage to Mary Ann Finnegan produced four sons: John, James, William and Joseph. The youngest of these children, Joseph (or Joe) Wilson, born in 1883, was, among other things, a piano-player. He fathered two children by Elizabeth Burgess: a daughter, Muriel, born in 1910, and John Burgess Wilson, who reinvented himself in 1956 as 'Anthony Burgess'.

Joseph Wilson's career was so haphazard that it is difficult to say precisely what his trade was. One family legend has him as a door-to-door encyclopaedia salesman, who was forced to run away to Scotland when his employers accused him of stealing money. The idea of being a 'piano-player', which is one of the titles he claimed for himself, is rich in its seedy associations – half a world away from the drawing-room or concert-hall respectability of the 'pianist'. The family tree describes Joseph, perhaps rather grandly, as a 'cashier'. Yet when John Burgess Wilson enrolled at the Xaverian College in Manchester in 1928, his father stated his occupation as 'tobacconist'. In February 1917 he was a lance corporal in the Army Pay Corps at Preston, and shortly after the war he found a job at Swift's Beef Market in Manchester. Joseph began as a musician and ended up as a shopkeeper, but his fondness for spending as much time as possible betting at race-courses and drinking in pubs meant that he found it not at all difficult to be given the sack on a regular basis.

Both Joseph Wilson and Elizabeth Burgess were involved with the music halls in Glasgow and Manchester, although the details of what they did there and when are far from clear. Joseph, according to his son, was an 'adequate' piano-player and 'a superb sight-reader'.* He sang badly but enthusiastically, especially when drunk. Elizabeth, born to a Protestant family in Scotland in 1888, was a professional singer and dancer – or, in the language of the time, a 'soubrette'. Joseph is said to have worked in Glasgow before the First World War as a piano-player for the theatrical impresario Fred Karno, who had famously discovered the brothers Sidney and Charlie Chaplin. It is more than likely that Joseph and Elizabeth met when they were performing together in Glasgow. Burgess suggests as much in *Little Wilson and Big God*, but in an earlier autobiographical fragment he identifies his mother as a Lancastrian and implies that his parents' first meeting took place at the Ardwick Empire in Manchester.† He consistently refers to Elizabeth as Joseph's wife, but they seem not to have married in Scotland or England: the files at the General Register Office in Edinburgh show no trace of any marriage between a Burgess and a Wilson in Scotland between 1900 and 1920; and the English public records are equally silent on the question of a legal union. Either Elizabeth and Joseph were unmarried, or else (as seems possible) they were married in church by a Catholic priest, and were unwilling to pay the required fee to make an official declaration of the fact.

What is clear is that, after Elizabeth Burgess had met Joseph, she abandoned her music-hall career in order to raise her children. The first of these, Muriel, was to die suddenly at the age of eight.‡ The

---

* Burgess, *This Man and Music* (London: Hutchinson, 1982), p. 11.
† See Burgess, 'You've Had Your Time: Being the Beginning of an Autobiography', *Malahat Review*, no. 44 (1977), pp. 10–16.
‡ Seven is the age that Burgess gives for her in his autobiography. But he also told Samuel Coale, who interviewed him for the journal *Modern Fiction Studies*, that

other child, a son, was given the traditional family name John (or Jack, sometimes Jackie). His mother's surname became his middle name, and later he was to take the confirmation name Anthony. John Anthony Burgess Wilson was to marry twice: once in 1942, to Llewela Jones (who died in 1968); and for the second time in 1968, to an Italian divorcee, Liliana Johnson, née Macellari. This second Mrs Wilson, also known as Liana Burgess, is now in her mid-seventies and flourishing in Monaco. Her son, Paolo Andrea, who renamed himself Andrew Burgess Wilson in adult life, was born in 1964 and died in 2002, at the age of thirty-seven.

This family tree is a characteristic Burgessian production in that it is largely based on family legend, rumour, speculation and wistful sectarian yearnings. The bold assertion that Burgess's great-great-great-grandfather was the illegitimate son of Prince Charles Edward Stuart (otherwise known as the Young Pretender or Bonnie Prince Charlie) is flimsy and undocumented. After the Jacobites were defeated at Culloden Moor in April 1746, Charles successfully evaded capture by the English and fled to France. He is connected to Manchester by nothing more substantial than a Jacobite folk song, 'Farewell, Manchester, Sadly I Depart', which stops well short of identifying him as the father of John Stuart or John Wilson.* Burgess failed to mention the Stuart connection anywhere in his

---

Muriel had expired at the age of four. His sense of chronology is equally uncertain when he tries to identify the year in which his mother and sister died. In various interviews, Burgess claims to have been anywhere between four months and two years old when they succumbed to the influenza epidemic. See, for example, Samuel Coale, 'An Interview with Anthony Burgess', *Modern Fiction Studies*, vol. 27, no. 3 (Autumn 1981), pp. 429–51; Geoffrey Aggeler, *Anthony Burgess: The Artist as Novelist* (Alabama: University of Alabama Press, 1979), pp. 1–29; Paul Boytinck, *Anthony Burgess: An Annotated Bibliography and Reference Guide* (New York: Garland, 1985), pp. x–xiii; 'Anthony Burgess: Unearthly Powers' in *Writers Revealed*, ed. by Rosemary Harthill (London: BBC Books, 1989), pp. 13–24.

* Charles Edward Stuart (1720–1788) was the grandson of King James II, claimant to the crowns of England and Scotland, and leader of the 1745 army of Scottish Jacobite rebels. He died in exile in Rome.

published work. The family tree, unmistakably in Burgess's handwriting, was discovered among his private papers after the contents
of his Monaco apartment were sold. Whether it was intended as a
joke or as a private piece of posturing, this implausible document
indicates that he was attracted by the idea of royal blood having
entered his family in the mid-eighteenth century. And it was particularly exciting, from the point of view of a writer ill-disposed towards
the monarchy of Protestant England, that this should be dissident,
Catholic blood.

Another doubtful claim to ancestry is worth considering. Burgess
stated in his memoirs that he believed himself to have been
descended from a sixteenth-century Jack Wilson, who was a singer
and boy-player in the Lord Chamberlain's company. He is named in
Shakespeare's First Folio as the actor who performs the song 'Sigh
no more, ladies, sigh no more' in *Much Ado About Nothing*. Again,
there is no real basis for this story, and it makes sense only in the
context of a twentieth-century England which was hypersensitive to
matters of class and heredity. If Burgess was troubled by a nagging
sense that his theatrical family lacked distinction, he could represent
them as being more significant by putting about the rumour that at
one time they had possessed impressive-sounding Shakespearean
connections. His anxiousness to claim grand ancestors might profitably be compared with Shakespeare's own attempts to acquire the
trappings of gentility – a subject which Burgess explores at length in
his Shakespeare biography (1970).

*

The story of John Burgess Wilson's early life is dominated by early
death. He was born when the First World War was at its height.
The Second World War erupted before he had completed his education. His father was dead before Burgess had turned twenty-one.
Perhaps the most significant losses were the earliest: his sister and
mother both died unexpectedly in November 1918, three months
before he reached his second birthday. They were victims of the so-
called Spanish influenza, a particularly deadly variant of the flu

virus, which killed 27 million people – more than twice as many as the First World War – in Europe, Africa, Asia and America between 1917 and 1919. The symptoms of the influenza which killed Elizabeth and Muriel are well documented: their temperatures rose; they began to cough blood; they developed high fever and delirium; their lungs filled with choking fluid; their lips turned blue from lack of oxygen; they developed pneumonia; and then their hearts failed. Most patients died within forty-eight hours of showing the first signs that they were ill.* Nobody knew how to treat the influenza, or how to prevent its spread. Nothing could be done except to wear masks in public places, and to bury the dead in mass graves. Joseph Wilson was back in Harpurhey, on leave from his barracks at Preston, when his wife and daughter fell victim to the influenza, which quickly manifested itself, according to their death certificates, as acute broncho-pneumonia. Muriel died first, on Friday, 15 November 1918. Elizabeth's end came four days later. Joseph registered both deaths, which had been certified by Dr J. Kerr-Bell, a Licentiate of the Royal College of Physicians.

Burgess always insisted that he had retained no direct memories of his mother and sister. Most of what he knew about them came from a photographer's sepia studio portrait, which must have been taken a month or two before they died.† Muriel is on the left, looking directly at the camera, a well-nourished child with a white ribbon in her blonde hair. The infant John Wilson, jug-eared and puzzled-looking, sits in the centre on his mother's knee.

---

* For a full account of the origins, symptoms and extent of the Spanish influenza epidemic, see Gina Kolata, *Flu: The Story of the Great Influenza Pandemic of 1918 and the Search for the Virus That Caused It* (London: Macmillan, 2000).

† Burgess writes in *Little Wilson and Big God: Being the First Part of the Confessions of Anthony Burgess* (London: Heinemann, 1987) that 'termites and damp heat destroyed any photographs I had of my family or own early life' (p. vi). This is not entirely true. A badly damaged album of his family photographs, including one of his father and several of himself as a boy, was discovered in his house on Malta after his death. It is now in the archive of the Anthony Burgess Center at the University of Angers in France.

Elizabeth herself, a slender and elegant woman of thirty, looks at her son with a slight smile, her hands clasped around his ribs to support him. Her long hair is neatly pinned up. She is dressed respectably, perhaps expensively for the time, and adorned with a wedding ring, a bracelet, and a large brooch on the front of her dress. She gives the impression of being a happy middle-class mother rather than the voluptuous theatrical blonde of whom Burgess spoke later on.

Interviewed in 1988 by Anthony Clare for the *In the Psychiatrist's Chair* series on BBC Radio 4, Burgess was asked how he thought the death of his mother had affected him as a child.

> I had to grow up without something I envied in others – you know, the mother, the home atmosphere . . . I wonder whether this does something to one in later life – whether one becomes less able to give affection or to take affection – because one never had this early filial experience.

'I was always frightened of declaring friendship,' he added, 'because I had no infantile cushion to which I could refer.'*

The motherless boy was sent to live with his maternal aunt, Ann Bromley, a war widow with two daughters, Elsie and Betty. They lived on Delaunays Road in Higher Crumpsall, another suburb of north Manchester, which lies to the north-west of Harpurhey. Burgess's most vivid memory of living with this aunt, whom he now called mother, related to a picture of a gypsy woman (captioned 'BEWARE') which hung above his bed. In his dreams, a flood of snakes and horse shit would cascade into the bedroom from behind the picture. He would wake up screaming, but his aunt would not take the picture away. He was still having nightmares about snakes as 'vitalized faeces' when he was in his seventies.

In his interview with Anthony Clare, he was prepared to concede that the death of the mother he never knew had impaired his

---

* Burgess, *In the Psychiatrist's Chair*, interview with Dr Anthony Clare, BBC Radio 4, 27 July 1988.

subsequent emotional development, engendering a reticence that had extended well into adult life. He said that he found it difficult to make unambiguous declarations of love, because he was not altogether sure what love was supposed to mean. Professor Clare later commented on Burgess's emotional vocabulary in this interview: 'He talks of *rage* and *lust*. He has difficulty talking of affection and love.'*

What Burgess ended up doing when he found himself deprived of maternal affection was to invent a dream-mother from the characters that he found in literature. He described the process to Clare:

> When I read Somerset Maugham's *Cakes and Ale*, I came across the character of Rosie Driffield. Rosie's a bit of a slut: she sleeps with any man to give him pleasure. She's totally generous. I often see elements of my mother – my mythical mother – in this character.

It's said of Rosie in Maugham's novel that 'She must have been dreadfully common', chiefly because she had worked as a barmaid before marrying the writer, Edward Driffield.† The book's narrator, John Ashenden, who meets Rosie as a boy and later becomes one of her innumerable lovers, describes her as 'a rather large blonde woman' who 'smiled with her lips and with her eyes and there was in her smile something that even then I recognized as singularly pleasant'. He is struck by her 'disarming frankness' and her 'zest of life'. Rosie is presented as a life-force: she has little time for literature, which is otherwise one of the book's main preoccupations, but seems to represent a vigour that is lacking among Maugham's genteel London bookmen and their boringly dependable spouses.

---

* *The Burgess Variations: Part One*, directed by David Thompson, broadcast BBC 2, 26 December 1999.
† W. Somerset Maugham, *Cakes and Ale, or, The Skeleton in the Cupboard* (London: Heinemann, 1930), p. 29.

These were the details that Burgess chose to invest with a private significance, fixating on Rosie as a robust earth-mother figure, and wishing to imagine that his real mother had in some sense resembled her. They are echoed in a brief sketch in Burgess's later novel, *The Pianoplayers* (1986), which – as he acknowledged – was an attempt to write in detail about his parents' lives in the music halls and silent cinemas. In the early typescript drafts of *The Pianoplayers*, the Manchester narrator, Ellen Henshaw, tells us that she, like Burgess, was born on 25 February 1917. Ellen's mother, who has died during the Spanish influenza outbreak, is said to have been a soubrette on the music-hall stage, a member of the chorus of provincial shows, though 'never in London', and part of a 'travelling pantomime company'. 'I shouldn't have been surprised if my mother had played around a bit in her time,' the breathless heroine tells us, 'but she was none the worse for that, who am I to talk?' It is said in her defence that the average life of an itinerant chorus girl 'wasn't as Moral as they said it was'.* The nature of this mother's 'playing around' is left deliberately vague, but the general impression of guiltless, liberated sexuality is hard to miss.

Burgess's basis for implying that his own mother was 'a bit of a slut' is unclear. Elizabeth was hardly ever mentioned by Burgess's widowed father, nor by his adoptive relations. Nobody in his childhood ever told him that he looked like her, and in any case he took after the male side of the family. Joseph Wilson was undemonstrative, even evasive, on the subject of his first wife, preferring where possible not to bring her up in conversation. 'My father,' Burgess told Clare, 'was good enough never to come in drunkenly and say, "You lived and she died." But I sensed a certain resentment.'

When Burgess was asked by others about his real mother later in life, he offered various accounts of her life and background, either derived from things he'd been told about Elizabeth or founded on his own imaginings. He told Samuel Coale:

---

* Burgess, *The Pianoplayers* (London: Hutchinson, 1986), p. 41.

My mother had no living relatives. Family disappeared. Didn't know her at all. . . . An unusual woman, judging from the photographs, a very beautiful blonde. . . . She was involved in the old music hall, as it was, in Manchester. She was a dancer and singer. She was for a time understudy to [José] Collins.*

When he published an early fragment of autobiography in 1977, Burgess went into more detail on the subject, claiming that Elizabeth had been 'the daughter of a respectable small tradesman and became a singer and dancer, chiefly in such Manchester music halls as the Gentlemen's Concert Rooms (popularly known as the Snotty Parlour)'. He added that her stage name had been 'The Beautiful Belle Burgess', and described her appearance in a surviving photograph as that of 'a comely smiling woman with a mass of fair hair'.† There is nothing to verify that Elizabeth actually performed under this name, since no theatrical posters or flyers referring to a 'Beautiful Belle Burgess' have so far come to light; the Gentlemen's Concert Rooms had been completely demolished by 1898, when she was ten years old; and Burgess is mistaken in thinking that his mother's father was a 'respectable small tradesman'.‡

According to the public records in Edinburgh, three Elizabeth Burgesses were born in Scotland in 1888, in Penninghame, North Leith, and Keith. The third of these is the likeliest candidate. She was the daughter of William Strachan, a journeyman blacksmith, and Christina Burgess, a domestic servant who gave her address as 82 Regent Street in Keith in the county of Banff (now Aberdeenshire). Her parents were unmarried, and neither of them was

* Burgess to Samuel Coale, 7 and 11 July 1978.
† Burgess, 'You've Had Your Time', pp. 11–12.
‡ He was thinking of the Gentlemen's Concert Hall on Lower Moseley Street, where Mendelssohn and Chopin had performed in the 1840s. The site was sold in 1897, and the Midland Hotel, where Burgess and his second wife often stayed on their return visits to Manchester in the 1980s, now stands there. See John Parkinson-Bailey, *Manchester: An Architectural History* (Manchester: Manchester University Press, 2000), pp. 63, 134.

recorded as still living in Keith when the 1891 census was taken. Given the absence of a marriage certificate for Elizabeth, the available records seem to have nothing further to say about her until her death on 19 November 1918. What became of her parents is also mysterious, but their trades would have allowed them a good deal of mobility.

The most poignant part of Elizabeth's story is that Burgess had no idea where she was buried. When he was interviewed for Granada Television in 1980, he said that he was thinking about the possibility of acquiring a grave in Moston Cemetery, where his father, mother and sister were buried.* St Joseph's Cemetery in Moston is the largest Catholic burial-ground in north Manchester, and a glance through the records confirms that the graves of Joseph Wilson and his second wife are indeed to be found there. What Burgess didn't know was that his mother and sister had been deposited in a common grave (number 5334) with no identifying headstone at the City of Manchester General Cemetery on Rochdale Road, which marks the western border of Harpurhey. He would have been surprised and embarrassed to discover that this is a Protestant cemetery, since it seems to disprove his assertion that Elizabeth had become a convert to Catholicism when she'd met Joseph.† But it also means that nobody can ever have taken him to visit her grave, or told him where he might find her remains. The hope that he articulated in the interview – that of a posthumous reunion at Moston Cemetery with his father, mother and sister – would have been impossible to fulfil.

In 1922, when Burgess was five years old, his father married a widowed Manchester Irishwoman, Margaret Dwyer (née Byrne). Joseph had known Margaret and her first husband when Elizabeth had been alive. Maggie already had two daughters by her previous marriage, Agnes and Madge, and the two newly conjoined families

---

* *Celebration: Burgess in Manchester*, Granada Television, broadcast 24 October 1980.
† Burgess, 'You've Had Your Time', p. 11.

moved into a series of rooms above a large pub on Lodge Street in
the Miles Platting district of Manchester. This was the Golden
Eagle, which Joseph and Maggie Wilson ran jointly for a couple
of years. It was a very large street-corner pub, now demolished,
containing three downstairs singing rooms, each of which had its
own piano. Hearing all three pianos being played at once while he
was in the upstairs flat was, Burgess said, his earliest experience of
cacophony.*

For Burgess, the crucial fact about his stepmother – for which
he refused to forgive her, even long after she was dead – was that,
although perfectly numerate, she was unable to read. He recalled
her habit of signing cheques by copying her name from a 'greasy'
bit of paper, whose letters were no more meaningful to her than a
string of hieroglyphics. Maggie Wilson, as she was known to her
family, is a palpable presence in the sequence of comic novels which
begins with *Inside Mr Enderby* (1963) and *Enderby Outside* (1968).
The poet Enderby is afflicted with a devouring stepmother, the hated
female figure who has supposedly ruined flesh-and-blood women for
him. As he sits alone, balding, toothless, masturbating heavily and
writing poetry on his lavatory, he puts the blame for this middle-
aged abjection on his traumatic memories of stepmotherly grossness:

> Oh, she had been graceless and coarse, that one. A hundred-
> weight of ringed and brooched blubber, smelling to high heaven
> of female smells, rank as long-hung hare or blown beef, her
> bedroom strewn with soiled bloomers, crumby combinations,
> malodorous bust-bodices. She had swollen finger-joints, puffy
> palms, wrists girdled with fat, slug-white upper arms that, when
> naked, showed indecent as thighs. She was corned, bunioned,
> calloused, varicose-veined. Healthy as a sow, she moaned of
> pains in all her joints, a perpetual migraine, a bad back,
> toothache. 'The pains in me legs,' she would say, 'is killin' me.'
> Her wind was loud, even in public places. 'The doctor says to

* *Burgess at Seventy*, directed by Kevin Jackson, broadcast BBC 2, 21 February
1987.

let it come up. You can always say excuse me.' Her habits were loathsome. She picked her teeth with old tram-tickets, cleaned out her ears with hairclips in whose U-bend earwax was trapped to darken and harden, scratched her private parts through her clothes with a matchbox-rasping noise audible two rooms away, made gross sandwiches of all her meals or cut her meat with scissors, spat chewed bacon-rind or pork-crackling back on her plate, excavated beef-fibres from her cavernous molars and held them up for all the world to see, hooked out larger chunks with a soiled sausage-finger, belched like a ship in the fog, was sick on stout on Saturday nights, tromboned vigorously in the lavatory, ranted without aitches or grammar, scoffed at all books except *Old Moore's Almanac*, whose apocalyptic pictures she could follow. . . . Hate? You've just no idea.*

As he observed his real stepmother's physical eccentricities – belching, farting, vomiting, pube-scratching, earwax-mining – with a cold and journalistic eye, Burgess was storing them away as potential future material. Although he did not vilify Maggie Dwyer in print until she had been dead for more than twenty years, her daughters and other surviving relatives in Manchester recognized the caricature when he sent them a copy of *Inside Mr Enderby* on publication in 1963, and they took justifiable offence.

*

The Wilsons' new family home, the Golden Eagle, was next door to a cinema called The Palace, managed by a Jew named Jakie Innerfield. Silent cinemas such as this allowed Joseph Wilson to earn money in the evenings as a piano-player, accompanying newsreels, Charlie Chaplin comedies, American nationalist epics and uplifting Biblical narratives. According to his son, Joseph rarely undertook such work without first drinking a skinful of beer. On one occasion,

---

* Joseph Kell [i.e. Anthony Burgess], *Inside Mr Enderby* (London: Heinemann, 1963) pp. 27–8.

he peered at the cinema screen through a drunken mist and discerned 'a scene of evident merriment', with a crowd of men eating and drinking around a table. He dutifully banged out a version of 'For He's a Jolly Good Fellow' on the piano. After the film had ended, he was told by the enraged cinema manager that he had been accompanying *The Last Supper*.*

Most of what is known of Joseph Wilson comes out of Burgess's memories and the oblique portrait of him which is given in *The Pianoplayers*. Certain details recur, and these may be regarded as the core of Burgess's narrative about his father. He was a smoker of Woodbines and a drinker of draught Bass. He did most of his drinking in the Alexandra Hotel, Manchester, until he was barred for some piece of bad behaviour. He was musical, with a certain facility for the piano. According to Burgess, Joseph would sometimes accompany his playing in pubs by singing out of tune, 'but that's what they wanted'.† Joseph gave his ten-year-old son what he remembered as the most important music lesson of his life. Sitting him down at the piano in the family home at 261 Moss Lane East, Joseph showed him where to find middle C on the keyboard and indicated the corresponding note in a collection of sheet music entitled *The Music Lover's Portfolio*. The lesson ended there because Joseph was on his way out to go boozing, but Burgess was able to puzzle the rest out for himself. Thinking back to this incident fifty-five years later, he wrote: 'Find middle C and you have found everything.'‡

Joseph is easily caricatured as a feckless drunk, but there are some indications that he encouraged his son to take an interest in the arts. At the age of seven, John was sent for violin lessons to Mr Bradshaw's School of Music, not far from the Wilson family home. It was a fairly joyless experience, as he later recalled: 'I

* Boytinck, *Anthony Burgess: An Annotated Bibliography and Reference Guide*, p. xii.
† *The Burgess Variations: Part One*.
‡ Burgess, *This Man and Music*, p. 18.

treated my violin very badly. I chipped the varnish and broke one of the pegs. My bow was a disgrace, unresined and filthy'.* He learned nothing, not even how to play the open strings, and mastered only the art of faking, as he mimed along with the other young students, without ever sounding a note. Mr Bradshaw, whose business depended on the accumulation of fees, was unwilling to expel any of his pupils, no matter how inept. After a while Burgess started skiving the lessons which his father was paying for, and the enterprise ended, inevitably, with a 'terrible row' when the deception was discovered.

But there was more gratification to be had from the twice-weekly concerts given by the Hallé Orchestra at the Free Trade Hall, which father and son attended regularly from about 1929, when John was twelve. It was at his first Hallé concert that Burgess heard the music of Richard Wagner, which he didn't warm to at first, though he retained a memory of the *Rienzi* overture. Nevertheless, he started to become reluctantly interested in the music he heard there. 'The initial Free Trade Hall experience,' he later said, 'was the most basic experience of my life.'† Listening to the Hallé, he acquired a knowledge of the standard classical repertoire: Bach, Brahms, Beethoven, Richard Strauss's *Don Juan*, Rimsky-Korsakov's *Scheherazade*. Burgess attended diligently to these, but he was genuinely moved and excited by the first performance of *Rio Grande* by Constant Lambert at the Free Trade Hall on 12 November 1929. Lambert's wildly eclectic piece fused jazz and classical music, bridging the supposed divide between 'high' and 'low' forms of music. A similar kind of fusion may be heard in Burgess's own Symphony in C, which aims to bring together the musical styles of Gustav Holst, Benjamin Britten and George Gershwin.

It is clear that Joseph passed on to his son a basic interest, though not a technical expertise, in serious music. He also provided the funds necessary for Burgess's early experiments in building his

---

* Ibid., p. 14.
† *Celebration: Burgess in Manchester.*

own crystal radio sets in his bedroom. Thus equipped, he was able to tune into the musical and cultural programmes of the British Broadcasting Corporation. Listening to the BBC on a Saturday afternoon in 1929, he chanced upon a broadcast of an early performance of Claude Debussy's *Prélude à l'Après-Midi d'un Faune*:

> Searching for Jack Payne and his BBC Dance Orchestra ... I got instead a kind of listening silence with coughs in it, and then a quite incredible flute solo, sinuous, exotic, erotic. I was spellbound. The velvety strings, the skirling clarinets, the harps, the muted horns, the antique cymbals, the flute, above all the flute.*

What this experience represented to Burgess was a moment of revelation which was to echo throughout his subsequent life as a writer and composer. His first encounter with Debussy's tone poem was, as he put it, a 'psychedelic moment ... an instant of recognition of verbally inexpressible spiritual realities, a meaning for the term *beauty*'.[†]

Burgess frequently mentions this moment as a turning point, but the full extent of his musical education through his self-assembled radio kit was much broader. Radio introduced him to the wider canon of early twentieth-century music, and it enabled him to hear works by composers such as Hindemith, Krenek, Honneger and Mossolov. Filled with enthusiasm, Burgess taught himself how to sight-read on the piano. By the time he was fifteen, he says, he could play 'any keyboard piece that did not have rapid runs in it'.[‡] As he advanced through his teens, he became increasingly persuaded by contemporary music. At some point after 1934, he went to the newly built Central Library in Manchester to look at the original

---

* Burgess, *This Man and Music*, p. 17.
† Ibid. Burgess writes in the same volume that he bought, with money given to him for his fifteenth birthday, a printed score of Debussy's *Prélude* (p. 18).
‡ Ibid.

manuscripts of two key Modernist compositions, Stravinsky's *The Rite of Spring* and Schönberg's *Pierre Lunaire*.

Modern drama was another important part of the BBC's output. As a young man, Burgess heard an unabridged radio production of Bernard Shaw's *Back to Methuselah*, a work at that time considered too long and too weighty for the commercial stage. Hungry to know more, Burgess began to read both the *Radio Times* and the *Listener*, a weekly magazine published by the BBC from 1928, which printed transcripts of general radio talks and exegetical musical lectures. The back pages of the *Listener*, edited for the magazine's first twenty-five years by J. R. Ackerley (the author of *Hindoo Holiday*), printed early poems by, among others, W. H. Auden, C. Day-Lewis, Louis MacNeice, Edith Sitwell and Dylan Thomas. The magazine also carried reviews of new novels, operas, films and plays.* The hitherto unexplored worlds of contemporary music and literature began to reveal themselves in detail to the eager and curious Burgess, at an age when he was prepared to be impressed by the shockingly new.

Like many incipient artists of his generation, Burgess was at least partly the product of Lord Reith's BBC. Reith, whose name has become synonymous in Britain with highbrow broadcast culture, was the corporation's founding director-general. He initiated a programming policy that was defiantly anti-popular, willing in principle to give airtime to 'difficult' new Modernist works. Reith's wider aim, as he said, was to 'give the public what we think they need – and not what they want'.† This was in a period when the BBC believed wholeheartedly in its mission (publicly and legally enshrined in the corporation's charter) to civilize and to educate its listeners. These high principles did not long outlast Lord Reith's

* For a full account of Ackerley's tireless promotion of new writing in the 1930s, see Peter Parker's diligently researched biography, *Ackerley* (London: Constable, 1989).
† Quoted in Kate Whitehead, *The Third Programme: A Literary History* (Oxford: Clarendon Press, 1989), p. 8.

retirement in 1938, but they survived long enough to have a formative effect on the young Burgess. Not that he was an uncritical subscriber to the high cultural ethos which Reith was disseminating: he retained a life-long interest in the popular music of the Twenties, Thirties and Forties, chiefly dance music, jazz and numbers from stage musicals. The lyrics of Cole Porter held a particular fascination for him, and he complained in his seventies that large sections of his memory were filled with what he called 'sub-art', meaning tunes and lyrics from the songs of his youth.*

The other area of cultural activity which Burgess inevitably associated with his father was the cinema, particularly the silent films of the 1920s. Joseph Wilson's approach to piano-playing in the Manchester bughouses which employed him is fictionalized very affectionately in *The Pianoplayers*. We learn a great deal about his craft in chapter 3 of the novel, when Billy Henshaw gives his daughter, Ellen, a lesson at the keyboard:

> Here's a chord you can't do without, he said, if you're a picture palace pianoplayer. You use it for fights, burst dams, thunderstorms, the voice of the Lord God, a wife telling her old man to bugger off out of the house and not come back never no more. And he showed me. C E flat G flat A. Or F G sharp B D. Or E G B flat C sharp. Always the same like dangerous sound, he said, as if something terrible's going to happen or is happening (soft for going to happen, loud for happening).†

There was more to it than that, of course. Cinema was one of the places – and the Whitworth Art Gallery on Oxford Road was another – where it was possible to encounter avant-garde European modernist art. In Burgess's memory, this was best exemplified by the futuristic cityscapes of Fritz Lang's *Metropolis*, which was first released in Weimar Germany in 1926. In *The Pianoplayers*,

---

* For Burgess on Cole Porter, see 'Cole Fire' (review of *The Complete Lyrics of Cole Porter*) in *Homage to Qwert Yuiop: Selected Journalism 1978–1985* (London: Hutchinson, 1986), pp. 345–7.
† **Burgess**, *The Pianoplayers*, p. 28.

Burgess revisits his memory of watching Lang's dystopia when it arrived in Manchester the following year:

> The images of the recessive Future that I hold will always be those of Fritz Lang, despite the manifest cut-out quality of his skyscrapers and raised motorways [. . .] No film has ever had better crowd scenes; no film has ever had bigger crowds. The combination of German Gothic and speculative futurism retains a terrible piquancy. The opening shot shows a 10-hour clock – as frightening as Orwell's clock that strikes 13 [. . .] *Metropolis* is the big mythopoeic film of my time.*

*

Throughout his schooldays, and while he was an undergraduate student at Manchester University, Burgess lived in Moss Side. From various flats above shops on Moss Lane East and on Princess Road, he was well placed to observe this district of Manchester throughout the 1920s and the 1930s. For at least a couple of generations before he was around to witness it, Moss Side had been a place of incomers. Although readers of *Little Wilson and Big God* are given the impression that it was largely an Irish Catholic district of the city, it had been known in the late nineteenth century as the epicentre of the Welsh community. The Prime Minister David Lloyd George had been born into a Welsh family in Moss Side in 1863, a few streets away from where Burgess's father and stepmother later kept their tobacconist's shop. Liberal politics were as much a part of the city's tradition as was immigration (from Wales, from Ireland, later from Central Europe and the Caribbean), and the city's liberal political tradition is reflected in the *Manchester Guardian*, a great regional newspaper which later translated itself into a national one. During the period when Burgess was at school in Manchester, the city became one of the places where European Jewish refugees migrated, fleeing the spread of fascism across Europe, and augmenting

---

* Burgess, 'My Seven Wonders of the World', *Sunday Times Magazine*, 16 October 1977, pp. 90–96, 96.

Manchester's Jewish population around West Didsbury and the Palatine Road. Louis Golding, the James Joyce scholar whose work was known to Burgess, wrote a long novel about Manchester's Jewish district, *Magnolia Street*, published by Victor Gollancz in 1932, the year before Hitler came to power in Germany.

In his book *Manchester, England*, Dave Haslam writes of Moss Side as 'an area full of history rubbed out, the kind of place [where] promises are postponed, good times fade and new beginnings are made every decade; hopes, like battered buildings, are regularly demolished'.* Haslam is thinking here of the area immediately surrounding what was once Wilson's the Tobacconist at 21 Princess Road. The shop itself has disappeared, redeveloped as the Royal Brewery. Immediately opposite the site of number 21 is an Asda superstore and a branch of Poundstretcher. The city planners are in the process of destroying Anthony Burgess's Manchester: the few nineteenth-century buildings which remain on the east side of Princess Road have a doomed look about them. The majority of these are now uninhabited and boarded up, and before long they are likely to be demolished to make way for more hangar-like shops.

Only one of the Wilsons' pre-war shops has survived the latest phase of reconstruction, the former off-licence at 47 Princess Road, which is now a Rastafarian gift shop specializing in joss-sticks and scented candles. It stands in a narrow terrace of shops, just across the road from the retail park, not far from a piece of wasteground full of dog shit and advertising billboards. The upstairs flat, once the site of John Burgess Wilson's early experiments in poetry and fiction-writing, is empty, and the windows have been smashed. The muddy back alley behind the shop is littered with broken bottles and flapping, eviscerated bin bags. As you walk along Moss Lane East from here, none of the streets appear to have names; somebody has stolen all the signs.

Burgess returned to Manchester with a television camera crew

---

* Dave Haslam, *Manchester, England: The Story of the Pop Cult City* (London: Fourth Estate, 1999), p. 221.

in 1980, to document how far the city had changed since he'd left it forty years earlier. He deplored the fact that so many of the slum streets that he had known as a young man had been allowed to survive. 'Why the hell did we put up with it,' he asked, 'and why are we putting up with it still? This is not worthy of man, especially not Mancunian man [. . .] City planners allow the junk to survive – and this is junk, God help us.'* He was thinking of those areas of Moss Side which Haslam documents at length: the 'sharp end', as he calls them, the 'other Manchester', half a world away from the pedestrianized respectability of the recent city centre development – with its public fountains and uplifting bits of civic sculpture – or the new waterside bars and warehouse-conversion apartments on the canal at Castlefield.† Many of the houses in Moss Side are lived in by students, since the rents are cheap. The rents are cheap because the risk of burglary is high. But the students are just passing through, staying in the run-down terraced houses off Moss Lane East for no more than a year or two, much like the Welsh and the Irish factory-workers who passed through here before them. For Burgess, getting an education, acquiring the literary culture which a university degree offered, was also a way of moving beyond these seedy-looking flats above shops. He was keenly aware that Catholics like him had been barred from attending English universities until 1829 (just a few generations ago, from his point of view), and that higher education was a way of transcending his class origins. Of course, he did more than merely become a student of literature: he ended up becoming part of what he had gone to Manchester University to study.

*

Between the ages of six and eleven Burgess attended Bishop Bilsborrow Memorial School, immediately next door to the tram depot on Princess Road. This building, now demolished, was the end of the line for city trams, and in 1923 it marked the outer limit of central

---

* *Celebration: Burgess in Manchester.*
† Haslam, *Manchester, England*, p. 222.

Manchester. To the south and the west were the green spaces of
Alexandra Park, bandstands, athletic grounds, and the sports fields
of Hulme Grammar School. Burgess's recollections of his primary
school were indistinct. He remembered being knocked over by other
children in the playground. He also recalled a sense of feeling
different from his peers because he could already read before he
arrived at the school. When he was about three years old, or so the
story went, his father had shown him a newspaper while they were
on a tram. After some straightforward letter-recognition, he found
that he could read aloud: first words, then sentences.

One of the teachers at the school – the only one he could
remember by name – was a sadistic nun, Sister Ignatius, who
administered random justice by beating the children on their hands,
frequently and vigorously, with a leather strap. As an adult, Burgess
looked back on the beatings he had received at Bishop Bilsborrow
and regretted that there had been so much 'brutal torturing of the
quintessentially human organ, nervous and well supplied with
blood'.* In general terms, he remembered childhood as 'a matter of
being frightened – frightened of hellfire, frightened of sex, frightened
of sensuality'.† But this was in the nature of a Catholic primary
education: catechisms and multiplication tables were ruthlessly
beaten into the young.

There were distractions from the gloom and brutality of school.
Joseph and Maggie had moved from Lodge Street to a rented
property at 21 Princess Road, Moss Side, where they lived above
the tobacconist's shop which they ran downstairs. At the top of the
building was an attic, 'primarily an annexe for junk and a stepson',
as Burgess wryly put it.‡ The other occupant of the attic was the
hired help, a young Irish housekeeper who had no objection to
warming the bed with a pre-pubescent boy. 'My father and step-

* Burgess, *Homage to Qwert Yuiop*, p. 111.
† *Celebration: Burgess in Manchester*.
‡ Quoted in Angela Lambert, 'The True Confessions of Anthony Burgess', *Independent*, 1 November 1990, p. 18.

mother were so innocent that they allowed me to share a room with the serving girl. She led me into a certain amount of sexual dalliance before I was ready for it,' he told Anthony Clare. This premature erotic experience – he'd have been about seven years old at the time – was the start of his career as what Martin Amis has called 'a remorseless puller of the women'.* Burgess said that his first inept sexual fumblings 'confirmed everything the Church had said about sex being a dirty business'. It was, he confessed, 'very shocking [. . .] It frightened me out of my wits.'†

Before he left his primary school, Burgess had begun submitting cartoons to local and national newspapers. He never had any real talent as an illustrator, as testified by the surviving notebooks of his amateurish doodles, now archived in the library at Angers University in France. Nevertheless, a couple of examples of his early work found their way into print, in the *Manchester Guardian* and the *Daily Express*. As he tells the story in his memoirs, these precocious appearances in the newspapers earned the admiration of his school-fellows. More importantly from Burgess's point of view, the fact of his being a published artist had a placatory effect on Sister Ignatius, who was persuaded to direct her attentions with the strap towards the less gifted.‡

*

By the time Burgess won a scholarship to his secondary school at the age of eleven, he had amassed his formative emotional experiences and established his credentials as an incipient artist, at least to his own satisfaction. His new school, the Xaverian College, still stands on the Lower Park Road, a residential street in the leafy district of Victoria Park, just to the east of Wilmslow Road. Victoria Park was originally intended as a self-contained estate of villas,

* Martin Amis, *The War Against Cliché: Essays and Reviews 1971–2000* (London: Jonathan Cape, 2001), p. 126.
† *Celebration: Burgess in Manchester.*
‡ Burgess, *Little Wilson and Big God*, p. 79.

constructed from 1840 onwards. The idea of placing these large houses within a walled park (the gates to be locked at night) was conceived by the architect Richard Lane, though the walls and gates have long since been removed. Three of these grand houses, acquired individually over a period of some years, formed the series of school buildings that Burgess knew, and the generous grounds which lay between and around them served as cricket fields and tennis courts.*

The Xaverian Brothers had arrived in Manchester in 1848. They bought 'Firwood', the first of the villas on Lower Park Road, in 1905. The adjoining villa, 'Sunbury', was bought in 1908 and put into use as a preparatory school. By 1922 the Xaverian College had 267 students, sixty of whom were boarders – some originally from Belgium, France, Spain and Mexico. By 1926, two years before Burgess's arrival, the number of pupils had risen to 318. A third building, 'Marylands', was purchased and added to the existing grounds in 1931. This final phase of expansion represents the full extent of the site today.† The main school villa is built in a dark red brick, further darkened by the effects of ageing and industrial soot. A stained-glass window in an upstairs room contains the motto of the Xaverian Brothers: 'Concordia res parvae crescunt'. Burgess writes in his autobiography of the schoolboyish glee he derived from holding up a hand to obscure all but the last four letters of this inscription. The interior of the building is cluttered with dusty-looking devotional pictures, and dominated by a large and ornate Gothic wooden staircase. Two large paintings – of the Blessed Virgin Mary and the crucifixion – occupy prominent positions on the walls, and both images are in full view as you descend the stairs towards ground level. The Xaverian Brothers no longer run the school, nor is it primarily a Catholic establishment: since 1977 it has been a co-educational sixth-form college, and

---

* Nikolaus Pevsner, *Lancashire: The Industrial and Commercial South*, The Buildings of England series (London: Penguin, 1969), pp. 325–6.
† 'The Xaverian Story', from the Old Xaverians' Association Golden Jubilee dinner menu, 18 November 1978.

many of the students today would identify themselves as Muslims, Hindus, agnostics or atheists. The culture of the college is entirely different from the hard-line Catholicism that Burgess experienced and absorbed there as a boy.

The Xaverian Brothers were a teaching order whose members were committed to an austere way of life. They took vows of poverty, chastity and obedience but they were not ordained, and were therefore unable to celebrate the sacraments. As one former pupil of the college remembers, 'This meant that they had the worst of both worlds. Quite a lot of masters actually left the order. It was not a satisfactory life. A number of them married and went into academic work.'*

Xaverian College in the 1930s was a selective Catholic boys' grammar school. Most of the pupils were the sons of grocers or fairly well-off businessmen. Manchester's Catholic community was very close in the 1920s and 1930s, and the boys' fathers tended to know one another, having met for reasons of trade or religion. (There was even a Catholic businessmen's association, set up in Manchester as a rival organization to the Freemasons.) A few boys from other religious backgrounds were also admitted. Manchester was one of the British cities where Jewish incomers and refugees had settled, establishing a large community.† Burgess recalls among his immediate contemporaries a Jewish boy called Harold Foreman, whose father kept a draper's shop on Princess Road.‡ At Xaverian College, as elsewhere, the gathering storm of European politics and the possibility of a second world war were hard to ignore. Inevitably, the politics of the wider world were reflected among the school's pupils: as well as the few Jewish boys, there were those who supported Oswald Mosley's British Union of Fascists, two of whom were involved with the Blackshirts. But there were not many

---

* Brian Bagnall to author, 22 June 2000.
† Sir John Barbirolli's memoirs note that a substantial proportion of the Hallé Orchestra was made up of Jewish musicians during these years.
‡ Burgess, *Little Wilson and Big God*, pp. 116–17.

Blackshirts to be found in Manchester, since the ideology of fascism was thought to be at variance with the city's long traditions of socialism and liberalism.

Although it was a grammar school, the college's ethos was not rigorously academic: the purpose of Xaverian at this time was primarily to turn out well-behaved citizens with good manners. It never enjoyed the academic reputation of its rival institution, the (largely Protestant) Manchester Grammar School. If the atmosphere was partly anti-academic, this was in large measure due to the influence of the colourful headmaster, Brother Martin, CFX, whose real name was Eugene McCarthy. The artist and architect Brian Bagnall, who was in the lower school at Xaverian when John Burgess Wilson was in the sixth form, remembers Brother Martin as a theatrical figure and a staunch disciplinarian:

> He was about six foot two or three, a very commanding presence, full of histrionics. He took snuff, and he always used to blow his nose with a large bandanna handkerchief. Brother Martin was a distant relative of Seymour Hicks, although he himself was almost entirely of Irish stock. I think he saw himself as a theatrical figure. His control of the school was absolute. I don't think there could have been anyone at the school who loved him. He was feared and respected in many ways. He was full of aphorisms, which never changed. He would say, 'Matter out of place is dirt.' That means 'Pick up rubbish.' Brother Martin was known as 'Nick' to a lot of people. I don't know why. Perhaps he *was* a bit of a devil. And I think that in many ways not stepping across the line of good behaviour was more important to him than academic excellence.*

Bagnall drew a caricature of the headmaster from memory a few years after he'd left the school, which shows an impressively tall and chinless figure, virtually hairless, who is wearing a black soutane and inhaling a pinch of snuff, while a long string of rosary beads

---

* Interview with Brian Bagnall, 22 June 2000.

dangles from his left-hand pocket. The cartoon is captioned 'Big Brother of the 1930s' – referring to the fear and respect which Brother Martin commanded. Burgess's description of him was rather more direct in its judgements: he summed him up as 'an Irishman, a liar, a character'.*

Burgess's account of his schooldays in *Little Wilson and Big God* suggests that he was stimulated by the academic curriculum – especially his history and English classes – but he gives little impression of other aspects of school life. Although games such as cricket, swimming and tennis were important to most of the boys who studied at the college at this time, Burgess appears to have taken little or no interest in these activities. Even at the age of eleven he was already a short-sighted, bookish boy, known to the other pupils as a 'weakly kid'. His antipathy to sport later hardened into a defiant, almost slobbish, anti-athleticism.† Nevertheless, he contributed to the life of the school in other ways. Bagnall remembers John Wilson playing the grand piano in school concerts in the early 1930s; and he wrote for a school magazine, the *Electron*, in which he published his first poem, 'That the Earth Rose Out of a Vast Basin of Electric Sea', a competent parody of Gerard Manley Hopkins, when he was eighteen:

> Rolled, rolled, rolled,
> And all being fills in it,
> Where fire flies, sparks gay with gold,
> Wash the lot, the tide swills, spills in it.
> Tying all, oh with what strings
> It binds, binds earth and air to all
> It shews and knoes, meets all, leaps and sings

---

* *Celebration: Burgess in Manchester.*
† For Burgess on football (one of his few utterances on the subject of sport), see his report on the Holland v. West Germany match in the 1974 World Cup, 'An Ancient Kickaround (Updated)', *Time*, 8 June 1974, p. 39: 'The *Fussballweltmeisterschaft* has brought nations together in unlethal rivalry, and that cannot well be shrugged off as a lot of fussball about nothing'.

> *Its way through the spray of it, the misty caul.*
> *Womb of all, tomb of all, the mass*
> *Where mighty fingers beat now, knead and mould,*
> *With a curling of tongues, a laugh and a mocking to pass:*
> *It ceases not, rolling in wash and glint of gold.* *

Apart from the pursuit of sporting success over other local schools and occasional musical events, the cultural side of Xaverian life seems to have been very limited. Bagnall recalls only one school play being put on while he was there, *The Story of Perseus*. 'I'm sure that it had absolutely no literary value whatsoever,' he says. 'I don't ever remember Shakespeare being performed.' As a student whose aptitude lay in the visual arts, Bagnall was disappointed by the school's failure to nurture his interest in drawing and painting: 'The facilities were really very poor. You did things like poker-work and bits of rug-making. It was more in the style of remedial occupational therapy than the visual arts.' The music department was better equipped. There was a violin teacher on the staff and a music master, Mr Sandiford, who was also a competent pianist.

The school careers of most writers are dominated by the memory of one or two charismatic teachers who caught their attention at an age when they were willing to have their characters moulded. Two of the teachers Burgess mentions seem to have made a lasting impression on him. The first of these was Dorothy McManus, always known among the boys as Dolly, who taught English and elocution: the 'received' accent which was considered necessary for entry into teaching, the priesthood, the armed forces or the civil service.

Later recordings of Burgess's speaking voice show us very clearly how far he had modified his Manchester accent in order to make his way in the world. The earliest surviving recordings, which are preserved in the National Sound Archive and in the audio library of the BBC, date from the mid-1960s. (Most of the radio broadcasts

---

* J. B. Wilson, 'That the Earth Rose Out of a Vast Basin of Electric Sea', *Electron*, 1935 (Archive of the Xaverian Brothers, Manchester).

that Burgess made in the 1950s and early 1960s went out live, leaving a handful of transcripts but no tapes.) Burgess's vowels show strong evidence of what linguists call 'correction', though his speaking voice altered in the other direction when regional accents came into fashion later on in the 1960s, with the rise of the Beatles and the Mersey Beat poets.* Burgess's own recording of passages from *A Clockwork Orange* – issued on vinyl by Caedmon in 1973 – deliberately reverts to the Manchester accent of his youth. This implies that he was, at some level, associating Mancunian English with yobbery and ultra-violence. It also raises the possibility that, when the author of *A Clockwork Orange* heard the hero-narrator's voice in his head, Alex spoke with a Manchester accent, as opposed to the south-of-England RADA accent employed by Malcolm McDowell in Stanley Kubrick's film adaptation.

To most of the boys whose vowels it was Dolly McManus's solemn duty to alter, elocution was bound up with the possibility of moving out of the shop-keeping class. For Burgess this was also his first introduction to phonetics, which he was later to study in a more formal way under the linguist G. L. Brook as part of his undergraduate degree in English. It was Dolly McManus who first opened the door for him on to the spoken language as an area of study in itself. Her influence led eventually to Burgess's two published non-fiction books on the subject, *Language Made Plain* (1964) and *A Mouthful of Air* (1992). As a novelist, especially in works such as *The Doctor Is Sick* (1960), Burgess shows himself – like his near-contemporary, Kingsley Amis – to be deeply interested in the sounds of speech, and he is concerned in virtually all of his fiction with making detailed phonetic transcriptions of how the characters talk.† The Mancunian English that Burgess grew up

---

* The 'Mersey Beats', otherwise known as the 'Liverpool Poets', were Adrian Henri, Roger McGough and Brian Patten. Their collections (both published in London) were *The Mersey Sound* (1967) and *The Liverpool Scene* (1967).
† For example, in *The Doctor Is Sick* (London: Heinemann, 1960) we find garlicky 'lowlife' passages such as this: 'Blimey, you 'ear? 'E spik lak good man. Why you

speaking and listening to was radically different from Standard English in terms of its grammar as well as its sounds ('I come' or 'I comed' as the past tense of 'I came', for instance). As a boy, Burgess had a wide vocabulary of dialect words which came more naturally to him than the Standard English forms: a 'cuddy' was a horse; a 'petty' was a lavatory; a back alley was an 'entry'.* And the other children at his primary school called him 'mardy' or 'mardarse', meaning one who was sulky or solitary, not part of the gang.[†]

The second influential teacher at Xaverian was the Liverpool Irish history master, L. W. Dever, known as Bill Dever. Not being a Xaverian Brother, he represented the secular wing of the staff. Dever's lessons on the history of the Reformation were an important trigger for the religious crisis that Burgess underwent in his middle teens:

> When I was at the Xaverian College in Manchester and was in the sixth form – I was seventeen – we had a Liverpool Irish Catholic history master, and we were studying the Reformation, and he put the case for the Reformation a bit too well. I'd done a lot of reading on my own about Luther. I wrote a play about Luther, long before John Osborne's play. It was pretty agonizing, chiefly because of the sacramental element in Catholicism. One can throw away certain of the doctrines, but one can't throw away the Eucharist quite so easily. And of course this was Joyce's situation.[‡]

Tellingly, the sequence of thoughts in this passage moves immediately from Dever to Burgess's own religious doubts to James

---

not spik lak 'im? *Señora*, 'e say. Bloody ole bag an fackin' oor, you say. Why you not be good man? No money you give one day, two, sree. One day I go. Blimey, yes, get good man. Lak 'im I get' (p. 53).

* See Burgess, *Homage to Qwert Yuiop*, p. 177.

[†] Burgess, *Flame into Being: The Life and Work of D. H. Lawrence* (London: Heinemann, 1985), p. 1.

[‡] Samuel Coale, 'Interview with Anthony Burgess', unpublished transcript, p. 2.

Joyce. What emerges clearly from Burgess's various accounts of his schooldays is that Bill Dever was a vaguely subversive figure, a man who was willing to engage with his pupils on a personal level and to become a drinking partner once they'd left the school.* According to one version of events, Dever did Burgess the favour of putting into his hands a piece of literary dynamite, the banned book which would inform all of his subsequent thinking and writing:

> When Joyce produced *Ulysses* it was promptly banned every-where except Paris [. . .] No British or American printer had been willing to risk jail by setting up the abominable text, and it had to be given to a printer in Dijon who knew no English. The book was published by the American owner of a Paris bookshop, and it was sent through the mails to such as relished highly wrought literature, or dirt [. . .] It was seized by the customs authorities at New York and Folkestone and seques-tered or burnt. The ban was still in force when, in 1934, my history master smuggled the Odyssey Press edition out of Nazi Germany and lent it to me.†

Dever did much to shape Burgess's adolescent consciousness, both by guiding his reading and, more generally, by encouraging him to question the Catholicism which was supposedly being nur-tured by the school. Yet the story of Dever having lent him his own copy of *Ulysses* is cast into uncertainty by a different version of events which Burgess gives in *Here Comes Everybody: An Introduc-tion to James Joyce for the Ordinary Reader*:

> Printed at last in France and published by a Paris book-shop, [. . .] it [i.e. *Ulysses*] began an unbelievable career of suppression, vilification, adulation, piracy, public and private burning, smuggling. (As a schoolboy I sneaked the two-volume

---

* *Little Wilson and Big God*, p. 161.
† 'Joyce as Centenarian' in *Homage to Qwert Yuiop*, pp. 431–7, 432; reprinted in *One Man's Chorus: The Uncollected Writings*, ed. by Ben Forkner (New York: Carroll & Graf, 1998), pp. 277–84, 278.

Odyssey Press edition into England, cut up into sections and distributed all over my body.)*

The claim that Burgess himself smuggled the book into England is repeated in his 1992 introduction to the Minerva edition of *Ulysses*, and in the 1994 Secker and Warburg edition, published after his death.

This Odyssey Press edition of *Ulysses* was published in Hamburg, Paris and Bologna in December 1932, in which year Burgess turned fifteen. The Bodley Head published an unlimited (and legal) London edition of the novel in September 1937, so there would have been no need for smuggling or secrecy after that date. There is no record of Burgess travelling outside of England before 1935, and he left the school in September of that year. It seems likely, then, that he was looking at Dever's copy of the novel at some time between 1932 and 1935. The most likely date is 1934, when he was in the sixth form at Xaverian. The date of his first exposure to *Ulysses* is important because he later spoke of it as an experience from which he had never fully recovered. Joyce, he said, was the writer against whom he 'hopelessly' measured himself whenever he sat down at his typewriter.† *Ulysses* and *A Portrait of the Artist as a Young Man* are the works which did more to form him as a writer than any of the other literature which came his way throughout his youth and early adulthood.‡

---

* Burgess, *Here Comes Everybody: An Introduction to James Joyce for the Ordinary Reader* (London: Faber, 1965), p. 83.

† Burgess, 'Favourite Novel' in *Homage to Qwert Yuiop*, pp. 429–31, 431.

‡ The full extent of Burgess's engagement with Joyce, both as critic and reader, has not yet been properly documented. This is not the place to make a detailed assessment of the works that Burgess produced in response to Joyce, but such a study would have to include, as a minimum: the two full-length critical books, *Here Comes Everybody* (1965) and *Joyspick* (1973); Burgess's edition of *A Shorter Finnegans Wake* (1966); the essays in *Urgent Copy* (1968), *Homage to Qwert Yuiop* (1986) and *One Man's Chorus* (1998); his *Monitor* documentary for BBC television, *Silence, Exile and Cunning* (1965); the Anglo-Irish radio musical, *Blooms of Dublin* (broadcast 1982; published 1986); other musical settings of

Approaching Joyce's *Portrait* at the age of either fifteen or sixteen (the exact date is uncertain), Burgess said that he was so scared by the hellfire sermon that, although he had been on the point of becoming an apostate, he diligently retreated back into the Church. Thinking back in 1985 to this adolescent moment of crisis, he recalled that

> I was losing my faith and I was told by my history master [. . .] that Joyce's *A Portrait of the Artist as a Young Man* might suggest a rational justification of a painfully irrational process. I did not know why I was apostatizing, but apparently Joyce's hero did. When I read Father Arnell's sermon on hell I was, like Stephen Dedalus, scared back into being a good son of the Church and, for at least six weeks, kept away from the occasions of sin, meaning chiefly great literature.*

It is not hard to see why such writing should have terrified Burgess to the extent that it did. As he contemplates the agonizing intensity and the boundless duration of the fires of hell, the priest in Joyce's *Portrait* builds up a detailed picture of what an eternity of torment might feel like from the viewpoint of the unrepentant sinner:

> Consider then what must be the foulness of the air of hell. Imagine some foul and putrid corpse that has lain rotting and decomposing in the grave, a jelly-like mass of liquid corruption. Imagine such a corpse a prey to flames, devoured by the fire of burning brimstone and giving off dense choking fumes of nauseous loathsome decomposition. And then imagine this sickening stench, multiplied a millionfold and millionfold again

Joyce's poems; the Joyce chapter in *Earthly Powers* (1980); the introductions to various paperback reprints of *Dubliners*, the *Portrait*, *Ulysses* and *Finnegans Wake*; an *Observer* review of Richard Ellmann's biography of Joyce (1982); a review of Peter Costello's *James Joyce: The Years of Growth 1882–1915* (1992); and the large number of newspaper articles on Joyce listed in Paul Boytinck's *Anthony Burgess: An Annotated Bibliography and Reference Guide*.
* Burgess, *Flame into Being*, p. 3.

from the millions upon millions of fetid carcasses massed together in the reeking darkness, a huge and rotting human fungus. Imagine all this, and you will have some idea of the horror and the stench of hell [. . .] The blood seethes and boils in the veins, the brains are boiling in the skull, the heart in the breast glowing and bursting, the bowels a red-hot mass of burning pulp, the tender eyes flaming like molten balls.*

Above all it is the gross physicality of this description that appals, the almost unbearable dwelling on the putrefying human body. This was a lesson that Burgess learned from Joyce and later applied to his own fiction, in which the emphasis is frequently on the weakness of corruptible human flesh. Although the minds of Burgessian heroes are stuffed with idealistic principles and grand aesthetic schemes, the physical body is what usually lets them down.

Two crucial formative episodes took place when Burgess was around fifteen: his reading of Joyce's *Portrait* and his actual confrontation with the Jesuit priests of the Church of the Holy Name of Jesus on Oxford Road in Manchester. One of the most striking elements in Burgess's description of this encounter at the Holy Name is the extent to which it echoes the plot of Joyce's novel: the hero of both narratives is having intellectual difficulties with Catholicism, and is horrified by the Church's response to his own scepticism. According to Burgess's version,

I thought I would argue out with these great Jesuit fathers at the Holy Name my objections to Christianity and they would say: 'Oh, my good God. You're right. I'd never thought of that before. Go in peace, my son.'†

Instead Burgess got what he described as 'the shock of my life'. The priest to whom he had confessed his doubts (chief

* James Joyce, *A Portrait of the Artist as a Young Man* (London: Secker & Warburg, 1994), pp. 124–5.
† *Celebration: Burgess in Manchester.*

among which was the idea that the sacraments were 'superficial') replied with condemnation, 'his dead, white face wet with the perspiration of anger'. The Jesuit reiterated the orthodox view that a Catholic who deliberately stopped communicating with his Church and receiving the sacraments would put himself at risk of eternal damnation. Expecting to be sent away with words of sympathy, Burgess found himself on the receiving end of a Joycean hellfire sermon.

The memory of Joyce's sermon stayed with Burgess well into adult life, and a version of it comes back as the prison chaplain's dream-vision in *A Clockwork Orange*. Although Burgess had been estranged from the Catholic Church for nearly thirty years by the time he came to write his own hellfire sermon, the affinities between the chaplain's discourse and Joyce's *Portrait* are clear:

> I have been informed in visions that there is a place, darker than any prison, hotter than any flame of human fire, where souls of unrepentant criminal sinners like yourselves – and don't leer at me, damn you, don't laugh – like yourselves, I say, scream in endless and intolerable agony, their noses choked with the smell of filth, their mouths crammed with burning ordure, their skin peeling and rotting, a fireball spinning in their screaming guts.*

Joyce's *Portrait* had articulated, in a concrete way, a series of vague doubts about Catholicism which had been present in Burgess's consciousness around the time that he read it. His self-identification with Stephen Dedalus, the novel's hero, was total. Looking back on Stephen's decision to leave the Church, and on his own parallel crisis of faith, Burgess commented that the condition of the lapsed Catholic was necessarily that of a man who believed himself to be an exile: 'One feels genuinely lost, abandoned. What does one

---

* Burgess, *A Clockwork Orange* (London: Heinemann, 1962), part 2, chapter 1, p. 80. Another sermon along broadly similar lines, a terrifying warning against the sinful pleasures of sex, is delivered to an audience of schoolboys in the opening chapter of *Tremor of Intent* (London: Heinemann, 1966), p. 6.

become? A Marxist? No. A Protestant? *No*.'* The hellfire rhetoric
of Joyce's novel scared him briefly back into the Church, but – on
subsequent readings – the defiant aestheticism he saw in Stephen
Dedalus seemed to provide an alternative system of belief, or at least
some kind of consolation for his lost faith. Joyce eased Burgess's
difficult transition from being a practising Catholic to being a
reluctant renegade. As Burgess puts it in his film about Joyce,
Silence, Exile and Cunning,

> I was drawn to a great Irish Catholic when he'd ceased to be
> either truly Irish or truly Catholic. He was a renegade. I myself
> at the age of 16 was a renegade. He'd made his world out of the
> materials of the world he'd rejected. I wanted confirmation that
> the agonies and elation I knew as a renegade had some sort of
> artistic significance, meant something. I should imagine that
> when an Anglican loses his faith it's a smooth sweet process,
> rather like the shedding of a skin. His church has as good as told
> him not to take its doctrines too seriously. But for a cradle
> Catholic to leave his Church, it's like the wrenching of palpable
> bone and muscle – it's like the draining of the very content of
> the skull. [. . .] Anyway it seemed to me that what I called reason
> was tugging one way, and emotion, instinct, loyalty and fear
> were tugging the other. James Joyce summed it all up for me.†

Despite his identification with the predicament of the hero (and,
implicitly, with the author) Burgess's first reading of *Ulysses* did not
provoke another religious crisis comparable to the one that the
Portrait had brought on. A good deal of the importance and
fascination of this work for him lay in the innovative approach it
took to literary form. Speaking, in a 1965 radio interview, of the
formal attractions of *Ulysses*, Burgess tried to explain why this was
the twentieth-century novel which mattered to him above all others.
In Joyce, he argued, there seemed to be something going on between

---

* *Celebration: Burgess in Manchester.*
† *Monitor: Silence, Exile and Cunning*, BBC 1, 20 April 1965. Script in BBC
Written Archives, pp. 4–5.

the author and the reader which is simply missing from the works of most popular writers. The language of *Ulysses* is always 'getting in the way [. . .] It's not a deliberate set of puzzles or tricks, it's not a thorny thicket, but an attempt to show that speech, the love of language, plays as much a part in our lives as other properties of life'.* In other words, puns, malapropisms, acrostics and other kinds of verbal trickery were worth pursuing for their own sake. Instead of wanting to satisfy the reader's desire for plot and action, Joyce had decreed that, in the novel, language itself should be one of the characters, perhaps even the central character. When you're reading Joyce, says Burgess, 'you're not reading clichés'.† It's a neat aphorism, and one which sums up Burgess's useful distinction between popular writing (which is easy to read because it 'indulges in clichés') and the modernism of Joyce, which he sought continually to emulate in his own fiction.

Coming into contact with Joyce's modernist masterpiece was the beginning of Burgess's engagement with serious literature. And it's at precisely this point, while he is still a schoolboy tortured by guilt at his dereliction of the family faith, that he stops being just a reader and starts to become a writer. One of his earliest poems was written at this time, probably when he was sixteen. In the long tradition of adolescent poetry, it is a melancholy reflection on his far-from-happy home life:

> My father, his wife,
> Too old to make decisions,
> Yet plotted revisions
> Of their life.
> Nor could this hope be
> More vain for
> It was left to me
> To open the oven door.

---

* *The World of Books*, interview with Peter Duval Smith, BBC Home Service, 9 November 1965. Transcript, p. 2.

† Ibid., p. 6.

> She at least, the mother.
> He in his apprehension
> Cut the knot of tension.
> She thought of other
> Uses, seeking a flame
> Stronger in her
> The instinct came
> To start the Sunday dinner.*

It's hard to do much with this poem beyond registering the vague note of domestic discontent which it sounds. It seems to describe a struggle between life-changing 'revisions' and the 'instinct' which wins out in the final lines, though it is not clear what kind of revisions might be at stake. From a literary point of view, it is unexciting stuff. Burgess's first poem in imitation of Hopkins, written in 1934, is a much more accomplished performance:

> Whether windowed a greycold welkin or a dawn that mounts
>   and breaks
> In a roseflush wave each day arises this working man,
> Heavy maybe but never for a thwarted life's plan
> Seen shaped to the pounding day: for the day's round he
>   awakes.
> He shakes sleep away. Day warms. He leaves and takes
> A snap of suller cheese, hunked bread, a brew for his can,
> And thrives in the air, strives, spits, swears. His breastcares
>   span
> But Saturday's care or bet. Naught deeper rankles or aches.
>
> When the violet air blooms about him, then at last he can wipe
> His hands sheerfree of swink, monarch of hours ahead.
> Hearty he eats and, full, he sits to pull at his pipe
> Or drag at his tube in the kitchen glow. The no-news read,
> He argues, sups, in the vault. To a plate of tripe
> Or crisp chips home returns, then climbs to a dreamless bed.†

---

* Quoted in Burgess, *Little Wilson and Big God*, p. 153.
† Box 121, folder 4, Harry Ransom Center, University of Texas at Austin.

Hopkins's poems were not properly published in a commercial edition until 1930, so Burgess must have found and absorbed them shortly after they appeared. This is the emergence of a fully formed Burgessian voice: confident, learned, language-loving. Everything he wrote after this date would be written under the twin shadows of Joyce and Hopkins. Burgess had always known that he wanted to be some kind of artist, but for many years – until the publication of his first novel in 1956 – he went on believing that his true artistic calling was that of composer, albeit a self-taught and eccentric one. The precocious schoolboy sonnet demonstrates that he was already, at the age of seventeen, developing and honing the literary technique that would eventually bear enormous fruit in the Malayan novels, the Enderby quartet, *A Clockwork Orange*, *Nothing Like the Sun*, *Tremor of Intent* and *Earthly Powers*. It was a modest enough beginning. But it was still a beginning.

2

University

Burgess left the Xaverian College on 23 July 1935, in possession of a Matriculation Certificate but without any fixed idea of how to pursue his creative ambitions. His immediate prospects were far from clear. His father and stepmother, who had supported him for four years beyond the minimum legal school-leaving age, decided that it was time for him to go out to work, and there was talk for a while of his entering the Customs Service. It's unlikely that anyone except Burgess saw the irony of his considering such a job at the same time that he was reading and relishing his smuggled copy of Joyce's *Ulysses*.

While he prepared to sit the entry examinations for the Customs Service – which he failed catastrophically, and perhaps deliberately – there was music to be composed, and by the end of 1935 he had written a long piece, his first symphony in the key of E major. The original manuscript of this symphony, which ran to 300 pages of thirty-stave scoring paper, is now lost, but Burgess wrote out a piano reduction from memory in the 1970s. This second manuscript, still unperformed, is archived with Burgess's other music in Texas.

Burgess remained on friendly terms with Bill Dever, and the two men met for an occasional drink and to exchange literary talk. Perhaps it was at Dever's suggestion that he decided to apply to read for an English degree, since he would have received little encouragement at home. Burgess knew that it would be down to him to find the necessary fees for a university course by working for a couple of years. As well as being an occasional pub pianist, he worked as a delivery boy for Wilson's, his father's Moss Side tobacco business. Joseph Wilson's health was beginning to fail: he suffered from respiratory difficulties and was unable to walk long distances. But Burgess had little or no interest in following his father into the tobacco trade. He was determined to find his own profession, and completing his education offered the best hope of breaking free from the small world of shopkeeping.

One of the important events of 1936 for him was the publication of T. S. Eliot's *Poems 1909–1935*. He writes in the autobiography that he bought this book during a visit to London and read it on the train back to Manchester. His attention was caught by the songs from Eliot's unfinished 'Aristophanic melodrama', *Sweeney Agonistes*, and he decided that these frivolous, cannibalistic numbers should be set to music.* The other musical project of that year also arose out of literature. He produced an unaccompanied setting, for soprano, alto, tenor and bass, of 'Compleynt, compleynt I hearde upon a day' from Ezra Pound's 'Canto XXX'. The choice of text seems to reflect something of Burgess's own sense of purposelessness and melancholy. Like the character who speaks in Pound's poem, his was a life still waiting to acquire a definite shape and direction:

> All things are made foul in this season,
> This is the reason, none may seek purity
> Having for foulnesse pity
> And things growne awry;
> No more do my shaftes fly

---

* His versions of the *Sweeney* songs were performed in 1980, with Burgess singing and accompanying himself at the piano, when he delivered the T. S. Eliot Memorial Lectures at the University of Kent at Canterbury. The lectures were broadcast on BBC Radio 3, but there have been no subsequent performances of these unpublished songs.

> To slay. Nothing is now clean slayne
> But rotteth away.*

Whatever private meaning these lines held for Burgess, it is likely that he came to Pound by way of Eliot, who had written an introduction to Pound's *Selected Poems*. In many ways this was a natural progression: private study of Pound, combined with his reading of Joyce, Hopkins and Eliot, would have given Burgess a solid grounding in modernist poetry and fiction.

This is not to say that his reading was in any sense ordered or programmatic. He was also reading Robert Herrick at this point, and he later gave a copy of Herrick's *Poems*, inscribed 'John Burgess Wilson, 1936', to an Army colleague, Bill Brian. On the flyleaf of this book, Burgess had copied out a quotation from Walt Whitman's 'Song of Myself':

> I hear the key'd cornet, it glides quickly in through my ears,
> It shakes mad-sweet pangs through my belly and breast.

Whitman, too, became another of his heroes, eventually to be celebrated in one of the essays in *Urgent Copy*. Burgess admired him for his innovation of 'the rhetorical catalogue, the enumeration in line after long line of visual phenomena'.† Whitman's technique of compiling extensive lists of things thought, felt, seen and recollected was one that Burgess would later borrow for his own novels. (In *Tremor of Intent*, for example, the banquet scene is presented as a Whitmanesque nightmare, in which Dennis Hillier and Mr Theodorescu, on board a Black Sea cruise-ship, devour – at a single sitting – lobster medallions in sauce cardinale, red mullet, artichoke hearts, fillets of sole, shellfish tart, soufflé au fois gras, avocado halves with red caviar, filet mignon with zucchini, roast lamb and onions, gruyère casserole, celery julienne, pheasant, harlequin sherbet, peach mousse, pears in chocolate sauce, cold Grand Marnier

---

* Ezra Pound, *The Cantos of Ezra Pound* (London: Faber, 1968), p. 152.
† Burgess, 'The Answerer' in *Urgent Copy: Literary Studies* (London: Jonathan Cape, 1970), pp. 48–53, 52.

pudding, strawberry marlow, nectarine flan, chocolate rum dessert with whipped cream, orange marmalade crème bavaroise with Cointreau and apple tart normande with Calvados. Hillier, whose digestive tract is more fragile than that of Theodorescu, empties his mutinous guts into the sea. After this he is lured into the cabin of his Indian mistress, who rides him into submission with alarming sexual manoeuvres: 'the half-moon on the buttocks, then the tiger's claw, the peacock's foot, the hare's jump, the blue lotus-leaf'.)* In spite of being temporarily cut off from formal education, it is clear that Burgess was reading and learning all the time.

*

The Victoria University of Manchester, originally known as Owens College, was founded in 1851 with a bequest from the philanthropist John Owens (1790–1846), who had made his fortune in the Lancashire cotton industry. In 1871 the college left its original site on Quay Street, Deansgate, and moved to the new Oxford Road premises, directly opposite the Church of the Holy Name, where Burgess underwent his apostasy. These new buildings were neo-Gothic in style, and they formed the core of the city campus. The university received its charter in 1880, and it was given the power to grant medical degrees three years later. In the final decades of the nineteenth century, student numbers climbed from just sixty-two in 1851 to over 1,000 by 1900.†

The official history of the university, published in 1951 to commemorate the centenary of Owens College, is full of uplifting rhetoric about the dignity of learning, and it gives a good impression of the ethos of the university as Burgess would have known it:

> In an academic community, men are joined in fellowship and freedom to a common high purpose, and the functions of learning to work and learning to live are not separate [. . .] Its

---

* Burgess, *Tremor of Intent* (London: Heinemann, 1966), pp. 70–76, 90.
† H. B. Charlton, *Portrait of a University 1851–1951* (Manchester: Manchester University Press, 1951), pp. 22, 164.

persisting manner must be the communication to the minds of youth not only science which is in a state of completeness, but also of science which is in a state of growth; in that way the student is brought into contact with the living elements that make up the progress of human culture.*

It is clear from the high-minded tone of these lines that the principles of Matthew Arnold's *Culture and Anarchy* and John Henry Newman's *The Idea of a University* were the keystones of higher education as it was administered at Manchester. The spirit of the university was genuinely outward-looking, with a strong emphasis on public lectures and adult education. The author of the passage quoted above was H. B. Charlton, a man despised by Burgess, who was Professor of English throughout the 1930s. Like Sister Ignatius and Brother Martin, he was another figure of authority with whom Burgess managed to fall out.

The lectures that Burgess attended in English, French, History and Latin (these last three being his subsidiary subjects) were held in the Arts Building, an impressive structure completed in 1919. It has a large neo-classical portico giving on to a grand, pillared entrance hall. Between the pillars stands a bust of Samuel Alexander, who was Manchester's Professor of Philosophy between 1883 and 1924, and whose statue Burgess remembered as a meeting place for courting couples. Directly behind the Arts Building on Lime Grove was the Arts Library, newly opened in 1937, flat-roofed and modern with tall windows.

The prospectus for 1937 shows which courses were available for study, as well as giving a full list of the university's teaching staff and detailed reading lists for undergraduate courses. In 1937 student numbers stood at 2,729, and of these just under 600 were women. In the Arts Faculty where Burgess studied, there were 1,211 men and 426 women. These figures remained more or less constant for the next three years, with a slight falling-off after the declaration of

* Ibid., pp. 68–9.

war in 1939.* The proportion of women students increased as young men of military age were conscripted into the armed forces, but those, like Burgess and his contemporaries, who had already begun their degree courses before the outbreak of war were given the opportunity to graduate before going off to be shot at or blown up.

The range of subjects taught in the 1930s was remarkably wide. The Arts Faculty offered degrees in Philosophy, Architecture, History, Economics, Politics, Law, Psychology, French, German, Italian, Spanish, English Language, English Literature, Greek, Latin, Art History, Russian, Chinese, Semitic Languages (Arabic, Hebrew and Aramaic), Military Organization and Tactics, Palaeography and Egyptology. Students seeking admission to Arts courses had to be at least sixteen years old, or seventeen if they were women; they were also required to produce 'a certificate of good character' from a headmaster or a clergyman, and to sign a declaration that they would observe the university's regulations. The minimum academic requirement for entry was a school Matriculation Certificate, and prospective students were warned that, once admitted, they would not be allowed to graduate without obtaining a pass in the university's intermediate examination in Latin or Greek. This would come to be especially problematic in Burgess's case. He came dangerously close to failing his BA honours degree because his competence as a Latinist fell short of the required standard.

The university's fees for undergraduates were steep, and hardly any scholarships were available. A 'composition fee' of £32 6d. was payable in October, at the start of each academic year. This was supplemented by an examination fee of £2, payable in March. Graduating students were charged an additional 8 guineas (£8 8s.) for the conferment of the BA degree. The university estimated that the cost of books would be around £5, bringing the minimum cost of a degree course to £114 14s. 6d. This did not include the cost of accommodation and meals in halls of residence, but Burgess was

* See ibid., pp. 166–7.

now lodging with his father and stepmother at 5 Leighbrook Road, a bland suburban street in Fallowfield. If Joseph and Maggie Wilson agreed to pay his examination fees, this was partly because they had been talked into it by Burgess's stepcousin, George Dwyer (later Archbishop Dwyer), who had recently completed a theology degree and entered the priesthood.

The English department at Manchester was a small but distinguished group of scholars. It was headed by Henry Buckley Charlton, who had gained his own degrees from Leeds and Manchester. J. D. Wright, a senior lecturer and eighteenth-century scholar, was another Manchester graduate. Two assistant lecturers were particularly important in shaping Burgess's conception of the literature of the Renaissance: Lionel Charles Knights, a graduate of the Cambridge English school, and John Davies Jump, who had taken his degree at Liverpool University. One surviving class register from the academic year 1937–8 shows that John Burgess Wilson went to all nineteen of his tutorials in the Michaelmas Term. In the Lent Term he was less diligent, attending fourteen out of a possible eighteen, and in the Summer Term of 1938 he missed one in five of his classes. Given the choice between scholarship and skiving, he was beginning to feel the attraction of the latter.

Looking back on his university days, Burgess acknowledged that the influence of L. C. Knights, the charismatic Marxist scholar, had been crucial. Reg Bate remembers him as 'a tall man with a prominent Adam's apple and a rather effeminate delivery'.* Knights sat on the editorial board of *Scrutiny*, the scholarly journal edited out of the Cambridge English department by F. R. Leavis, and Burgess's contact with him put him in touch with one of the significant intellectual movements of his day.† Knights was a fre-

---

* R. G. Bate to author, 24 May 2001.
† Frank Raymond Leavis (1895–1978), critic and teacher. For many years he was regarded as the most influential literary commentator of his day. As a fellow of Downing College, Cambridge, Leavis edited the quarterly review *Scrutiny* from 1932 until 1953. His publications include *New Bearings in English Poetry* (1932),

quent contributor to *Scrutiny*, and the essays he'd been publishing in that journal – and in *The Criterion*, a rival magazine edited by T. S. Eliot – were the basis of his first book, *Drama and Society in the Age of Jonson*, which Burgess certainly read as an undergraduate.* Knights is a key figure in the history of 1930s criticism. He is remembered, in particular, for a ground-breaking lecture entitled 'How Many Children Had Lady Macbeth?', in which he set himself, deliberately and contentiously, against the standard character-based approach to Shakespeare, defined by A. C. Bradley in his book *Shakespearean Tragedy* (1904) and continued in Manchester by Professor Charlton.† Burgess found himself caught in the academic crossfire between the traditionalist Charlton, whose lectures he said were exercises in 'disinspiration', and Knights, the young challenger of established orthodoxies. Knights's method of approaching a text came out of his belief that 'the total response to a Shakespeare play can only be obtained by an exact and sensitive study of the quality of the verse, of the rhythm and imagery, of the controlled associations of the words and their emotional and intellectual force'.‡ While Charlton insisted that criticism shouldn't enquire into moral or philosophical values, Knights saw these as being at the heart of any literary text.

In his third year of study Burgess took the 'Elizabethan Drama and Society' course with Knights and Jump, which was to lead to a lifelong preoccupation with Christopher Marlowe. He wrote a 100-page dissertation on Marlowe's *Doctor Faustus* as an index to

---

The Great Tradition (1948), *The Common Pursuit* (1952), *D. H. Lawrence: Novelist* (1955) and *Two Cultures?* (1962). From 1965 he was Professor of English at York University. For his association with L. C. Knights, see Ian MacKillop's biography, *F. R. Leavis: A Life in Criticism* (London: Penguin, 1995).

* *Drama and Society in the Age of Jonson* (London: Chatto & Windus, 1937).

† Originally published as a pamphlet by the Minority Press in 1933, Knights's lecture is reprinted in his book *Explorations: Essays in Criticism, Mainly on the Literature of the Seventeenth Century* (London: Chatto & Windus, 1946; Penguin, 1964), pp. 13–50.

‡ Ibid., p. 21.

Elizabethan popular religious beliefs. His central argument was taken from William Empson's commentary on *Doctor Faustus* in *Seven Types of Ambiguity* (1930).* Empson argues that Faustus's apparent denial of the Christian framework of damnation is either an elaborate bluff, or else rooted in a fundamental uncertainty about the possible existence of hell. So when Faustus sells his soul to Mephistophilis and tells him, 'Come, I think hell's a fable,' he is simply trying to brazen it out. The key moment in the play, according to Empson, is when Faustus, at the very point of being dragged off to hell by the demons who have come to convey him there, says the words: 'Ugly hell, gape not! Come not, Lucifer; / I'll burn my books! – Ah, Mephistophilis!'.† The crucial point about the first of these lines, says Empson, is that the rules of metre demand that the emphasis should fall on the words 'gape' and 'come' ('Ugly hell GAPE not! COME not, Lucifer'). Those *not*s are weak, half-hearted. Marlowe's play, says Empson, is an example of the seventh type of ambiguity, in which the words mean both what they say and the opposite of the apparent meaning, 'so that the total effect is to show a fundamental division in the writer's mind'.‡ Following the Empsonian interpretation, Burgess claimed that Faustus is unpersuaded by his own words, and that he secretly desires damnation in order to satisfy his intellectual curiosity about the nature of hell. It is possible that Burgess saw in the play a shadow of his own apostasy. Like Marlowe's hero, he was both sceptical about the Christian notion of hell and simultaneously not entirely persuaded by his unbelief.

The figure of Marlowe appears repeatedly in the fifty years that

---

* William Empson (1906–1984), poet, critic and professor. His two books of verse, *Poems* (1935) and *The Gathering Storm* (1940), are reprinted in John Haffenden's edition of Empson's *Complete Poems* (London: Penguin, 2000). Empson's most important critical book is *Seven Types of Ambiguity* (London: Chatto, 1930; Penguin, 1995).

† Marlowe, *Doctor Faustus*, scene 19, lines 189–90.

‡ William Empson, *Seven Types of Ambiguity* (London: Chatto, 1930; reprinted Penguin, 1995), p. 271.

followed the composition of Burgess's pioneering dissertation. He has a bit-part in *Nothing Like the Sun* (1964), a hallucinatory modernist novel which arises out of, but wickedly deviates from, the known facts of Shakespeare's biography. He also occupies an important place in Burgess's script on the life of Shakespeare, which went under the working titles *Will!* and *The Bawdy Bard*. Burgess's Marlowe, an incorrigible blasphemer and enthusiastic buggerer of boys, is given many of the best lines in this script. He wanders around the London of the 1590s, full of insolence and wine, shouting that Christ was a conjuror and his mother dishonest, and that all those who love not tobacco and boys are fools. Burgess's Shakespeare witnesses Marlowe's murder at the hands of government agents, although he manages to avoid the assassins' daggers. The screenplay loses a good deal of its momentum after Marlowe has been killed.

Marlowe's *Tamburlaine* stands solidly behind Burgess's proposed television mini-series on the life of Attila the Hun, which survives in typescript. This later provided the basis for the novella 'Hun', published in *The Devil's Mode* (1989). Burgess imagines Attila as a reworking of Tamburlaine, the garrulous hero-figure whose unstoppable rhetoric drives the action forwards. The debt becomes obvious when Attila, in a frenzy of bloodthirsty insolence, declares that he has become 'the scourge of God'. These words are lifted directly from Marlowe's play – 'For Tamburlaine, the scourge of God, must die' – an homage to the original on which Burgess modelled his drama of an overreaching hero.*

Marlowe is also the hero of the last novel that Burgess published before his death, *A Dead Man in Deptford* (1993), a gleeful homosexual romp in which the amoral Marlowe penetrates the Elizabethan underworlds of theatre and espionage. Although the novel is propelled by the vulgar energy of its hard-swearing principal characters, it is far from being Burgess's best work. 'You are a lover of breasts?' Marlowe is asked early on. He replies, 'The swinging

---

* Marlowe, *Tamburlaine the Great*, Part Two, Act V, scene 3, line 248.

udders I was nursed at? I am given otherwise'.* This is a particularly clumsy way of establishing the fact of Marlowe's queerness, and Burgess writing at the height of his powers would surely have suppressed such an exchange. Nevertheless, this novel represents the final working-out of an interest which can be traced all the way back to his undergraduate dissertation at Manchester. Writing it was possibly a way of closing the circle.

*

The reading list for Burgess's Part One examinations in 1939 was wide and demanding. It was a traditional degree course, requiring examinees to demonstrate a detailed knowledge of English literature from the earliest Anglo-Saxon texts to 1760. This was well before the invention of literary theory as an academic discipline in its own right, but such theory as was available came out of Leavis's *Scrutiny*, I. A. Richards's *Practical Criticism* (1929) and T. S. Eliot's book of essays, *The Sacred Wood* (1920). Among the major set books were *Beowulf*, *The Saga of Burnt Njal*, *The Canterbury Tales*, *Piers Plowman*, *The Fairie Queene*, Jonson's *Volpone*, Donne's *Satires*, *Paradise Lost*, *Robinson Crusoe*, *Gulliver's Travels*, Pope's *Essay on Man*, Fielding's *Tom Jones*, Johnson's *History of Rasselas* and Goldsmith's *Citizen of the World*. Burgess was also following nineteenth-century History courses under A. J. P. Taylor, and wrestling with the *Epistles* of Horace and the *Annals* of Tacitus for his General Latin paper. His awareness of the literary canon was expanding all the time, laying down a fund of knowledge which he would draw on when he wrote his own history of English literature in 1958.

In the first volume of his confessions, Burgess looks back on his undergraduate days with guarded affection. He recalls in particular his involvement with the Stage Society and with the *Serpent*, a student magazine which flourished in the late 1930s until wartime paper shortages closed it down. What Burgess's

---

* Burgess, *A Dead Man in Deptford* (London: Hutchinson, 1993), p. 10.

autobiography cannot reveal is how his fellow students saw him, but a few of them are still alive to tell us. They knew him as 'John B' or 'JB', to distinguish him from a flamboyant student named John A. Wilson, who had arrived at the university the year before Burgess, and who had already established himself as a poet whose work had appeared in the *Serpent*. John A. Wilson sat on the editorial board of the magazine, and was therefore one of those responsible for publishing Burgess's earliest stories, criticism and poems.

According to the novelist Douglas Mason, who was his contemporary, Burgess was usually dressed in 'a long grey/black raincoat and a black hat with a floppy brim'.* Mason suspected that this rather dandyish appearance was possibly a disguise borrowed from Stephen Dedalus, the aesthete-hero of Joyce's *Portrait* and *Ulysses*. Burgess 'felt that he had much in common with Stephen,' says Mason. 'Music and James Joyce were the engines which drove his mind. Maybe Joyce was the more potent force of the two.' The new friends he made in the autumn of 1937 quickly became his drinking partners. Mason recalls that he and another English student, Denis Crowther Gaunt, met Burgess in the Men's Union during their first term as undergraduates, and at once formed themselves into a friendly trio. They shared an interest in poetry (which all three were writing and publishing in the 1930s), amateur theatricals and crawling around the city's pubs. 'It was necessary to get drunk in Manchester,' Burgess later told a television interviewer. 'If you found it was no longer possible to estimate how you felt, you knew you were having a good time [. . .] I liked the atmosphere of pubs,

* Douglas Mason to author, 14 June 2001. Born at Hawarden in 1918 and educated at Chester Grammar School, Douglas Rankine Mason trained as a schoolteacher and worked as a headmaster in Cheshire before he began writing novels in his early forties. His many science-fiction novels, which he wrote at the rate of four per year and published under the pseudonym John Rankine, include *The Weisman Experiment* (1969), *The Ring of Garamas* (1971), *Astral Quest* (1975) and *Last Shuttle to Planet Earth* (1980). Under the name R. M. Douglas, he has also written a romantic-historical novel, *The Darkling Plain* (1979).

the talk, the jokes. Behind it all was the noise of the piano.'*
Douglas Mason remembers that 'we spent many evenings wandering
about in the Shambles area of the city, where half a crown was
enough to finance an evening in a tavern'. Burgess was an awkward
drinking companion: not an aggressive one, but nevertheless prickly.
Another of his student friends from Manchester, Reginald Bate,
recalls that

> he was a person who did not find it easy to fit into the normal
> social life of a group of undergraduates. He was an extrovert
> person, and I often felt that he would express an opinion on
> some matter which we were discussing solely because it was
> controversial and different. He seemed to be always rather on
> the fringe of our group.†

Burgess was a theatrical figure, then, who wanted to give the
impression of being a vaguely Joycean artist, but he's remembered as
having been a marginal presence, too. The other defining characteristic that Douglas Mason notes is Burgess's dislike of his stepmother.
Disenchanted with his home life, Burgess was, as Mason puts it, 'very
much a lone figure'. Perhaps he was merely seeking to overcome his
sense of outsiderness by making outrageous statements in front of his
new literary friends. 'John was always inclined to turn idle chat into
a serious discussion,' says Mason. On one occasion in the Men's
Union, he suddenly asked his companions: 'If Jesus Christ came in
through that door, would you be surprised?'

Imaginatively, at least, the spectre of the Church still seemed to
be with Burgess. His ongoing preoccupation with Christianity is
only dimly reflected in the relevant section of his autobiography, but
elsewhere he said that he felt rebuked by the Church of the Holy
Name whenever he walked past it on his way to lectures. With
hindsight, he represented himself as a more secular young man than

---

* *Celebration: Burgess in Manchester*, Granada Television, broadcast 24 October
1980.
† R. G. Bate to author, 24 May 2001.

he seemed to those who knew him at the time. Although he considered himself to be a lapsed Catholic after 1933, he retained a keen interest – Mason calls it an 'obsession' – with the Church which he had rejected. Hence his self-identification with Joyce's Stephen Dedalus, who finds himself infected by a similar nagging guilt. Burgess summed up his own position – emphasizing his sense that rejecting the Church was a betrayal – when he wrote that

> The family suffered, apparently, so that I could achieve apostasy: an ironical end to the fight for freedom of worship. I am far from happy about this situation, but nobody can actively *will* loss of faith.*

Becoming an artist was, or promised to be, one way of filling the void that Catholicism had left behind it. Mason recalls: 'The general expectation amongst his friends was that John Wilson would have a career in music. Much of his conversation was about music and musicians. He was often working on some arrangement or setting which he would play on the piano at the Student Union.' Around this time, Burgess worked for a few evenings as a piano-player in one of the pubs in the Shambles, but he was sacked after performing the entire 'Jupiter' section from Gustav Holst's *The Planets*. Holst was not in heavy demand in the Shambles, and Burgess's taste was too upmarket for him to remain employed for long as a popular musician. He was temperamentally and artistically unsuited to pursuing his father's trade.

Douglas Mason remembers that he and Burgess contributed mildly indecent poems to the *Rag Rag*, a student magazine published and sold in aid of the university's charities appeal. They borrowed a suggestive limerick from the works of the composer Peter Warlock:

> *The girls who frequent picture palaces*
> *Know nothing of psychoanalysis.*

---

* Burgess, 'On Being a Lapsed Catholic', *Triumph*, vol. 2, no. 2 (February 1967), p. 31.

> *But Herr Doktor Freud*
> *Is not really annoyed.*
> *Let them cling to their long-standing fallacies.* *

Mason recalls that the limerick was published 'with a cartoon of broken classical columns and the caption "Ancient fallacies exposed".'† Burgess later wrote that his involvement in Manchester's Rag Day in 1939 was (along with his meeting with his second wife and the performance of his symphony in Iowa) one of the few moments of unmixed pleasure that he had experienced.

Mason also ran the university's Stage Society, and in 1938 Burgess provided original music (now lost) for his production of James Elroy Flecker's orientalist drama, *Hassan*.‡ What Manchester lacked, however, was any obvious trace of what Burgess termed the 'epicene'. Although there was a hard core of hard-drinking, hard-smoking men, and a smaller number of women students to be pursued, there were few aesthetes and dandies in evidence. The culture he inhabited was predominantly heterosexual, and if there were any same-sex fumblings going on among the artistic student crowd, they were all happening discreetly and out of sight.

Another of Burgess's associates at the university was Jack Allanson, an engineering student who had an interest in politics and the arts. Allanson was an active member of the Communist Party, the debates secretary of the Men's Union, an undergraduate journalist and a prominent member of the university's Socialist Society, in which capacity he was well known for his ability as an extravagant

---

* Warlock's real name was Philip Heseltine. The limerick appears, without acknowledgement and with minor alterations, in *The End of the World News* (London: Hutchinson, 1982), p. 209. For Burgess on Peter Warlock, D. H. Lawrence and homosexuality, see *Flame Into Being: The Life and Work of D. H. Lawrence* (London: Heinemann, 1985), pp. 78–9.
† Douglas Mason, letter to Burgess, 5 March 1987.
‡ James Elroy Flecker, *Hassan: The Story of Hassan of Bagdad and How He Came to Make the Golden Journey to Samarkand: A Play in Five Acts* (London: Heinemann, 1922).

speech-maker. According to his widow, Grace, Burgess's memory of Jack Allanson carrying around a complete set of the works of Lenin is 'slightly exaggerated'.* Even so, Marxism and Communism were very much in the air in the late 1930s. This was the period of the Spanish Civil War, and a number of left-leaning English intellectuals, including Stephen Spender, W. H. Auden and George Orwell, had gone to Spain to work with the International Brigade and the Republican army in the fight against General Franco's Fascist militia.† Auden's sixpenny pamphlet-poem, *Spain*, published in 1937 to raise funds for a Republican medical charity, was reviewed at length in the undergraduate newspaper at Manchester. The Spanish war presented British intellectuals with the problem of aligning themselves with one side or the other. Should they support Franco or the Communists? The neutral position barely seemed tenable. It was widely believed that Spain represented a small-scale version of the European anti-Fascist war which was undoubtedly on its way. Many of Burgess's literary heroes contributed to a *Left Review* pamphlet entitled *Authors Take Sides on the Spanish Civil War* (1937). Evelyn Waugh supported Franco. Graham Greene was on the side of the Republicans. Eliot declared himself to be neutral, but neutrality in this context was construed as a form of right-wing non-interventionism. Orwell dismissed the *Left Review*'s questionnaire as 'bloody rot', but his response was not published.‡ After 1936, Spain was an issue on which almost everyone seemed to have an opinion. This is reflected in the Manchester chapters of Burgess's

---

* Grace Allanson to author, 28 August 2001. For the reference to Jack Allanson and the works of Lenin, see Burgess, *Little Wilson and Big God: Being the First Part of the Confessions of Anthony Burgess* (London: Heinemann, 1987), p. 182.
† For a detailed account of the British literary response to the Spanish Civil War, see Valentine Cunningham, *British Writers of the Thirties* (Oxford: Oxford University Press, 1988), pp. 419–61. For Orwell's involvement in the war, see Bernard Crick, *George Orwell: A Life* (new edition, London: Penguin, 1992), pp. 313–52. A wider survey of Franco and the Civil War may be found in Piers Brendon, *The Dark Valley: A Panorama of the 1930s* (London: Jonathan Cape, 2000), pp. 307–50.
‡ See Cunningham, *British Writers of the Thirties*, pp. 438–9.

novel, *Any Old Iron* (1989), in which left-leaning students interrupt their university courses to go and fight for the Republican cause. Burgess himself did nothing of the sort.

If international politics were hard to avoid, Burgess seems to have remained unconvinced by any particular ideology as an under-graduate, though he certainly participated in the general feeling of anti-Fascism. His sympathy for Manchester Jews, especially the Jewish musicians who played in the Hallé Orchestra, comes through very strongly in *Any Old Iron*. Yet there is no indication in his published writing of the 1930s that he was ever persuaded by the argument (fashionable at the time) that Communism offered the only hope for defeating the Fascist advance in places such as Abyssinia and Spain. At the end of a decade characterized by political extremes, and in an intellectual climate which insisted on the necessity of making ideological choices, Burgess remained stead-fastly uncommitted. Fifty years later he wrote that he had 'never, not even as a university student, written anything that could be construed as politically progressive'.* He did, however, contribute a large volume of critical writing against the censorship of films, plays and literature. Burgess drew a firm distinction between direct politi-cal action and the absolute right of artistic free expression. But he was reluctant to concede that declaring himself to be against censor-ship might be seen as a political gesture.

Burgess's university years were pivotal to his development as a journalist and story-writer, and much of his progress can be traced to his involvement with the *Serpent*. One of his formative influences was the work of Alun Lewis, the remarkable mid-century Welsh poet who died during the Second World War.† Lewis had com-

---

* Burgess, *You've Had Your Time: Being the Second Part of the Confessions of Anthony Burgess* (London: Heinemann, 1990), p. 140.
† Alun Lewis (1915–1944) was born in Cwmaman, Mid-Glamorgan, and educated at Aberystwyth College. In his lifetime, Lewis published one volume of poems, *Raiders' Dawn* (1942), and a book of stories, *The Last Inspection* (1943). He enlisted in the British Army in 1940 and died suddenly in Burma in 1944, possibly

pleted his MA dissertation, on thirteenth-century religious history, and left Manchester – a city which he seems to have hated – shortly before Burgess began his degree course. But he left his mark in the form of published poems and short stories. Burgess's early experiments in verse have a certain amount in common with Lewis's Manchester poems, and it is likely that he read them in back numbers of the *Serpent*. Lewis, for example, wrote in his poem, 'Corfe Castle':

> *Those to whom life is a picture card*
> *Get their cheap thrills where here the centuries stand*
> *A thrusting mass transfigured by the sun*
> *Reeling above the streets and crowing farms.*
> *The rooks and skylarks are okay for sound,*
> *The toppling bastions innocent with stock.*
>
> *Love grows impulsive here: the best forget;*
> *The failures of the earth will try again.*
> *She would go back to him if he but asked.*
> *The tawny thrush is silent; when he sings*
> *His silence is fulfilled.* *

Picking up on the bird images in these lines, Burgess produced his own poem, no less apocalyptic in tone:

> *'Caution, caution,' the rooks proclaim,*
> *'The dear departed, the weeping widow,*
> *Will meet you in the core of flame.*
> *The running tap casts a static shadow.'†*

The imperatives recur throughout Burgess's poem: 'Act' say the ducks; 'Prudence' warn the pigeons. But who is the 'weeping

---

by his own hand. Robert Graves edited a posthumous collection of his poems, *Ha! Ha! Among the Trumpets* (1945).

* Alun Lewis, *Ha! Ha! Among the Trumpets: Poems in Transit* (London: Unwin, 1945), pp. 14–15.

† 'Joseph Kell' [i.e. Anthony Burgess], *Inside Mr Enderby* (London: Heinemann, 1963), p. 34.

widow'? Possibly this is a reference to the woman he mentions in the autobiography, who had picked him up in Manchester Central Library when he was in the sixth form at Xaverian College.* She taught Marxist political theory for the Workers' Educational Association and, having lost her husband in the First World War, was keen to instruct the young Burgess in the art of rubber-insulated sex in front of the gas-fire in her sitting room.† The other figure who stands behind this poem is Louis MacNeice, from whose 'Trilogy for X' Burgess borrowed several of his rhymes. His evident indebtedness to poets such as Lewis, MacNeice and William Empson (whose complicated, riddling verse was another important influence) reveals a good deal about the gradual evolution of Burgess's own literary voice.‡

The *Serpent* had been published since 1917, and its purpose was to act as a record of events at the university and in the wider world of culture: it published reports on student debates, concerts and plays; it carried reviews of new books; and it circulated poems and stories by Manchester writers. Bound volumes of the *Serpent* are preserved in the university's archives, and there is a full run covering the years when Burgess was a student. The magazine appeared five or six times a year, in issues of between twenty-eight and thirty-two pages, and was circulated free of charge to members of the Men's Union and the Women's Union. Burgess's potential readership in the

---

* William Boyd also makes this association in his radio play *Homage to AB* (BBC Radio Scotland, broadcast 21 August 1994).

† Another possible sexual encounter is worth recording here. Burgess claimed in a 1980 interview: 'I was seduced at the age of thirteen on a slag heap, somewhere around Moss Side, as I remember. It was very shocking. It frightened me out of my wits. It confirmed everything the Church had said about sex being a dirty business [. . .] I had my initiation early to the delights and terrors of sex.' This story may be pure fabrication: no such incident is mentioned in *Little Wilson and Big God*, and Burgess, who was not much given to reticence when it came to describing other sexual encounters, never referred to it elsewhere.

‡ For Burgess on Empson, see 'Television: The Arts', *Listener*, 18 February 1965, p. 275.

years 1937–1940 was around 2,700. After 1939 the magazine was sold for a charge of 3d. Readers who objected to the alarmingly modernist tone of *Serpent* poetry were not slow to complain, as the letters pages testify. Lance Godwin, a postgraduate student who was editing the magazine in Burgess's first academic year, seems to have viewed it as a vehicle for publishing his own poems, which he wrote under the pseudonym 'Walter Blent'. The poetry he favoured was Empsonian in its difficulty, and Blent's poems, like Empson's, often required footnotes to explain what they were driving at. A few lines from his 'Symposium' give a fair example of what this poetry looked and sounded like:

> *Icicles tinkle in the ruby wineglass.*
> *The rough linen is swathed in snow*
> *And the dried blood of the slain season*
> *Cuts a red gash in the frozen snow flesh.*
> *But in the corpses of those feasters*
> *The phallic germ is alone unwithered.*
> *Will snakelike strike that ice heart*
> *And turn it with fear to running water.*
> *In the untouched womb of the recumbent virgin*
> *Germ plasms come and go.* *

This poem provoked so many complaints that the following issue of the magazine carried a line-by-line commentary, explaining its ambiguities. Defending himself against his uncomprehending critics, Godwin wrote that 'the University has a gymnasium for strengthening the mature body; and it has a magazine for strengthening the young uncertain mind'.† The 'Walter Blent' poems influenced Burgess, who set at least one of them to music ('The rattle basket dry / Hung in the summer dust'), and they set the standard for his own undergraduate poems. Blent was one of the poets he knew he was up against.

---

* 'Walter Blent' [i.e. G. L. Godwin], 'Symposium', *Serpent Poetry Supplement*, vol. 22 (1937–8), p. 10.

† 'Editorial', *Serpent*, vol. 22 (1937–8), p. 63.

Writing as 'J.B.W.', Burgess contributed fourteen poems, three stories and five reviews to the *Serpent*. He also wrote unsigned pieces, subbed other contributors' articles, and sat on the magazine's editorial board. Some of his poems appear to be space-fillers, in which he makes a profound-sounding noise for the duration of five or six lines. Of the longer works, 'September 1938' is well known, since Burgess attributes it to his poet-hero, Francis Xavier Enderby, in *Enderby Outside* (1968). It begins: 'There arose those winning life between two wars, / Born out of one, doomed food for the other.' This sentiment is borrowed from Stephen Spender's poem 'In 1929', which asserts that 'A whim of Time, the general arbiter / Declares the love, instead of death, of friends.'* Even as early as 1929, Spender believed his generation to be suspended between two wars, and Burgess acknowledged the truth of this gloomy prognostication in his 'September 1938'. This was the year of Neville Chamberlain's Munich agreement with Hitler – the notorious last gasp of appeasement – and the annexation of Austria by Germany. An editorial in the *Serpent* from the same year indicates that Manchester's science labs were short of essential equipment because Britain's industrial production had already been turned over to the manufacture of armaments. Burgess's poem ends with a description of what will be left after the imminent apocalypse: 'Engines rusting to world's end, heirs to warfare / *Fonctionnant d'une manière automatique*.' This final line is borrowed from Flaubert's *Un Cœur Simple*, and the technique of collage (pasting bits of other literary works into his own poems) is one that Burgess had picked up from studying Eliot's *The Waste Land*.

The other long poem that stands out from this period is 'Wir Danken Unsrem Führer'.† Published in October 1939, the month following Britain's declaration of war with Germany, it speaks alarmingly of a possible future England ruled by the Nazis. The

---

* Stephen Spender, 'In 1929' in *Collected Poems 1928–1985* (London: Faber, 1985), pp. 35–6.
† Burgess, 'Wir Danken Unsrem Führer', *Serpent*, vol. 24 (1939–40), p. 4.

lines operate entirely through irony and negative suggestion, to give a clear impression of what Britain and France were fighting against:

> We thank our Führer for redeeming us
> From the ignoble sluggish slough of peace:
> For striking down the sleek, insidious
> Serpents that choked us; working our release
> From the semitic bondage of our race.
> Sun symbol held aloft, we climb still nearer
> To the pure sun, the one God-granted place;
> We thank our Führer.
>
> [. . .] We thank our Führer that he prophesied,
> 'Yours is the kingdom. You shall inherit earth.'
> Fulfilling that, men will have starved and died
> Gladly with pride in death through pride in birth.
> Shadowing space our fylfot will have told
> History's spring and end to the eager hearer,
> Our earth's first blood, our titles manifold.
> We thank our Führer.

This poem suggests that, despite his later denial of 'politically progressive' writing, Burgess, too, was engaged – in an ironic and roundabout way – with the politics of the time.

Burgess was pleased enough with some of his early poems to reprint them later, both in his novels and in the autobiography, where they are reproduced totally without commentary or explanation. Many of his Manchester poems are said, in the novels, to have been written by the poet Enderby – indeed, a generous selection appear in an appendix at the end of *Enderby Outside*, complementing those which appear in the main text.* But in presenting them as the work of a fictional character, Burgess distances them from the younger self who had written them, thereby prompting Gore Vidal

---

* See Burgess, *Enderby Outside* (London: Heinemann, 1968), pp. 239–43.

(reviewing *Little Wilson and Big God* in the *New York Review of Books*) to make the interesting assertion that 'Burgess himself is not much of a poet but his invention, the poet Enderby, on the showing of *his* poems is one of the finest of contemporary poets and ought to be anthologized as himself.'*

Burgess published three stories in the *Serpent* under his own initials, 'J.B.W.'† 'Children of Eve', written in 1938 or 1939, takes its title from the Catholic liturgy ('Hail, Holy Queen, Mother of mercy [. . .] To thee do we cry, poor banished children of Eve'), and is a fragment which imitates Joyce's *Dubliners*.‡ Burgess imagines a nun, Sister Veronica, who is in bed and on the point of sleep. The emphasis throughout the story is on her uneducated piety:

> When she was a child she had never thought that she would become a nun, and she tried to think what she would have been like if she had still been Annie Clafferty. She might have got married, like Peggy, who had been married two years, or like her cousin Nancy, who had just written two days ago to say that she was going to get married.

In her dream, Sister Veronica tries to concentrate on the image of the crucified Christ, but her thoughts keep wandering to the splendid bodies of the centurions at the foot of the cross. Forty years later, Burgess resurrected 'Children of Eve', and inserted it into the text of his longest novel, *Earthly Powers*.

Another story, 'Grief', was awarded the Sidebotham Prize of

---

* Gore Vidal, 'Why I Am Eight Years Younger Than Anthony Burgess', *New York Review of Books*, 7 May 1987; reprinted in Vidal, *United States: Essays 1952–1992* (London: André Deutsch, 1993), pp. 404–12, 412.

† The 'J.B.W.' stories are 'Elegy', *Serpent*, vol. 22 (1937–8), pp. 173–4; 'Children of Eve', *Serpent*, vol. 23 (1938–9), pp. 71–2; 'Grief', *Serpent*, vol. 24 (1939–40), pp. 75–6.

‡ Sean Finnegan, *A Book of Hours and Other Catholic Devotions* (Norwich: Canterbury Press, 1998), p. 343. The original Latin text reads: 'Salve, Regina, mater misericordiae; vita, dulcedo, et spes nostra, salve. Ad te clamamus exsules filii Hevae. Ad te suspiramus gementes et flentes in hac lacrimarum valle.'

5 guineas by the writer Harold Nicolson.* This prize was the *Serpent*'s annual literary competition, in which a practising author was invited to read that year's crop of new stories. 'Grief' is another modernist vignette about two schoolboys, Gerald and Leonard, who have saved their pocket-money to buy a boxful of fireworks to celebrate the Fifth of November, 'smooth brittle-sticked rockets and tightbound ripraps and pin-wheels, all heavy with powder and tantalizing with promise'. The boys are looking forward to letting them off when disaster strikes, 'the end of the world . . . a fifty-voice fugue, a deafening dazzling counterpoint of noise and light'. A pig-faced, thuggish youth deliberately throws a firecracker into their box of fireworks. Everything goes off at once, and Burgess narrates the catastrophe with a pyrotechnic display of his own, in a style borrowed from Joyce:

> Barraboom Leonard didn't dare look at Gerald hisssss as wheeee Geraald ssssssstooood there wyowwwwww aiaiaiaim-lessly thunderssssstrrrruck for brrrrroooommm neither Leonard nor Gerald had ever seen the other cry ever barrabooom.†

Throughout his Catholic childhood, Burgess had always been troubled by Guy Fawkes Night. As a boy, he 'had to pretend that the Guy Fawkes I burned in effigy on November 5 deserved to be burnt for failing to blow up the English parliament'.‡ In this story he takes evident delight in coining new compound words, as if trying to write a kind of Hopkins poem in prose: 'The chokethroat fogfilth of the day before yesterday,' and 'an agonizingly sweet alldrowning blurred sunset of grief [. . .] the allembracing allsubmerging ocean of grief'. This is the grief of innocence suddenly lost, and of the boys' self-pity in response to a random act of cruelty. Yet it is

---

* Harold Nicolson (1886–1968), author of biographies, travel books and novels, including *Some People* (1927). He married Vita Sackville-West (1892–1962) in 1913.
† 'Grief', p. 75.
‡ Burgess, 'You've Had Your Time: Being the Beginning of an Autobiography', *Malahat Review*, no. 44 (1977), p. 15.

Burgess's linguistic ingenuity that rescues the story from the oily swamp of sentimentality.

'Elegy' is the most obviously personal of the *Serpent* stories. It deals with the death of a father as witnessed by his son, and its publication in the summer 1938 links it to Joseph Wilson's death, from pleuro-pneumonia, on 18 April of the same year, at the age of fifty-five. Once again the writing reveals a debt to James Joyce, but this time it is the Joyce of *Ulysses*:

> I saw his death like this. He was as good as dead already. But the form and ceremony of dying had still to be observed. Frayed cords to untwist. A gasping pump. The heart's conceit to work itself out with flat logic. Meanwhile he had to continue to bear the terrible but mere offshoot of it.*

The influence of Joyce may be seen in Burgess's focus on the mechanics of dying, the reduction of the body's processes to a set of failing organs and dwindling sensory perceptions. The narrator observes from a position of detachment, and is distracted by the sound of barking dogs and children playing in the street outside the death-room. There is a coldness in this account, as well as a curiosity about how death goes about its work:

> Death began to use the body. There was to be observed the art or craft of death, the strangeness of its quiet expertness or efficiency [. . .] It bulged the eyes out of their sockets (all prayed, they pulled me to my knees), and breath puffed out the flesh of the spent mouth, the lips clothed in scum. Agony shook the throat. (Desperate, they sprinkled holy water on his pillow). The glow reblew faintly when I tried to close one of the eyes, and the nerves protested and worked life to the face. Then it was all over. The bowels and bladder gave way.†

The business of kneeling to pray is an echo from *Ulysses*, a reference to the moment in Joyce's novel when Buck Mulligan says

---

* 'Elegy', p. 173.
† Ibid.

to Stephen Dedalus: 'You wouldn't kneel down to pray for your mother on her deathbed when she asked you.'* Burgess's narrator genuflects in the story, but only when he is pulled to his knees by others. (When Burgess remembers the moment of his father's death in *Little Wilson and Big God* it is rather differently, claiming that, like the hero of Joyce's novel, he had refused to kneel as Joseph expired: 'All knelt except me, who knew my *Ulysses* too well. All remained kneeling for the collapse of the excretory system and the filling of the room with a stench that had to be termed diabolic'.†)

The true horror of death as he represents it here lies not in the body's physical collapse but in the objects which are left behind afterwards: the father's false teeth, his hairbrushes, his glasses, an unreturned library book. Leaving the corpse in the death-room, the narrator goes out and immerses himself in the stuff of life. He finds himself moved by voices, 'problems and syllogisms', the flavours of food, 'colours and sound'. Life goes reassuringly on. Clearly, the story is an attempt to come to terms with his father's death. At the age of twenty-one, Burgess was already using fiction as a way of making sense of catastrophe and loss.‡

Looking back on his early stories in 1983, at a French academic conference devoted to investigating the short story as a literary genre, Burgess was inclined to dismiss them as minor works. He referred back to 'Grief' and 'Children of Eve', but he neglected to mention his best story, 'Elegy', as if he had forgotten ever having written it. Making a distinction between the short story and the novel, he told his audience:

---

* James Joyce, *Ulysses* (London: Bodley Head, 1960), p. 8.

† Burgess, *Little Wilson and Big God*, p. 192.

‡ The autobiography tells us that his father's ghost appeared to him on several occasions in Manchester between 1938 and 1940, both in dreams and in person. Burgess saw Joseph, or a bowler-hatted man who resembled him, while listening to a concert at the Free Trade Hall. He also claimed that, after he'd watched his father die, he suffered from nocturnal ejaculations. This complaint seems to have been entirely psychosomatic. See ibid., pp. 192–5.

I deeply regret that I cannot tackle the form of the short story
... and I think this has something to do with timing – a simple
matter like musical timing, the telling of a joke and knowing
exactly how long to pause before the punch line. I've written
short stories, and I've known that they're wrong because they
don't end at the right point. Should they end later? Should they
end earlier? My timing has somehow gone wrong ... It's
ultimately an instinctual matter, and one's instinct may run to
either the short story or one's instinct may not. Mine, unfortunately, doesn't.*

Yet Burgess was a more accomplished short-story writer than he
thought. He regularly turned out stories for magazines throughout
his career as a writer, though he chose not to reprint most of them
in book form. His only book of stories, *The Devil's Mode*, appeared
in 1989, when he was seventy-two. The stories he wrote after he'd
left university are useful from a biographical point of view, since
they frequently show him working unguardedly and at great speed.
The lack of polish is part of their appeal, and Burgess often exposes
himself to an unexpected degree, particularly when he is writing,
directly or indirectly, about his first wife.

*

As a student book reviewer, Burgess's most notable achievement
was that of offending the poets Laura Riding and Robert Graves,
who were at this time living and writing together.† Burgess's

---

* 'Anthony Burgess on the Short Story', *Les Cahiers de la Nouvelle*, no. 2 (January
1984), pp. 31–47, 46–7.
† Laura Riding (1901–1991), born Laura Reichenthal, American poet, critic and
short story writer. She collaborated with Robert Graves on *A Survey of Modernist
Poetry* (1927). A collected edition of her *Poems* was published by Carcanet in 1980.
Robert von Ranke Graves (1895–1985), poet, novelist and critic, is best known for
an autobiography, *Goodbye to All That* (1929), a sequence of historical novels,
including *I, Claudius* (1934), and a reference book, *The Greek Myths* (2 vols, 1955).
For Burgess on Graves, see 'The Magus of Mallorca', *Times Literary Supplement*,
21 May 1982, pp. 547–8, and 'Graves and Omar' in *Urgent Copy*, pp. 203–9.

dealings with them began in September 1938, when he reviewed Riding's *Collected Poems* in the *Serpent*. Burgess compared Riding's work favourably with that of Eliot and Ezra Pound. He praised her, too, for not having succumbed, like Auden and C. Day-Lewis before 1939, to the fashionable temptations of Leftism or Communism. Much of Burgess's aesthetic vocabulary in the review is borrowed from Stephen Dedalus:

> Laura Riding practises an artistic asceticism which denies to her work all meretricious, all inessential graces and much of the old poetic clothing. Her verse, if one may use terms fast becoming clichés, is lean, sinewy, rugged, economic to the point of angularity: it strives towards a single active quality, an essence.*

Registering the spectres of William Blake and Gertrude Stein in Riding's poems, the review concludes with the statement that 'Miss Riding is essentially a woman poet, not a mere woman writing poetry [. . .] The idealized woman of these poems is one of those great-loined Females out of Blake's prophetic books.'

Riding read this review and was not displeased by it. Accompanied by Robert Graves, she visited Manchester before the end of 1938 to give a talk to the university's Literary Society. This event is recorded in Burgess's subsequent review of Graves's *Collected Poems*, published a few months later, early in 1939:

> Mr Graves is a disappointing poet. He has not developed much, even after meeting Laura Riding [. . .] I remember now how he came along last year when Laura Riding lectured to the Literary Society. A burly six-foot-two red-faced farmer-like figure, he sat on the edge of a sofa [. . .] making the sofa creak. And flicking cigarette-ends into the fire from that distance, he invariably missed. So with his poetry: he seems always to be hitting the fringe of his target.†

---

* Burgess, 'Proper Art', *Serpent*, vol. 23 (1938–9), pp. 21–2, 22.
† Burgess, 'Wood Not Trees', *Serpent*, vol. 23 (1938–9), pp. 50–51, 51.

There's no doubt that this is a suave performance on Burgess's part. And no doubt, either, that it's the work of a pushy lad, too anxious to tell the famous war poet, critic and autobiographer (the celebrated author of *Goodbye to All That*) how to go about the job of writing. What he didn't anticipate was that Graves would write an outraged letter for publication in the next number of the magazine. Graves fulminated against Burgess's suggestion that he had lifted a series of images from Auden's *Poems* (1930) – pointing out that the poem in question had appeared in print seven years before Auden's first book had been published. He ended with a point-by-point reply to Burgess's Literary Society gossip:

> Yes, I am tall, perhaps even burly. No, I have not a red face by any standards of colouring. And I am sorry if the arm of the sofa creaked: but nobody offered me a chair. And I am sorry if I threw my cigarette ends into or near a fire, but nobody offered me an ash tray, and manners forbade me to grind them into the floor with my heel. I think this is enough. If your reviewers cannot be courteous they should at least be accurate; and/or if they cannot be accurate, they should at least be courteous; and if they cannot be either, they should at least be apologetic.*

This letter sparked the beginning of Burgess's off-and-on campaign against the poet, which he pursued in reviews of Graves's *Collected Short Stories* (1965) and his translation of Omar Khayyám's *Rubáiyát* (1967). The vendetta was resumed in 1971, with dismissive remarks on Graves's 'pot-boiling' fiction in *The Novel Now*, and again in 1982, when Burgess wrote a long article for the *Times Literary Supplement* on Martin Seymour-Smith's biography of Graves.

Another of his slashing book reviews was of T. S. Eliot's play, *The Family Reunion*, in 1939.† Much as he admired *The Waste*

---

* Robert Graves, 'Correspondence: The Poet Replies', *Serpent*, vol. 23 (1938–9), pp. 55–6.
† Burgess, 'Rats and Bones', *Serpent*, vol. 23 (1938–9), p. 130.

Land and *Ash Wednesday*, Burgess found that the poet's imagination was not a dramatic one. He said that Eliot's plays, with the
sole exception of *Sweeney Agonistes*, were full of 'superficial profund-
ities' and inferior to the Auden–Isherwood plays, from which they
nevertheless borrowed a great deal. He complained that the characters were mere stereotypes, inhabiting the familiar English country
house of stage convention. Eliot, who had been born an American
and a Unitarian, had reinvented himself as an Englishman and an
Anglican. Burgess argued that he had also adopted the drawing-
room comedy, an English theatrical form, but this was already a
burnt-out tradition. These were harsh words, and his attitude
towards Eliot's plays had mellowed considerably by the time he
directed an amateur production of *Murder in the Cathedral* in 1948.
But it is likely that his decision to direct this verse drama about the
twelfth-century martyr Thomas Becket was motivated by something
more powerful than his aesthetic respect for Eliot's poetry. One of
the actors from this 1948 production writes: 'I remember discussing
Roman Catholicism with [Burgess] on one occasion when he claimed
that he could never throw off its discipline much though, in practice,
he defied it.'* Perhaps the Eliot play represented a form of Catholic
nostalgia, and a means by which Burgess could imaginatively revisit
his childhood in Manchester, where there had been frequent talk of
martyrs in the Wilson family.

*

Along with literary journalism, the most important activity of
Burgess's student days was the courtship of his first wife, Llewela
Jones. She was born in Tredegar, Wales, in 1920, and her family
history combines literary, scientific and academic elements. Llewela's
grandfather, Joseph Jones (born in 1867) was an inventor from
Bolton, Lancashire. He had made a small fortune from his patent
for a chemical fire extinguisher, which was widely used on the
Manchester Ship Canal. His son, Edward Jones (1886–1963), took

---

* Peter Walker to author, 5 September 2001.

a science degree at Manchester University and became a schoolmaster. He joined the staff of Tredegar County School in 1908, and taught science and sport there, although his teaching career was interrupted by the First World War. Serving as a sanitary officer in the Royal Army Medical Corps, he saw action in Egypt and Palestine, where he was wounded. Returning to civilian life in 1919, he taught in Kingston-upon-Thames and Newbridge before being appointed headmaster at Maescwmmer Secondary School in 1934, and of Bedwellty County Secondary School in Aberbargoed when it opened in 1937. On his retirement in 1949 the local newspaper, the *Blackwood Weekly Argus*, reported that he had never missed a day through illness in forty-one years.*

Edward was married to Florence Jones (1867–1956), and both were practising Anglicans. Their first daughter, Hazel, born in 1914, later became the dedicatee of Burgess's novel, *One Hand Clapping* (1961). The second daughter, Llewela, born in November 1920, was educated, like her sister, at local schools, and eventually she became one of her father's sixth-form pupils at Bedwellty. Llewela is pictured sitting on the arm of a bench next to Edward Jones in a photograph of the school's 1938 women's hockey team. This was the year in which she left the school and became a student at Manchester University. A cheerful-looking girl, she wears a striped school tie over her hockey kit, and her long, fair hair is tied back. Although she was seventeen when the picture was taken, Llewela looks a year or two younger than the other girls. She beams at the camera, whereas the others scowl or smirk. Her cousin Evelyn, who was six years her junior, remembers her as 'bright, intelligent and physically attractive [. . .] I seem to remember she was also a good mimic . . . I always thought as a child that she was great fun. Llewela and her sister were someone to look up to.'†

Llewela's family photograph album shows a branch of the

* Anon., 'Gwent Headmaster Never Missed a Day Through Illness', *Blackwood Weekly Argus*, 3 September 1949.
† Evelyn Jones to author, 4 October 2001.

Joneses who were well off in the 1920s and 1930s. In one early photograph, Llewela – who was always known to her immediate family as 'Liz' – is aged about five, on a family motoring holiday. She stands in front of a large and new-looking car, one of several such vehicles owned by her father. In another picture, Llewela is sixteen and on a holiday with Geneviève, her French pen-friend. She sits shyly on a harbour wall, wearing a cotton, floral-print dress and a white cardigan, her figure evidently no longer a child's. According to Llewela's niece, Ceridwen, she contracted hepatitis on this visit to France, and her liver was damaged by the illness. In an undated cutting from the *Manchester Guardian*, she grins toothily above the caption: 'The smile that collected £1,000 for the hospital'. The picture was taken during Rag Week in either 1938 or 1939. There is also a formal graduation picture from 1941, which shows Llewela wearing her BA gown and furry graduate's hood. The profile captured in the photographer's studio is gaunt-looking, almost undernourished. But there is a certain confidence about her bearing, which is not evident in the earlier photographs from her schooldays. Llewela looks ready to face an immediate future of responsible war work. Her left arm protrudes from the black gown; and an engagement ring can be seen on her fourth finger.

Apart from a handful of photographs, fragments of a diary, and a few letters which she sent home from Malaya, Llewela Jones left remarkably few visible traces. There is a solitary reference in one of Burgess's letters of the 1950s to her being at work on a girls' school story which he was typing up, but no typescript has survived. Her only known published works are the three novels she translated out of French: *The Olive Trees of Justice* by Jean Pelegri (1962), *The New Aristocrats* by Michel de Saint-Pierre (1962) and *The Man Who Robbed Poor Boxes*, a translation of *Deo Gratias* by Jean Servin (1965). These translations were made in collaboration with Burgess and, in the absence of any manuscripts, it is impossible to be sure how much of the text is Llewela's work.

Easier to verify is the fact that Llewela was not, as Burgess claims in his autobiography, a 'cousin' of the writer Christopher

Isherwood.* A family tree inherited by her niece shows that the connection was tenuous and distant at best. Llewela's father was descended from a female Isherwood (the mother of Joseph Jones, the inventor), whose married name was Frances Burdett Birch, which means going back four generations, to the beginning of the nineteenth century, before encountering any Isherwoods. If the rumour of an Isherwood affiliation signifies anything, it is that Burgess wanted people to believe that he was connected by marriage to another famous writer. It is clear from the birth-records that Llewela's family name was Jones, not (as Burgess often liked to suggest) 'Isherwood Jones' or 'Isherwood-Jones'. The other recurring myth about the Joneses is that they were fluent Welsh speakers. Hazel's daughter, Ceridwen, is adamant that this was not the case: 'My mother knew the Welsh for "Shut the door." That was about it.' According to Ceridwen, Edward Jones never fully lost his Manchester accent. Although the family was well liked in Bedwellty, they were always regarded as displaced English, or at best Anglo-Welsh.† The name Llewela is cognate with Llewelyn, but in Manchester Llewela shortened her name to 'Lynne' for the benefit of English speakers who had trouble pronouncing the consonantal double-L.

Burgess and Lynne met in the autumn of 1938, during her first term as a student at Manchester, where she was studying Economics, Politics and Modern History. She first set eyes on him when he was performing in a play for the Stage Society, playing

---

* Christopher William Bradshaw Isherwood (1904–1986), novelist and playwright. He published his first novel, All the Conspirators, at the age of twenty-four. Two volumes of Berlin stories followed, Mr Norris Changes Trains (1935) and Goodbye to Berlin (1939). He collaborated with W. H. Auden on three plays, including The Ascent of F6 (for which Burgess composed music for an amateur production in 1948). In 1939 he sailed to America with Auden, and became a US citizen in 1945. For Burgess on Isherwood, see 'Character Called Isherwood', Yorkshire Post, 8 March 1962, p. 4; 'Why, This is Hell', Listener, 1 October 1964, p. 514; 'Candid Camera', Spectator, 18 February 1966, p. 201.
† Ceridwen Berry, interview with author, 12 October 1999.

the part of a Ruritanian captain. According to the review in the *Serpent*, it was a lousy production. For Burgess, this new relationship meant frequent and vigorous sex after his long years of solitary creativity, which had been punctuated occasionally by guilty, furtive couplings with women. His discovery of regular sex brought with it a new set of anxieties, including the constant threat of accidental pregnancy. 'As a university student,' Burgess recalled, 'I indulged, as we all did, in the erotic act. Sex went delightedly on in the background, probably *because* it was forbidden. However, the guilt was always there [. . .] It was like testing Hell to see if it was hot.'* Most of their assignations took place in Lynne's study-bedroom at Ashburne Hall, the women's hall of residence, which was patrolled by fierce female wardens. None of the internal doors had locks, so Burgess and Lynne were in constant fear of discovery and recriminations.

The most erotic poem he published at this time was 'A History', which records a qualified delight in the fact of copulation:

> [. . .] he at least was amazed at the futility,
> Thought the whole thing overrated; out of mind
> Were the sweat and labour to compass an ecstasy.
> But with her an unpurposed external heat
> Had achieved the loosening of the icefloes.†

Burgess now began to write about sex with the confidence of someone who could claim a certain amount of experience in the matter. He also began to write earnest love poems in the style of Hopkins. One of these, whose title is simply 'Girl', characterizes the loved one as 'Brittle crystal'. Her hair is described as 'harvested sheaves', and her body reveals 'the flash / Of the flesh of a summer river'.‡ Another love poem, 'To Amaryllis After the Dance', ends on a note of frustration, with a riot of phallic images:

---

* *Celebration: Burgess in Manchester*, Granada TV, 24 October 1980.
† Burgess, 'A History', *Serpent*, vol. 24 (1939–40), p. 56.
‡ Burgess, 'Girl', *Serpent*, vol. 24 (1939–40), p. 26.

> *One never gets to know anything really, having no word*
> *To body forth a thought, no axe*
> *To reach flagged soil, no drills*
> *To pierce to living wells.* *

All this metaphorical talk of axes and drills seems to be in the service of a wider point about the impossibility of truly possessing the female lover. You can seduce her on a physical level, the poem complains, but how far can you ever know what's going on in her head? The other point made in the poem is one about the futility of words: they can't 'body forth' or capture the lovers' thoughts, since there is no ready verbal equivalent for the physical sensations of erotic love. If Burgess believed this in his early twenties, his later work rejects it out of hand. In mature novels such as *Tremor of Intent* (1966) he tries hard to find a prose-style that will be true to the experience of sex, even (or especially) in its wilder, sado-masochistic varieties.

*

By the summer of 1939, Czechoslovakia had fallen to the Nazis and Poland seemed to be the next target of their territorial ambitions. A second European war was looming. Burgess, having passed his Part One examinations, was by now living in the flat above 47 Princess Road with his stepmother, who kept an off-licence in the shop down-stairs. It was probably in a spirit of innocent recklessness – as well as wanting to avoid her unliterary company – that he and Llewela took themselves on a walking tour of France, Belgium and Germany. They were lucky to get out without being interned as citizens of an enemy power. In late August they were still in Germany. Chamberlain declared war on the first day of September, as they were returning through France and heading for the Channel. They came back to Manchester to find a blackout in force and air-raid defences in place. The new term began in October, but when Burgess resumed his

---

* Burgess, 'To Amaryllis After the Dance', *Serpent*, vol. 24 (1939–40), p. 89.

studies he knew that he would probably be conscripted within eight months, as soon as he had graduated. Reg Bate remembers a night spent on fire-watching duty with Burgess on the roof of one of the university buildings. 'We were never quite sure what our presence there would had achieved had any fire bombs been dropped,' he says. But when the air-raids came to Manchester, the results, though often catastrophic, were not always displeasing. After a particularly bad bombing raid, Bate recalls that 'it transpired the following day that almost every labour exchange in the city had been hit – and since this was where all the records about military call-up were held, we all enjoyed a year's postponement in our call-up'.*

As Burgess typed out his 100-page BA thesis on Marlowe in the summer of 1940, he was preparing to sit his Part Two exams. The syllabus placed a heavy emphasis on the history of criticism and the literature of the eighteenth and nineteenth centuries. For the criticism course he was asked to read Plato, Aristotle, Coleridge's *Biographia Literaria*, Walter Pater and I. A. Richards. For the literature courses he mugged up on Thomas Hobbes, Tennyson, Browning, Coventry Patmore, Hopkins, De Quincey, Keats, Shelley, Wordsworth, Crabbe and Byron, as well as Carlyle, Matthew Arnold, Ruskin and the major Victorian novelists. Having absorbed these works in the space of a single academic year, and having undergone eighteen hours of examinations in June, Manchester's English students were entitled to call themselves educated.

Burgess passed his courses in English, History and French. But the pass-list for summer 1940, now in the University Library at Manchester, indicates that he failed his General Latin paper. Against the name 'WILSON, J. B.' is written 'Failed in subsidiary subject, otherwise would have been II (i)'. The university regulations allowed for an oral examination to take place in the event of a failed Finals paper, but the purpose of his *viva* was never disclosed to Burgess. He believed, mistakenly, that it was to decide between a First-class degree and an Upper Second. Whatever was said in the examination

* Reg Bate to author, 13 September 2001.

room, he did enough to satisfy the professors of English and Classics and secured his 2.1. He was now John Burgess Wilson, BA (Hons), and ready to be absorbed by the British war machine.

For a few blissful months he simply waited, neither a student nor a soldier. There was still time, before the Army got hold of him, to undertake a secret engagement to Lynne. They were both aware that the prospect of such a union would distress her Anglican family and what remained of his Catholic one. Given the sectarianism of Manchester in the 1940s – a division reflected in the constituency of the city's two football clubs, Manchester City and Manchester United – they acted bravely in persisting with their relationship. From one point of view, he might have been said to be returning to his mother's Protestant roots by offering to marry Lynne.

*

The death of his stepmother that autumn, though not in itself the cause of undue distress to Burgess, was unexpected. Maggie died suddenly, just after he had brought her a morning cup of tea in bed. Later he replayed this death-scene in fiction. The poet Enderby fantasizes about poisoning his loathed stepmother in *Inside Mr Enderby* – he considers spiking her tea with rat-poison, but he lacks the courage to go through with the plan. Maggie, who had known both of Burgess's parents, was his last surviving link to them. He now believed himself to be fully orphaned.

He moved out of Princess Road to lodgings on Ducie Avenue, not far from the Whitworth Art Gallery, where his landlady was a good-hearted woman who raised no objections if unmarried couples such as Burgess and Lynne wanted to cohabit. While Lynne pursued her third year of studies under A. J. P. Taylor and Lewis Namier (considered to be two of the finest historians of their day), Burgess worked as private tutor for the eleven-year-old son of a Manchester garage owner. The boy had a heart condition and was too ill to attend school. This was undemanding work and not badly paid, since the boy supplemented Burgess's hourly fee with extra money from his own pocket.

Burgess continued to write music during the early months of the war, though it is unclear whether any of it was performed. 'Blackout Blues' was a collection of original cabaret songs, which promised laughter in the dark. He set T. S. Eliot's 'Lines for an Old Man', intending the words to be sung by an old man 'with wrinkled breasts', accompanied by a four-piece band, and he began and abandoned a short opera based on *Doctor Faustus*.

Finally, in the middle of October 1940, his call-up came. He was ordered to report to the barracks at Eskbank, near Edinburgh. He took few possessions with him, but his kitbag contained Hopkins's poems and Joyce's *Finnegans Wake*, published a few months earlier by Faber and Faber with a cover price of 21 shillings. This was considered steep, but Burgess reasoned that a novel which had taken Joyce seventeen years to write and virtually destroyed the author's eyesight in the process was probably worth the money.

He left Manchester, then, and never properly returned. None of his subsequent visits to the city lasted longer than a few days. In his early sixties he spoke about wanting to come home to Manchester, to be buried in Moston Cemetery. Returning with a television camera crew in October 1980, exactly forty years after he'd left, he said that the city made him feel both 'guilty' and 'wronged'. He felt the guilt of a self-elected 'exile'. If he hadn't left, he speculated, then he might have turned into a respectable Mancunian, ending up as a schoolmaster, or an insurance clerk, or 'a small journalist'. But he felt 'wronged', too, because he thought that the city had failed to satisfy many of the appetites which its own university had encouraged in him. Looking back on the formative years that he'd spent there, Burgess believed that Manchester lacked 'human potentialities, a measure of beauty, a measure of dignity'. He said: 'You come back and it is as it was – totally hopeless – and you want to get out again.'

Eight years after this melancholy return to the sites of his boyhood, Burgess submitted to the probing of Jeremy Isaacs for a *Face to Face* interview on BBC television. Isaacs asked him, shrewdly, what the boy from Moss Side would have said to Anthony

Burgess, the grand old wordsmith of Monaco, if the two of them could have met. 'I'd have said "Come off it,"' Burgess replied. 'Or I'd have said "He's turned into an opinionated, stuck-up *bastard*" – because that's the Mancunian response to anyone who's left the city and tried to achieve something in the bigger world.'* The vowels he used in making that phrase 'stuck-up *bastard*' were Mancunian vowels: 'stook oop'. For a moment it was as if little Jack Wilson had been resurrected to challenge his suave, cosmopolitan, cigar-puffing older self.

---

* Burgess, *The Late Show: Face to Face* (interview with Jeremy Isaacs), BBC 2, broadcast 21 March 1989.

3

The Army and Gibraltar

Boarding the train from Manchester with a degree and a few works of modernist literature in his kitbag, John Burgess Wilson entered a future in which war was the only certainty. Frank Kermode, who was conscripted into the Royal Navy at roughly the same time, writes in his autobiography that the possibilities of an indefinitely protracted war, or a sudden and disastrous Nazi invasion of mainland Britain, seemed all too real to those who were called up in 1940.* Burgess had written a respectable number of poems, a few stories, and a couple of book reviews. He had composed music, but had found difficulty in getting it performed in public. If he had been killed in the war, he would not now be remembered for any particular artistic accomplishment. Yet the Army, as well as being an organization he quickly grew to hate, gave Burgess ample raw material for three novels: *A Vision of Battlements* (published in 1965 but written shortly after the war), *Napoleon Symphony* (1974) and *Any Old Iron* (1989). Along with school and university, it was one of the institutions which shaped his character and his fiction.

Although Burgess's account of his war years is narrated in an ironic voice, his military service must have been full of discomforts.

---

* Frank Kermode, *Not Entitled: A Memoir* (London: HarperCollins, 1996), p. 84.

He represents the Army as a fundamentally absurd institution in which rank and promotion were unrelated to ability – resembling the disreputable private school in Evelyn Waugh's *Decline and Fall*, staffed entirely by maniacs and incompetents. The emphasis throughout his writings about the war is on the purposelessness of most Army activities. He describes his basic training in terms of endless shit-shovelling in freezing Scottish weather, with no particular aim in mind other than that of lowering the morale of new conscripts. A medical lieutenant named Empson took a dislike to his foreskin – which was said to be too tight – and decided that it had better be removed. Burgess refused to be operated on, but this episode contributed to his reputation as an awkward bugger. His respect for Army discipline was, even at a generous estimate, non-existent. The constant threat of being put on a charge for insubordination merely made him more bloody-minded. Later he summed up his resentment concisely: 'When I was a soldier I was taught: "If it moves, salute it; if it doesn't move, whitewash it."'* Possibly it was the practical, anti-intellectual side of military life that he took exception to. The autobiography might be thought of as a prolonged act of revenge-taking against everyone by whom he had been 'buggered about', as he put it, during these years of reluctant service for king and country. It evidently pained Burgess deeply that, as a young man in possession of a university education who at least *felt* well qualified, he was nevertheless expected to defer to career soldiers and public school men whom he judged to be his intellectual inferiors. He was never much of a warrior at heart – his reservations about violence are well attested – and it is no coincidence that, by the end of his six years of military service, he had failed to achieve a rank higher than that of Warrant Officer. Other university men who were more inclined than Burgess to suck up to their masters were able to enter the officer class with comparatively little difficulty, but his truculence kept him down

---

* Burgess, 'Thoughts on the Present Discontents' in *Homage to Qwert Yuiop: Selected Journalism 1978–1985* (London: Hutchinson, 1986), pp. 17–19, 17.

in the lower ranks. Still, he was relieved at being conscripted into the Ambulance Corps, where the likelihood of being shot at was fairly low.

Among other things, the Second World War presented hitherto unimagined opportunities for sexual dalliance. The maxim 'There's a war on' provided, or seemed to provide, a justification for any amount of venereal adventuring, and this phenomenon of the wartime easy pick-up is well documented. We can see it in the 1940s paintings of James Fitton, who published his work in *Lilliput* magazine. One of his images, 'West End – Two Doubles', shows two women sitting at a table in a London pub. They are eyeing up, and being eyed up by, a pair of men standing at the bar, one red-faced and clutching his glass, the other smoking and leaning on the counter.* There's a similar brand of easy sexuality to be found in wartime caricatures by the artist Edward Burra, which usually show grotesque, obese men leering at ample-bosomed women, who are strutting around on impossibly high heels with their cleavages jutting out. Many of Burra's gleefully saucy pictures are set in pubs, cafés or streets, the public places where sexual transactions were most likely to begin.

By his own admission, Burgess dallied at various points during the war: with the nurses at a mental hospital in Winwick, with a woman on Gibraltar named Conchita, and possibly with others as and when the opportunity presented itself. He remained in contact with Lynne by letter, but it was easy to make written protestations of fidelity while participating in discreet liaisons on the side. Many of those who knew Burgess later on have expressed surprise or disbelief at the account of his extensive erotic activities throughout the war. But in seizing the day as he (probably) did, he was behaving no differently from many thousands of other men and women who found the moral and social fixities of peacetime temporarily suspended.

* Fitton's painting is reproduced in Andrew Sinclair's *War Like a Wasp: The Lost Decade of the Forties* (London: Hamish Hamilton, 1989).

From Eskbank he was sent temporarily to Morpeth, Northumberland, but as the winter of 1940 drifted into the January of 1941, he was still waiting for a permanent posting. It was a depressing time of mindless Army routine, of the kind which he recollected in his late novel-in-verse, *Byrne*:

> *Once, in an army cookhouse, with the pans a-*
> *Wash in spuds I'd peeled, the thought arose*
> *That I was a mere adjunct. (See, that man's a*
> *Spud-peeling fist, no more.) So I suppose*
> *I'm now an iron pen.* *

One other melancholy episode stands out from this time. After a long illness, James Joyce died in Zurich on 13 January 1941 from a perforated duodenal ulcer – but Burgess, having no easy access to newspapers or a radio, did not learn of his hero's death until a week after the event, when he was looking out at the snow in Morpeth and attempting to clean the window of the Sergeants' Mess with an old copy of the *Daily Mail*. Next to an account of the bombing of Plymouth, he found the grim news. He recollected his next words as follows:

'Good God, James Joyce is dead.'
'Who the hell's he?' asked a sergeant.
'A writer. Irish. The author of *Ulysses*.'
'Aaaaah, a *dirty* book that is. Get on with the job.'†

Burgess dutifully crumpled the paper and went on polishing, as instructed. There was no possibility of finding anyone with whom to discuss the significance of Joyce among his fellow soldiers in snowbound Morpeth. As Burgess remembered it, Joyce, along with writers such as Radclyffe Hall and D. H. Lawrence, signified little to his comrades-in-arms except filth and the potential for sly, onanistic

---

* Burgess, *Byrne: A Novel* (London: Hutchinson, 1995), p. 47.
† Burgess, *Here Comes Everybody: An Introduction to James Joyce for the Ordinary Reader* (London: Faber, 1965), p. 18.

pleasure. Literature with a capital L was the yardstick with which Burgess measured his Army colleagues, not always entirely fairly, and the lack of comprehension between the artistic and the military mindsets is one of the underlying themes of his autobiography. But this was a failure of sympathy which clearly worked in both directions.

The Army did at least teach him how to swear properly. On one occasion Burgess overheard a mechanic performing a diagnosis on a broken-down motor vehicle. 'Fuck it. The fucking fucker's fucking fucked,' was the verdict.* This, he recognized, was a kind of obscene poetry. What was more, Burgess, with his recently acquired interest in the structure of language, couldn't help noticing that the word 'fuck', in its various declensions, was being used as imperative, adjective, noun, adverb and verb. Part of his Army uniform was a hat which was known to the men as a 'cunt cap', because of its vaguely labial shape, because it was a 'felt' hat, and (as he recollected in his memoirs) 'because [it] made you look a cunt'.†

Much later, he drew on his knowledge of the language of Second World War soldiers in a novel, *Napoleon Symphony* (1974), transposing the idiom of the 1940s on to the Napoleonic infantry of the 1790s. The liveliest sections of this novel are narrated by anonymous footsoldiers, who are intended to function as Everyman figures caught up in the international politics of the Napoleonic period, although speaking in a language appropriate to the ordinary man participating in any war, anywhere, and at any time:

> The fact is, lads, that those bastards in Marseilles did a fine fucking job of swindling the army, fat-arsed civilians who depend on us for our fucking lives, so get ready for starvation rations, horseflesh not too bad really as you already know, a bit sweetish but nourishing, we've got to hold out though, that's

---

* Quoted in Burgess, *A Mouthful of Air: Language and Languages, Especially English* (London: Hutchinson, 1992), p. 263.
† Burgess, *Little Wilson and Big God: Being the First Part of the Confessions of Anthony Burgess* (London: Heinemann, 1987), p. 245. See also Jonathon Green (ed.), *Cassell's Dictionary of Slang* (London: Cassell, 2000), p. 301.

the point [. . .] What's happened is that this General Melas has separated General Massena's lot, that's us, from General Suchet's lot and forced General Suchet's lot back to the Var. Well, you know where that is, lads, and you know what it all means. It means if we don't hold on here until General Berthier gets over the Alps and rams his bayonets up those bastards' arses, then the bastards will go marching into France and, as the song says, fucking our wives and sons and daughters. So we have to hold on. Any questions? Yes, when do we get some fucking leave, how about our back pay, I've got this pain in the balls citizen sergeant.*

This passage, delighting in its coarse inventiveness, tells much about the British Army as Burgess experienced it. Lacking, or failing to comprehend, the bigger picture about the war, the soldiers refer to matters which are purely pragmatic, their own pay and conditions. The political future of Europe means, in this context, fuck all to them. This 'lowlife language' (Burgess's preferred term for it) had a subversive function in the Second World War: it was what divided the men from the hated officer class. Amidst the many deprivations of military life, this language was one of the few aspects of working-class culture that couldn't be taken away. It offered a kind of consolation in the face of mass conscription and the risk of violent death.

Burgess's own war was far from Napoleonic. While serving in the Royal Army Medical Corps, he found himself posted to a military mental hospital at Winwick, which specialized in what was then termed 'General Paralysis of the Insane'. This was a euphemism for syphilis, a disease which, in its tertiary stage, leads to a softening of the brain tissues. What he found among these GPI patients was remarkable: approaching death, they suddenly developed new creative talents which they had not previously possessed. Years later, Burgess described some of what he had witnessed on the GPI ward to John Cullinan, who interviewed him for the *Paris Review*:

---

* Burgess, *Napoleon Symphony* (London: Jonathan Cape, 1974), p. 83.

I discovered that there was a correlation between the spirochete and mad talent ... There was one man who'd turned himself into a kind of Scriabin, another who could give you a day of the week for any date in history, another who wrote poems like Christopher Smart. Many patients were orators or grandiose liars. It was like being imprisoned in a history of European art. Politics as well.*

The idea of syphilitic creativity was one that he filed away for later use in fiction – it's there, in a modified form, in his Shakespeare novel, *Nothing Like the Sun*, in which Shakespeare dies of syphilis in the final chapter. In the interview Burgess went on to claim, though without much supporting evidence, that Richard Wagner, William Shakespeare, John Keats and King Henry VIII were all examples of prominent statesmen and creative artists who had been familiar with the symptoms of tertiary syphilis.

*

Burgess's phoney war extended for almost three years, until the end of 1943. He was posted to the mobile Entertainments Section of the 54th Division of the Royal Army Medical Corps. This touring concert party had been established by the Division's commanding officer, General John Priestland, and the musicians were therefore known as the 'JPs' or 'Jaypees'. Burgess's reception among them was frosty at first, since he was replacing a brilliant pianist called Tommy Smith. One of his colleagues, W. C. (or Bill) Brian, recalled that Smith's departure was the cause of deep gloom among the concert party and that, initially at least, they had their doubts about his successor.† Yet Burgess soon charmed them, and he was reckoned to be a more than adequate replacement, who brought with him the ability to write new arrangements of the band's existing

* John Cullinan, 'Anthony Burgess' in George Plimpton (ed.), *Writers at Work: The Paris Review Interviews: Fourth Series* (London: Secker & Warburg, 1977), pp. 323–58, 341.
† Bill Brian, letter to Burgess, 28 February 1987.

repertoire, as well as his competence as a self-trained composer of original music. One of the songs they performed to entertain the troops went like this:

> *We are the members of the band,*
> *We do not dance or sing,*
> *But we can play a nifty tune,*
> *And rhythm is the thing.*
> *I'm Ted. I'm Dick. And I am John.*
> *My name is Harry Walkling.*
> *They call me Styx – I do the tricks.*
> *I'm Bill – the trumpet's talking.* *

Whereupon Bill Brian – another self-taught musician, like Burgess – launched into a solo on his B flat trumpet. 'Styx' Williams was the band's percussionist and xylophone-player. Richard Nutting, who played double bass, remembers his fellow musicians as 'a very mixed and motley crowd', but he liked and admired Burgess for his musical aptitude and because 'he came from a very modest background'.† Mr Nutting writes:

> I found John extremely friendly towards me. Maybe I was in awe of his intelligence and various talents: he arranged music for the band and could always tell a good story. He was always ready to help Bill Brian and myself with our music. He was rather acid towards some of the 'prima donnas' who entertained, and aloof to the three ENSA girl dancers. Most of the group found him to be rather eccentric but Bill and I liked him because he was always straight to the point and honest.

In a post-war letter to Bill Brian, Burgess mentions some of the songs which formed the band's repertoire: 'Sophisticated Lady', 'Mood Indigo', 'Creole Lovesong', 'Folks' and 'If We Ever Meet

---

* Quoted in Burgess's letter to Bill Brian, 12 March 1987. The authorship of the song is uncertain, but it is likely to have been a collaborative effort.
† Richard A. Nutting to author, 5 January 2002.

Again'.* He also recalls in the letter that his concert party piano-playing was done 'without very much skill'. One of the band's original numbers provides a good example of concert party bawdiness:

> Caviar is the roe of the virgin sturgeon
> And the sturgeon's a very rare fish.
> The virgin sturgeon doesn't take much urgin'
> So caviar's a very rare dish.†

This song shows us what was demanded of Army musicians, chiefly lyrical cleverness and the gentle suggestion of indecency. Bill Brian recalled their touring band days with some fondness: 'We were young, there was a bit of magic about doing our thing whilst the rest of our age group spent their youth learning how to kill or be killed and, seemingly more importantly, how to polish, parade and bullshit.'‡

The Jaypee concert party travelled widely around England – to Chesham in Lancashire, to Moreton-in-Marsh in Gloucestershire, and to Eye in Suffolk, among other venues. At their Suffolk barracks the men were regularly woken before dawn by a sadistic sergeant who would shout, 'Out of them wanking pits!' or, more sinisterly and enigmatically, 'You've had your time, I'll have mine.'§ This expression continued to resonate long after the event, and eventually formed the title of the second volume of Burgess's confessions.

*

In the summer of 1941, Lynne had completed her degree. After finishing her thesis on the colonial history of Morocco before the

---

* Burgess, letter to Bill Brian from City College, New York, dated 28 April [1972 or 1973]. Collection of Mary Brian.
† Quoted in Bill Brian, letter to Burgess, 25 March 1987 (box 71, folder 1, Harry Ransom Center, University of Texas at Austin).
‡ Bill Brian, letter to Burgess, 25 March 1987.
§ Quoted by Burgess in his interview on *The John Dunn Show*, BBC Radio 2, 31 October 1990.

First World War, she graduated and found a job with the Board of Trade, working first at Bournemouth and later in Manchester. The exact nature of her duties is now hard to establish, but it is thought that she was involved in planning the Normandy landings of June 1944.*

Burgess and Lynne were married at the Register Office in Bournemouth on 28 January 1942 while he was visiting her on leave. This first marriage was followed by two more: a Welsh Protestant wedding in the winter of 1942 to satisfy Lynne's parents, and a Manchester Catholic ceremony carried out in the summer of 1943, to keep the peace with Burgess's remaining Dwyer relations. A photograph of Burgess and Lynne taken in 1942 shows him in uniform, looking cheerful but terribly gaunt as a result of war rations and the Army's compulsory exercise regime, which he resented and described bitterly in A Vision of Battlements. He was becoming accustomed to a diet of thin stews which nevertheless resulted in acute constipation. A combination of the war economy and German U-boat patrols around the coast of Britain had led to a regime of rationing and widespread undernourishment. Fresh eggs and milk were replaced by their powdered substitutes. In the absence of authentic ground coffee, everyone (except for more fortunate American servicemen) was forced to drink a vile mixture which was said to be derived from crushed acorns. Tea was still available but in short supply.

Characteristically, Burgess responded to these straitened circumstances by writing music. He produced a piece entitled 'Song for a Northern City', a nostalgic homage to Manchester, and a setting of Siegfried Sassoon's First World War poem, 'Everyone Suddenly Burst Out Singing'. Sassoon's text is not so much a poem about combat as an idealistic yearning for a better place. Written immediately after the Armistice of November 1918, it evokes a moment of sublime unison, in which the soldiers of the trenches are transformed into free-flying birds:

---

* Ceridwen Berry to author, 12 October 1999.

Everyone's voice was suddenly lifted;
And beauty came like the setting sun:
My heart was shaken with tears; and horror
Drifted away. *

The poem ends on an impressive note of affirmation, with the idea of an unstoppable and endlessly sustained song. In composing this melody, Burgess was asserting an opposition between the military present tense in which he found himself and the bigger realm of aesthetics (music, he was fond of saying, was a matter of pure structure) that he felt to be more relevant to his own existence. In its way, the song was about the values that the soldiers fighting the war were meant to be defending.

Burgess and Lynne's war wasn't unremittingly gloomy on all fronts. In 1943 Lynne's job moved to London, and she rented a top-floor flat at 122 Baron's Court Road. This flat is remembered by her friend Molly Currie, who visited her there, as 'sort of slutty'.† In spite of the danger of bombardment, London was an exciting place to be, especially for those who operated on the margins of the literary world or possessed an ambition to write. Alone at first, Lynne infiltrated the bohemian scene of poets and little magazines which centred on Soho. One of the friends she acquired there was Sonia Brownell, who worked at *Horizon* magazine for Cyril Connolly. Sonia became better known after the war, when she made a sudden marriage to Eric Arthur Blair (George Orwell) in the final days before his death from tuberculosis in 1950.

Lynne was Burgess's mode of entry into the bohemian milieu of poets, artists, fiction-writers and journalists who drank long, loudly and deeply at pubs such as the Wheatsheaf, the Duke of York, the Black Horse, the Bricklayer's Arms and the Fitzroy Tavern. She introduced him to the painter Nina Hamnett and the journalist James Tambimuttu, editor of *Poetry London*, who achieved notoriety for

---

* Siegfried Sassoon, *The War Poems* ed. by Rupert Hart-Davis (London: Faber, 1983), p. 144.
† Mollie Currie to author, 22 January 2000.

forgetting to pay his contributors. Alan Ross, the future editor of the post-war *London Magazine*, was another key member of this hard-drinking, hard-smoking crowd. At its centre was the esoteric figure of Julian Maclaren-Ross, a short-story writer, autobiographer and gifted raconteur who gained legendary status when Anthony Powell fictionalized him as the novelist X. Trapnel in his twelve-volume roman-fleuve, *A Dance to the Music of Time*, published between 1951 and 1975. Powell gives a semi-affectionate account of Maclaren-Ross in his wartime memoir, *The Strangers All Are Gone* (1982):

> An habitual *tenue* of semi-tropical suit, ancient suede shoes, teddy-bear overcoat (in winter), stick with silver (gold when in funds) knob, gave the air of a broken-down dandy, though just what breed of dandyism was not easy to define. There was something Mediterranean about the get-up, hints even of more distant climes.

Maclaren-Ross was rarely, if ever, seen without a pair of dark green sunglasses, which Powell thought gave him the air of a 'security agent or possibly terrorist'.*

In the 1930s Maclaren-Ross had worked as a vacuum-cleaner salesman in Bognor, but the war provided him with the material he needed to turn himself into a writer. After a short stint in the Army, from which he was discharged for health reasons, he published a successful book of topical short stories, *The Stuff to Give the Troops* (1944). He spoke fluent French and was well known among fellow drinkers for his repertoire of impressions, including a popular one of Boris Karloff as the creature from *Frankenstein*. Peace, according to the poet Alan Ross, 'did for him', because it deprived him of a transient audience willing to listen to his small repertoire of mono-logues. In spite of the critical neglect into which his works have now

---

* Anthony Powell, *The Strangers All Are Gone* (London: Heinemann, 1982), p. 7. For Burgess on Powell, see *The Novel Now: A Student's Guide to Contemporary Fiction* (London: Faber, 1967), pp. 82–5.

fallen, Maclaren-Ross was a character whom Burgess, Powell and others found enchanting and memorable. He was also the first proper writer with whom Burgess had been on drinking terms. Some of his traits are visible in Burgess's post-war professional Man-of-Letters persona, as persistent chat-show guest and tireless interviewee. It may be going too far to say that Burgess turned himself into a version of Maclaren-Ross; but certainly he admired his writing and acquired something resembling his haphazardly theatrical fashion sense.

The other wartime writer who made a large and lasting impression on Burgess and Lynne was Dylan Thomas, whose poems Burgess admired and whose bed Lynne briefly shared. Around the time that Lynne first met him, Thomas was writing his apocalyptic wartime poems about the fiery destruction of London during the Blitz, and a number of erotic poems which record and affirm the physical act of love in a calculatedly mystical language. It's impossible to say whether any of these refer directly to Lynne, since they address a general female principle rather than speaking in detail about individuals. Thomas's friend, the poet George Fraser, summed him up when he wrote, a few years after his death, that 'He used all his fire, his passionate dense imagery, in the celebration of all human and material experience. He wrote genuinely for the glory of God, as he understood God, and for the love of man.'*

The poet Gavin Ewart commented, a little sceptically, on the 'booming bardic readings' that Thomas gave in public. He brought something of the same style to his pub conversation. Soho pubs were his natural environment, and in one of these he met or was introduced to Lynne. In spite of his obesity, non-stop drinking and non-stop talking, women seem to have found his advances hard to resist. On the question of his sexual habits, Burgess wrote in 1980 that Thomas was, or had been, a 'great masturbator', presumably a piece of intelligence passed on to him

---

* G. S. Fraser, *The Modern Writer and His World* (revised edition, London: Penguin, 1964), p. 335.

by Lynne.* We don't know exactly when or in what circumstances Lynne began her affair with Thomas, but they went to bed together on at least one occasion while Burgess was away in Gibraltar.† It's likely that the encounter meant more to her than it did to Thomas, for he appears to have left no written record of ever having known her. Burgess seems not to have been unduly distressed by the knowledge of their affair, and the story of Lynne having bedded Thomas became part of his standard interview patter after she was dead. When Burgess returned to England on leave from Gibraltar in 1945, he established a cautious friendship with Thomas: they were on first-name terms, and Burgess recalled that he once watched the poet drinking lime juice in the bar at Richmond railway station to prepare his stomach for the day's drinking that lay ahead. (In America, Thomas breakfasted on beer and cigarettes, according to the biographer John Malcolm Brinnin.) Kingsley Amis, who knew Thomas slightly and disliked him at once, remarked that 'Being a poet meant for Thomas being his own man, being above convention, especially the tiresome sort'.‡ He adds that Thomas and his wife Caitlin were devoted 'not only to booze but also to petty criminality, minor fraud, stealing from friends and messing up their houses, cheating, cadging, above all [to] a shared conviction that rich, complacent people, i.e. those living off their own earnings, deserved to have anything movable taken off them by Mr and Mrs Dylan Thomas'.§

Nonetheless, Burgess's estimation of Thomas's poems was high, and he ventured the judgement that he was 'the greatest lyric poet of the twentieth century', defending his position with reference to Thomas's habit of cutting, shaping and reworking

---

* Burgess, 'The Celtic Sacrifice' in *One Man's Chorus*, pp. 172–75, 173.
† Burgess told his literary agent Deborah Rogers that the affair was a one-night stand (Deborah Rogers to author, 4 January 2002).
‡ Kingsley Amis, 'On the Scrounge' in *The Amis Collection: Selected Non-Fiction 1954–1990* (London: Hutchinson, 1990), pp. 208–10, 208.
§ Kingsley Amis, 'Life with Dylan Thomas', ibid., pp. 210–11, 211.

his poems.* 'Fern Hill' reportedly went through 300 drafts before it was finished to the author's satisfaction. In a long magazine article on Thomas, Burgess writes that 'it is the deliberate exploitation of ambiguity that makes his poems as densely rich as they are'.† He adds that the published letters, especially the begging ones, are a crucial part of Thomas's literary work; as are his short stories, parodies, and radio plays, especially the play for voices, *Under Milk Wood*. Thomas, who had worked in all of the available genres, was a true man of letters of the kind that Burgess became after he had abandoned his ambition to be known as a composer.

Dylan Thomas was not the only writer with whom Lynne was carrying on during the war. She also had an affair with a journalist named Archie Currie, a married man not much younger than her father. He was tubercular, ill-nourished and, by all accounts, entirely charming. Under the pseudonym 'Agag', he wrote a regular satirical column for G. K. Chesterton's magazine, *G. K.'s Weekly*. (Chesterton, a proselytizing Catholic, once referred to him as 'Currie the non-practising atheist'.) He also contributed to *Punch* under the initials 'AMC'. Eventually he divorced and made a happy second marriage in 1954 to a young former public school girl called Molly. Burgess and Lynne remained on visiting terms with the Curries, and the two couples often went away for weekends together in the 1950s. Archie and Burgess had a common interest in literature, which seemed to override any residual jealousy on Burgess's part. The knowledge of Lynne's wartime infidelity appears to have done nothing to sour their friendship. This affair and the subsequent amicable relations enjoyed by all parties give a good example of how open the Wilsons' marriage was, unusually so by the standards of the time. Molly Currie, the sole survivor of this quartet, still

---

* Burgess, 'The Writer as Drunk' in *Urgent Copy*, pp. 88–92, 89. Burgess quoted from Thomas's most famous poem when he spoke to Anthony Clare in 1988: 'I still feel rage, but it's a rage against the dying of the light.'

† Burgess, 'Man and Artist', *Spectator*, 25 November 1968, pp. 693–4.

remembers Burgess and Lynne with affection: 'Lynne had obviously been one of Archie's girlfriends before me, so the relationship between the three of us was always benign.'*

Burgess said his farewells to Lynne and to Soho literary life at the end of 1943. He had been offered the chance to transfer into the Army Education Corps in Gibraltar. He had vacillated at first, reluctant to abandon his musical friends, and he asked their advice as to what he should do. Bill Brian told him that, for his own sake, he should get out. If he stayed with the RAMC, there was a strong chance of being killed in action while carrying the wounded out of a combat zone, whereas the Education Corps would be a relatively safe posting.† Burgess followed Brian's advice and applied for the transfer. It was a slow process, and for some months he was stuck in rural England, although his musical duties there were congenial.

When he finally left it was on a hazardous outward journey which carried the threat of German torpedo boats. Burgess's troop-ship sailed west, out into the Atlantic, before looping back to the Straits of Gibraltar. The Rock was regarded throughout the war as a key strategic point: if Gibraltar fell to the German armies, then it would allow them to occupy North Africa with comparatively little difficulty. After the fall of France in 1940, all but 4,000 of Gibraltar's civilian population of 20,000 had been evacuated, most of them to Casablanca, Tangier and other towns in French North Africa. Meanwhile the Nazis had drawn up 'Operation Felix', a plan to invade Gibraltar via Spain, with the cooperation of General Franco and the supposedly neutral Spanish.‡ (When the imprisoned Hermann Goering was interviewed by Sir Ivone Kirkpatrick in Nuremberg in June 1945, he claimed that Hitler had ignored his advice to take Gibraltar. Hitler, he said, 'was determined to show

---

* Molly Currie to author, 22 January 2000.
† Bill Brian, letter to Burgess, 25 March 1987.
‡ On the military significance of Gibraltar during the Second World War, see George Hills, *Rock of Contention: A History of Gibraltar* (London: Robert Hale, 1974), pp. 420–38, 479–81.

the Spanish dictator that Germany could get on very well without Spain'.)* Although Operation Felix was never put into effect, the perceived threat of a land invasion was real enough, at least until the Normandy landings of June 1944. Burgess's first few months in Gibraltar were necessarily anxious ones. It was rumoured, for example, that up to 12,000 Nazi secret agents were working across the border in neutral Spain, many of them carrying false Spanish papers. This figure was probably exaggerated, but there is no doubt that there was a covert German presence in the port of La Línea, a few miles from Gibraltar. Burgess writes about this situation in his novel *Any Old Iron* (1989), in which one of the book's heroes, Reginald Jones, knifes and kills an unarmed Gestapo agent in Spain. His commanding officer is horrified by this act, and arranges for his immediate posting elsewhere. Sergeant Jones protests that killing Nazis is what he has joined the Army to do, but this argument cuts little ice with his military masters.

Burgess's immediate problem in 1943 was the infestation of his barracks by fleas, lice and bed-bugs. They persisted in spite of his energetic attempts to kill them off. On Sundays he would carry his sturdy iron bedstead outside and set it alight (producing 'a Magritte-like apparition', he said).† In the sergeants' mess at the Moorish Castle he also acquired a pet chameleon, regarding its colour-changing ability as one of his personal seven wonders of the world. He tested the legend about chameleons bursting into flames if they were placed on a piece of tartan. It refused to combust, but grew 'palpably unhappy'.‡

His new commanding officer was Major Bill Meldrum (1912–1996), a professional soldier who spent most of his career in

---

* Quoted ibid., pp. 429–30.
† Burgess, *On Going to Bed* (New York: Abbeville Press, 1982), p. 43.
‡ Burgess, 'My Seven Wonders of the World', *Sunday Times Magazine*, 16 October 1977, pp. 90–96. The full list of Burgess's seven wonders was: Tiger Balm massage oil; the chameleon; the pre-decimal British monetary system; *The Mikado* by Gilbert and Sullivan; the Petrarchan sonnet form; champagne; and Fritz Lang's *Metropolis*.

the Army Education Corps. Burgess conceived a deep and unreasonable hatred of Meldrum, who for his part seems to have regarded Burgess as an undisciplined waste of space, and something of an embarrassment in military terms. The confident and cocky Burgess threatened to be a subversive piece of grit in Major Meldrum's otherwise orderly military machine. As the officer in charge of Army Education on the Rock, Meldrum was in daily contact with Sergeant John Burgess Wilson, who was to serve under him as a junior instructor for nearly three years. Meldrum was an athlete and a redhead (thereby betraying his north-eastern Scottish ancestry), with a plum-wine voice and a reputation as a good organizer. He was a reading man whose bookish enthusiasms included detective stories, the works of Anthony Trollope and George Eliot, and Edward Gibbon's *Decline and Fall of the Roman Empire*. His son-in-law, Patric Curwen, recalls that Meldrum 'wasn't interested in music at all. To him music was just something people listened to. But theatre he loved.'* He would have had little or no sympathy for Burgess's ambition to be known as a composer.

Meldrum later served as Burgess's model for Major Muir in the Gibraltar novel, *A Vision of Battlements*. Muir (a Scottish name, like Meldrum) is a figure of scorn, mocked for his zealous attitude and half-educated malapropisms: 'You have violated instructions. Fragrantly,' he says.† Major Muir, we're told, has 'beautiful brown eyes' and speaks 'ungrammatically, with a home-made accent in which Cockney diphthongs stuck out stiffly, like bristles'.‡ The book dismisses him as an ignorant enemy of high culture, although the real Bill Meldrum, with his love of theatre, could hardly be written off in such terms. Within the novel, Muir embodies the senseless buggering about which the Army invariably represented to Burgess. The character is at the same time a comic triumph and an outrageous libel. Fortunately for both author and

---

* Patric Curwen to author, 9 October 2001.
† Burgess, *A Vision of Battlements* (London: Sidgwick & Jackson, 1965), p. 29.
‡ Ibid., p. 27.

publisher, Meldrum himself seems to have been unaware of the novel's existence.

Burgess's most important task on Gibraltar was to deliver regular lectures on 'The British Way and Purpose'. He drew his material for these talks from a series of eighteen booklets published under the same title by the Directorate of Army Education. The 'BWP' scheme, as it was widely known, had been in place since 1942, when the Army Council had given permission for every combatant to be released from other duties for up to three hours per week to be instructed in 'citizenship'.* It was felt necessary to explain to the men how the Nazi conquest of mainland Europe had come about, so they were asked to learn a great deal of political history. In spite of its jingoistic-sounding title, BWP was a remarkably liberal and forward-looking educational programme. The BWP booklet entitled 'You and the Empire' was more than an attempt to justify British rule in India and elsewhere. It looked forward to a post-colonial time when India would begin to govern itself.

Many of the BWP booklets anticipated the end of the war and its consequences. Working from this material, Burgess delivered lectures which asked serious questions such as 'What would you do with the war criminals?', 'Who will take over in the liberated countries?' and 'How can Europe avoid further wars?'.† With regard to the reconstruction of post-war Britain, BWP set out tentative proposals for full employment and a new Welfare State. This nakedly socialist agenda has been cited as one of the reasons why Clement Attlee's Labour government was returned in the General Election of 1945. Burgess took a more pragmatic view of the election: Labour had promised to get the men demobilized more quickly than Churchill's Conservative administration. The desire to go home was stronger than party politics, he claimed. It was as simple as that.

---

* *The British Way and Purpose* (consolidated edition, Directorate of Army Education, 1944).
† Ibid., p. 8.

In practice, Burgess's lectures often deviated from the official line. He recalled a particular lecture which ended abruptly when he told the men: 'You don't need me. What you need is a drink.'* One possible reason for his sceptical approach to the material is that the BWP booklets are virtually silent on the question of high culture. They have plenty to say about economics, justice, education, the Colonies, and the glories of parliamentary democracy – but it is likely that Burgess had ideological difficulties with the Leftist policies which BWP authors were advocating. Summing up his attitude to the Second World War in his seventies, Burgess quoted from C. Day Lewis's wartime poem, 'Where Are the War Poets?':

> It is the logic of our times,
> No subject for immortal verse –
> That we who live by honest dreams
> Defend the bad against the worse.†

This, in short, was what Burgess thought the 'British Way and Purpose' was really about: he was defending the bad against the worse, with no firm belief in the rightness of the cause for which he was required to speak. Day-Lewis, who had been a fervent recruit to Communism in the 1930s, expressed a deep scepticism that chimed with Burgess's own hesitations and reservations about the British Empire. Looking back on his Gibraltar years, Burgess poured scorn on BWP lecturing in two novels, *A Vision of Battlements* and *Inside Mr Enderby*. In the second of these, Mr Enderby, who is deeply drunk at a posh literary dinner, delivers a rambling speech which is intended as a parody of uplifting British Way and Purpose rhetoric:

---

* Burgess, *Little Wilson and Big God*, p. 307.
† C. Day Lewis, *The Complete Poems of C. Day Lewis*, ed. by Jill Balcon (London: Sinclair-Stevenson, 1992), p. 335. C. Day-Lewis (1904–1972) was a schoolmaster, poet, Oxford Professor of Poetry (1951–6), classical translator and publisher. As 'Nicholas Blake', he wrote a long series of crime novels featuring the detective Nigel Strangeways. Day-Lewis was appointed Poet Laureate in 1968.

We look forward to a time when the world shall be free of the shadow of oppression, the iron heel with its swastika spur no longer grinding into the face of prone freedom, democracy a reality, adequate health services and a bit of peace hovering dovelike in the declining days of the aged. And in that belief and aspiration we move forward . . . And thereto . . . I plight thee my truth.*

The point of this passage is that Enderby doesn't mean a word of it. He is speaking on autopilot, recalling his own wartime stint as a BWP lecturer, stringing together platitudes merely for the sake of making a noise. 'I didn't know what I was saying,' he explains afterwards. Burgess, on the other hand, knew exactly what he was saying, but he struggled to conceal his private doubts about its socialist agenda.

Burgess's other wartime jobs on Gibraltar were less demanding. Between 1944 and 1946 he worked as a film critic for the *Gibraltar Chronicle*, the oldest newspaper in Europe – and, at this time, the only anti-Fascist paper openly publishing on mainland Europe. By his own account, he did the job badly, and he eventually stopped going to the cinema altogether, preferring to write about films of his own invention.† The job came to an end, but Burgess had lost interest in film criticism long before he was sacked.

Around this time he made his only contribution to the *Rock*, an Army-run magazine which existed primarily to entertain the troops on Gibraltar. Most of the editorial matter was concerned with sport, with a heavy emphasis on regimental boxing competitions, but the magazine also ran an occasional poetry column. Burgess's article (which he signed 'J.B.W.') deplored the poor standard of wartime verse. He began with some general remarks on the state of poetry:

---

* Joseph Kell [i.e. Anthony Burgess], *Inside Mr Enderby* (London: Heinemann, 1963), p. 62.

† Burgess, speech delivered at Sardi's restaurant, New York, December 1971. Recording and transcript in Anthony Burgess Center, Angers.

Nowadays . . . [the poet] is lucky to be able to sing at all, and he certainly never expects his voice to be heard above the amplified dance band. The cruder but more insistent rhythms of an industrial age override his. There is little money, little glamour, little acclaim awaiting the end of his labours.

. . . But in art we cannot have, as in sport, one set of criteria for the amateur and another for the professional . . . If poetry is to progress the critic must have more whips than pennies. The amateur will never become a professional if criticism dotes and becomes overtolerant.*

This was a prelude to Burgess's stinging line-by-line critique of the poems published in the *Rock*'s 'Poetry Gibraltar 2' supplement. He accused one poet of producing 'wooden crudities' which had been lifted from Rupert Brooke and *Hymns Ancient and Modern*. He wrote of another poem: 'You would never think it possible. And in cold print too. As for the second line ["Such a large throne, such a small stool"], has the author the cloacal obsession or have I?' Elsewhere he castigated 'Worn images, imprecise expression of flocculent thinking, the obscurity not of compression but of ellipsis'. Of a poet named Paxman he wrote: 'I have nothing to say.'

The tone of his article was lofty and dismissive. This piece was Burgess's first and last contriubtion to the *Rock*. The magazine quickly found another writer to handle the poetry criticism, who was willing to take a tactful approach to the job. For Burgess this represented an undignified sacking. It was clear that he was not yet willing or able to take journalism seriously. He still intended to make his name as an orchestral composer, and this ambition is reflected in the central position that music occupies in his earliest surviving novel, about a frustrated composer who spends the war on Gibraltar.

*

---

* Burgess, 'Poetry Criticized', *Rock*, vol. 4, no. 8 (October 1944), p. 9.

A Vision of Battlements is Burgess's first sustained attempt at fiction. He completed a first draft a few years after he had been demobilized from the Army, at a time when wartime Gibraltar was still fairly fresh in his memory. The exact date of composition is difficult to establish. Burgess's introduction to the 1965 edition gives the date as 1949. In *Little Wilson and Big God*, published twenty-one years later, he states that the book was written while he was suffering from mumps in the winter of 1953, and in a later newspaper article about his first novel, again gives this date.* However, he also mentions that he has succumbed to the 'mumps pandemic' in a letter to the headmaster of Banbury School, Douglas Rose, written on 4 January 1952, making December 1951 or January 1952 the likely date when the novel was begun. An internal memo in the Heinemann archive (dated 17 May 1961) confirms that the book was 'originally offered to us in 1952 and rejected'. The editorial papers at Heinemann suggest that the book was rewritten at least twice – and rejected – before its eventual publication, by Sidgwick & Jackson, in 1965. Although it is one of Burgess's shorter novels, it is nevertheless long on ideas, and the brevity of the published text is partly disguised by the large typeface, and by Edward Pagram's full-page charcoal illustrations.

The novel takes its title, as the epigraph reveals, from an entry in *The Illustrated Family Doctor*, which lists the symptoms of migraine as 'tingling sensations in the limbs, impairment of vision, flashing lights, a vision of battlements, noises in the ears, mental depression or other phenomena'. Burgess suffered from migraines while he was on Gibraltar, but in wider terms the war, like a migraine, is seen in the novel as an episode of mental disturbance, a mass hallucination, or a collective feeling of unease. Burgess lifted the bones of his plot from Virgil's *Aeneid*. The novel's version of Aeneas, Richard Ennis, is a sergeant in the fictional Army Vocational Cultural Corps, which nevertheless bears many resemblances

---

* Burgess, 'Great Expectations', *Observer*, 'New Beginnings' supplement, 28 March 1993, p. 4.

to the Army Education Corps in which Burgess served. The German bombing of Manchester stands in for the destruction of Troy, and there is a flashback in which Ennis remembers carrying his father's body through the flames of the city. Gibraltar is reimagined as a version of Carthage, and Dido finds her equivalent in a Spanish woman called Concepción. The founding of Rome in Virgil corresponds to the prospect of post-war reconstruction in Burgess's updated version of the myth. Specifically, the music that Ennis proposes to write once the war is over is seen as the great hope for building a new civilization. In both cases the war is perceived as a necessary evil, a rite of passage on the way to building the Just City.

The precedent for updating a story borrowed from a classical epic had been established by Joyce, who had set out to modernize Homer's *Odyssey* in his *Ulysses*. Unlike *Ulysses*, however, *A Vision of Battlements* maintains a consistent narrative tone throughout, and the reader is free either to recognize or to discard the epic scaffolding, the important point being that a prior knowledge of the *Aeneid* is not really necessary in order to comprehend Ennis's humiliations and utopian ambitions. A few autobiographical elements are discernible in the novel. Ennis spends several chapters trying to write a passacaglia, and Burgess himself composed an overture for large orchestra (the 'Gibraltar Overture') in 1945, while he was still stationed on the Rock. He had also composed a passacaglia of his own in 1959, before the novel was rewritten for publication. Ennis, like Burgess, is asked to deliver a series of lectures on the 'British Way and Purpose'. And the letters Ennis receives from his absent wife bear a close resemblance to Lynne's letters, which Burgess quotes from in his autobiography.

Burgess set the pattern for his future novels by including a homosexual character, the ballet dancer Julian Agate, who shares a room with Ennis. Julian represents the epicene, or the twin Wildean devotions to decadence and Art for Art's sake. Ennis, confined within the predominantly single-sex community of the Gibraltar garrison, feels he is temporarily cut off from the peacetime sphere of women and sex, but he resists Julian's advances. The composition of music, as the novel sees it, allows him to assert his suppressed heterosexual drive. Ennis's weirdly libidinous art is the earliest expression of a recurring Burgess theme, namely that of maleness and creativity. This idea of 'masculine' music seems to prefigure Alex's interconnected enthusiasms for gang-rape, ultra-violence and listening to Beethoven in A Clockwork Orange. Ennis dreams of music that will be 'as elemental as water splashing or rocks falling, as brutal as the grind of heavy chains, something which would strike at the diaphragm'.*

Ennis – the maverick, thwarted artist – conspicuously fails to behave according to the pattern of traditional heroism in classical epics. He lacks the necessary bloodlust and clearly defined sense of duty, except to himself and to his music. In fact he has less in common with Virgil's Aeneas than with the character Jim Dixon in Kingsley Amis's Lucky Jim (1954). Dixon quickly established himself in the popular imagination as a new kind of bungling post-war hero: an intelligent and fundamentally decent man, but also one driven into spasms of fury by the university which employs him, and specifically by the complacent fossil of a professor who is his immediate superior. Whether or not Burgess's book owes anything to Amis must remain an open question. A first draft of A Vision of Battlements was in existence before Lucky Jim was published, but this early typescript is now lost. It's certain that Burgess carried out substantial revisions to his book after its first rejection by Heinemann, and equally certain that Amis had become a prominent figure on the English literary scene before he did so.† Burgess suggested in

---

* Burgess, A Vision of Battlements, p. 117.
† Christopher Ricks points out that the 1965 version of A Vision of Battlements contains the phrase 'the perils of hypergamy'. This is a word-for-word borrowing from Geoffrey Gorer's long article on Kingsley Amis, published in the New Statesman on 4 May 1957. We can be sure, then, that Burgess knew the article and was aware of Amis's reputation. In the circumstances, it would be astonishing if Burgess had not also read Lucky Jim before A Vision of Battlements was rewritten. See Ricks, 'Rude Forerunner', New Statesman, 24 September 1965, pp. 444–5.

his 1966 radio interview with Roy Plomley that his Gibraltar novel had actually anticipated other manifestations of the so-called 'Angry Young Men' of 1950s drama and fiction.

> PLOMLEY: You were one of the first to develop the now fashionable figure of the anti-hero?

> BURGESS: My first novel did have an anti-hero in it, but I've often felt that the anti-heroes of Kingsley Amis and John Wain and so forth came very late. It was during the war and especially in the services that young men began to feel that they were being fed a great deal of . . . a lot of . . . about the future, the great future that lay ahead, that didn't really exist and this quiet stoicism and irony began to develop.*

The missing word, nervously suppressed because it was considered unspeakable on the radio at this time, is either 'bullshit' or 'bollocks'.

There is a serious point to *A Vision of Battlements*, too, but Burgess deals with it so lightly and swiftly that the reader could be forgiven for failing to notice that it is there at all. The novel refers, in chapter 13, to a crucial meeting which took place at the end of the war. In a Gibraltarian bar, Burgess met the Spanish-American soldier whom he fictionalized as 'Captain Mendoza'. It was a brief encounter, but one which crystallized his thinking about religion and politics. 'Mendoza' put forward a theory about the well-known theological dispute between St Augustine and the fifth-century heretic Pelagius. Pelagius had famously disagreed with Augustine's notion of Original Sin, which states that man is born in a fallen state, naturally predisposed towards evil, and that it is impossible to proceed towards goodness and salvation without the intervention of a Christian God. The Pelagian heresy claims that it is possible, in broad theory, to perform acts of goodness while remaining ignorant of revealed religion – in other words, that Original Sin is not a

---

* Burgess, *Desert Island Discs* (radio interview with Roy Plomley), BBC Home Service, broadcast 28 November 1966.

universal phenomenon, and that man is born with an inbuilt procliv-
ity towards goodness and charity.*

Mendoza's refinement of this historical controversy was to equate
the Augustinian belief in Original Sin with political conservatism,
and Pelagianism with liberalism and socialism. Ultra-conservative
'Augustinians' believe that the individual is incapable of behaving
well without the repressive intervention of the state and its laws;
political 'Pelagians' believe that we are all equipped with an instinct
to love and tolerate our fellow human beings. Utopianism, free
speech, the pursuit of individual freedom and the just redistribution
of wealth are essentially Pelagian ideas. The repressive, bureaucratic
or totalitarian state is seen as an Augustinian construct. This is putting the idea crudely, but the important point is that Burgess believed
it, totally and uncritically. Later he dramatized the clash between
Augustinian and Pelagian ideals in a futuristic novel, *The Wanting
Seed* (1962). The hero of that book, Tristram Foxe, a history teacher,
is given the task of explaining the theory of the Augustinian state to
an audience of bored schoolchildren:

> If you expect the worst from a person, you can't ever be
> disappointed . . . The pessimist, which is another way of saying
> the Augustinian, takes a sort of gloomy pleasure in observing
> the depths to which human behaviour can sink. The more sin
> he sees, the more his belief in Original Sin is confirmed.[†]

On the subject of Pelagianism, he says:

---

* St Augustine formulated the 'dogmatic truth' of Original Sin, ratified by the
Council of Carthage in 418. This affirmed 'the immortality of Adam before the fall,
the transmission of sins to his descendants, the necessity for infants to be baptized
[. . .] and the impossibility for non-baptized infants to enter the kingdom of heaven'.
Pelagius (none of whose actual writings survive) is represented as having taken
a different view, arguing that mankind was predisposed towards goodness and
charity, and that it was possible to achieve salvation by works alone. See Eugène
Portalié, *A Guide to the Thought of Saint Augustine*, trans. by Ralph J. Bastian
(Westport, CT: Greenwood, 1975), pp. 190–91.
† Burgess, *The Wanting Seed* (London: Heinemann, 1962), p. 11.

Because of the fundamental thesis that the citizen's desire is to behave like a good social animal, not like a selfish beast of the waste wood, it is assumed that the laws will be obeyed. Thus, the Pelagian state does not think it necessary to erect an elaborate punitive apparatus ... Your failure to obey does not spring from Original Sin, it's not an essential part of the human fabric. It's a mere flaw, something that will be shed somewhere along the road to final human perfection.*

All this is implicit in *A Vision of Battlements*, the germ of an idea outlined almost at random by a stranger in a Gibraltar drinking-den, and Burgess would make it his obsession and his hallmark in his later novels. The Augustine/Pelagius distinction might be thought of as the engine which drives Burgess's mature imagination; it gave him a set of home-made theological spectacles with which to view history and politics. His attitude to the world, as he articulates it in his fiction, is deeply informed by an Augustinian pessimism about human intentions and behaviour. The Burgessian picture of humankind assumes that we are all predisposed towards committing acts of wickedness. The paradox is that he makes outrageous comedy out of this.

When *A Vision of Battlements* was finally published, it met with a warm reception, though one or two reviewers questioned the wisdom of publishing it with Edward Pagram's illustrations. Christopher Ricks wrote that Burgess had done well to capture the 'dreary impatience' of war, and that he had faithfully evoked the dialogue of barrack-rooms and the indignity of compulsory parade-ground exercise.† Jocelyn Brooke, writing in the *Listener*, praised the book's seedy atmosphere, with particular reference to 'the drabness, the squalor, the vomiting drunks, the beggars, the used french letters in the gutters'.‡ A. C. Cockburn, who reviewed it under the cloak of anonymity for the *Times Literary Supplement*, was less sympa-

* Ibid., p. 18.
† Ricks, 'Rude Forerunner', p. 444.
‡ Jocelyn Brooke, 'New Fiction', *Listener*, 30 September 1965, p. 505.

thetic. He said that the novel suffered from 'premature ejaculation' in its verbal effects.*

There is a scene in the novel in which Ennis is reunited with his wife after a long separation, and their love-making comes to a sudden and disappointing end. There is also some evidence to suggest that Burgess, too, had suffered from the same complaint. According to Moyna Morris, who was a teaching colleague of Burgess's in the 1950s,

> He told me that he was in the Rock Hotel in Gibraltar with a friend, watching a WREN having tea. He saw her crossing her black-stockinged legs. And he had that problem where boys can't hold back, which he writes about in the autobiography.†

This is an affliction which is visited on several of his fictional heroes, including the homosexual writer Kenneth Toomey in *Earthly Powers*. From a physical point of view, Burgess was in bad shape in Gibraltar: he was ejaculating uncontrollably in public places, dyspeptic, bitten by bed-bugs, tormented by migraines, and regularly smoking eighty cigarettes a day. His tobacco habit was a small gesture of defiance in response to the Army's compulsory fitness sessions, which, for reasons that remained unclear to the men, intensified after the actual fighting was over.

*

Lynne remained in London for the duration of the war, but in April 1944 a catastrophic piece of news reached Burgess in Gibraltar, via a letter written by Lynne's friend, Sonia Brownell. Walking home from her office one night during the blackout, Lynne had been viciously attacked by a small gang of American men, presumably deserters, who had robbed her in the street and kicked her as she lay screaming on the ground. One of these assailants tried to break

---

* A. C. Cockburn, 'The Ennead', *Times Literary Supplement*, 30 September 1965, p. 850.
† Lady Morris to author, 22 November 1999.

her finger to remove her gold wedding ring. She had been pregnant, but she miscarried as a result of the beating she received. She was told that the dead child would have been a boy.* When Burgess received Sonia Brownell's letter, he went to Major Meldrum and asked for permission to go to England on compassionate leave to visit his hospitalized wife. This was refused, and Burgess's resentment of Meldrum intensified.

The consequences of the attack on Lynne were immense. She began discharging an unusual amount of menstrual blood (the medical term for her complaint was 'dysmenorrhea') and she became anaemic. Ten years later, Burgess told a teaching colleague in Malaya that she was still suffering from 'perpetual menses'.† Her doctors recommended that she should drink pints of Guinness, known to be rich in iron, to replenish her lost red blood cells. Partly as a consequence of this medical advice, she developed a fatal enthusiasm for pubs and for heavy drinking, which began her long descent into the alcoholism which killed her. After the assault, her sex-life with Burgess lost its pre-war innocence. Although she continued to sleep with other men, she told Burgess that she now found intercourse with him painful and difficult.‡ The short-term physical injuries that she sustained in the attack were traumatic enough, but its enduring psychological effects cast a permanent shadow over their marriage.

---

* This is Burgess's preferred or authorized version of the story. His literary agent, Deborah Rogers, heard at least three conflicting accounts of it from him. Sometimes he merely claimed that Lynne had been 'attacked'. On another occasion he told Rogers that she had been raped by the deserters. In a third version of the story, Lynne had become pregnant as a result of the rape and deliberately engineered an abortion. 'I could never work out the details of the GI rape,' says Rogers. As so often with Burgess, it is difficult to establish where the truth stands in relation to his fictions (Deborah Rogers to author, 4 January 2002).
† Leslie Jones to author, 10 January 2002.
‡ Burgess told Christopher Burstall, who became a close friend in the 1960s, that his sex-life with Lynne was entirely finished by about 1965 (Christopher Burstall to author, 7 June 2000). And in *Little Wilson and Big God* he writes that their physical relationship declined after they left Brunei in 1959.

A few years after Lynne's death, Burgess described her symptoms in an interview with C. Robert Jennings:

[The attack] was followed by a disease that was very hard for the gynecologists to explain. It brought on perpetual loss of blood, perpetual menstruation, so there had to be a corresponding intake of fluid. She was not able to have children or even to have intercourse for a long time. Things never got really right again. And so she just resigned herself to the idea of wanting to die and drank steadily. I couldn't stop her. Finally she got what she wanted.*

Although Burgess states that it was impossible for Lynne to become pregnant after 1944, there is a letter that she sent to her sister on 28 March 1952 (two days after the birth of Ceridwen, her niece), in which she says that she and Burgess were hoping to start a family in the near future. It didn't work out that way, but Lynne was evidently still thinking and writing about the possibility of motherhood eight years after her miscarriage. Is her letter an optimistic piece of self-delusion? Or is Burgess's later account of her illness misleading? These are hard questions, and the only people qualified to answer them are now dead.

*

For Burgess, the final months of the war were filled with hack journalism, the writing of melancholy war poems and BWP lecturing. He celebrated the end of the European war on 7 May 1945 by going across the border to Spain and getting incapably drunk. He was arrested by the Spanish police for making insulting remarks about General Franco. He spent a couple of days in the jail at La Línea before being allowed back to Gibraltar without any charges being brought.

In the long summer of 1945, between the end of the European

---

* C. Robert Jennings, 'Playboy Interview: Anthony Burgess', *Playboy*, September 1974, pp. 69–86, 70.

war and the Japanese surrender, Burgess found and read a little-known novel which had a decisive influence on his later works. This was *The Aerodrome* (1941) by Rex Warner, a schoolmaster and classical translator who is sometimes described as the English Franz Kafka.* The novel is a dystopia in which a small corner of England is taken over by a gang of Fascist airmen, led by a charismatic and vaguely Hitlerish Air Vice-Marshal. Yet Warner's book is far more than a piece of crude wartime propaganda. Its cleverness lies in transposing the kind of paranoid situation found in a Kafka novel on to an English pastoral setting. Warner, though writing from the standpoint of a convinced Leftist, presents a serious analysis of the possible attractions of Fascism.† *The Aerodrome* offered Burgess a series of nightmarish ideas which he replayed in his own dystopias, notably *The Wanting Seed*, *1985* and *The End of the World News*. Nine years before George Orwell published *Nineteen Eighty-Four*, Warner had presciently hit on the theme of totalitarianism and dramatized it in a way that had a deep appeal. Burgess wrote a critical introduction to the 1982 reissue of Warner's novel, and the two writers struck up a correspondence (Warner admired the achievement of *Earthly Powers*, and he urged Burgess to write a novel about the Boer War). Decoding the allegory of *The Aerodrome* in his preface, Burgess writes: 'the village is the human family with its palimpsest of interlinked atomic families. Outside the village there is a great aerodrome dedicated to cleanliness and efficiency [. . .] The earth is dirty, and so are the men who work on it and live off it; the future lies in the unsullied empyrean.'‡ Warner was

---

* Rex Warner (1905–1986), schoolmaster, novelist, poet, and translator. His other novels are *The Wild Goose Chase: An Allegory* (1937), *The Professor: A Forecast* (1938) and *Why Was I Killed?: A Dramatic Monologue* (1943).

† Another Fascist dystopia which impressed Burgess was Sinclair Lewis's *It Can't Happen Here* (London: Jonathan Cape, 1935), a novel about the rise of Fascism in the United States. For a full discussion, see Burgess, 'Utopias and Dystopias' in *The Novel Now* (second edition, London: Faber, 1971), pp. 38–48.

‡ Burgess, introduction to Rex Warner, *The Aerodrome* (Oxford, 1982; reissued Harvill, 1996), pp. 6–7.

playing with fire here, as Burgess wasn't slow to realize: the novel appears to justify the murderous actions of the airmen while quietly exposing their ideology as dangerous nonsense. *The Aerodrome* is a remarkable feat of negative suggestion, and Burgess admired the craftsmanship that lay behind it.

Following the defeat of Germany and the liberation of Europe, news of the Nazi concentration camps was slow to reach Gibraltar. When it came, it did so in the form of newsreels. Like everyone else, Burgess was appalled by the images of mass graves, death-camp squalor and the terrifyingly emaciated Jewish men and women who had somehow survived. Once seen, these pictures were unforgettable, and the Holocaust was a subject that Burgess returned to in his historical novels about the twentieth century. The Nazi experiments in mass-extermination confirmed what he had long suspected about humankind's capacity for evil: he regarded the Holocaust as concrete evidence that Original Sin was still an active force in the modern world. He makes this point in *Earthly Powers*, when his character Kenneth Toomey is sent on a fact-finding mission to a concentration camp at the end of the war. His report presents the cold facts of mass killing:

> In a laboratory we saw shelf after shelf crammed with dusty glass jars with livers, spleens, kidneys, testicles, eyes in them [. . .] Then we saw the trapdoor and the chute to the basement of the mortuary block. They threw the rebellious and the mortally sick down there, ready for execution. We saw the forty gibbets with their forty hooks. There was a bloodstained Herculean club for finishing off the slow to die. Crematorium ovens. Calcined ribs, skulls, spinal columns.*

Toomey is shown a series of photographs which depict 'the smashed womb and the filthy slogans written in bits of entrail [. . .] Semen in the skull. The sexual apparatus torn out at the root and stuffed laughingly up the anus'.† His conclusion is that the Holocaust

---

* Burgess, *Earthly Powers* (London: Hutchinson, 1980), p. 456.
† Ibid., p. 457.

is merely a foretaste of other horrors to come: 'Man had not been tainted from without by the prince of the power of the air [i.e. the devil]. The evil was all in him and he was beyond hope of redemption.' It was a gloomy prognosis, but Burgess believed that the twentieth century was characterized by such outrages. He was doubtful that they could be averted by liberal political or educational programmes. He regarded the impulse to carry out large-scale acts of war and destruction as an irrepressible part of the human psyche.

The Second World War came to its horrifying end with the destruction of Hiroshima and Nagasaki on 6 and 9 August 1945. The Japanese government formally surrendered to the Allies on 14 August. Shortly after the news was announced on Gibraltar, Burgess witnessed a fight with broken bottles between British soldiers who could not agree about whether the word 'donkey' referred to the same thing as 'ass'.* Newsreel pictures of the atomic bombs found their way in due course to the cinema on Gibraltar. Watching them, the troops were in no doubt that they were witnessing a historical turning point. From now on, they would be inhabiting an age in which the threat of a wider nuclear holocaust would be the central, unavoidable political fact. Burgess composed a piece entitled 'Music For Hiroshima' at some point in the second half of 1945, but this is now thought to be lost. His most considered response to the era of the atomic bomb came in the form of a long poem, written nine years later, and at his instigation, by the sixth-formers he was teaching at Banbury Grammar School in Oxfordshire. Burgess acted as editor, and the poem, a free-verse piece entitled 'Sonata in H', was published in the school magazine, *The Banburian*. It is hard to be sure who wrote which sections of this work, but it is certain that Burgess had a hand in it:

> The squeeze of a button, the pressure of a thumb
> The windpipe of humanity wheezes asthma and phthisis

---

* Burgess, *Language Made Plain* (London: English Universities Press, 1964), p. 3.

Dark, clotted blood trickling, the convulsive world hears and
    constricts
Choking on radio-active air over Hiroshima, Nagasaki,
London, Paris, Rome, Cairo, Bombay . . .*

('Phthisis' is a hallmark Burgessian word, which also occurs in
one of his undergraduate poems and in several of the novels.) The
aim of 'Sonata in H' was to produce a nuclear-age collage vaguely
in the style of Eliot's *The Waste Land*, with Burgess carrying out
the Poundian function of paster-together and arranger of the fragments. The poem combines the vocabulary of science lessons ('The
hydrogen nuclei / Fuse forming helium nuclei and there is a /
Tremendous generation of energy') with a more thoughtful and
elegiac tone of voice:

> *There is no more crying to be done.*
> *You who lie*
> *In fleshrags gibbering now fly*
> *Beyond the reach of the stolen sun.*
>
> *Leaving a whimper of foiled questions, laughs*
> *Echo in the desert sand.*
> *The thrown ball, the child's raised hand*
> *Stand monstrous on the wall, the devil's photographs.*
>
> *But even the child's days begin*
> *With promise of the man,*
> *And this final thunder can*
> *Be heard echoing in*
> *The newborn gasp, the first tantrums of*
> *The primal sin.†*

These last lines, identifying the H-bomb as another manifestation of Original Sin, sound characteristic of Burgess. Whoever wrote

---

* Anon., 'Sonata in H', *Banburian*, vol. 12, no. 2 (May 1954), pp. 5–8, 6. The
poem is unsigned, and identified only as being the work of '6B English'.
† Ibid., p. 7.

them – whether it was Burgess himself or one of his pupils – did so with a knowledge of his theological views. His attitude to the politics of nuclear weapons is more difficult to interpret. By the early 1960s he tended to regard the anti-nuclear peace movement more critically, suspecting its Leftist leaders of being crypto-Communists. Yet some of his Eastern European novels (such as *Tremor of Intent* and *Honey for the Bears*) are closely engaged with the Cold War which began in 1945, and these books communicate his unease about the nuclear stockpiling that was symptomatic of the prolonged Americo-Russian stand-off.* The character Edwin Roper, an English nuclear scientist who defects to the Soviets in *Tremor of Intent*, functions as a metaphor for espionage, betrayal and double-dealing. The atomic age, as Burgess sees it, is a troubled time in which loyalty can easily be bought and sold. The 'final thunder' of which the poem speaks reminds us that the Cold War was more than a game between the superpowers, and that its consequences could be terminal and catastrophic. Although the Second World War was over, the threat of Armageddon was still present. But the idea of a global catastrophe was also attractive to Burgess as a subject for fiction, and in 1982 he published *The End of the World News*, an apocalyptic fantasy which speculates about the final destruction of the earth. A handful of survivors blast themselves into space, but everyone else is killed by the after-effects of a crash-landing asteroid.

*

In spite of the armistice, Burgess was far from being out of Army Education. When he was informed by the War Office in London that he would not be demobilized for at least another year, his disappointment was matched by that of Major Meldrum. The two antagonists were stuck with each other's company, but both faced the immediate task of organizing some kind of provisional

* For Burgess on the Cold War, see 'The Human Russians', *Listener*, 28 December 1961, pp. 1107–8; 'A Metaphysical City', *Listener*, 4 July 1963, p. 30; and 'Funeral in Berlin', *Saturday Review*, 15 September 1979, p. 10.

education system for Gibraltar's returning civilian population. Burgess was given responsibility for running the Gibraltar Evening Institute, an adult education facility, and he volunteered to give lectures and recitals for the British Council, the YMCA and the Gibraltar Literary and Debating Society. As the Army switched its attention from adult to child education, he was involved with re-equipping local schools, and he taught classes in English, Spanish and French. This was an opportunity to pick up teaching experience which might make him more employable in civilian life. He delivered lecture courses on phonetics, English drama, the modern novel and the techniques of journalism. He also taught philosophy, philology, German and music, including a piano-playing course for beginners. The haphazard education that he had acquired mostly through wide and random private reading was at last beginning to pay some dividends. More importantly, he was gathering the material which would later be deployed in *A Vision of Battlements*, and writing the music which would become Ennis's music in the novel. One consequence of the peace was that he was ordered to attend a training course so that he could learn how to shoot. The irony of being instructed in the art of efficient killing when there was no longer an enemy to kill wasn't lost on him. This episode seemed to confirm what he had long suspected about military logic. Although he achieved a marksman's score on the firing-range, it was too late to deploy this skill to any practical purpose.

Sailing home to England, Burgess stood on the deck of his troop-ship and watched Gibraltar as it seemed to vanish into the sea. Later he wrote: 'The Rock sank, englutted to the fading of slow chords, raising not a bubble.'* When he returned there for a holiday with Lynne in 1966, he enjoyed his visit because Gibraltar no longer represented unpleasurable incarceration by the Army. He said of this later visit: 'I don't know whether I like Gibraltar or not, but it became an aspect of my private mythology, and I can claim a minor

---

* Burgess, *A Vision of Battlements*, p. 266.

part in its history.'* He told his friend Anthony Froggatt that, as he disembarked from the ship in England in 1946, a loose filling fell out of one of his teeth and bounced down the gangway ahead of him.† It was a moment of low comedy and humiliation, a kind of mini-defeat in the jaws of victory that wouldn't be out of place in a Burgess novel. Gloomily, he followed his filling to the quayside and prepared to re-enter civilian life.

---

* Burgess, 'Rock of Ages', *Guardian*, 9 November 1966, p. 18.
† Anthony Froggatt to author, 20 July 2000.

4

Schoolmaster

Burgess's reunion with Lynne was far from joyful. She had been carrying on a complicated affair with two brothers, Eddie and Herbert Williams, and she did not propose to end it merely because her husband had returned from Gibraltar. When Burgess attempted to resume sexual relations with his wife, they discovered that one of them (they weren't sure which) had passed on crab-lice to the other. They shaved each other's pubic hair with a safety razor in the bedroom of a cheap hotel. Then Lynne returned to the arms of the brothers Williams.

In August 1946 Burgess found a teaching job in England. Although he was delighted to be out of the Army, this was not quite a civilian job. Employed by the Central Council for Adult Education in His Majesty's Forces, he was a full-time lecturer working, under the umbrella of Birmingham University's extra-mural department, to equip demobilized military conscripts with qualifications and experience suitable for civilian life. He moved to Brinsford Lodge, a residential college near Wolverhampton. It was an all-male institution, and there was no accommodation there for Lynne. His students were members of the Royal Army Education Corps, and Burgess's main task was to give preliminary instruction in teaching techniques. In addition, he gave lecture courses in 'civics' and cultural subjects, including government and politics, international affairs, English literature, drama, the appreciation of music, and European history. In many respects this was a continuation of the haphazard post-war teaching work that he had done on Gibraltar. He also arranged timetables, booked visiting lecturers, and looked after the welfare of the residential students.

While Lynne was pursuing erotic adventures elsewhere, Burgess met and fell in love with a Jewish woman from London. She was a sergeant in the Auxiliary Training Service who had been posted to Brinsford Lodge. Although he never disclosed her name, he said later that, if he had been single, he would certainly have wanted to marry her. Yet he retained a vestigial Catholic belief in the idea of marriage as an indissoluble bond, and he regarded divorce from Lynne as out of the question. The liaison was passionate and indiscreet: everyone at the barracks knew about it, with the sole exception of Lieutenant-Colonel Scriven, Burgess's commanding officer. Their affair lasted until the woman received another posting. Lynne had by this time broken up with the brothers Williams, and she and Burgess agreed to restart their married life in earnest.

In 1948 he moved to a second teaching post, a lectureship in Speech and Drama at Bamber Bridge Emergency Training College, near Preston in Lancashire.* He was again training teachers as part of the Labour government's post-war initiative to convert returning military men into qualified schoolmasters. Over the course of two years, Burgess was responsible for educating 360 men. Most of the students at Bamber Bridge were former fighter pilots, infantry men and munitions workers. They undertook an intensive one-year teacher-training course, and Burgess was ideally placed to instruct them, deploying his by now considerable experience as an Army lecturer. It suited him to be back in his native Lancashire, and as a Catholic he was pleased to be working near Preston (the name is a contraction of 'priest town'), which had been one of the centres of

* For Burgess's short (and strangely uninformative) memoir of Bamber Bridge, see 'The Brigg' in *One Man's Chorus: The Uncollected Writings*, ed. by Ben Forkner (New York: Carroll & Graf, 1998) pp. 42–8.

recusancy in the sixteenth and seventeenth centuries. Lynne had difficulty understanding Lancashire dialect, but Burgess recognized it as part of his heritage, the language he had heard spoken by his Wilson grandfather. When Burgess and Lynne went into a pub on a rainy day, she was asked by one of the locals: 'Art witshert?' He was able to translate this as 'Art [thou] wet-shod?', meaning 'Are your feet wet?'*

One of his students at Bamber Bridge, Don Briddock, remembers Burgess and Lynne as 'great socializers' who were 'well known for their somewhat Bohemian lifestyle'.† Mr Briddock was particularly impressed by Burgess's sharp ear for language:

> One thing that stands out in my memory about John Wilson was his extraordinary grasp of dialect [. . .] I was born quite close to his own place of birth in Manchester and I remember him going round the class asking each in turn to say something and identifying with uncanny accuracy the part of the country from which the speaker came [. . .] With all of those who came from Manchester he not only identified them as Mancunians but pinpointed the district, almost the very street in which they lived. It was an amazing performance.

Another Bamber Bridge student, Noël Makin, became a personal friend, and he continued to correspond with Burgess after they had both left the college. Makin, who had been a conscientious objector serving with the Merchant Navy during the war, remembers Burgess for his relaxed approach to teaching:

> John used no notes; there was just an effortless, articulate flow with enough humour to make what was (to me) a really boring subject tolerable [. . .] He thought we might be surprised to see him, a youngish male, lecturing in a subject which was usually the province of 'unfructified duennas'. There was an element of

---

* Burgess, *Language Made Plain* (London: English Universities Press, 1964), p. 144.
† Don Briddock to author, 18 January 2001.

shock because, for all of us (I think) our last teaching had been by stuffy grammar school teachers.*

Noël Makin remembers Burgess's classes as being 'a laugh', and he was delighted that this eccentric lecturer seemed willing to treat his students as adults, even to the extent of getting drunk with them after hours in a local pub, the Red Bull: 'He showed a capacity for beer and for both good argument and polemic.' But when the students congregated in Burgess's flat at the college, they had to contend with Lynne. Her presence often meant that 'arguments could become unpleasantly aggressive and personal, with John trying to calm things without ever putting her down'. Makin's abiding memory of Lynne is that she was 'generally vicious' and argumentative. Yet he remained fond of Burgess himself, and introduced him to a number of friends who were 'enormously impressed' by his powers of conversation.

The main part of Burgess's work involved teaching basic courses in phonetics and voice production. He held individual corrective sessions for students who suffered from speech defects such as cleft palates, lisping, or 'rhotacismus' (the technical term for a mispronunciation of the phoneme 'r'). Beyond this, he supervised teaching practices, gave advanced courses in the history of drama and dramatic technique, and took full responsibility for student drama productions within the college. He organized a debating society, a gramophone club and an informal group known as the Chaucer Society, whose purpose was to investigate the history of English pronunciation.† He found time in the evenings to run another drama class for the Workers' Educational Association in Chorley.

The dramatic activities of the college consumed a good deal of his energies. Between 1948 and 1950 he directed six stage plays. In order of production, these were: T. S. Eliot's *Murder in the*

---

* Noël Makin to author, 10 December 2001.
† More than forty years later he included a chapter on the phonetics of Shakespearean English, 'How Did Shakespeare Speak His Lines?', in *A Mouthful of Air* (London: Hutchinson, 1992), pp. 217–21.

Cathedral (with Lynne playing the chorus of the Women of Canterbury); Auden and Isherwood's *The Ascent of F6*; Marlowe's *Doctor Faustus*; Eliot's *Sweeney Agonistes*; *Lord, I Was Afraid* (which he adapted from the novel by Nigel Balchin); and an ambitious full-text version of Shakespeare's *Hamlet*, performed in two parts, with two separate casts, on consecutive evenings. Since Bamber Bridge was an all-male college, Burgess decided that men should take the women's parts in *Hamlet*, as the boy players had done in Shakespeare's own theatre companies.

The actor who played Michael Ransom in *The Ascent of F6* and St Thomas in *Murder in the Cathedral* was Peter Walker, who has written about his memories of Burgess and Lynne in a pamphlet, *Bamber Bridge Training College: Fifty Years On*. He recalls Burgess's theatrical ventures as rather amateurish enterprises. Such good qualities as they possessed came not from the director but from his more gifted students. One of these was Frank Holden, who had been a professional actor with a repertory company before the war. Among the others were Fred Hodgkinson, an 'extremely competent' stage electrician, and Syd Cross, a 'brilliant' artist who was responsible for designing the sets. Peter Walker remembers appearing opposite Lynne in *Murder in the Cathedral* and in Bernard Shaw's *The Man of Destiny*: 'She was a Welsh girl and unlike her country folk, not much given to smiling. The reputation throughout the college was that neither [Burgess nor Lynne] was happy in their marriage and there were frequent quarrels.'* Another student, Cliff Metcalf, who lived in the same residential block as the Wilsons, also witnessed their loud, late-night arguments. He remembers Burgess 'returning from the pub in Bamber Bridge and playing beautiful music on the piano in his flat whilst having a violent row with his wife'.†

---

* Peter Walker to author, 5 September 2001.
† *Bamber Bridge Training College: Fifty Years On* (privately published, 1998), p. 57.

In spite of his reservations about Burgess as a theatre director, Peter Walker remembers his old tutor as

> a friendly, sociable person with a fine command of words [. . .] The John Wilson we knew was a more likeable character than the persona of Anthony Burgess which he became and in the cloak of which, from time to time, he flickered across our TV screens. A rather better person than perhaps he gives himself credit for in his autobiography.*

One of the few pieces of Burgess's writing to have survived from his years in Bamber Bridge is a two-page fragment from an undated letter which he sent to his in-laws, Bill and Hazel Looker. The letter thanks the Lookers for sending a present before launching into a semi-literate postscript in Lancashire dialect, supposedly written by Suky the dog:

> this is suky writin wot hasnt written for a long time becos as ow the boss as not ad time to tek down wot i have to say not as ow ther is a lot to say these days with my ome and my garden avin nobody in like ther was why ther was hundreds of people ere once all men like an walking about to lechers wot the boss used to give an i used to bark at them but i let them stay in the colige which is my ouse an now they is all gone.†

Beneath the postscript is a pen-and-ink drawing of Bamber Bridge College in Burgess's hand. It shows a collection of crumbling brick buildings and wooden sheds, black smog, dirty windows, dustbins, barbed wire, litter, empty tin cans, spiders and cobwebs. A goods train trundles through the middle of the wreckage. The general impression is one of gloom and desolation. It's not surprising, given such surroundings, that he was busily applying for other jobs and looking forward to getting out.

*

---

* Ibid., p. 32.
† Burgess, undated letter to Bill and Hazel Looker. Collection of Ceridwen Berry.

When Burgess wrote his application to Banbury Grammar School on 10 June 1950, he mentioned that a book he had jointly authored (apparently in Danish) with Dr H. P. Bridges, entitled *Engelsk Grammatik*, was awaiting publication in Denmark. There is no record of such a work in the Royal Library in Copenhagen, and Dr Bridges's name fails to show up in any of the major library catalogues in England, Scotland, Denmark and the United States. Possibly the book was rejected by its intended publisher and the typescript subsequently lost; or more likely both Dr Bridges and *Engelsk Grammatik* were fictions, created to help Burgess get the Banbury job. Whatever the truth of the matter, his application and interview favourably impressed the headmaster and governors, and he was offered the post of English master on 21 June 1950. He was now thirty-three years old, and this was his first permanent job.

Burgess and Lynne initially considered renting a flat in Banbury from a clergyman named Mr Carpenter, but they kept him waiting too long for a decision and he let it to another tenant. Armed with a substantial loan from Lynne's father and a small building society mortgage, the Wilsons were instead able to buy a small two-up-two-down cottage in the outlying village of Adderbury. This modest house, 4 Water Lane, became their centre of operations for the next four years, and it was here that Burgess wrote his first two full-length novels, as well as orchestral music, poems, a stage play and occasional pieces of journalism for the school magazine.

Even before Burgess arrived there, Adderbury could lay claim to an impressive literary tradition. The debauched Restoration poet John Wilmot, second Earl of Rochester, had lived at Adderbury House in the seventeenth century. Burgess was an admirer of Rochester's writing (especially 'A Satire Against Reason and Mankind') and he warmed to the 'strong sensuality' of his erotic poems.* Part of the appeal lay in the scurrilous and blasphemous nature of Rochester's work. His louche, bisexual love poems – bawdy

---

* See Burgess, *English Literature: A Survey for Students* (London: Longman, 1958; new edition, 1974), p. 124.

celebrations of alcoholism, marital infidelity, inexpensive whores and sex with boys – anticipate at least some of the antics that were going on in Burgess and Lynne's marriage.

Lynne made a vivid impression in Adderbury, and even after half a century her behaviour is still the subject of local gossip. One of her former neighbours claims that the back garden of their cottage on Water Lane was full of empty bottles. An unreliable village rumour that Lynne was in the habit of cavorting naked in the garden persists to this day. According to another local legend, she once got hopelessly drunk and disappeared for a few hours. A search party was sent out, and she was finally discovered sleeping in an empty field behind the village petrol garage. One of their neighbours, Vera Wood, who still lives in Adderbury, remembers: '[John Wilson] had all these way-out ideas [. . .] They were a bit of an embarrassment, being drunk so much. I mean, Lynne died of it. Chronic. He was a likeable chap, very popular with the landlords, as you can imagine.'* Another neighbour, who asks not to be named, says that Burgess and Lynne kept pictures of naked men in their upstairs bathroom. Presumably these were Lynne's, or else a joke of Burgess's devising, intended to scandalize his fellow villagers.

The house, which they renamed 'Little Gidding', after T. S. Eliot's poem, stands directly opposite a pub, the Bell. The retired Anglican vicar of Adderbury, the Rev. Peter Dance, whose father was one of the Bell's owners, remembers meeting Burgess there two or three times a week for a drink in the Oak Room.† After Burgess and Lynne were barred from the Bell for some misdemeanour or other, they had to walk a short distance up the hill to do their drinking in Adderbury's other pub, the Red Lion, a large former coaching inn on the main Oxford road. After they were barred from the Red Lion, they drank in the house, or took the bus to pubs in Banbury.

*

---

* Vera Wood to author, 20 July 2000.
† Peter Dance to author, 7 October 2001.

Banbury Grammar was a co-educational state school of a kind that scarcely exists today. All but a few of the British state grammar schools were dismantled for political reasons, following an edict from the Labour education minister Shirley Williams in the late 1970s. Prospective pupils sat an entrance exam at the age of eleven, which ensured that the calibre of the students was high. The headmaster of Banbury Grammar School, Douglas Rose, believed that the purpose of education was to propagate culture in the widest sense. He regarded class teaching as only part of an English master's work. Music and drama were thought to be important aspects of school life. Burgess obligingly wrote piano music for Valerie Tryon, the teenage daughter of a fellow teacher, which she performed at the Town Hall in Banbury. The school magazine, *The Banburian*, shows that he was involved in a number of play productions. He composed an overture and entr'acte for the school production of *A Midsummer Night's Dream* in December 1950, and he directed William Douglas-Home's play, *The Chiltern Hundreds*, in July 1951. The *Banburian*'s drama critic wrote: 'Many people seemed to enjoy it. It proved itself to be not a bad play, but not really a play at all – a mere flaccid mass of stock situations, lifeless characterization and limp dialogue, hung like a lot of wet raincoats on a richly antlered prop-list.'* The script called for a live duck, which could not be prevented from moulting on stage. After the production, Burgess claimed to have killed the duck and roasted it for his Sunday dinner.

As a schoolteacher, Burgess was almost universally well liked, and his eccentricities endeared him to his students in Banbury, whose ages ranged from eleven to eighteen. One of them, Jackie Adkins, remembers: 'He was my teacher and I thought he was great. He used to wear outrageous clothes – gaudy waistcoats and a terrible ginger tweed suit. His fingers were stained with nicotine.'† Another pupil at the school, Susie Kerridge, found his enthusiasm

---

* I. V., 'The Chiltern Hundreds', *Banburian*, vol. 9, no. 3 (December 1951).
† Jackie Adkins to author, 3 October 2001.

for literature infectious. After she left the school she found a job as a bookseller, and she attributes her pleasure in reading to Burgess's inspiring presence in the classroom. Graham Wilton, who was also taught by Burgess, writes: 'I remember him as a smoker, with a quiff of hair rambling down off his forehead, and being quite gently spoken, although he could get quite annoyed by what he thought was stupidity or the inability to grasp something quickly. I liked him mainly because he had a very good sense of humour.'*

Sonia Blinkhorn, who studied under Burgess in the sixth form, says: 'We regarded him as extremely clever. He exerted control because he was unpredictable. He gave us an awareness of the joy of learning and made us feel good about English literature.'† She remembers his lessons on the metaphysical poets as 'a huge adventure'. Sonia was surprised and amused by Burgess's description of 'wholly nubile' sixth-form girls such as herself in his autobiography.‡ 'We thought he was distinctly unsexy,' she says. 'He was quite a gent where women were concerned.' Unlike some of the other male teachers at the school, Burgess 'never made a lewd pass'. The headmaster seems to have been less restrained. According to Sonia Blinkhorn, Mr Rose 'would make a pass at any woman who came within reach'.

Some of Burgess's impressions of his life in Banbury (and his opinions on the world in general) are recorded in his answers to a questionnaire, published in the school magazine in July 1952:

Q: Would you advise your pupils to become teachers?
A: Only those I dislike.

Q: Describe your favourite pupil.
A: Must suffer from the delusion that he knows less than I.

---

* Graham Wilton to author, 7 October 1996.
† Sonia Blinkhorn to author, 28 April 1997.
‡ Burgess, *Little Wilson and Big God: Being the First Part of the Confessions of Anthony Burgess* (London: Heinemann, 1987), p. 354.

Q: How would you live if you were rich?
A: On some palm-fringed, sun-baked shore watching the sweat trickle down my tummy.

Q: What do you think is the greatest menace at the present time?
A: Neo-Pelagianism (refusal to believe in Original Sin) which produced Russia, America, youth organizations and holiday camps.

Q: What are the main attractions of Banbury?
A: Certain houses with zoomorphic signs.

Q: What epitaph would you choose?
A: Him the Gods had made neither a digger nor ploughman, nor otherwise wise in aught, for he failed in every art.*

This last quotation was from the 'Ode to Pan', a pseudo-Homeric fragment of Greek poetry. Twenty-two years later, he told another interviewer that he had always been impressed by this epitaph, and said he was 'determined to have it' on his gravestone, because it seemed to express an eternal truth about the literary life: 'We *do* fail if we attempt art. We're happier if we can do things like digging and ploughing, just putting our hands to the ground, reaching Walden Pond.'†

*

Amateur drama was Burgess's main preoccupation from 1950, when he formed a theatre group called the Adderbury Players. They operated out of the village hall, a ramshackle structure with few facilities except a stage and an upright piano. Working with local actors in Adderbury, and also with the Old Banburians' Society, Burgess directed productions of *A Phoenix Too Frequent*

---

* 'What the Staff Really Think', *Banburian*, vol. 10, no. 2 (July 1952), pp. 4–8.
† Robert C. Jennings, 'Playboy Interview: Anthony Burgess', *Playboy*, September 1974, p. 86.

by Christopher Fry, *The Gioconda Smile* by Aldous Huxley, *Engaged* by W. S. Gilbert, *The Adding Machine* by Elmer Rice, and *Sweeney Agonistes* by T. S. Eliot. Martin Blinkhorn, who played Sweeney in the Eliot play, remembers that, as Burgess's leading actor, he had 'great difficulty' understanding the play and 'acted as an automaton almost [. . .] Quite frankly, I hadn't a clue about what I was doing in the play, it was all his direction and we were just puppets.'* Sweeney's central monologue about 'birth, copulation and death' was considered risqué by its village audience, but the play received an enthusiastic notice from the drama critic of the *Oxford Mail*, and the production toured around a number of Oxfordshire villages in the summer of 1951.

Martin Blinkhorn, who was in his early twenties at this time, found Burgess to be a genial companion, and the pair often drove around Oxfordshire in Blinkhorn's Aston Martin sports car. After a theatre rehearsal, followed by a Banbury pub session involving many pints of rough cider (which, being cheaper than beer, was Burgess's drink of choice), Blinkhorn gave him a lift back to Adderbury. He remembers:

> Usually he sat in the front seat holding on to the dashboard with white knuckles but on this occasion he stood up, holding on to the windscreen with the wind blowing into his face and he shouted long chunks of Chaucer and Shakespeare into the wind. He said the oncoming wind and the outgoing voice cancelled each other out [. . .] He enjoyed himself at the parties we held in each other's houses, often getting quite drunk and holding forth about his latest theories (Elizabethan education, our inability to appreciate good literature and so on). I don't think we honestly appreciated his brilliance and regarded him as a somewhat weird academic, out of his place as a grammar school teacher.[†]

---

* Martin Blinkhorn to author, 29 September 1996.
† Ibid.

In 1952 Burgess directed a production of Sean O'Casey's flamboyant Irish Republican play, *Juno and the Paycock* (1925), for the Adderbury Drama Group. The part of Mrs Tancred was taken by Lynne, and Burgess played both Jerry Devine and 'The Mobilizer'. In a programme note, signed 'J.B.W.', he wrote:

> Although rightly described by the author as a tragedy, *Juno and the Paycock* is full of humour and contains some of the most brilliant character-drawing of all time. Once seen, Juno, 'Joxer' and the 'Captain' are not easily forgotten. We find our brains full of their speech and we feel we know them even better than we know ourselves. This is as it should be for, in a sense, they *are* ourselves.

Although the play was judged a success by local standards, not everyone in the company had a high opinion of Burgess's ability as a director, as had been the case at Bamber Bridge. Moyna Morris, who acted in his production of *Juno*, says: 'He was not a good producer at all. He fancied himself as a producer, but he just couldn't do it.'* But another witness remembers the play more fondly. Graham Wilton, a photographer who worked for the local newspaper and knew Burgess socially, maintains that the production was 'outstanding', largely due to its 'exciting and inventive' director.†

In 1952 Burgess wrote his first original play, a three-act theological comedy called *The Eve of Saint Venus*. He had first planned it as an opera libretto after Lynne delivered an ultimatum. She demanded that he should either write a long piece of music, as he had been promising to do since the end of the war, or else stop talking about being a composer. But the libretto grew too long for an opera, and Burgess saw that it would work better as a stage

---

* Lady Morris to author, 22 November 1999.
† Graham Wilton to author, 7 October 1996.

play.* Once the script was complete, he tried to get the play performed in Oxfordshire, but the local drama groups were unwilling to take it on.† Disheartened, he put the typescript away in a drawer, and it finally emerged thirteen years later, rewritten as a novella.

The Eve of Saint Venus is Burgess's most optimistic statement about love and marriage, but he wrote it when his own marriage was under intense pressure. The action takes place in a large country house which is intended to stand as a microcosm of England. The cast includes a comic working-class servant and an Anglican vicar who is plagued by doubts. On the eve of his wedding, Ambrose Rutterkin playfully puts a wedding ring on the finger of a statue of Venus in the garden. The stony finger curls up, and the ring cannot be removed. The goddess then descends to claim him as her husband. Meanwhile his wife-to-be, Diana, is being seduced by a lesbian journalist, and the two women agree to run away to the Continent. The Rev. Norman Chauncell arrives to perform a Latin rite of exorcism on the house, in an attempt to drive out the pagan gods, but Venus is too powerful for him. Disgusted by his own weakness, the vicar renounces his faith and tries to tear off his dog-collar – a difficult job because he finds it tricky to unfasten the rear collar-stud. Shortly after he has hurled the symbol of his office across the drawing room, a bolt of lightning strikes the garden, and the statue is destroyed by a falling tree. We are never entirely sure whether the lightning is a coincidence or a timely intervention on the part of a Christian God. Whatever the true cause, it is enough to drive Mr Chauncell back into the arms of his Church.

The ring is recovered, the two lovers are reconciled, and the wedding is set to go ahead the following day. The novella ends in

---

* The opera was later completed, although it has never been performed, and the score forms part of the Burgess music collection at the Harry Ransom Center, University of Texas at Austin.
† A pencilled note of rejection (partially erased) is visible on the first page of the play typescript in the archive at Texas. The signature is illegible.

verse, with the characters reciting Burgess's free translation of the
Pervigilium Veneris ('Cras amet qui numquam amavit quique amavit
cras amet').* It is an uplifting hymn to love, though primarily sexual
rather than religious:

> Tomorrow will be love for the loveless, and for the lover love.
> The day of the primal marriage, the copulation
> Of the irreducible particles; the day when Venus
> Sprang fully-armed from the wedding blossoms of spray
> And the green dance of the surge, while the flying horses
> Neighed and whinnied about her, the monstrous conchs
> Blasted their intolerable joy.
>
> [. . .] The bed will be no monster's labyrinth,
> But spirals winding to a blinding apex,
> Sharp as a needle, when the last shred of self
> Is peeled off painlessly, and space and time are bullied
> Into carrying their own burdens. Tomorrow
> Shall be love for the loveless and for the lover love.†

The laughably inadequate vicar and his religious crisis are cruel
pieces of satire against Anglicanism. In one scene Mr Chauncell
argues with Ambrose's friend, Jack Crowther-Mason, about the
existence of pagan gods. Is Venus a real presence here or an
imaginary one? Crowther-Mason is Burgess's mouthpiece in the
text. He says:

> Everything's made by men [. . .] We've got to admit it. The
> objective and the eternal are alike in that they're inseparable
> from the observer [. . .] The eternal isn't any less eternal because
> a fallible mind conceives it. Divine revelation has to end up in
> the mind of a human observer. In that sense we make our
> gods.‡

---

* For a full text of the *Pervigilium Veneris*, see H. W. Garrod (ed.), *The Oxford
Book of Latin Verse* (Oxford: Oxford University Press, 1912), pp. 375–8.
† Burgess, *The Eve of Saint Venus* (London: Sidgwick & Jackson, 1964), pp. 124–7.
‡ Ibid., p. 97.

Burgess does not seriously attempt to unravel the conflicting Christian and pagan theologies in his story. As the pantheon of pagan gods roams around the English garden, Anglicanism is powerless to resist them because it no longer knows what it believes in. Unlike Catholicism, the Church of England has lost sight of the old absolutes, such as evil and sin. *The Eve of Saint Venus* is best understood as a work that is nostalgic for a system of absolute belief. Yet the reality of Burgess's own life in 1952 was more complicated and troubling than the play is willing to acknowledge. This was not simply a question of feeling exiled from his Church. At the very point that he was writing in celebration of married love, he considered himself to be one of the loveless.

*

Shortly after Heinemann had rejected *A Vision of Battlements* for the first time in 1952, Burgess decided to attempt another novel. This time he drew his material from his immediate surroundings, assembling a comic caricature of Oxfordshire. The book's hero is a lapsed Catholic schoolmaster. *The Worm and the Ring* is a novel whose history has been troubled by scandal – even more so, in some respects, than *A Clockwork Orange*. Two important facts have got in the way of an appreciation of the book on its own considerable merits. First, it was on the receiving end of a libel writ, thereby generating the harmful journalistic publicity that normally attends any kind of literary legal action. Second, and disastrously, the publisher admitted the libel, and agreed to settle out of court for £100. The unsold copies of the first edition were immediately recalled from bookshops and destroyed. The book has never been reprinted in its original form and it is the most difficult of Burgess's novels to find. Second-hand copies are offered for sale at between £600 and £1,000.

The novel is set around the time of the Festival of Britain in 1951, roughly three years before the first draft was written, though the book was not published until 1961. The central character, Christopher Howarth, is recognizably a Burgess-figure. He teaches

1. Elizabeth Burgess Wilson with her daughter Muriel and the infant John, 1918. (Liana Burgess/International Anthony Burgess Foundation)

2. John Burgess Wilson, aged six, outside the Golden Eagle in July 1923. (Collection of Sheila Mather)

3. Joseph Wilson with his second wife, Margaret Dwyer (née Byrne), the stepmother hated by Burgess. (Collection of Sheila Mather)

4. The Golden Eagle, 69–71 Lodge Street, Miles Platting, Manchester. (Manchester Central Library)

5. Joseph and Margaret Wilson on holiday (probably in Blackpool) with Agnes, Dan and Sheila Tollitt in 1935 or 1936. (Collection of Sheila Mather)

6. The Bedwellty School Ladies'
Hockey Team, summer 1938.
Edward Jones is in the centre.
His daughter, Llewela, is sitting
next to him, at the far left of
the middle row.
(Collection of Ceridwen Berry)

7. Llewela (Lynne) Jones on
her graduation day, summer
1941. Her engagement ring,
a gift from Burgess, is just visible
on her left hand.
(Collection of Ceridwen Berry)

8. Captain (later Major) Bill Meldrum, Burgess's commanding officer in Gibraltar, at the beginning of the Second World War. (Collection of Patric Curwen)

9. John Burgess Wilson and Llewela Jones on their wedding day in Bournemouth, 22 January 1942. (Collection of Ceridwen Berry)

10. The Entertainments Section of the 54th Division, otherwise known as the 'Jaypee' dance band. John Burgess Wilson, their piano-player and musical director, is third from the right. (Collection of Richard Nutting)

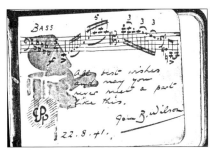

11. Burgess's signature in Richard Nutting's wartime autograph book.

12. Burgess and Lynne in the back garden of their house at 4 Water Lane, Adderbury, in 1954. (Collection of Joan Bussingham)

13. (*above left*) Archie Currie, Lynne and Burgess on holiday in the early 1950s. (Collection of Molly Currie)

14. (*above right*) The cast of Burgess's production of *Juno and the Paycock*, Adderbury, March 1952. Lynne is in the back row, second from left. Burgess and Moyna Morris are seated at the front. (Collection of Vera Wood)

15. Burgess (seated at centre of front row) with the staff and students of the Malayan Teachers' Training College in Kota Bharu, where he worked between 1955 and 1957. (Collection of Joan Bussingham)

16. Lynne with the Mentri Besar (Prime Minister) of Kelantan province, Malaya, at the Remembrance Day dance, November 1955. (Collection of Joan Bussingham)

17. Time for a Tiger: Lynne at the airport bar in Kelantan, Malaya.
(Collection of Joan Bussingham)

at a secondary school not entirely unlike Banbury Grammar School (for example, both schools are built of yellow-white stone and have a Palladian portico). Several of the incidental characters – Roberts, Pocock, Lowther, Potter, Lees and Sykes – are named after pupils who were at the school when Burgess taught there. The book mentions a Major Horton-Smith and a Dr Briggs, both of whom were well-known characters in Banbury. Although Banbury is not named as the location of the novel, Burgess's text mentions two outlying villages, Charlbury and Ratley, which are the real names of villages not far from Banbury. The presence of so many local references in Burgess's text allowed the lawyers to claim that the book was rooted in an identifiable place, and that it had deliberately presented itself as a roman-à-clef. There is no doubt that it draws in strong and immediate ways on the details of Burgess's life in Oxfordshire.

Peter Howarth, Christopher's son, who is a pupil at the school, is persecuted for his Catholicism and confused by what he learns in history lessons about Martin Luther and the Reformation. Howarth himself is unhappily married to Veronica, a devout Catholic who resents his apostasy and refuses to sleep with him because of some ill-defined medical complaint: she suffers from 'mild hysteria', which is possibly psychosomatic. Her doctor tells Howarth that 'A woman's system is a queer thing. Delicately balanced. Mind and body are intermixed, more so than in a man.'* Burgess seems to have been projecting his deep-seated fear and horror of Lynne's illness on to Veronica, and he certainly borrowed a number of Lynne's symptoms for fictional purposes here. The sexually frustrated Howarth transfers his attentions to a young female teacher. She is Hilda Connor, a voluptuous tennis-player ('Her cyclamen lipstick made her look whorish,' we are told).† Hilda is married to an engineer, who is performing feats of heroic construction at some

---

* Burgess, The Worm and the Ring (London: Heinemann, 1961), pp. 93–4.
† Ibid., p. 77.

distance away. In his absence she seems all too seducible, and Howarth contemplates initiating an affair with her:

> But was it safer to court Hilda Connor? Indiscreet, also a double adultery. He saw her sturdy legs in hockey dress. 'Come on, girls!' Yet he had smelt Schiaparelli's *Shocking* on her (having first seen the vial in her handbag), and had admired the slim blood-tipped fingers that gripped a vicious marking pencil. Her eyes had been warm lately . . . Her home, in the village on the other side of the town, was antipodeal to his own. The name of the village – Rodforth – crackled in his mind, crepitated like silk underclothes. She would be marking maths books now, her body fallow. Did the coming of spring simmer in her?*

Rodforth, it's worth pointing out, is not a real place in Oxfordshire, but a phallic creation of Burgess's own. Moyna Morris put it bluntly and simply: 'I *am* Hilda Connor.'† This is merely to say that she recognized elements of herself in the character, not that the events of the novel are 'true' in all respects. In her view, Burgess had acted irresponsibly by mixing recognizably real people and fictional situations in the book. Even so, she refused to have any part in the libel action when Gwen Bustin, the woman who issued the writ, asked her to 'join in'. Understandably, Moyna Morris had no wish to draw undue attention to herself by being involved in a legal case. She insists that she had no intimate dealings with Burgess.

Events work out rather differently in the novel. Howarth pursues Hilda and eventually persuades her to sleep with him. But, at the moment of consummation, while they are locked illicitly in the school library one lunchtime, Howarth's son Peter falls from the roof while retrieving a lost football. He lands on some spiked railings, which pierce his chest. In Burgess's unpublished first draft

---

* Ibid., p. 67.
† Lady Morris to author, 6 November 1999.

of the novel, the son dies and Howarth is consumed by guilt. The consequences of his lust are clear for all to see. In the published version, Peter recovers from his injuries and the newly reconciled Howarth family decides to leave England for Catholic Italy. Christopher does not exactly return to the faith of his fathers, but he does the next best thing: he becomes a wine salesman, distributing the blood of Christ in its non-sacramental form.

The libel writ arose from the novel's sub-plot. Burgess borrowed this from Wagner, who had in turn lifted it from the old Germanic legend, *The Ring of the Nibelungs*. Here is another mythical substructure at work, as in Burgess's earlier updating of Virgil in *A Vision of Battlements*. A headmaster called Mr Woolton runs the school. He is intended to stand in for Wotan, the supreme ruler of Valhalla in the myth. The schoolchildren are characterized as malevolent dwarves: Wagner's Alberich is transformed into Albert Rich.* There is no stolen ring in *The Worm and the Ring*, but there is a stolen diary, originally belonging to a schoolgirl who has written down her fantasies of being seduced by Mr Woolton. The novel's villain is Dr Gardner (Gardner being the surname of a hated shopkeeper in Banbury, according to Burgess), who uses the stolen diary for the purpose of blackmailing Woolton. The headmaster's secretary is Alice, a middle-aged spinster who circulates gossip around the school and secretly desires to begin sexual relations with Woolton. It was the real secretary of Banbury Grammar School,

---

* For more detail on the Wagnerian sub-text in *The Worm and the Ring*, see Burgess, *Little Wilson and Big God*, pp. 368–9; 'Ring' in *One Man's Chorus*, pp. 180–89; and 'Wagner's "The Ring": Anthony Burgess on a Number of Interpretations', *Listener*, 17 September 1964, pp. 419–21: 'I opened out with the three Rhine-daughters turned into schoolgirls splashing through puddles, the horrible dwarf Alberich into an ugly, randy, eventually love-renouncing brat called Albert Rich [. . .] *The Ring* is symbolism, and only artists who are not sure what they believe indulge in it, since symbols are good at reconciling opposites, resolving ambiguities, suggesting archetypes.' Burgess later spoke, in his T. S. Eliot Memorial Lectures (1980), about the use of Wagnerian images in Eliot's *The Waste Land* and in James Joyce's *Ulysses*.

Gwendoline Stella Bustin, who made the claim for libel damages against Burgess and Heinemann.*

Gwen Bustin (or Alderman Bustin, to give her her full title) was in her early fifties when Burgess knew her. She was one of the pillars of Banbury society: she had served at various times as the town's mayor, deputy mayor and 'mayoress to a woman mayor'.† Born in 1902, she was educated at Banbury Grammar School, and subsequently worked as the school secretary for forty-two years until her retirement in 1962. She lived at Orchard House, one of the oldest houses in Banbury, with her parents. She never married, was keen on horticulture and was said to be an expert on orchid-growing. Vera Wood, a former pupil at the school, remembers: 'She was a horrible thin spinster. She always looked miserable. We all took the mickey out of Miss Bustin. "Crusty Bustin" we used to call her.'‡

Under English law, a novel (or a stage play, or a poem, or a film) may be held to be libellous if an individual can prove that he or she is recognizably present in the text, and that publication of the work in question is likely to damage his or her reputation among right-thinking people. If a case comes to court, the jury will decide, following the judge's summing-up of the evidence, whether or not the work is libellous, and will award damages accordingly. In practice, the overwhelming majority of libel cases are settled out of court.§

It seems likely, to judge from the large pile of letters and internal memoranda relating to libel in the Heinemann archive, that Burgess simply didn't understand what libel was, and therefore had little idea of how to avoid it. Arthur Crook, the former editor of the

---

* A copy of the writ, which was served on 5 January 1962, is on file with the Burgess papers in the Heinemann archive.

† Report on the *Worm and the Ring* libel case, *Evening Standard*, 7 August 1962.

‡ Vera Wood to author, 20 July 2000.

§ Most fictional characters are, of course, composites of actual people. Marcel Proust wrote about the process of merging or 'mitosis', whereby a single real-life figure could become several characters, or a number of 'real' individuals could collapse into one character.

Times Literary Supplement, who regularly commissioned anonymous reviews from Burgess in the 1960s, remembers that Burgess
'had a propensity to introduce something libellous [into his copy]
which one would naturally have to deal with'.* And one of the
lawyers who compiled a libel report on *Little Wilson and Big God*
for Heinemann spoke of its author's known 'libel problem'. Unlike
Auberon Waugh, who had an acute sense of what could and could
not be got away with in print, Burgess attracted writs in much the
same way that magnets attract iron filings. Usually he was acting
out of innocence rather than malice.

*

Gwen Bustin has been dead since 1974, but it seemed to me that the
person best placed to comment on Burgess's Banbury years was
Moyna Morris (later to become Lady Morris), who had identified
herself as the original for 'Hilda Connor'. Even before I visited Lady
Morris at her home in Bath, I knew that it was likely to be a delicate
occasion. She had told me that she possessed a large number of
intimate poems and letters from Burgess, and I suspected that,
despite her hesitations, she was keen not to be left out of his story.

When I met her in 1999 (on the sixth anniversary of Burgess's
death), she was living in a large, double-fronted Georgian town
house on one of the most elegant streets in Bath. She was a tall,
athletic-looking, politely spoken woman in her early seventies, full
of good humour and entirely fearless. After she had shown me her
collection of paintings in the drawing room, we went downstairs
into the kitchen, where we sat at opposite ends of a long pine
kitchen table. Lady Morris's husband, Sir Alec, excused himself and
went off into the garden. I could see him through the window,
battling in the November wind with piles of leaves. I wondered
whether he'd been propelled outside by a love of gardening, or by
the wish to make himself absent while I was speaking to his wife

---

* Arthur Crook to author, 30 September 2001.

about her involvement with Burgess.* She had made a few notes in preparation for my visit, and she sat with a pile of Burgess's letters in front of her. We proceeded cautiously at first: she read me a few extracts from the correspondence, but was reluctant to let me look at the letters for myself. After a couple of hours she relented, and I was allowed to inspect a few pages, but by no means all of them.

Moyna Morris (as she was then known) had been teaching at Banbury Grammar School for a couple of terms before Burgess arrived in 1950. She was twenty-three years old, a recent graduate in History who had done a two-year course to gain her teaching qualification. She came to Banbury as a temporary science teacher, and stayed there for three years while her husband was training to be a pilot. She lived at Well Cottage in Chipping Warden, Oxford-shire. As a private joke, Burgess invented a place called 'Chipping Wellwater' in the first chapter of *The Worm and the Ring*.† Moyna recognized other echoes of real life in the novel. While Lynne was teaching a class for the WEA, she and Burgess went to watch *La Ronde* at the cinema in Banbury.‡ He recollects this incident in precise detail in the book, when he writes about 'that trip to Charlbury, late in the afternoon in the cinema (a French film), the drinks and dinner afterwards, no funny business at all on the homeward journey'.§

---

* Air Marshal Sir Alec Morris, KBE, CBE, FR Eng, was born in 1926 and married Moyna Patricia Boyle in 1946. In a long and distinguished Royal Air Force career (1945–83), he worked as an engineer with radar and guided weapons, and served as Director of Air Signals, Director of Strategic Electronic Systems, and Chief Engineer of the RAF.

† Burgess, *The Worm and the Ring*, p. 3.

‡ There is an odd circularity here: *La Ronde* (directed by Max Ophüls, 1950) is adapted from the play *Reigen* (1900) by the Austrian writer Arthur Schnitzler (1862–1931). In October 1976 Stanley Kubrick wrote to Burgess with a request to adapt another Schnitzler text, *Traumnovelle* (or *Dream Novel*, first published 1926), for the screen. Kubrick eventually made the film, with a script by Frederic Raphael (born 1931), as *Eyes Wide Shut* (1999).

§ Burgess, *The Worm and the Ring*, pp. 96–7.

Moyna had spent the Easter holiday of 1950 in Spain and Gibraltar, where her husband was recalibrating the radar for the RAF. When she first met Burgess in the staff room in September of that year, they got talking and discovered that they had Gibraltar in common. 'He asked me what I thought of Andalucia, pronouncing it the Spanish way,' she said.* A firm friendship was quickly established. Lady Morris remembered Burgess as a charming eccentric and a good talker, though she took the view that he was 'not organized enough' as a teacher, because she 'didn't feel [that] he prepared properly'. He earned the admiration of the other staff when he courageously put one of his own poems (unsigned) into a fifth-form English exam and invited the pupils to comment on it. Although Burgess was 'very well liked' by his colleagues, it seems that he was not altogether devoid of prejudice when it came to questions of class:

> He was frightfully conservative in politics. He complained that he'd been to a dance at a drill hall at Adderbury. He objected to the working-class people there. He was naturally conservative. Maybe he found working people threatening. He had this toffee-nosed attitude to people he didn't think were of his own social or intellectual class.

This account of Burgess's politics is echoed by Anthony Froggatt, Burgess's friend and occasional drinking partner, who lived in the house next door on Water Lane in Adderbury. He recalls: 'They were *not* socialists. They were quite the opposite.'†

Most of Lady Morris's memories of these Banbury years were cheerful ones. 'We were all the most marvellous friends,' she told me. 'It was an enchanted place and time.' One evening Moyna and Alec went out drinking with John Burgess Wilson and Lynne. Both couples were childless at this time. Somebody asked what it would

---

* Lady Morris to author, 22 November 1999. All further quotations are from this interview.
† Anthony Froggatt to author, 20 July 2000.

feel like to have a child. Burgess replied: 'I can feel the milk welling up in my breasts.' 'We all thought this was terribly funny – even Lynne,' said Lady Morris. There was evidently a playful side to their social dealings. Burgess and Lynne took pleasure in winding up Thomas Atkinson, the games master who taught rugby at the school. According to Moyna, 'They were talking about it as if rugby was something that gave him homosexual pleasure.'

She remembered drinking mead with Burgess and Lynne at the Winter Garden in Banbury. Burgess had not passed a driving test, so Moyna often drove him around in her car, usually from one pub to the next. 'When he caught the bus from Banbury to Adderbury, he got so drunk that they warned him that he wouldn't be allowed to take the bus any more.' Burgess eventually bought himself a motor-assisted bicycle, for which no driving licence was required. After a couple of glasses of wine, Lady Morris's other memories of Burgess began to tumble forth, in no particular order. He was known around the school for his outstanding powers of memory, and his ability to quote long passages from Shakespeare's plays, especially *Richard II*. He confided to Moyna that one day he planned to write a book about Shakespeare. In fact he published two books on the subject: *Nothing Like the Sun*, in 1964; and a semi-fictionalized illustrated biography, *Shakespeare*, in 1970.

One of Lady Morris's memories of Burgess at the school is particularly revealing. Various members of the teaching staff, including Moyna and Burgess, were taking coffee in the Men's Common Room after lunch. Out of the blue, Burgess asked: 'If you could produce a symphony or write a book but the price was that you had a terrible disease, which would you choose?' Everyone replied that they would rather be healthy, with the sole exception of Kathleen Winfield, who later became the school's Deputy Head. Burgess refused to answer his own question. However, the idea of creativity being spurred by a fatal illness is one that returns frequently in his writing.*

---

* See, in particular, *The Doctor Is Sick* (1960), *Enderby Outside* (1968), *Beard's*

This moment of common-room talk anticipates the story Burgess later circulated about his medical 'misdiagnosis' in 1959, when (according to his version of events) he was told that he had a brain tumour and was likely to die within the year. It seems weirdly prescient that Burgess was already talking about a fatal illness in the early 1950s, and one possible explanation is that he had been reading, either in German or in English translation, Thomas Mann's novel, *Doctor Faustus* (1947), in which the composer-hero, Adrian Leverkühn, strikes a bargain with the devil.* The price of his worldly success is that he must die a painful death from syphilis. Burgess was certainly familiar with Mann's novel, since he discussed it at length in a radio broadcast on 'The Novelist and Music' in 1962.†

When Lady Morris heard that Burgess was about to publish the first volume of his *Confessions* in 1987, she sent an anxious letter to his Monaco address. 'Everyone knew that Hilda Connor – that silly woman – was based on me. It was *so* thinly disguised.' Her letter asked Burgess what he was planning to say about their friendship and the background to *The Worm and the Ring*. He replied, a little evasively, that he had not mentioned her name in his text. What he actually wrote was this: 'There was not much opportunity for adultery [. . .] and I was the one to commit it spectacularly if discreetly with a fellow member of staff.'‡ Lady Morris didn't read the autobiography until a few years after it was published, but she was angered by the imputation. She told me: 'I don't know what counts as adultery in these post-Clinton days. As far as I know, I was the only woman he made a pass at.' But she insists that nothing

---

Roman Women (1976), *Little Wilson and Big God* (1987), *You've Had Your Time* (1990), and the posthumously published verse-novel, *Byrne* (1995).

* See, in particular, chapter 25 of Mann's *Doctor Faustus*.

† Burgess, *The World of Books*, BBC Home Service, broadcast 14 April 1962. The text of this radio talk was published as 'The Writer and Music', *Listener*, 3 May 1962, pp. 761–2.

‡ Burgess, *Little Wilson and Big God*, p. 352.

ever happened between them except for a single innocent kiss under the mistletoe one Christmas. When she came to read Burgess's first published novel, *Time for a Tiger* (1956), she recognized a fictional version of this episode. Victor Crabbe, the hero of the Malayan trilogy, says: 'You can't call kissing fornication. Otherwise I shall have to admit that I fornicated with your wife last Christmas. Under the mistletoe.'* These lines are in effect a letter home to Moyna from Malaya.

Burgess wrote a more directly confessional series of letters to Moyna while they were both living in Oxfordshire. She took care to preserve them, resisting what must have been a powerful urge to throw them away and erase the record entirely. Yet she was reluctant to see them published in full during her lifetime. 'I suppose they *will* eventually be published,' she told me, 'but I don't want to live to see it.' The correspondence runs to about fifty pages, mostly in the form of long, handwritten letters, with a few typewritten poems scattered among them. Moyna was adamant that the poems are 'love poems, *not* sex poems'. She allowed me to look at only one of them, a dramatic monologue about a student who is sitting an examination, answering questions on the subject of Love (the first line is 'No tobacco, infinite retention of urine'). The examinee's confinement is said to be a parallel for the tortured waiting of the unrequited lover. The candidate struggles with the question of why he loves the woman of his fantasies. His answer parodies the famous 'Rose is a rose is a rose is a rose, is a rose' from Gertrude Stein's 'Sacred Emily'. He writes: 'I love because I love because I love'. The poem ends with an oblique reference to T. S. Eliot's 'Coriolan', which ends with the words 'RESIGN RESIGN RESIGN.' The last line of Burgess's exam poem is 'FAIL FAIL FAIL.' Lady Morris's commentary on this was: 'You couldn't be subjected to such affection without being moved by it.' In another letter, Burgess accuses her of cruelty, of preventing a starving man from entering a lavish

---

* Burgess, *Time for a Tiger* (London: Heinemann, 1956), p. 54.

feast. He tells her: 'I go on being aware of a tremendous void which only you seem to be able to fill.'*

One theme that runs consistently through the letters is his fear that Lynne will find him out. The true nature of their friendship, he keeps saying, must be a guilty and unguessable secret between writer and reader. In spite of these protestations, Moyna wondered whether Burgess was in fact hoping to be discovered: 'He left the letters pinned to the noticeboard in the staff room. They were not in envelopes. Anyone could have read them.' Trying to make sense of Burgess's 'outpourings', as she called them, she said: 'He was obsessed. I sometimes think it wasn't much to do with me. He wanted *someone*.' Burgess's fixation was noticed by at least one senior member of the school staff, who warned Moyna (as she recalls): 'You should beware of him. He's always watching you.'

Re-reading Burgess's love letters half a century after they were written was, she told me, a 'painful' experience. 'They're so sad. There's this feeling that nothing can come of it, that it's a lost cause [. . .] He often says in the letters how enduring his love will be, that he'll love me for the rest of his life.' Nearly all of the letters are addressed to 'My darling' or 'My love'. In at least one of them Burgess makes his intentions perfectly clear: Moyna must leave Alec and run away with him. Lynne knows nothing of his true feelings, but he doesn't want to break the news to her until Moyna has agreed to the elopement. Other letters contain elaborate fantasies about seduction. In one, Burgess imagines Moyna in her black teacher's gown, and says that she resembles a yashmaked Islamic woman. He tells her that he wishes to become her 'sheik' – presumably thinking of himself as Rudolph Valentino's exotic seducer from the silent films. In a way Burgess was experimenting, in this correspondence, with the rhetoric of literary courtship – even, on occasion, reaching for forms of language which might sound excessive or ridiculous. But Moyna insisted that most of the affair took place

---

* Burgess, unpublished letter to Moyna Morris, dated 'Adderbury, Tuesday'.

entirely inside his head: 'The thing I can't emphasize enough is that, despite the letters, it was *not* a physical relationship.'

What Burgess discovered – though not without considerable pain and embarrassment – was that words are sometimes not enough, and that no amount of passionate letter-writing was going to get him the girl in this case. The fact that both Burgess and Moyna were already married was a serious obstacle, since divorce was still thought to be an unusual and vaguely scandalous activity in the England of the early 1950s. Beyond this, there was another insuperable problem. 'If we'd both been free,' said Lady Morris, 'I don't think we'd have got together. I couldn't imagine marrying a man I wasn't sexually attracted to.'

In spite of her anxiety about being identified in the autobiography, she later became regretful that Burgess had chosen the path of discretion when it came to writing about his involvement with her, and that he referred to her in detail only in *The Worm and the Ring*. 'He never talked about his friendship with me. He never dedicated a book to me [. . .] I don't think he loved Lynne, but he was wonderfully loyal to her. He nursed her for years.' Burgess's prolonged attempt at seduction by letter remained a mystifying episode to Moyna. 'He devoted two or three years of his life to these outpourings – but he makes no reference to them in *Little Wilson and Big God*.' Whatever the reason for his silence, Lady Morris was right to believe that she had been written out of the official story of Burgess's life which he published six years before he died.

The flow of letters ended, as it had to, when Moyna left the school in July 1953. The last poem Burgess wrote to her, which I was not allowed to see, is dated that month. Within a year of her departure, Burgess and Lynne went off to live in Malaya. He and Moyna exchanged a handful of letters after 1953, but these lacked the passionate tone of his Banbury correspondence.* The affair,

---

* For example, Burgess wrote to Lady Morris on 11 August 1982, ostensibly to congratulate her on her husband's recent knighthood. It is a grudging and ill-tempered letter, in the course of which he complains that the British state has failed

such as it was (if an affair is what it was), was over. Yet it acquired a new significance when Burgess produced an embellished version of it in *The Worm and the Ring*. Lady Morris kept a first edition of the novel on her bookshelf (one of the few copies not to have been pulped after the libel action), with a handwritten dedication from the author. The novel, written out of nostalgia for Oxfordshire, and with a strong element of erotic wish-fulfilment, doesn't give an accurate account of their friendship. But the surviving letters and poems – which speak eloquently and unguardedly of Burgess's hopeless, unconsummated desire – offer more insight into his state of mind during these troubled years. Even so, we will not know everything about this important correspondence until Lady Morris's heirs decide to allow access to the collection. She died of cancer, after more than fifty years of marriage to Sir Alec, in 2001.

*

Burgess and Lynne's disenchantment with their Oxfordshire life had been growing for some time, and it was exacerbated by the phoney nationalistic optimism of the Festival of Britain in 1951 and the Coronation in 1953. As a literate, music-loving man, Burgess became resentful that his salary of £500 per year (around £350 after tax and national insurance had been deducted) was not enough for him to be able to afford new books, records or a subscription to the *New Statesman*. He argued that the gradual devaluation of school-teachers' salaries was part of a wider government conspiracy against the intelligentsia.* Many of his pupils appeared to be wealthier than he was. Without the support of Lynne's wealthy father (who had retired in 1949 and invested his money shrewdly), the Wilsons would have struggled to make ends meet. Lynne often complained

---

to honour him for his services to literature. Lady Morris comments: 'He seemed to think that you got a knighthood in return for putting on a couple of cocktail parties. It was obvious that *he* would never get one because he was a tax exile.'
* See Burgess, 'The Pinball Peninsula', *Guardian*, Weekend section, 10 January 1981, p. 9.

in her letters to her sister that they were short of money, even though she was also teaching regularly for the WEA. Molly Currie recalls that Burgess considered himself too poor to go to a proper barber, and that Lynne would cut his hair using the kitchen scissors and a pudding basin. It was a mean economy, as the photographs of Burgess from this time testify. A decade later he described how he had paid the chemistry master at the school to manufacture tonic water, to save himself the expense of buying it in shops.* The cost, including quinine and saccharine to flavour it, was about a penny per gallon. (On the other hand, it can't have been cheap to keep Lynne supplied with the large amount of drink that she demanded.) Constantly anxious about bills and money, Burgess saw prosperous farmers, factory workers and market stall-holders in Banbury pubs who could afford to buy lavish rounds and doubles of spirits, as he could not. He wrote a resentful poem about this: 'Here ruined farmers, in new hacking-coats, / Pour Scotch and ram fat bacon down their throats'.† The suspicion that he was undervalued – which was connected with his nagging sense that middle-class schoolmasters with literary ambitions ought to be paid more than working men – continued to grow.

His exit from Banbury seems to have come about more or less by accident. By his own admission, Burgess was in the habit of getting wrecked on cheap cider at weekends and replying to job advertisements while under the influence. He retained a dim memory of having applied for a teaching post on Sark (one of the Channel Islands) late in 1953. He applied with no expectation of being appointed, and sent his application, as he put it, 'into the usual great silence'.‡ Then Christmas came, and he was struck by a bout of influenza. In January 1954 he was pleasantly surprised to receive

---

* Burgess, 'Rationality in Drinks', *Guardian*, 16 November 1966, p. 20.
† Burgess, 'Adderbury' in *Revolutionary Sonnets and Other Poems*, ed. by Kevin Jackson (Manchester: Carcanet, 2002), pp. 30–31.
‡ Burgess, 'Twelve Hours That Were Different', *Woman's Hour*, BBC Light Programme, 15 January 1962.

a letter from the Colonial Office, inviting him to attend an interview at an address in Great Smith Street in London. The letter did not mention Sark, but he assumed that this must have been the job in question.

Burgess wrote up the story of this job interview as a radio script for *Woman's Hour* in 1962, eight years after the event. According to this version of the narrative, he pawned his cigarette case in order to raise the train fare to London. Arriving at the Colonial Office, he was met by a committee of functionaries who greeted him cordially. They then asked him why he wished to work in Kuala Hantu. He recollected the conversation which followed:

> I said, in a small voice, 'Where *is* Kuala Hantu?'
> 'In Malaya,' said one of the junior men. 'Now may we proceed with the interview?'
> 'But,' I said, 'I never applied for a job in Kuala Hantu.'
> 'Oh, yes you did,' said the senior men.
> 'Oh, no I didn't,' I said. This went on for some time.

The interview panel then showed Burgess his neatly typed letter of application. His signature was indeed at the bottom. Had he applied, he wondered, in a state of delirium, or when drunk on cider? He told his interrogators that he had come to London expecting to be interviewed for a job in Sark, and they dissolved in laughter. 'It seemed evident,' he wrote, 'that some of the senior men were going to dine out on that.' One member of the panel expressed relief that he was proposing to teach English and not colonial history. The interview proceeded, he was offered the job, and he immediately said yes. He agreed to sail to Malaya that summer. As he was on his way out of the door, he heard somebody say the word 'Sark'. Noises of helpless mirth pursued him from the room.* The

---

* In his autobiography, Burgess suggests that the interview for the Malayan teaching job took place on the same day that Roland Gant of Heinemann rejected *A Vision of Battlements*. I think this must be a false memory. The records in the Heinemann archive indicate that the novel had been turned down two years earlier. See *Little Wilson and Big God*, pp. 366–7.

story sounds implausible, as Burgess himself recognized, but he sent a covering letter with the radio script to his producer, Jean Burns, assuring her that it was true in all respects.

He returned to Banbury, wrote a letter of resignation to Douglas Rose, and got down to the hard job of learning to speak Malay. He bought a copy of *Teach Yourself Malay* by M. B. Lewis, and claimed to have mastered the basics in six weeks. The Adderbury house was put on the market, and Burgess and Lynne prepared to put their possessions into crates for the voyage out. They had little idea of what to expect in Malaya, but they were not entirely sorry to be getting out of Oxfordshire. All they knew for certain was that they would not be coming back for at least three years.

Shortly after Burgess had left the school, a brief note about him appeared in the *Banburian*:

> Mr Wilson, that truly remarkable man, will by now be in Malaya, where he has taken a post in a college for the sons of Malay aristocrats. We hope he will find the climate a little more to his liking. Certainly we shall never forget his original and unconventional contributions to the life of the school.*

He was not altogether forgotten. A couple of weeks after Burgess died in 1993, an obituary appeared in the *Banbury Guardian* under the headline 'Former Banbury Teacher Dies at 76'.† Little attention was paid to his literary works. The local paper spoke as if his life, or the only part of it that mattered, had really ended in 1954.

---

* 'School Notes', *Banburian*, vol. 12, no. 3 (September 1954), p. 3.
† *Banbury Guardian*, 2 December 1993.

5

Beds in the East

Burgess and Lynne sailed from Southampton with Lalage, their
Siamese cat, on a Dutch passenger liner, the *Willem Ruys*, at twelve
noon on Thursday, 5 August 1954. They had planned to spend the
night before their departure at the Star Hotel in Southampton, but
when they arrived there a hatchet-faced manageress informed them
that animals were not allowed in the bedrooms. She was unmollified
by Burgess's words of protest ('Good God, woman, this is our last
night in England'), so they were forced to find a room elsewhere, in
'a kind of dosshouse' which served only revolting cold fried food. If
this was Burgess's last taste of England, he was not sorry to be
emigrating, and he felt sure that they would not be coming back in
a hurry. Lynne, who had left her family behind in Leicester, was
more doubtful.

A few days before he left, Burgess wrote a final letter to Agnes
Tollitt, his stepsister in Manchester. He thanked Agnes and her
husband for their various acts of kindness, and promised to do
whatever he could to help their children in the future.* The letter
ended with a rhetorical flourish: 'With the help of God & his Holy

---

* The promise was not fulfilled. He fell out of touch with the Tollitts shortly
afterwards, and the correspondence was not resumed until he and Lynne were back
in England in the early 1960s.

Mother, Wilson shall not be found wanting where glory and right shall lead [. . .] Good-bye! God bless you! *Salamat Tinggal*! Your loving brother, John.' He had not altogether disowned his extended family in Manchester, but it is hard to know whether the pious-sounding utterances of his valediction were sincerely meant, or whether he was merely acting the good Catholic in order to flatter the woman who had recently sent him a cheque for £100 in response to a begging letter.

The sea journey to Singapore, threading slowly through the Suez Canal and the Indonesian islands, took five weeks, and the Wilsons passed the time by trying to learn a few words of Dutch, so as to communicate with the ship's crew, and expanding their Malay vocabulary. They travelled first-class at the expense of the Colonial Service, acquired the new habit of drinking gin rather than bitter or cider, and were required to dress for dinner. 'For the first time in my life,' Burgess said later, 'I became a gentleman.'* Among their fellow passengers were the first colonials they had encountered – a collection of English rubber planters and expatriate civil servants, returning from home leave. Burgess was on the whole unimpressed by his travelling companions, but he acknowledged that he had a certain amount in common with these people: nobody was in any doubt that Malaya represented the fag-end of the British Empire, and most of those who administered it had, like Burgess, gone abroad because they had failed to make their mark in England. But there were positive reasons for going to live in south-east Asia, too: he was already feeling middle-aged at thirty-seven, and it might soon be too late to see what he called 'the exotic East'. He approached his colonial future with a certain sense of optimism. Here, evidently, was an opportunity to make a fresh start, perhaps even to reinvent himself entirely in the tropics.

The Malaya he was sailing towards was a country – or a loose federation of semi-autonomous Islamic states – in the middle of a

---

* Burgess, 'The Pinball Peninsula', *Guardian*, Weekend section, 10 January 1981, p. 9.

civil war. An official 'state of Emergency' had been in place since June 1948. This was a euphemistic designation for jungle warfare between Communist guerrillas and the Malay Regiment, an assortment of British and Malayan troops. The guerrillas, all of whom were Chinese, were armed with weapons left over from the Second World War, and wished to bring about a Communist Malaya ruled from Peking. The Emergency was a war conducted on more gentlemanly lines than the later American involvement in Vietnam: a series of amnesties allowed the Communist terrorists free passage from their jungle hideouts to China. Nevertheless, British civilians in Malaya knew that they were always possible targets for ambush and summary execution by the Communists, especially if they travelled outside the major towns and cities. Just before Burgess and Lynne had left Leicester, the English newspapers had reported the murder of a Scottish rubber planter on an estate less than two miles from Kuala Kangsar. He had been garrotted by Chinese terrorists, who had (according to witnesses) sung an uplifting ballad about the Brotherhood of Man as he expired.*

Although the nine principal states within the Federation of Malaya (Johore, Kedah, Kelantan, Negri Sembilan, Pahang, Perak, Perlis, Selangor and Trengganu) were theoretically governed by sultans, the Straits Settlement of 1875, engineered by Sir Stamford Raffles, had installed a British 'adviser' in each of these territories. Two other British-ruled settlements, Penang and Malacca, were also attached to the Federation. Both Singapore and Malaya had been occupied by the Japanese between 1941 and 1945, and those members of the European population who were not interned in prisoner-of-war camps were sent to Burma as forced labourers to construct the notorious railway commemorated in the film *Bridge Over the River Kwai*. When the British returned after the Japanese surrender in July 1945, it was clear that home-rule for Malaya could not be far away. The Imperial Japanese Army, who had invaded almost effortlessly (on bicycles, not in tanks), had demonstrated that

---

* See Burgess, 'The Emigrants', *Punch*, 12 June 1968, pp. 852–4.

THE REAL LIFE OF ANTHONY BURGESS

the British presence on the peninsula once known as the 'Gibraltar of the East' was a haphazard and temporary affair. Burgess said, with reference to the Japanese invasion of 1941, 'The British had shown their weakness. Their Empire was not impregnable. It was just a few white men, sitting on verandas.'*

Strictly speaking, the post-war Federation of Malaya was never a colony (although it came under the jurisdiction of the Colonial Office in London), since sovereignty remained with the sultans. Yet the voice of the democratic Independence movement – whose slogan was '*Merdeka*', meaning 'freedom' – was becoming steadily louder in the early 1950s. After protracted negotiations with the British government, a new constitution was drawn up in 1956, and Malaya became fully independent at midnight on 30 August 1957. The period of Burgess's stay there, from September 1954 to August 1957, coincided exactly with the final three years of the British presence. As an education officer whose job took him on frequent excursions around the country, he was well placed to observe the anxieties of the Emergency, the dismantling of the colonial civil service, and the pre-natal traumas of a fully independent state. This is the turbulent political situation which is lavishly and affectionately chronicled in his three Malayan novels.

Burgess was not the only British writer who spent time in Malaya during the Emergency.† Alan Sillitoe was sent there while he was on National Service in 1955, and he wrote about it in a novel, *Key to the Door*.‡ Reviewing Sillitoe's book in the *Yorkshire Post* in October 1961, Burgess declared:

---

* *Writers and Places: A Kind of Failure*, BBC television documentary, broadcast 15 January 1981.
† Leslie Thomas, whose first novel, *The Virgin Soldiers* (1966), is also set in Malaya during the Emergency, appeared with Burgess in a radio discussion about the end of Empire, broadcast on the BBC Home Service on 22 February 1966.
‡ Alan Sillitoe, Nottingham-born novelist, poet and short-story writer, best known for two early works, *Saturday Night and Sunday Morning* (1958) and *The Loneliness of the Long-Distance Runner* (1959). Burgess said of the first of these books: 'Sillitoe catches the grumbling and the touchiness, the traditional radicalism,

Key to the Door is Mr Sillitoe's attempt at a big *Bildungsroman*
[. . .] abutting between depressed pre-war life in Nottingham
and disaffected RAF other-rank down-with-the-bleddy-boggers
grousing in Malaya [. . .] The Malayan sections chilled me.
Young Brian seems to grouse through a dripping and frightening jungle-and-mountain-scape completely without (if we except
his grousing mates) human figures. We hear of Malayans, and
wonder which of the Malayan races he means. Occasionally a
Malay, clad for some reason in a sari, glides through [. . .] It is
the complete lack of interest in people other than the ingrowing
group of working-lads that appals. But one is also appalled
morally. Brian cannot see the Chinese Communists as enemies.
His failure to kill off a terrorist who eventually snipes at his
own mate meets no condemnation. The political naiveté of the
book is incredible.

Burgess resumed his assault on Sillitoe in another article for the
same paper two months later:

The, to me, most infuriating novel of the year was Alan Sillitoe's
Key to the Door. This proletarian book created a moonscape
Malaya almost devoid of people (there are no greater wog-
snobs than your Nottingham working-lads) and falsified completely the Communist jungle-war. For those of us who, living
in terrorist territory, saw the garrotted bodies of our friends,
the political naiveté of a book like this is nauseating. I am
aware, of course, that this is not an aesthetic judgment.*

There is no reference to 'the garrotted bodies of [his] friends' in
Burgess's surviving letters, and he does not mention any such

---

the beer, fights, fornication and skittles in a novel whose form is imperfect but
whose dialogue is very much alive.' In the second, 'we really learn what makes
juvenile delinquents tick' – evidently a subject close to the heart of the author of *A
Clockwork Orange*. See Burgess, *The Novel Now* (1971 edition, London: Faber),
pp. 149–51.
* Burgess, 'Best of the Spate: Looking Back at the Year's Fiction', *Yorkshire Post*,
28 December 1961, p. 3.

incident in his autobiography. He may have been dramatizing a story he had heard from a fellow British colonial who had witnessed it; Leslie Jones, who worked with Burgess from 1955 when they both taught at the Malayan Teachers' Training College in Kota Bharu, says that the regions of Kelantan and Perak, where Burgess lived, were 'not at all dangerous'. He adds: 'The Emergency only really affected Johore. I'd be surprised if Burgess had any direct experience of it.'* Burgess's account of the Malayan Emergency sounds like a traveller's tale, an imagined version of a war that he knew only slenderly and distantly.

Neither Burgess nor Lynne had travelled outside of Europe before, and most of what they knew about Asia and the British colonial territories came out of other people's books: George Orwell's novel, *Burmese Days* (1934); Somerset Maugham's Malayan short stories; Joseph Conrad's trilogy of Malayan novels (*Almayer's Folly*, *An Outcast of the Islands* and *The Rescue*); and the works of Rudyard Kipling. Kipling's poems had a particular resonance for Burgess. 'No writer, except Shakespeare and James Joyce,' he said of Kipling in 1986, 'has so thoroughly exploited the resources of the English language.'† He recited Kipling's poem 'Mandalay', which he knew by heart, during the outward voyage to Malaya:

> *Ship me somewheres east of Suez, where the best is like the*
> *   worst,*
> *Where there aren't no Ten Commandments an' a man can*
> *   raise a thirst;*
> *For the temple-bells are callin', an' it's there that I would be –*
> *By the old Moulmein Pagoda, looking lazy at the sea.*

Burgess discussed Kipling and colonialism with V. S. Naipaul in 'The High Noon of Empire', a BBC radio feature broadcast on

---

* Leslie Jones to author, 10 January 2002.
† Burgess, 'Rudyard Kipling and the White Man's Burden' in *One Man's Chorus: The Uncollected Writings*, ed. by Ben Forkner (New York: Carroll & Graf, 1998), pp. 291–4, 292.

24 July 1965. Burgess said: 'Possibly like yourself, I was brought up on Kipling [. . .] The particular image of Kipling was a jelly belly flag-wagger [. . .] The cartoon image of the imperialist has been imposed on Kipling, hasn't it? When we start reading the poems and even the stories – and *Kim*, for instance, his only real novel – we get a very different image [. . .] of a man who is, well, *scared* of the Empire in some ways.' Naipaul agreed that Kipling had 'this great grasp of a society [i.e. Anglo-Indian society], which of course he was looking at under very special circumstances.' He added: 'I think the view which will eventually come to be held is that Kipling was a very good writer. Those early stories – they're as good as Angus Wilson – different in that they do portray an entire society.' Naipaul made an explicit comparison between Kipling and Burgess when he talked about 'the ambiguous [. . .] rather confused elements of imperialism – the commercial element, or the idealistic element – which Kipling had, and an educationalist like yourself [had]'.*

Burgess's admiration for Kipling does not necessarily imply that he agreed with him in regarding colonial subjects as 'captive' races, 'half devil and half child'. Anti-establishment by temperament, he shared many of Orwell's liberal doubts about imperialism – they both despised the aloof apartness of the Europeans in their whites-only clubs – at the same time as believing that the British Empire was being dismantled prematurely, before its 'civilizing' purpose had been fully accomplished. His position was an ambivalent one, not easily reducible to any clear party line or ideology. Unlike Orwell, who had worked in Burma as a colonial policeman in the 1920s, Burgess was taking up a teaching job which would at least give him

---

* For Burgess on Kipling, see 'Kipling and the Kuch-Nays', 'Kipling: A Celebration in Silence' and 'Said Rudyard to Reader' in *Urgent Copy: Literary Studies* (London: Jonathan Cape, 1968), pp. 101–12; and 'Rudyard Kipling and the White Man's Burden' in *One Man's Chorus*, pp. 291–4. For Burgess on Naipaul, see 'Raw Matter' (review of *Finding the Centre: Two Narratives*) in *Homage to Qwert Yuiop: Selected Journalism 1978–1985* (London: Hutchinson, 1985), pp. 519–21.

the opportunity to pass on some of the broad, humanistic culture that he had acquired in England.

When the Wilsons disembarked from the *Willem Ruys* in Singapore, Lynne immediately collapsed, apparently suffering from nervous exhaustion. A local doctor was unable to determine whether this was a consequence of the heat, the gin, or the long journey. Lynne felt guilt at having left her parents in England, and she had persuaded herself that they would both be dead before she returned home. Burgess telegrammed ahead to the headmaster of the Malay College to warn him of their late arrival. Stuck in Singapore City for an unforeseen couple of days, and with the first instalment of a hefty colonial allowance in his pocket, he visited a Chinese brothel in the Bugis Street red-light district, where he was able to verify Shakespeare's dictum that the beds in the East are soft. The smells of Singapore ('hot wet dish-rags, cat-piss and turmeric') provided a brief foretaste of what was to come in Malaya itself.* Then, when Lynne had recovered from her unexplained illness, they took the night train to Kuala Kangsar, changing at Ipoh.

Kuala Kangsar lies in the estuary of the River Perak in the north-west of Malaya (now Malaysia), a few degrees above the equator and not far from the border with Thailand. It is a centre of the rubber and tin-mining industries, and the home of the Sultans of Perak. Burgess and Lynne lived in a grand building called the King's Pavilion, an annexe of the Malay College which also served as a dormitory for some of the school's pupils. The King's Pavilion had been used for the purposes of torture during the Japanese occupation, and indelible bloodstains on the bathroom floor testified to its gruesome history. Burgess and Lynne were told about a local superstition that the ghosts of the war-dead still haunted the building, and their cook reported occasional spectral manifestations in the kitchen and garden. One of Burgess's teaching colleagues from Malaya comments:

---

* Burgess, 'The Corruption of the Exotic', *Listener*, 26 September 1963, pp. 465–7, 466.

There was a lot of talk about ghosts and black magic and *bomohs* [witch doctors]. I think Burgess exaggerates its significance. The local belief was that ghosts were very beautiful but that their feet did not touch the ground. Hair and nail-clippings were used in Malay magic. There was a genuine and widespread belief in this.*

The Wilsons were now better off than they had ever been, since Burgess's annual salary had risen substantially from the £500 he had been earning in Banbury to a tax-free £1,900. They bought a refrigerator and, local wages being low, hired three servants: a cook, a part-time gardener, and an *amah* (housekeeper). Their formidable *amah* was called Mas. Married at the age of eleven during the Japanese occupation, she had been widowed at thirteen after giving birth to two children, and she was nearly twenty when she came to work for the Wilsons. In a radio talk on Malayan women, Burgess said: 'Most tenderly I remember Mas, the first *amah* we ever had. She spoke English, Malay, Tamil, and three dialects of Chinese. She could sew, embroider, knit, cook, nurse. She was less than five feet high, but she ruled our house – *Tuan* must not wear this shirt, it has a hole in it; *tuan* has paid too much for this article, he must go back to the shop and throw it in the shopkeeper's face; *mem* is too ill to go to Ipoh, she must stay in bed all day.'† The Wilsons submitted meekly to her non-negotiable demands, and they began to wonder whether the traditional European idea of Islamic women as frail flowers might be a myth.

The other significant character in their ménage was Yusof the cook, a homosexual and occasional transvestite, who soon began to direct his amorous attention towards his new employer. In a letter to Kathleen Winfield, Burgess wrote: 'He [Yusof] is probably hermaphroditic. He is also too fond of bringing hot water into my

* Leslie Jones to author, 10 January 2002.
† Burgess, 'Malayan Fashion' (radio feature), *Woman's Hour*, BBC Light Programme, broadcast 8 July 1960.

bathroom when I'm already bathing.'* One evening in Kuala Kangsar town square, Burgess and Lynne saw Yusof taking part in a
ronggeng dance in full drag. Although openly gay men were thin on
the ground there in the 1950s, same-sex relationships were regarded
as a harmless eccentricity, and Chinese lesbian sororities were also
said to be common.† Burgess declined his cook's advances as politely
as he could, and later claimed that Yusof had spiked his food with
a love-potion procured from a local witch-doctor. This episode finds
its way into the first volume of the Malayan trilogy, in which
Ibrahim, Victor Crabbe's Malay cook, tries unsuccessfully to seduce
him using the same method. Burgess took a risk in saying such
things in public, even under the cloak of fiction, but he must have
calculated that Yusof, who was virtually illiterate, was unlikely ever
to read the novel.

With some reluctance, the Wilsons were talked into buying a car
– a second-hand Austin A70 – by a police lieutenant and amiable
con-artist called Donald (or 'Lofty') Dunkeley, who promptly volunteered his services as chauffeur, since neither Burgess nor Lynne
possessed a driving licence. The truth of the matter, of course, was
that Dunkeley had wanted to acquire a car for himself without having
to pay for it. He was six feet eight inches tall, and his background
was mysterious. Nobody was sure whether he was Northamptonshire
English, Anglo-Indian, or something else again. His accent was also
hard to place, which reinforced the impression that he was a man
from nowhere. He had served in the Palestine police force during the
war, and although he could speak fluent Hindi, Punjabi and Urdu,
he barely understood a word of Malay. He was unhappy about his
English and preferred, whenever possible, to speak Urdu. His constant companion was another police lieutenant who acted as his
interpreter. (This second man is called 'Alladad Khan' in the memoirs,

---

* Burgess, letter to Kathleen Winfield from Kuala Kangsar (no date but 1954 or
1955).
† Burgess, 'The Corruption of the Exotic', *Listener*, 26 September 1963, pp. 465–7.

but it is not his real name.*) Donald Dunkeley is the original for the anti-heroic character Nabby Adams in *Time for a Tiger*, a committed drinker who has renounced women in favour of beer: 'His real wife, his houri, his paramour was everywhere waiting, genie-like, in a bottle. The hymeneal gouging-off of the bottle-top, the kiss of the brown bitter yeasty flow, the euphoria far beyond the release of detumescence.'† Dunkeley himself was rather less fixed in his loyalties than his fictional counterpart. Burgess heard Lynne loudly copulating with him on at least one occasion when he stayed overnight at the King's Pavilion. Dunkeley's associate 'Alladad Khan' was no more successful in avoiding Lynne's erotic overtures. She fixed her blue eyes on him (he said that they were '*sa rupa pisau*' or 'sharp like a dagger') and invited him to share her bed.‡

Burgess was clearly impressed by the sights and smells of Malaya – the 'winds of garlic and dried fish and turmeric'; the 'sweating, breathless, obscene, sunless greenery' of the deep jungle; the cigarettes that tasted 'damp with the night air'; the 'flying-ant wings in the whisky glasses' – all of which he diligently recorded on paper.§

---

* Who *was* 'Alladad Khan'? Burgess took the precaution of changing his name in the typescript of *Little Wilson and Big God*, but the publisher's lawyer was nevertheless worried that he might sue for libel because of a reference to his heavy drinking habits. Burgess reassured his editor at Heinemann, Fanny Blake, that the real police lieutenant 'does not exist on the level of reading books'.

† *Time for a Tiger* (London: Heinemann, 1956), pp. 68–9. I reject the theory that Nabby Adams is a caricature of the South African pro-Fascist poet Roy Campbell (1901–1957), which has no basis beyond the fact that Campbell and Adams were both *tall*. There is no evidence to suggest that Campbell ever met Burgess, and his well-publicized hatred of the gay English writers much admired by Burgess (Auden, Isherwood, Spender) would surely have prevented them from getting on if he had done so. Burgess does not mention Campbell in the autobiography, or in his otherwise thorough history of English literature (1958). Nor are there any copies of his works in Burgess's private library, now housed at the University of Angers.

‡ Quoted in *You've Had Your Time: Being the Second Part of the Confessions of Anthony Burgess* (London: Heinemann, 1990), p. 70.

§ Burgess, *Time for a Tiger*, pp. 50, 143; *The Enemy in the Blanket* (London: Heinemann, 1958), pp. 118, 111.

From the beginning of their time there, he and Lynne broke the unwritten colonial code by rejecting 'the world of the [European] Club, the week-end golf, the dinner invitations, the tennis parties', preferring to spend their off-duty hours drinking with Asian friends.* His ambivalent responses to Malaya – elation, dejection and a number of states in between – are clearly visible in the fiction that he wrote there: 'I love this country. I feel protective towards it [. . .] I feel that it needs me'; 'Life in Malaya is impossible [. . .] Civilization is only possible in a temperate zone'; 'The white man's day is coming to an end. *Götterdammerung*. You've had it'; 'What a madhouse Asia was. He would be glad to be out of it'; 'If Malaya were left to the Malays it wouldn't survive for five minutes [. . .] Without the Malays it would be a good country perhaps.'† The swirl of languages fascinated him, of course, and stimulated his novelistic instincts. But he also knew that he was a European out of his context (in such a place, he said, 'a white skin was an abnormality'), and his knowledge of Lynne's boredom, heavy drinking, homesickness and experiments in adultery depressed him to such an extent that he worried that he might be in danger of running amok and dealing out random violence with a *parang* or machete. Yet it was through words, not violence, that he exorcized the nagging internal voices of guilt, rage and frustration, transforming his unpromising situation into artful comedy and farce.

*

The Malay College in Kuala Kangsar, founded in 1905, was known in the old Malay Federation as 'the Eton of the East'. Its Latin motto is 'FIAT SAPIENTIA VIRTUS', which translates as 'Let manliness come through wisdom'. This, the first residential school established in Malaya, was originally intended to be a public school on the British model, whose purpose was to give the sons of sultans and

---

* *Time for a Tiger*, p. 88.
† Ibid., pp. 57, 59; *The Enemy in the Blanket*, p. 117; *Beds in the East* (London: Heinemann, 1959), p. 101.

their future Malay advisers a distinctively English education, 'encouraging them to focus their sights beyond the river and the jungle and the kampong'.* It was intended that boys should graduate able to speak fluent English with an accent appropriate to the ruling class. Although places at the school were reserved for Malay boys (the other races of the country were excluded), by 1954 entrance was by competitive examination. The sons of the aristocracy were exempt from the exam, but it was theoretically possible for boys from lower down the social spectrum to win scholarships. Burgess recognized that one of the things he was being paid for was to manufacture the new Malay elite, which would be running the country after Independence. Lessons were given in English by a mixture of expatriate and local teachers. The headmaster between 1953 and 1958 was a Welshman, Jimmy Howell, who is caricatured as the headmaster in *Time for a Tiger*. In the novel he is a fat, dwarfish, red-haired man called Boothby, with a whining voice and a third-class Durham degree, 'a paunchy sportsman with a taste for whisky-water and fast cars, who subscribed to a popular book-club and had many long-playing records, who invited people to curry tiffin and said, "Take a pew." '† Burgess detested Howell for referring to the Malay boys as 'wogs'.

The college still exists, although there are no longer any British teachers there, and Malay has displaced English as the language of instruction. The main building is a peeling white neo-Palladian school-house redolent of faded colonial elegance, surrounded by a cluster of palm trees. A map of the college grounds shows extensive cricket and rugby pitches, and courts for tennis, squash and fives. As at the Xaverian College in Manchester, team sports were supposed to occupy a central place in the curriculum of the Malay College. Burgess, who had become a habitual slob since leaving the Army, made it his business to avoid such pursuits.

One of Burgess's former pupils, Abdullah Ahmad, who was in

---

* Burgess, 'The Pinball Peninsula'.
† *Time for a Tiger*, p. 31.

the fifth form in 1954 (and who went on to become a United Nations ambassador and the executive editor of the *Straits Times*), has written, in a short memoir, about the first time he met Burgess, who arrived in the classroom 'red-faced', 'perspiring and smoking', wearing a crumpled shirt and, shockingly, 'without a tie'.* The boys were delighted by this shambolic, bohemian-looking figure, who taught them 'apparently with some reluctance', as Ahmad puts it. 'We knew right away that he was not a typical colonial [. . .] He was in many ways a throwback to the social class the British colonials had scrupulously tried to shield us from.' When Ahmad received generous praise from Burgess for an essay he wrote on the subject of Communism ('He did not know how I had struggled during that 45-minute period to write it [. . .] I got seven marks out of a possible ten for my effort'), he was 'elated' by his teacher's critical comments and 'grateful for his advice' on spelling and English usage. 'By all accounts,' he writes, 'Wilson was a good and, simultaneously, an unconventional teacher.' Before Ahmad left the school in December 1954, he asked for his teacher's autograph, and was impressed when 'he obliged by writing it in Jawi', the calligraphic Arabic form of Malay. Burgess used the same Arabic script when he embellished the typescript of *Time for a Tiger* with a dedication (in Jawi) 'To all of my Malayan friends'.

Burgess had arrived with a firm belief in the liberal educational ideals which he felt it was his duty to disseminate. English literature, meaning the works of William Shakespeare, T. S. Eliot and Graham Greene, was supposed to be an international commodity, and Burgess subscribed to the universalist view that the values of that literature would be readily comprehensible to all readers in all places, regardless of their cultural background. Malaya forced him

---

* Abdullah Ahmad, 'Ruffled Feathers at MCKK [Malay College Kuala Kangsar]'. Ahmad mentions that another of his schoolmates, Abdul Rahim Ismail, 'vice president of the Lake Club and a great Rotarian', corresponded with Burgess for many years 'when both had become rich'. What happened to him? And does he still have Burgess's letters?

to reconsider his opinions about all that. His students laughed at Greene's tortured presentation of an adulterous triangle in *The Heart of the Matter*. If Mr Scobie was in love with two women, they argued, why didn't he simply convert to Islam and marry both of them? Shakespeare was problematic, too. Burgess watched the film of Laurence Olivier's *Richard III* in a kampong, and was alarmed when the Malay audience treated it as a straight documentary about the bloodthirstiness of political life in twentieth-century England.* Working with a Malay friend, he tried to translate Eliot's *The Waste Land* into Malay ('*Bulan April ia-lah bulan yang dzalim sa-kali / Membawa bunga lilac daripada tanah mati / Memchamporkan ingatan dengan hafsu*'), but the English text presented too many difficulties. From the Malay reader's point of view, it would make no sense that April was 'the cruellest month', since in the tropics every month is exactly the same. They abandoned the translation when they came to the expression 'spring rain' in the fourth line. When Burgess looked into Richard Winstedt's *Practical Modern English–Malay Dictionary*, he discovered that there was no Malay word for 'spring'.†

Burgess's teaching career in the East was, as he admitted twenty years after he had left the Colonial Service, 'a kind of failure'. He felt that his efforts as a teacher had been misunderstood or underappreciated. Part of his original ambition was 'to import the traditional British liberal virtues: tolerant, sceptical, humanistic, dedicated to truth, beauty and justice'.‡ But clearly this was too big an ideal. Burgess was distressed by the technocratic (or, as he saw it, 'philistine') way of thinking that characterized Malaysia's postcolonial development after 1957. 'The Malays,' he said in 1980, 'were eager to absorb technology from the West, but not art, not

---

* Burgess, *European Culture: Does It Exist?*, BBC Radio 3, broadcast 4 April 1990.
† Sir Richard Olaf Windstedt (1878–1966), *A Practical Modern English–Malay Dictionary* (Singapore: Kelly & Walsh, 1952).
‡ *Writers and Places: A Kind of Failure*.

philosophy.' A good proportion of his students at the Malay College
went on to become industrialists, lawyers, diplomats, civil servants
and the leaders of the United Malay Nationalist Party. Yet his eccentric teaching methods, fuelled though they were by an unquenchable
passion for literary learning, did not, in the event, produce the cohorts
of published poets and novelists that he had hoped they might.*

The production of new literature was a more urgent task than
trying to make the existing European canon intelligible to Malay
readers. Burgess was determined either to write, or to encourage one
of his students to write, 'a *Ulysses* of the East'. In this respect he
was entirely successful, for he returned to England five years later
with three Malayan novels already published: *Time for a Tiger*, *The
Enemy in the Blanket* and *Beds in the East* (the trilogy known as
The Long Day Wanes in America). One of his early aspirations in
Malaya was to turn himself into a mid-twentieth-century Somerset
Maugham, a truly internationalist man of letters, a 'man at home
in Paris and Vienna but also in Seoul and Djakarta, convivial and
clubbable, as ready for a game of poker as for a discussion on the
Racine alexandrine, the antithesis of the slippered bookman'.†
Although he had his doubts about Maugham's agnosticism – he felt
that the novels and short stories projected a world in which 'God
probably does not exist: there is no heaven after death, and there is
enough hell on earth' – Burgess was attracted by his 'charity', his
'great human virtue' of tolerance, and his liberal attitude to sexual

---

* The career of the poet–novelist D. J. Enright (1920–2002), who taught English at
the University of Singapore while Burgess was nearby in Malaya, offers a useful
point of comparison. Several of Enright's students went on to establish themselves
as university teachers and writers, the most prominent of whom is Shirley Chew,
Professor of English at Leeds University. Enright gives a picaresque account of his
teaching career in Egypt, Japan, Thailand and Singapore in his autobiography,
Memoirs of a Mendicant Professor (London: Chatto & Windus, 1969). His
Egyptian novel, *Academic Year* (a satire on English teaching in remote places, and
much admired by Burgess), was published in 1955.
† Burgess, 'W. Somerset Maugham: 1874–1965', *Listener*, 23 December 1965,
p. 1033.

matters.* He prepared an edition of Maugham's Malayan short stories with an enthusiastic introduction, and followed this up with a fair-minded obituary and long reviews of various Maugham biographies. And Maugham's life was to provide the basis for Burgess's fictional hero, Kenneth Toomey, in *Earthly Powers*. As much as he admired the naturalism of Maugham's writing – he claimed that 'the short stories are the nearest thing we have in English to the *contes* of Maupassant' – he was nevertheless disappointed by Maugham's cursory treatment of the Malays and Chinese: 'The stories of Somerset Maugham deal only with the lives of the British planters, miners and administrators. The natives are reduced to quacking voices in the distance or padding feet on the verandah'; 'Maugham belonged to an age in which the only people to be taken seriously in fiction were people of European stock [. . .] If Maugham had started writing Malayan short stories in, say, 1954 [the year in which Burgess himself arrived in Kuala Kangsar], his plots and characters might have been very different.'† The crucial point of difference between Maugham and Burgess in Malaya is that Burgess was willing to pick up the languages of the country, and was therefore able to move beyond the claustrophobic society of European expatriates going to seed in the tropical heat.

He got down to the hard business of learning proper idiomatic Malay, with the help of a *munshi* or language teacher. His imperatives for doing so were both pragmatic and financial, since the Colonial Office was willing to increase his salary after he had passed each of three examinations (Standard I, Standard II and Standard III Malay). Anxious to prove his linguistic competence by learning the

---

* Burgess, introduction to *Maugham's Malaysian Stories*, ed. by Anthony Burgess (Kuala Lumpar: Heinemann Asia, 1969), pp. vi–xvii. The stories which appear in Burgess's edition are 'The Vessel of Wrath', 'The Force of Circumstance', 'The Door of Opportunity', 'The Four Dutchmen', 'P. & O.' and 'A Casual Affair'.
† Burgess, 'Tanah Melayu' in *Homage to Qwert Yuiop*, pp. 59–63, 60; *Maugham's Malaysian Stories*, p. xvi.

language as quickly as possible, he invented a system of mnemonics to help him memorize the extensive vocabulary required for the exams. He explains how he did it in *Language Made Plain*:

> Some mnemonics are essentially personal. *Kowan* is 'friend': I had a friend called Cowan. Others are ultra-ingenious. *Bermas-tautin* is borrowed from Arabic and means 'to settle in a country, be domiciled'. I formed an image of a stout-drinking Scotsman lying in someone else's bed, saying 'Ah'm settled here. Bear ma stout in.' To remember *mualif*, another Arabic loan-word meaning an editor of a newspaper, I had to make a tortuous rhyme: 'If you've been drinking, chew a leaf / Of mint before visiting the *mualif*.' This had to be pinned down in my head with an image of a hard-drinking newspaper reporter.*

Language-learning, he decided, required a good memory for sounds and syntactic structures, but it did not demand any high degree of intelligence. He met Chinese bar-boys who spoke three languages without difficulty, and an interpreter in Port Said who spoke fifteen. To acquire a foreign language was, he said, not much different from being an actor and having to learn your lines. He embraced his new role as a Malay-speaking colonial with relish.

He also benefited from the intervention of what was known among the Europeans as a 'sleeping dictionary'. Burgess calls her 'Rahimah' in the autobiography (although this is not her real name), and she was a Malay divorcee who lived in Kuala Kangsar with her young son, working as a hostess in a low-grade dance and cabaret bar. He pursued a discreet affair with her for just under a year, and she was later fictionalized as Victor Crabbe's Islamic mistress in *Time for a Tiger*. Lynne knew nothing of the affair at first, and she failed to notice that small sums of money were disappearing from their joint bank account. She was told that Burgess was attending meetings of a non-existent school debating society while he was secretly spending at least one evening a week with 'Rahimah'. His

---

* Burgess, *Language Made Plain* (English Universities Press, 1964), pp. 127–8.

attitude towards adultery bears many similarities to that of Crabbe in the Malayan trilogy: 'Physical pleasure is in itself a good [. . .] and one should not withdraw from the proffered good, despite morality, honour, personal pride.' Guilt came into it, too, and there was always 'the knowledge that sooner or later there will be a hell of a row'.* For Burgess, as for his fictional hero, the idea that he was merely exacting revenge for his wife's adulteries provided an easy justification for his own infidelities. He said later, 'With regard to my first marriage, I would have been tortured by this guilt if my wife had not been almost philosophically unfaithful, if she had not established the general principle that to sleep with anybody was in order, but what was not in order was the declaration of love to anybody else'.†

*

Although Burgess does not attempt to depict the actual Malay College in *Time for a Tiger*, the fictional 'Sultan Mansor School' is presented as a microcosm of Malaya itself, with its uneasy mixture of races and religious customs. The novel views the melting-pot aspect of Malaya in broadly comic terms:

> The pupils themselves, through their prefects, pressed the advantages of a racial division [of houses within the school]. The Chinese feared that the Malays would run amok in the dormitories and use knives; the Malays said they did not like the smell of the Indians; the various Indian races preferred to conduct vendettas only among themselves. Besides, there was the question of food. The Chinese cried out for pork which, to the Muslims, was *haram* [Arabic: forbidden by religion] and disgusting; the Hindus would not eat meat at all [. . .]; other Indians demanded burning curries and could not stomach the insipid *lauk* of the Malays [. . .] Allocation to houses was

---

* Burgess, *The Enemy in the Blanket*, p. 84.
† Burgess, 'Unearthly Powers' (interview with Anthony Clare), *Listener*, 28 July 1988, pp. 10–12, 11.

arbitrary – the dormitories buzzed with different prayers in different tongues – and everybody had to eat cold rice with a warmish *lauk* of buffalo-meat or vegetables. Nobody was satisfied but nobody could think of anything better.*

The idea of the school as a miniature Malaya communicates the prevailing spirit of compromise very deftly. As Burgess sees it, the only thing that unites the various Malay peoples is their common hatred of the British – a negative unity, perhaps, but it is still better than nothing.

In other respects, Burgess's Malaya is an alarming place, and not just because of the political Emergency. Black scorpions and an expanding family of venomous king cobras infested the King's Pavilion and its grounds. Lizards colonized the interior of the house. Malarial mosquitoes could not be avoided even with the most elaborate of mosquito nets, but the presence of quinine in tonic water (a known cure for malaria) provided an excuse for Burgess and Lynne – especially Lynne – to drink as many gin-and-tonics as they could afford. Bottled beer, usually Tiger, Anchor or Carlsberg, was served unchilled, indeed at the temperature of tea, in Chinese drinking-shops or *kedais*. The trains to Ipoh and Kuala Lumpur, rumoured to be targets for terrorist attack, carried signs saying 'In the Event of Firing on the Lineside, Passengers are Advised to Lie on the Floor'. Books and photographs disintegrated in the humid air, or were devoured by termites. Mould flourished inside Burgess's leather briefcase. His collection of gramophone records, which had been acquired second-hand in Banbury, were warped into concavities by the heat. A black magician with whom the Wilsons were on friendly terms stuck pins into wax effigies of his enemies and tried unsuccessfully to hypnotize Lynne.†

---

* Burgess, *Time for a Tiger*, pp. 31–2.
† He is called 'Mr Pathan' in *Little Wilson and Big God*, but the libel correspondence in the Heinemann archive indicates that this was not his real name. Another version of this story may be found in the black magic episode in *Earthly Powers*

In Burgess's memoirs the streets seem to be festooned with Malay prostitutes, the unhappy victims of Islamic divorces which were all too easily obtainable. (Prostitution was supposed to be against the law, but the police in larger towns invariably turned a blind eye.) He was frequently perplexed and annoyed by what he saw as the inefficiency of the colonial administration – 'the shambles, [. . .] the obscurantism, the colour-prejudice, the laziness and ignorance'.* When dealing with the Malays themselves, he found that he had to adjust to an unfamiliar system of ethical codes and customs: 'If a Malay lied to me, this had to be interpreted as a mere withholding of the truth – something too precious to be handed over without ceremony. If he borrowed money from me, I must regard his failure to repay as a sign of friendship.'† The unique mixture of races and cultures – Malaya was, as he put it, 'the most remarkable multi-racial society in the world' – cried out to be transcribed in a long work of fiction, the '*Ulysses* of the East' that Burgess had envisaged before he had arrived. When he made a return visit to Kuala Kangsar in July 1980, he spoke about the initial impulse to embark on his sequence of Malayan novels. His purpose, he said, had been 'to record one white man's Malayan experience before it was too late, before the white man was thrown out of this final corner of the British Empire, as he was being thrown out of everywhere else'.‡

According to Abdullah Ahmad's memoir, it was common knowledge among the boys at the Malay College that Jimmy Howell (who is described by Ahmad as a 'feisty Welshman' and 'a disciplinarian') had clashed with 'the intellectual Wilson' soon after they met. One area of contention between them was linguistic: Howell was unapologetic about his failure to learn anything more than

---

(chapters 37–8). In the novel the magician is called 'Mr Mahalingam'. His name means 'large penis' in Tamil.

* *Time for a Tiger*, p. 57.
† Burgess, 'The Emigrants'.
‡ *Writers and Places: A Kind of Failure.*

basic Malay, whereas Burgess, who was energetically fraternizing with local Malays and Chinese, soon picked up an impressive command of the language. A more immediate cause of grievance was that he and Lynne were unhappy about living in the King's Pavilion, in close proximity to the schoolboys who disturbed them with noise and urinated intermittently from their balcony into a shared courtyard. The Wilsons' sleep was regularly disturbed by Malay boys having loud nightmares in the dormitories. Even the school holidays were punctuated by interruptions in the water supply, dawn visits from construction workers and more noise. A major row erupted early in 1955 when Howell declined their request to move into another house owned by the school, which was standing empty. The dispute ended acrimoniously, with Burgess no longer on speaking terms with his headmaster. Howell lost little time in demanding that he should be transferred elsewhere. It is clear that the antipathy between the two men was fierce, mutual and long-lasting. Speaking about Burgess some years after his retirement to Newport in Wales, Howell said: 'Wilson lets the side down badly. Amoral and a liar.'* 'Letting the side down' in this colonial context probably meant socializing with local people instead of doing his drinking at the European club. Burgess recalled, in a 1966 radio interview with Kenneth Allsop, 'I was very frequently, and so was my wife, told off by the authorities for going into small drinking shops and talking with the people. When I did really well in my Malay examinations, that was regarded as a kind of affront. One should do very badly in one's Malay examinations'.†

Burgess's students were unsurprised to learn that their subversive English master would be leaving them after having spent just one academic year at the Malay College. Abdullah Ahmad remembers: '[Wilson] mocked Howell and other fellow expatriates as philistines, obsessed with sports and the latest American movies and, in the case

---

* Quoted in Abdullah Ahmad, 'Ruffled Feathers at MCKK'.
† Burgess, *The World of Books* (radio interview with Kenneth Allsop), broadcast on BBC Home Service, 21 February 1966.

of Howell, with rugby in particular. Howell and the others were disappointed with him for lowering their "society and mores" in the estimation of the locals.'*

His new posting to Kota Bharu had been arranged by April 1955 and is mentioned in a letter to Susie Kerridge, one of his former pupils at Banbury Grammar School. Here Burgess also recorded, with self-evident enthusiasm, his more general impressions of working in Malaya:

I'm very busy here. One does more work than in England despite the intense heat, and my teaching day begins at 7.30 a.m. This College is for Malays only – no Chinese or Indians – and as the Malays are Mohammedans they need a long holiday at the time of Puasa – the big fast which lasts from sunrise to sunset – not even a glass of water! This holiday has just started and so I'm able to write. Apart from teaching and other work I have to study languages and I've already taken my first Malay exam, for which I got 82%. Soon we're being moved to Kota Bharu, across mountain and jungle, where I am to be English Lecturer at the new Training College. If you look at your atlas you'll see this place in the north-east corner – very near to Siam.

You'll be interested in what we eat here. There are many different races and many different kinds of food. My cook is a Malay, but he's very good at European dishes. However, we're fond of Chinese food, especially sharksfin soup, and we like curries. Men go round with little braziers on which they cook sateh – sticks with little slices of meat on them – and at one Chinese shop you can eat pan – bread which has been baked with curried meat in the middle. I'm afraid I'm getting fat, despite sweating so much in the hot sun. There are red peppers cooked with everything, especially with mee – a mixture of rice spaghetti, meat, prawns, vegetables and cucumber in a thick hot sauce.

The war against the Communist bandits still goes on. It's very hard to kill them, because the jungle is terribly thick and

---

* Abdullah Ahmad, 'Ruffled Feathers at MCKK'.

strong. If I look from the tower of our house I see that we're only in a little clearing in the jungle, and, if we let it, the jungle would march in from all sides very quickly. Malaya is nearly all mountain and jungle. There are snakes, scorpions, tigers and mosquitos, and other horrible things, but I love the country.*

Burgess and Lynne celebrated their departure from Kuala Kangsar with Donald Dunkeley and 'Alladad Khan'. The four of them got wrecked on a gallon of toddy, an illegally distilled spirit which reeked of sewers and burnt brown paper. 'If it wasn't for the smell and the taste,' comments a toddy-drinker in *Time for a Tiger*, 'it would be a damn fine drink.'†

Just before they set off for Kota Bharu, Burgess and Lynne both received letters from a neighbour who signed him or herself 'The Voice of the East'. These catalogued (separately) the vices of Mr and Mrs Wilson:

> And here I refer to your husband the teacher whose brain, though it contain knowledge to bestow in overflowing measure and bounty on eager learning youth, it can yet stoop to base act of sexuality. For it is known that he has for many months sated uncontrollable lust on simple Malay girl [. . .] You ask others here and they telling you the selfsame story.

This was too good to waste and is faithfully transcribed in the opening chapter of *The Enemy in the Blanket*. As in all of Burgess's early novels, the lack of invention in the Malayan trilogy is remarkable. With the possible exception of Christopher Isherwood, there was no other modern English writer who utilized his or her experience so economically for the purposes of fiction. We do not know what 'The Voice of the East' had to say about Lynne, but the sanctimonious charge-sheet – multiple adultery, immodest behaviour in public, occasional fits of drunken aggression – would be easy enough to draw up.

---

* Burgess, letter to Susie Kerridge from Kuala Kangsar, 20 April 1955.
† Burgess, *Time for a Tiger*, p. 22.

Kota Bharu, where Burgess was to work for the next two academic years, is the capital of the province of Kelantan. The Malayan Teachers' Training College there was newly established in September 1955, with a staff of twenty-five and 200 students. There were ten lecturers in the English 'option group', of whom seven were Malay and three (including Burgess) expatriate Englishmen. The head of the English department was Edwin Hilton – a bespectacled 'bullshitting' Lancastrian with a 'boy-gangster face' and a reputation for being 'pompous to a leaden degree', according to his former colleague, Leslie Jones, who says that 'John Wilson and Hilton took a dislike to each other. There was an element of jealousy on Hilton's part. He was a dreadful character.'* Yet, according to one of Lynne's letters home to her sister, Burgess got on reasonably well with Hilton at first – they had common origins in the north-west of England and a shared enthusiasm for the music of Richard Wagner – and Lynne cooked him a Lancashire meat and potato pie when he visited their house for dinner. In practice, Hilton had little contact with the lecturers who worked under him, and they were left to go their own way, using whichever teaching methods they preferred. Another of his expatriate colleagues writes that Burgess, who had been studying the Koran in his spare time,

> would amuse himself by asking his class, who were mostly Malay Muslims, 'When a Muslim man marries a non-Muslim woman, must she convert?' They shouted, 'Yes!' He would say, 'Louder!' They would shout 'YES!' After a bit more of this Burgess would roar, 'No, NO!' and proceed to quote chapter and verse [from the Koran] to the effect that if the woman is a woman of the book, i.e. Jew or Christian, the man must make provision for her to worship in her own faith. This did not go down well with certain people in Kelantan.†

---

* Leslie Jones to author, 10 January 2002.
† Denis Cartwright to author, 3 February 2002.

His knowledge of Malay continued to widen, and he presented himself as a candidate for the Standard III examination (the equivalent of degree-level), administered by the colonial government. This was a purely voluntary gesture on Burgess's part, since civil servants from overseas were not compelled to take their chosen language beyond Standard Two. To demonstrate his command of spoken Malay, the candidate was required to carry on a conversation at a suitable level with a native speaker. In Burgess's case this was the Town Clerk of Kota Bharu. The other examiner who was present, Denis Cartwright, gives this account of Burgess's performance:

> When the Town Clerk asked Burgess for his name he answered, 'Nama saya Abdullah bin Mohamed!' When the examiner recovered from this he began the conversation. Burgess took over entirely, as I recall, and spoke rapidly, fluently and loudly for several minutes in a monologue of Malay so mixed with Arabic that both the Town Clerk and I were lost. After Burgess had gone the rules required the examiner and myself (the adjudicator) to agree on the result. We passed him.*

Burgess and Lynne soon established a small and multi-racial social circle with three local couples: Haji Latiff (an Afghan Muslim) and his Saudi wife Sharifah; Cyril Brown (an Anglo-Indian) and his wife Isa, originally from Sumatra; and a man called Bangsir, whose ancestry was a mixture of Malay, Chinese and Dutch, and his wife Fatimah from Singapore.† The three women spoke no English, but the Wilsons were able to communicate with them in Malay. Friday is the Muslim Sabbath (enforced at that time by the Malayan police, with a stiff fine for anyone caught failing to observe it in public places), and so on Thursday nights the four couples would have drinks together at one or other of their houses, eat a meal of *sateh*,

---

* Denis Cartwright to author, 27 January 2002.
† Burgess names Fatimah, probably wrongly, as 'Normah' in *Little Wilson and Big God: Being the First Part of the Confessions of Anthony Burgess* (London: Heinemann, 1987), p. 407. I have followed the more reliable memoir he wrote in 1960, when the events of Malaya were fresher in his mind.

then visit the small cabaret at Biarritz Park in Kota Bharu. Here they would dance the *ronggeng*, 'in which, following Islamic custom, the man and the woman must keep their distance, facing each other, but never, never touching'.* Burgess had other, more discreet, encounters with women of whom Lynne knew little or nothing. One of these, a widow known as Che Hitam – because she was very dark-skinned, and *hitam* means 'black' – told Burgess that she had had many lovers. '*Berapa*?' he asked her ('How many?'). She replied: '*Kalau semua kerani di-Kelantan choba bilang, dia tidak boleh*' ('If all the clerks in Kelantan tried to count them, they couldn't do it'). He was probably thinking of Che Hitam when he wrote that he had encountered women in Malaya who were 'blacker than Africans'.† The honorific 'Che' (a short form of the Malay word *enche*) indicates that Hitam came from a low caste, but nothing more is known about her.

Looking back on his time in Kelantan, Burgess said: 'The very name of the place always conjures up for me an image of a host of head-high beauties, proud, strong-minded, self-willed, fitting consorts for the tough men of that state, men who have muscular bodies, all seem to be out of work, and kill their enemies (or yours, for a trifling charge) with little axes'.‡ The Malay axe-men – gangs of hired assassins who administered unofficial justice, though not always of a lethal kind – were no invention. Another lecturer from the college remembers: 'The little axe-men were said to be available for contract assaults or killings. For ten [Malay] dollars they would inflict an inch-deep wound in the victim's head. For twenty dollars you could get two inches.'§ It was rumoured that a senior politician in Kelantan had some influence with the axe-gangs, and they attacked and seriously injured the headmaster of a local private school while Burgess was working in Kota Bharu. His account of

---

* Burgess, 'Malayan Fashion'.
† *Little Wilson and Big God*, p. 386.
‡ Burgess, 'Malayan Fashion'.
§ Leslie Jones to author, 10 January 2002.

the axe-men in *The Enemy in the Blanket* ('Crabbe felt in antici-
pation the sharp axe-edge pierce his skull or, at best, the thud of the
dull heavy blunt back') looks like nothing more than straight
reportage to those who were there at the time.* This was rich
material for an incipient novelist, and there was little need for
Burgess to invent fictional scenarios when his daily life was so full
of outrageous episodes.

Leslie Jones, another English lecturer at the Training College
who later taught at Manchester University, has strong memories of
Burgess and Lynne in Kelantan:

> He was plain John B. Wilson when he joined the staff of the
> Kota Bharu T.T.C. as an English lecturer [. . .] He told me that
> when he started as an English teacher he had ideals and didn't
> want to cram his pupils for their School Certificate exams. They
> got bad results. 'Thereafter I dictated notes,' he said. He was
> way-out but conscientious, a very diligent member of staff. He
> turned up on time and marked his essays and set exercises.
>
> Lynne Wilson had a weakness for alcohol. When they came
> to my house for dinner, Lynne sat at the table, took a spoonful
> of soup and shoved it away as disgusting. She called for another
> gin and tonic and said 'Less tonic this time'.
>
> The English people who staffed the college were very cliqu-
> ish. They were not nice people in many ways. Kota Bharu was
> a small town – there were only about 150 Europeans – and
> they were a mean-spirited bunch. When *Time for a Tiger* was
> published there were reactions of envy and jealousy. They were
> not delighted. Some of the Malayan trilogy is journalistic,
> simply reporting what happened [. . .] They were a funny lot at
> that college and I've often wondered why Wilson didn't make
> more use of that material.
>
> I've always thought of John Wilson as a showman, a
> charlatan and a bullshitter. As for being a Don Juan, I think
> he's bumming his load [in the autobiography], showing off,
> exaggerating. *Little Wilson and Big God* doesn't ring true. I

---

* *The Enemy in the Blanket*, p. 10.

would be inclined to scoff a bit. Lynne was reported as saying that he was 'no good in a thunderstorm'. She was casting aspersions on his manhood, or something. He used to frequent the Bukit Bintang amusement park, which was a place of ill repute. He used to go down there to chat and drink with the locals. I don't know if he went alone or with Lynne.

I was ten years younger than Burgess and have always assumed that he was well disposed to me and my wife as I couldn't find myself in his novels! He used one or two of our colleagues in a fairly ruthless way. One woman's heart-to-heart went straight into *Beds in the East*.* Any one of his associates could find themselves in a book [. . .] But he was basically a nice, kind fellow in my opinion. I liked his whimsical and often self-mocking humour. He doted on our new-born baby. He had this tender and sensitive side, but it was often hidden under irony.

His fast study of the Malay language was remarkable and he passed Government Standard III with ease – spoken and written forms [. . .] The woman who taught Malay in the college asked John Wilson to take part in a debate, and she was impressed because he did so in Malay. I think he had a healthy contempt for his less literate colleagues who regarded him with some fearful distaste. They hated his use of obscure, ostentatious and sesquipedalian lexis.

I last met Burgess when he came to Manchester to get an honorary Ph.D. [on 12 May 1982]. I was on the staff there and he recalled me as soon as we met and spoke in a very friendly manner. I was impressed that he remembered me after so many years.†

---

* Denis Cartwright, another teaching colleague from Kota Bharu, writes that the character Rosemary Michael in *Beds in the East* is 'a cruel and very close representation of Celine Arnold, who was a physical education lecturer at MTTC Kelantan. I believe Burgess borrowed much of a letter she had received from someone jilting her, a letter which she showed to Burgess.' Denis Cartwright to author, 3 February 2002.

† Leslie Jones to author, 4 October 2001 and 10 January 2002.

Early in 1956, Burgess reported in a letter to a friend in England that he had started learning Chinese, a tonal language and 'very difficult' to the European ear.* Although he had been excited by his reading of Ezra Pound and Ernest Fenollosa's critical writings on Chinese poetry, his studies did not progress far into the written form of the language: 'I think the Chinese way of writing is a stupidly outmoded, insufficient technique [. . .] The sounds of Chinese are different because there you use musical intonations to determine meaning, and this has always been tremendously interesting to me, but I was drawn more to the Islamic culture and the languages of Islam.'†

Lowlife culture had its attractions, too. While he was working in Kelantan, Burgess experimented with smoking opium, which was easily and semi-legally obtainable, since opium dens were tolerated by the police and hardly ever raided or closed down. This was to some degree a response to the difficulties of his marriage, and an enthusiasm that he shared with other prominent writers of his generation, notably Graham Greene and William Burroughs.‡ In *Ways of Escape*, Greene gives an account of his opium-smoking adventures in Saigon, which probably corresponds with Burgess's own experiences in Malaya:

> After two pipes I felt a certain drowsiness, after four my mind felt alert and calm – unhappiness and fear of the future became like something dimly remembered which I had thought import-ant once [. . .] And then suddenly without warning one sleeps. Never has one slept so deeply a whole night-long sleep, and

---

* 'The sentence "*Ma ma ma ma ma ma*" [in Chinese] can mean "Has mother scolded the horse?" This sounds like a joke analogous to the Latin "*Malo malo malo malo*" ("I would rather be in an apple tree than a bad man in trouble") but it is no joke.' Burgess, *A Mouthful of Air* (London: Hutchinson, 1992), p. 65.
† Burgess, interview with Geoffrey Aggeler in Stratford, Ontario, 30 July 1969.
‡ Graham Greene (1904–1991), English novelist best known for his trio of 'Catholic' novels: *Brighton Rock* (1938), *The Power and the Glory* (1940) and *The End of the Affair* (1951). William Seward Burroughs (1914–1997), American novelist, sexual dissident, long-term opium addict and scandalous author of *Naked Lunch* (1964).

then the waking and the luminous dial of the clock showing
that twenty minutes of so-called real time have gone by.*

Later, in the autumn of 1957, Burgess, who had arranged to meet
Greene for the first time in London, flew from Kuala Lumpur with
a bundle of Chinese silk shirts in his luggage. These were a gift for
Greene from a mutual friend, Trevor Wilson, a British diplomat
stationed in Singapore and Malaya.† Arriving at Greene's bachelor
flat at the Albany, just off Piccadilly, he handed over the shirts,
which Greene immediately attacked with a razor blade. Opium
pellets had been sewn into the cuffs. Burgess had been duped into
acting, however unwittingly, as Greene's drug mule. The source
for this story is Nigel Lewis, a former radio journalist from the
Canadian Broadcasting Corporation, who knew both Greene and
Burgess. (Lewis, who was born in Belize, is the 'Canadian academic'
mentioned on page 4 of *Little Wilson and Big God*, whose proposal
to write Burgess's biography in 1985 prompted him to begin his
memoirs.) Burgess's own account of his first meeting with Greene
elegantly avoids fully admitting or denying the opium-pellet story:
'A rumour was later to put it about that the silk shirts had opium
pellets sewn into the cuffs, but this was not, I think, true.'‡ Nigel
Lewis's version is rather different: 'When I asked Burgess if the story
was true, he admitted it but begged me not to print it. He looked
appalled.'§ Wherever the truth of it lies, it would have been impossible for Burgess to make a public admission of his part in a drug-
smuggling episode, even thirty years after the event, without inviting
trouble from Her Majesty's Customs and Excise whenever he travelled back to England from Monaco. But it is worth noting that
Burgess also told Kingsley Amis that he had smuggled opium for
Greene.

---

* Graham Greene, *Ways of Escape* (London: Bodley Head, 1980), p. 168.
† For a detailed account of Trevor Wilson's friendship with Greene, see Norman
Sherry, *The Life of Graham Greene*, vol. 2 (London: Jonathan Cape, 1994).
‡ 'Graham Greene: A Reminiscence' [1991] in *One Man's Chorus*, p. 252.
§ Nigel Lewis to author, 8 March 2002.

His visits to opium houses were balanced by occasional invitations to mingle with the Malay aristocracy. Lynne reported in a
letter to her sister in November 1955 that she and Burgess had
attended a 'Poppy Day' dance at the residence of the Mentri Besar
(or Prime Minister) of Kelantan. She enclosed a photograph of
herself shaking hands with the diminutive minister, who was less
than five feet tall ('I look a bit fat because I am bending over – the
Mentri Besar is very small & I am as always tactful!').* Burgess
invariably felt uncomfortable at these functions, where he sweated
in a white tuxedo while 'a couple of rajas would argue about the
respective merits of the [London] Savoy and Claridges'.† Given a
choice of social milieux, he preferred drinking in cheap *kedais* to
banqueting or dancing at royal residences. He reserved his deepest
resentment for the European clubs, and he suggested that the
expatriates who hid themselves away in such places 'wanted to be
in the fastness of the club, [or] the little dinner parties on Saturday
evening in the bungalows' because they were frightened of ordinary
Malayans. 'They didn't want to get to know the people, and I felt
very bitter about that because the people were worth knowing, and
of course one was there to know the people and [for] nothing else, I
felt.'‡

He recollected the events of late December 1955 or 1956 in a
short story titled 'A Colonial Christmas', published in *Punch* in
1968.§ Christmas in Malaya was a feast not well understood by
Burgess's Muslim, Hindu and animist neighbours, who regarded it
as a pretext for calling at his house in search of a free drink. The
first visitor, 'a sophisticated black magician of *magister templi* rank',
arrived at seven in the morning. He was followed by one of the local
prostitutes, a *haji* and his wife, and a 'small electrician' of mixed
race, who drank an entire bottle of Benedictine at a single sitting.

---

* Lynne Wilson, letter to Hazel Looker from Kota Bharu, 3 November 1955.
† Burgess, 'The Emigrants', p. 854.
‡ Burgess, *The World of Books* (radio interview), 22 February 1966.
§ 'A Colonial Christmas', *Punch*, 4 December 1968, pp. 801–2.

(In another account of this *haji* and his wife, Burgess writes: 'Haji
Latiff was an Afghan who, when making his pilgrimage to Mecca,
had met his wife Sharifah in that holy city, and had married her
when she was only fourteen [. . .] Latiff was loud and quarrelsome
and fond of telling me – with a loving arm round my shoulder –
how much he hated the British.' Latiff and Sharifah, 'a good
daughter of Islam' with a 'glossy Chinese perm' and a liking for
brandy with ginger ale, were on very friendly terms with Burgess
and Lynne in Kota Bharu.)* The early-morning Christmas boozing
gets underway in the story, with predictable results:

> The haji, high-flown, told the prostitute she was a prostitute,
> and the prostitute alleged that his wife was an adulteress, and
> the electrician was sick into an ashtray. The magician said
> nothing but turned off his shadow – a common and ominous
> trick of black magicians. At eleven am I had to turn everybody
> out, since I was due at my boss's house for Christmas drinks.
> The haji accused me of race prejudice (a white man had bidden
> him to leave his house) and the prostitute offered me a whis-
> pered free short time and then was offended because I would
> not accept.

Running late for the next drinks party, Burgess's narrator
decides to take a short cut using a dangerous road by the seashore.
But he has misread the tide-table, and his car sinks in crocodile-
infested waters. He climbs on top of the half-submerged vehicle and
kicks nervously at the encroaching crocodile snouts. Rescued by a
passing fishing boat, he arrives dripping at the party, where he is
awarded third prize in the fancy-dress competition as 'A Castaway'.
The story ends with a bitter Christmas carol, the words adjusted to
reflect local customs:

> *Silent night, tropical night:*
> *Dogs howl, sandflies bite.*
> *Some are busy with bottles and knives,*

---

* Burgess, 'Malayan Fashion', BBC radio, 8 July 1960.

> *Others sleeping with other men's wives.*
> *The mosque is losing its dome.*
> *There's nothing to do but go home.* *

This story conveys many of the farcical aspects of Burgess's Malayan years: the drunkenness, the confusion, the hostile climate and wildlife, the petty social humiliations and the discords of racial collision. Although Burgess was able to make implausible comedy out of all this, other aspects of his life in Malaya provided fewer opportunities for laughter.

Serious trouble with Lynne was on its way. Late in 1955, she was distressed by a letter from her sister in England, which told her that her mother was suffering from an inoperable cancer of the throat. The Jones family gathered in Leicester for Christmas, and they recorded their celebrations on an early reel-to-reel tape machine ('The worst part is not being able to swallow,' said Lynne's mother, Florence Jones) for the benefit of the Wilsons in Malaya. Ted Jones, Lynne's father, read bawdy passages from Chaucer's *Miller's Tale* into the microphone, and her niece Ceridwen, then aged three, sang adenoidally to her absent aunt. Burgess misrepresents the details of this tape when he claims in his autobiography that Lynne's sister had 'ghoulishly' recorded her mother's dying words 'before her throat closed forever'.† The idea of a posthumous tape-recording later resurfaced in a novel, *Beard's Roman Women* (1977), in which a widowed author receives a series of apparently spectral telephone calls from his recently deceased Welsh wife. Eventually it is revealed that her crazed sister has been playing recorded voices down the phone line. The connection with the Jones family is made explicit in

---

* This carol appears in a rewritten form in the novel *Beard's Roman Women* (London: Hutchinson, 1977), where Burgess alters the last two lines to 'The curry's making me cough. / There's nothing to do but eff off' (p. 76).
† For Burgess's accounts, see *Little Wilson and Big God*, p. 419 and *You've Had Your Time*, p. 19. I have a copy of the tape, sent to me by Lynne's niece, and Burgess's descriptions of it are so inaccurate that it seems highly unlikely that he had ever heard it.

the final chapter when the fictional writer marries his niece, whose name (like that of Burgess's own niece) is Ceridwen.

Florence Jones died on 2 January 1956, and the news sent Lynne into an intense and prolonged depression. Towards the end of the year she tried to kill herself by swallowing an overdose of sleeping tablets. Burgess discovered her in their bedroom when he returned home from school at lunchtime, and he was able to make her vomit the tablets out by administering a solution of mustard and water. It was her first attempt at suicide, but there would be others to follow. She spent the following months in bed, re-reading the works of Jane Austen and drinking iced gin, emerging occasionally to go on messy, shambolic drinking binges. Leslie Jones remembers: 'They used to go to the bar at Kota Bharu airport. She was notorious. She would take her clothes off, stand on the tables and dance in her bra and pants.'* A photograph from the time, in which Lynne is fully clothed, shows her drinking with Burgess in the airport bar, apparently in some danger of falling off her chair.

Along with the necessity of looking after Lynne, Burgess's duties at the Teacher Training College made large demands on his time, as he reported to a friend back in England: 'I've been overworked and have hardly written anything except official letters and scripts for the Education Dept. of Radio Malaya. Every week they broadcast a talk of mine to the School Certificate forms, to help them with their set books, and this means extra work – sitting up till long after midnight every night.'† Understaffing at the college was another complaint. The groups Burgess taught contained more than forty students, which made individual tuition and speech-work difficult. 'Much as I like Malaya,' he wrote, 'the educational system isn't all that efficient, and I've worked harder here than I've ever worked in my life before.'

The task of training teachers required Burgess to make excursions to English-language schools in Penang, Seramban and Kuala

---

* Leslie Jones to author, 10 January 2002.
† Burgess, letter to Susie Kerridge from Kuala Lumpar, 11 March 1956.

Lumpur to supervise his students who were doing teaching practice there. Writing to Susie Kerridge in March 1956 from the Paramount Hotel in Kuala Lumpur, he gave the impression that his own future was as uncertain as that of Malaya after independence:

> Malaya is in something of a political ferment at the moment, as you may have read in the papers, and everybody is crying 'Merdeka!' which means 'Freedom'. In Singapore British civil servants like myself are getting pulled out fast, and people here in the Federation itself are getting worried about the future. Will they be able to stay in Malaya? they keep asking. I may have to go to some other colonial territory for my next tour of duty, possibly Africa, but there's so much work to do here that I think they would be wasting me if they didn't send me back here. One gets a little sick, however, of reading in the papers about the 'bloodsucking British' and hearing people say that every white man should have his throat cut. It is believed that the real trouble when Malayan independence comes will be between the Malays and the Chinese, who don't like each other, and people are talking of the monsoon-ditches running with blood! I hope that my and my wife's blood will stay in our veins and arteries.*

He mentioned in passing that both he and Lynne were off their food, and that Lynne had been suffering from 'vomiting' and 'fever'. 'So you see, we pay a price for going to live in the tropics [. . .] I can't say we're really enjoying it.' Heat-induced anorexia was common among Europeans in Malaya, and Lynne was certainly suffering from some kind of eating disorder, but in other letters Burgess mentions that he had been putting on weight. It is possible that they were suffering from food-poisoning, malaria, or some other tropical disease such as dengue or sandfly fever. Lynne, according to everyone who met her in Malaya, was rarely to be seen without a glass of gin in her hand unless she was actually unconscious. Her letters home to her sister are punctuated by regular

---

* Burgess, letter to Susie Kerridge, 11 March 1956.

complaints about shakes and fevers (probably the early signs of alcoholism): 'I wrote to Pa some days ago and intended writing to you the next day but since then I have had another go of fever and this is the first day "the shakes" have allowed me to write.' Writing in a shaky hand, Lynne continues: 'John says he's now definitely made up his mind to finish at the end of this tour [i.e. in 1957], partly because of the new education policy [. . .] & partly because I can't seem to get rid of this fever.'* She was still depressed about her mother's death, and continued to drink heavily and self-destructively in spite of her precarious health, mistakenly believing that the heat would allow her to sweat the alcohol out of her system before it reached her liver.

*

The opening scene came to Burgess somewhere between sleeping and waking, at dawn on a thundery morning in 1955. As the voice of the muezzin floated through the window, crying 'There is no God but Allah', the names of his creditors floated guiltily through his mind, together with how much he owed them. The mental collage of debts and voices went something like this:

> La illah illa'lah
> *Lim Kean Swee $395*
> *Chee Sin Hye $120*
> *Tan Meng Kwang $250*
> La illah illa'lah.

'Here,' he thought, 'was the beginning of a novel': a white man is lying in bed in the brontoid dawn, far from home, listening to the muezzin's call to prayer and worrying about his debts.† Working from this starting point, Burgess began to write ('with suspicious ease') the first volume of his Malayan trilogy. He later claimed that a line from Arthur Hugh Clough's long poem *Amours de Voyage*

* Llewela Wilson, letter to Hazel Looker from Kota Bharu, 26 May 1956.
† Burgess, 'The Corruption of the Exotic', *Listener*, 26 September 1963, p. 465.

(1858) provided a commentary on all three novels: 'Allah is great, no doubt, and juxtaposition his prophet.' The juxtaposition of Europeans, Malays, Chinese, Sikhs, Tamils, Bengalis, Bugis and Eurasians (with all the consequent problems of cultural mistranslation) is the consistent and unifying theme of the trilogy as a whole.

Burgess spoke in detail about the process of composing his Malayan fiction in his earliest surviving radio interview (with Patricia Brent):

> Of course I have very little time to write. I have a full-time job
> [. . .] but I have to dedicate about two hours of the ordinary
> siesta time in the afternoon to writing. Just have to get down to
> it, sweat over the typewriter, slither over the keys, and hope
> that words will pour themselves out with the sweat [. . .] I can
> think better with a typewriter, I find, than with a pen or pencil
> [. . .] A fan is a great nuisance when you're typing. It blows the
> paper out of position, you can't see what you're writing. I make
> periodic excursions to the refrigerator and gulp down coconut
> milk or plain water. But, of course, there's nobody there, there's
> nobody waiting on me. At that time of the day everybody's
> asleep [. . .] The servants' quarters are resounding with snores.
> One's just on one's own.*

The comedy of the trilogy was, he said, a way of venting the feelings of 'irritation' and 'bad temper' that colonial life had aroused in him.

> I think D. H. Lawrence said something about working off one's
> sickness in books. This wasn't exactly sickness, but I did feel
> that it was easier to tolerate the people of the East if one could
> see them in a comic light. And it's possible [that] the writing of
> these books was in some measure a catharsis [. . .] I smoke very
> heavily, smoke through a holder, and I usually got through one
> cigarette-holder a day, having bitten through the mouthpiece by
> the end of the day [in exasperation].

---

* Burgess, *The World of Books* (radio interview with Patricia Brent), BBC Home Service, broadcast 9 May 1959.

With the typescript completed and sent to London in the autumn of 1955, there was a final difficulty to be resolved. Burgess's superiors in the Colonial Service were unwilling for him to publish a novel under his own name. He explained the position to Samuel Coale in an unpublished interview: 'You were not allowed to use your name if you were writing anything of a frivolous nature [. . .] It was recommended strongly, indeed it was enjoined, that I use another name.'* (His literary history book, *English Literature: A Survey for Students* [1958], was in fact the only work that appeared under his legal name, John Burgess Wilson.) Lynne suggested two pseudonyms: 'Anthony Powell' (clearly unsuitable, because there was already another novelist of that name) and 'Anthony Gilwern'.† In a state of indecision, he wrote to Roland Gant, fiction editor at Heinemann, enclosing a list of possible literary identities. Gant replied that the one he preferred was 'Anthony Burgess'. It seems appropriate to the man who had come to Malaya by accident that the name under which he was to become known throughout the world was decided so haphazardly. But it is also fitting that Burgess's Catholic background should be signalled by both halves of his *nom de plume*: 'Anthony' was the name he had taken at his first confirmation; and the Elizabethan and Jacobean priests who were sent to infiltrate England (whose martyrdoms Burgess commemorates in his fiction) had also disguised themselves by adopting their mothers' maiden names.‡

Heinemann was a shrewd choice of publisher on Burgess's part. The firm was doing well out of its fiction list, which boasted best-

---

* Burgess, unpublished interview with Samuel Coale in Monaco, 11 July 1978 (collection of Samuel Coale).
† The Powells were cousins of Lynne's in Wales, who had kept a pub in a village called Gilwern, near Abergavenny. See *You've Had Your Time*, p. 111.
‡ The poet Francis Xavier Enderby also adopts his mother's maiden name (Hogg) in *Inside Mr Enderby* (1963) and *Enderby Outside* (1968), which provides a point of connection between Burgess and his fictional hero. The identification is reinforced by the fact that Enderby is said to have written Burgess's own undergraduate poems.

selling authors such as Nevil Shute, Somerset Maugham, J. B. Priestley and Eric Ambler.* Michael Joseph, an imprint of Heinemann, had sold more than a million copies of Paul Gallico's novella, *The Snow Goose* (1941), and the collected works of D. H. Lawrence also continued to generate a substantial income. The success of these popular writers subsidized the literary end of the Heinemann list: in the 1950s their stable of novelists included Henry Miller, Olivia Manning, A. E. Ellis and Vladimir Nabokov.† Burgess had originally approached Heinemann with *A Vision of Battlements* in 1952 because at that time he was an enthusiastic admirer of Graham Greene. The firm had published all of Greene's novels since *The Man Within* (1928), and Burgess regarded himself, however loosely, as a fellow 'Catholic' novelist.

Preparations for the publication of *Time for a Tiger* went smoothly, and no revisions to Burgess's text were thought to be necessary. The typescript was initially sent to Heinemann's chief in-house reader, Maire Lynd, who wrote an enthusiastic report. Roland Gant offered Burgess a meagre advance of £50 (which was a good deal less than he would have been paid if he had approached

---

* See John St John, *William Heinemann: A Century of Publishing 1890–1990* (London: Heinemann, 1990). For Burgess on J. B. Priestley, see his review of Vincent Brome's biography in *Times Literary Supplement*, 21 October 1988, p. 1163.

† 'A. E. Ellis' was the pseudonym of Derek Lindsay, who also wrote plays under his own name. His novel, *The Rack* (the title comes from Shakespeare's *King Lear* – 'the rack of this tough life'), is an impressive attempt to transpose Thomas Mann's *The Magic Mountain* on to a set of English characters. Burgess believed that Ellis's novel, a forgotten masterpiece, was 'better than Thomas Mann'. Vladimir Nabokov (1899–1977), whose novel *Pnin* was published by Heinemann in 1957, took his subsequent books to Weidenfeld & Nicolson after A. S. Frere, the chairman of Heinemann, refused to risk a prosecution over the scandalous *Lolita* (1959). Olivia Manning (1908–1980) is best known for her Balkan trilogy: *The Great Fortune* (1960), *The Spoilt City* (1962) and *Friends and Heroes* (1965). Burgess said that Manning's trilogy 'seems to me perhaps the most important long work of fiction to have been written by an English woman novelist since the war' (*The Novel Now* [1971 edition], p. 95).

Heinemann through the intermediary of a literary agent). Ann Hill, the company's art editor, sent a copy of the typescript to the artist R. F. Micklewright with a request to design a dust jacket: 'This is a first novel and a fairly light-hearted one with a Malayan background [. . .] I suggest we might have a drinking scene on the jacket with the school master and the police sergeant in a rather fly-blown bar – bare electric light bulbs, bush jackets, empty glasses, etc.'* Micklewright was paid 14 guineas for his cover design, but the accidental demotion of Nabby Adams from lieutenant to sergeant was a mistake for which the reviewers blamed Burgess.

Time for a Tiger was published in an edition of 5,000 copies on 8 October 1956, with a cover price of 13s. 6d. It attracted a surprisingly large number of reviews for a first novel, and the critical comments, though mixed, were mostly encouraging. David Hughes wrote in the *Times Literary Supplement*: '[Malaya] is truthfully seen by the author as an arid and fatiguing society of mixed races [. . .] Mr Burgess is at his best in the drinking scenes.' The *Observer*'s fiction critic said that 'Like all good comic writers Mr Burgess loves his creations as much as he mocks them.' Peter Quennell of the *Daily Mail* described it as 'one of the most enjoyable first novels I have read for many months'. And George Daniel wrote in the *Spectator*: 'The reviewer who, according to the advertisement, said "Mr Kingsley Amis and the Red Brick boys will have to look to their laurels" may be right [. . .] As for declaring that one was not amused by it – unthinkable'.†

Less than a week after *Time for a Tiger* had been published, Burgess sent the typescript of a second Malayan novel, *The Enemy in the Blanket*, to Roland Gant at Heinemann. In a covering letter, written on 16 October, he explained that this book completed the story of Victor Crabbe and his wife. By 29 January 1957 he had

---

* Ann Hill, letter to R. F. Micklewright, 14 May 1956 (Heinemann archive).
† David Hughes, 'Burning Bright', *Times Literary Supplement*, 9 November 1956, p. 670; George Daniel, 'New Novels', *Spectator*, 26 October 1956, p. 582; Peter Quennell, *Daily Mail*, 27 September 1956.

changed his mind, and was proposing to resurrect Crabbe for a third volume: 'I am in fact working on a third and longer novel about Malaya called provisionally *Tremor of Intent*. This will definitely be the end of Crabbe. Theme: the inter-racial problem in pre-independence Malaya. The milk-and-water neutral Englishman as the only medium for rapprochement. Crabbe up river. Crabbe's death by drowning'.*

Buried somewhere amongst the broad comedy of the Malayan trilogy is a remarkably melancholy and self-critical portrait of Burgess's own marriage. He projects Lynne's unhappiness on to the bored, seedy, desperate character of Fenella Crabbe, who lies list-lessly in bed with a bottle of gin, sliced limes, a bout of fever and a copy of Jane Austen's *Persuasion*.† Burgess commented:

> I must confess that some of the unhappiness of that character is drawn from my wife's own, shall I say, boredom. Most women become terribly bored in the East [. . .] There are so very few other women to meet, and, well, the climate does seem to have a very bad effect on the health of women [. . .] Most white women, I think, become languid, thin, can't eat, lose interest in life. I'm afraid my own wife has suffered a little from that.

Yet the Malayan novels also contain what looks like a painfully honest disclosure of Burgess's own shortcomings as a husband. The multiple adulteries of Victor and Fenella Crabbe provide a precise reflection of the extra-marital affairs that Burgess and Lynne were pursuing in Malaya. In *The Enemy in the Blanket*, he dramatizes a domestic argument between the Crabbes, deploying the all-too-familiar verbal clichés of a married couple who both know (but are unwilling to acknowledge) that they have spent the evening trying to engineer new affairs at a party:

---

* Burgess, letter to James Michie from Malayan Teachers' Training College, Kota Bharu, Kelantan, 29 January 1957.
† *Time for a Tiger*, p. 58.

'I didn't see much of you this evening.'

'Nor I of you.'

'What was going on anyway?'

'Exactly. What was going on?'

'I was just being sociable.'

'One can take sociability too far. Everybody was looking at the pair of you.'

'Everybody was looking at the pair of *you*.'

'Oh, well, it doesn't matter.'

'No. I don't suppose anything matters.'*

The novel does not tell us who said what in this dialogue, for the guilty, evasive discourse of one adulterer addressing another is more important (and more revealing) than the identity of the speaker. There is a total lack of connection between Victor and Fenella. As the words fly back and forth, it is clear that nothing heartfelt, nothing of any value or significance, is being said on either side.

The second and third volumes of the Malayan trilogy were published by Heinemann on 3 February 1958 and 6 April 1959. The British and American reviews were generous. Thomas C. Wheeler wrote in the *New York Times*, 'This [i.e. the full trilogy] is a hugely informative book in which Asian hatred of Asian, a resentment of the white race stronger than any national bond, and the impulse toward national independence turning into a fantasy of self-indulgence become fictional truths.' Bernard Bergonzi made the bold claim (in the *New York Review of Books*) that 'Among contemporary writers no one is blacker, or more comic, than Anthony Burgess [. . .] He combines a unique sense of humor with a desolate philosophical despair in a way that makes him one of the more remarkable of living novelists.'†

---

* *The Enemy in the Blanket*, p. 102.

† Thomas C. Wheeler, 'Twilight of Empire in the Malay States', *New York Times*, Book Review section, 30 May 1965, p. 14; Bernard Bergonzi, 'Funny Book', *New York Review of Books*, 20 May 1965, pp. 15–16.

Not all of the Malayan trilogy's readers shared the delight of these reviewers. On 21 November 1958 James Michie, who was now Burgess's editor at Heinemann, wrote a stern letter to him in Malaya:

> I come now to what may be very bad news. Despite your disclaimer to me in a letter last year that 'literally all characters (in *The Enemy in the Blanket*) are made up from within', we have received a letter from lawyers in Kota Bharu acting for a client, Gilbert Christie, who claims to be libelled in the character of Rupert Hardman. From the passages they quote the claim looks to be a serious one and all I can say is that we have passed the matter over to our lawyers. Before *Beds in the East* finally goes to press, I would like a solemn assurance on your part that there is no possible chance of a similar situation recurring over that book. Could you write to me by return? Meanwhile I am worried for both your sake and ours over the present impending action: as I say, Mr Christie certainly appears to have a case – how good a one I am not in a position to say – and we find this mystifying in the light of your previous guarantee concerning the complete imaginariness of all the characters in the book.

This threatened libel action was a major embarrassment, and (as with *The Worm and the Ring*) it underlines the direct way in which Burgess's early fiction refers to recognizably real-life characters and events. Gilbert Christie was an English expatriate who worked as a colonial servant in Kota Bharu. He had served as a fighter pilot in the Royal Air Force during the Second World War, and had suffered serious burns to his face when his plane had crashed. He recognized himself as the character Rupert Hardman, of whom Burgess writes: 'his face had been ravaged by fire. He still remembered the smell of the Sunday roast, he the joint, the cockpit the oven [. . .] The doctors had done a marvellous job [. . .] It was an acceptable face, especially under the officer's peaked cap which hid the pale hair.'* This

---

* *The Enemy in the Blanket*, p. 20.

description is not libellous in itself, but there is no doubt that Burgess acted recklessly in transposing Christie's physical features on to the character of a notorious bankrupt who marries a wealthy Islamic widow for her money and then absconds to England with the fortune. In the circumstances, it is hardly surprising that the disfigured war hero believed himself to have been libelled. Burgess claimed in his own defence that he had shown the typescript of the novel to Christie before publication, and that no objections had been raised at that stage; but it was careless of Burgess to rely on his verbal assurances that he would not take legal action. Christie won an injunction against *The Enemy in the Blanket* in the High Court in Singapore, but the judgement was later overturned on appeal. This was a lucky escape for Burgess and his publisher, who would otherwise have been liable to pay damages at the discretion of the court.

Gilbert Christie was not the only reader to take offence. Another letter arrived at Heinemann's offices at 15 Queen Street, Mayfair, from a Mr Graham Williams of 9 Adam Street, Adelphi, London WC2:

Having been many years in Malaya and seeing a novel purport-ing to be about life in that part of the world, I took out from the local Library a book called 'The Enemy in the Blanket' by Mr A. Burgess, published by your firm.

I think it only right to inform you of the trick being played by Mr Burgess on his readers and on yourselves, if you are not aware of the translations of some of the Malay words he uses.

I give you three examples: Page 6 he calls the chief town of the state 'Kenching'. This means 'Urine'. On page 78 he tells of a youth asking for time off to attend a rally at 'Tahi Panas'. 'Tahi' means excreta, very colloquially put, and 'Panas' means 'hot'. On page 209 he mentions a Malay called 'Inche Mat bin Anjing'. 'Anjing' is the Malay for 'Dog' and is quite unsuitable to apply to a Mohemmedan, as you are aware.

There are so many oddities about this book and the way Mr Burgess's characters behave that I shall not expand on them except to let you know that the picture of life in Malaya is a very sordid and nasty travesty of what is happening to the Colony that after gaining its freedom, remains our friend and where the British are still welcome and respected.*

Dwye Evans, the senior fiction editor at Heinemann, replied emolliently that 'As no one in this office speaks Malayan [sic], we had no means of knowing what these words meant and if they have caused you any offence, we are sorry.' But it is significant that Evans did not bother to pass on this complaint to Burgess, and it seems likely that he regarded the concealed obscenities as harmless jokes, unintelligible to most of the novel's readers. Denis Cartwright, who knew Burgess in Kota Bharu, comments: 'The Malayan trilogy is intended to be offensive to readers who speak Malay. Most of the place-names are obscene.' He cites several examples of coded scur- rilities in Burgess's Malayan fiction: the River Lanchap ('lanchap: slippery, hence masturbation'); Musang ('a civet cat, figuratively a philanderer'); the Iblis Club ('Iblis: the Devil'); Negeri Dahaga ('state or province of great thirst'); Mr Mahalingam (whose name means 'large penis').† This kind of semi-encrypted bawdiness is a recurring feature of Burgess's novels from first to last, and he delighted in inventing evasive ways of making his characters swear that fell just about within the limits imposed by the English obscenity laws. Nabby Adams has a dog who answers to the name 'Cough'; 'For cough,' suggests the poet-hero of *Inside Mr Enderby*; 'Fackin oor,' shrieks Carmen in *The Doctor Is Sick*; 'omnifutuant' is the euphem- ism used to describe Dr Tiresias in *Honey for the Bears*. Recognizing and responding to such indecencies is part of the game that readers

---

* Graham Williams, letter to Messrs William Heinemann Ltd, 4 December 1959 (Heinemann archive).
† Denis Cartwright to author, 27 January 2002. Mr Cartwright adds: 'I have heard that Burgess, when challenged about the name of a Chinese shop (kedai), insisted that he had actually seen "Wun Fatt Tit" on a sign [see *Time for a Tiger*, p. 179]. The nearest I ever saw to this was thirty miles south of Kuala Lumpur: Koo Tit Quail Farm.'

are invited to play. Who else but Burgess would insist on the fine distinction between 'coprophilia' and 'coprophagia', both of which refer to messy sexual practices?

By contrast, the other book that Burgess wrote in Malaya was a scholarly and wide-ranging work of non-fiction, which turned out to be one of the most commercially successful books he ever published, remaining continuously in print for nearly forty years. Dissatisfied with the available textbooks on the history of English literature, he proposed to the educational publisher Longman in London that he should write a new one, to be used specifically by students of English as a foreign language. *English Literature: A Survey for Students* is written with characteristic Burgessian brio, and it is remarkable both for the generosity of its critical judgements and for the deep fund of literary knowledge that stands behind it. Written over the course of several months in Kota Bharu, the book contains a number of engaging autobiographical digressions:

> Sitting here now, a degree or so above the equator, I look round my hot room and see nothing that will last. It won't be long before my house collapses, eaten by white ants, eroded by rain and wind. The flowers in front of me will be dead tomorrow. My typewriter is rusty already. And so I hunger for something that is permanent, something that will last forever.*

Only through the creation of music, art or literature (the reader is solemnly assured) can we hope to cheat death, or to pass on an individual artistic vision to those who have not yet been born. Burgess's artistic credo as a writer finds eloquent expression in his reflections on the poets, novelists and dramatists of the past, whose words are continually modified in the guts of the living. Presciently – and surprisingly, for a writer working in the 1950s – he acknowledges that the term 'English literature' refers not to a nation but to a flourishing worldwide language: 'Joseph Conrad was a Pole,

---

* John Burgess Wilson, *English Literature: A Survey for Students* (London: Longman, 1958; revised edition, 1974), p. 2.

Demetrios Kapentanakis was a Greek, Ernest Hemingway was an American, Lin Yutang was a Chinese, but English is the medium they have in common [. . .] Chinese, Malays, Africans, Indians reading this book may well one day themselves contribute to English literature.'* Burgess's literary history stands, along with the 600-page Malayan trilogy and the omnilingual *Earthly Powers*, as a monument to the internationalism and multifariousness of his enthusiasms. (The 1,000-page typescript of a more ambitious work of literary history, *They Wrote in English*, published in two lavish paperback volumes in Milan by Tramontana but now out of print and long-forgotten, is in the Burgess manuscript collection at the University of Texas. This 'lost' book is still waiting for a mainstream British or American publisher.)

Burgess's various writing projects did not prevent him from composing new music in Malaya. He provided a piano score for a local amateur production of the melodrama *Maria Marten*, and he also set five Malay *pantuns* (quatrain poems) for soprano and native instruments under the general title 'Kalau Tuan Mudek Ka-Hulu', which translates as 'If you, my lover, go upriver'.† As the date of Malayan Independence drew nearer, Burgess decided to mark the occasion with a full-scale orchestral work, composed under the title 'Symphoni Malaya'. He sent the score to Radio Malaya in the hope that they would broadcast it in August 1957, but it has never been performed. A description of the symphony appears in *Beds in the East* (1959), where it is said to be the work of a gifted young Chinese composer, Robert Loo:

> The first movement had seemed to suggest a programme, each instrument presenting in turn a national style – a gurgling Indian cantilena on the 'cello, a kampong tune on the viola, a

---

* Ibid., p. 9.
† He translated another *pantun* about the easy-going way of life among the *kampong* Malays: 'White men hurry, yellow men hurry. / The grave's the end of all their fuss. / We sit in the shade, eat rice, eat curry, / Wait for the grave to come to us' (quoted in the documentary *Writers and Places: A Kind of Failure*).

pentatonic song on the second violin and some pure Western atonality on the first. And then a scherzo working all these out stridently, ending with no resolution. A slow movement suggesting a sort of tropical afternoon atmosphere. A brief finale, ironic variations on a somewhat vapid 'brotherhood of man' motif [. . .] It held together, it was coherent, and it showed remarkable technical competence.*

Burgess cited three principal musical influences on this work – Mahler, Berg and Schönberg – but its claim to originality lay in unorthodox combinations of instruments: xylophone, harps, piccolo and three trumpets, for example.

In a programme note for the first performance of his later Symphony in C (1975), Burgess gives a misleading account of the history of the 1957 Malayan symphony:

In the last movement, as an infinitely extensible coda, the timpanist rolled indefinitely on C and the crowd was encouraged to shout 'Merdeka!' which means freedom, liberty, the yoke of the tyrannical white man has dropped from us, etc. The crowd could not be dissuaded from turning this shout into a free fight, so the timpanist stopped rolling and the whole orchestra went home in disgust. Thus, the symphony never really ended. It is still, in a kind of Platonic sense, waiting for its final chord.†

Although this anecdote is entertainingly narrated, it has little basis in fact. There was no fist-fight among the audience, for there was no audience, no orchestra and no performance. The headmaster of the Sultan Ismael College in Kota Bharu remembers Burgess mentioning in conversation that he had written a symphony, but none of his colleagues from the small expatriate community have any recollection of a public performance, riotous or otherwise, and

* Burgess, *Beds in the East*, p. 26.
† Burgess, untitled programme note for University of Iowa Symphony Orchestra, 22 October 1975.

they would surely have got to hear about it if it had actually taken place. Furthermore (and bafflingly), Burgess appears to refute his earlier version of events when he writes in the first volume of the autobiography that his Malayan symphony 'was never to be played'.* The programme note offers a good illustration of Burgess's harmless tendency to misremember the events of his own past for comic or dramatic effect. In this respect, he might be thought to participate in a recognizably Irish form of story-telling, in which the shape of the narrative takes precedence over factuality and reliability. ('Do you want the truth or do you want the big music?' is a question often heard in Irish and Anglo-Irish places, such as the Dwyer household in Manchester where Burgess was raised. His preference, almost invariably, was for the 'big music'.)

Burgess's three-year teaching contract with the Colonial Office expired in the summer of 1957, and he flew out from the airport in Kuala Lumpur with Lynne on 5 August. They took a short holiday in Rome on their way back to England, and the local detail Burgess gathered here was to provide the background to Enderby's Roman honeymoon in *Inside Mr Enderby*. Few of his foreign excursions were wasted: they were usually absorbed into his fiction at some future point. Before he left Rome, he threw a few coins into the Trevi fountain and vowed that one day he would return.

He lived for the next five months in Lynne's father's house at 2 Franklyn Road in Aylestone (a suburb of Leicester), a location that was later commemorated, not altogether generously, as 'the Franklyn Road Temporary Detention Centre' in *The Wanting Seed*.† Burgess knew that there was no further possibility of finding work in Malaya after the formal declaration of independence, so he began scanning the small ads in newspapers in seach of another teaching job. He had written only half-seriously to Kathleen Winfield about the possibility of returning to Banbury Grammar School, but there are no letters in the school files to suggest that he

---

* *Little Wilson and Big God*, p. 416.
† Burgess, *The Wanting Seed* (London: Heinemann, 1962), p. 162.

actually reapplied for his old post in the English department there. Besides, a large part of his purpose in going to Malaya three years earlier had been to escape from the unbearable dullness of village life in Oxfordshire and the meanness of teaching salaries in England. Nevertheless, Lynne was proposing, in spite of his reasonable objections, that he should become a schoolmaster in or near Leicester, and she had sent a letter from Kota Bharu to her sister, Hazel, asking whether her husband, William Looker (the headmaster of a school in Broughton Astley, Leicestershire), knew of any teaching vacancies in the area.

Burgess's own ideas about his future were rather more ambitious and exotic: he applied unsuccessfully for a Readership in Phonetics at the University of Punjab – a post for which he was hopelessly unsuited, having no publications in the field of linguistics, and no formal qualifications beyond a first degree in English Literature – and for a British Council teaching job in Jakarta.* As these job applications turned into rejections and disappointment, the Wilsons took to spending much of their time in the pub just around the corner from Franklyn Road, the Black Horse on Narrow Lane (a back-street drinking den whose name is misremembered in Burgess's memoirs as 'the Black Swan or Mucky Duck'). Yet these long months of enforced idleness in Aylestone were not altogether wasted. Lynne passed on a scrap of local gossip, and Burgess expanded it into The Right to an Answer, his black comedy of interracial adultery and murder in the English Midlands. He had the bones of a plot, but no clear idea of how it should be resolved.

The story was of two English married couples – Mr and Mrs A, Mr and Mrs Z – who played the weekend game of swapping spouses. Unfortunately the game was taken too seriously by Mr A and Mrs Z, who fell in love and thus disrupted two marriages. A character entered the fiction from nowhere – a Mr Raj, a Singhalese ignorant of the principles of English adultery,

---

* Burgess, letter to James Michie from Sultan Omar Ali Saifuddin College, Brunei, 10 February 1958 (Heinemann archive).

who resolved the unfinished tale bloodily. This I had not expected when I commenced writing, but I knew something would emerge out of the unconscious.*

He told Patricia Brent that this book was 'meant to bridge the gap between the novels about the East and the novels about England I intend to write, because it has as its main character a man who's lived in the East, and who sees what's happening in post-war England through the eyes of a man who's really an exile.'† This man is the narrator of *The Right to an Answer*, J. W. Denham, who returns to England after working abroad for some years to look after his dying father. His diagnosis, on looking around the nameless Midlands city where his father is now living – Burgess later admitted that he had been thinking of Leicester – is that the post-war West is in a hell of a mess:

> I lack the mental equipment and the training and the termin-
> ology to say whether the mess is social or religious or moral,
> but the mess is certainly there, certainly in England, and prob-
> ably in the Celtic fringe and all over Europe and the Americas
> too. I'm in a position to smell the putridity of the mess more
> than those who have never really been expatriated from it – the
> good little people who, with their television, strikes, football
> pools and *Daily Mirror*, have everything they want except death
> [. . .] I can feel damnation being broken in like a pair of shoes,
> myself becoming a citizen of the mess.‡

The fact that 'J. W.' Denham shares Burgess's own initials suggests that the author and his character might share this gloomy diagnosis. Yet there are substantial comic interludes in the long sections dealing with the escapades of Mr Raj, and in truth this is a novel about a foreign visitor who attempts with only limited success to integrate into English life. Mr Raj is Victor Crabbe in reverse, a

---

* Burgess, *One Man's Chorus*, p. 262.
† *The World of Books* (radio interview), 23 April 1959.
‡ Burgess, *The Right to an Answer* (London: Heinemann, 1960), p. 1.

touchingly innocent picaresque hero abroad, and indeed the French translation of this novel changes its title to *Monsieur Raj*, for he (not Denham) is the true focus of Burgess's imaginative interest. When *The Right to an Answer* received a lukewarm review from the critic Marghanita Laski, Burgess retaliated by giving her name to one of the undesirable streets in *A Clockwork Orange*. It must have given him quiet amusement to imagine Alex and his three droogs tolchocking, crasting and dealing out the old ultra-violence on Marghanita Boulevard.

In January 1958 the Wilsons flew back to the East, where Burgess was to take up another teaching post at the Sultan Omar Ali Saifuddin College in Brunei Town. He described his first impressions of Brunei in a letter to James Michie on 10 February:

> I don't think I like Brunei very much so far, chiefly because we are stuck in a hot Chinese hotel room with little prospect of a house for a long time and a chicken slaughter-house below our window. It's hard to get any writing done [. . .] The set-up isn't a very happy one either – the administration has more money than sense and spends it on the wrong things, and we have the usual colonial bitchiness all around us. However, my aim was to do another 3 years here and try to get another 3 novels written, and if possible come back to England and try and make some sort of living out of writing.

One of his fellow teachers at the school, Margery Fishenden, remembers:

> My husband [Roy Fishenden] met the Wilsons at the airport. Lynne demanded to be taken to a local shop, and came out with two bottles of gin. Their neighbours were crude Australian road-menders. It was a house poorly furnished to Malay standard. John Wilson was very crude, chatty and unafraid. He had a beautiful speaking voice, but he didn't fit in with the other Europeans. He was not a member of the Yacht Club. He wasn't invited to Christmas parties among the Europeans. He was cast

out. He was outspoken and feared, even by the British Resident. Not a happy man at all.*

Lynne (or 'his gruesome wife', according to Mrs Fishenden) soon earned herself a reputation among the expatriates as an uncontrollable piss-artist. In a café-bar called The Snowman she was observed putting her breasts on the bar and asking her Australian fellow-drinkers: 'Have you ever seen a better pair than this?' She was arrested after a street-fight with broken bottles, and on the day of her court appearance she sat on the bumper of a jeep outside the court-house with a bottle of gin and a thermos flask full of iced water, swigging away and shouting, 'Is it my turn yet?' She got off with a fine, but the episode did little to improve Burgess's standing in Brunei. Mrs Fishenden says:

> I remember her as ugly, poorly dressed, quite plump, with her hair scraped back. She mingled a lot with the Australian roadmen. She had a reputation for fighting – she would accuse you of ignoring her. When drunk, she'd shout you down. She'd be throwing chairs at anyone foolish enough to take her on. John Wilson and Lynne were always having sexual traumas in their house, audible to all around. She used to shout, 'Hurry up! If you don't come now you'll be too late.'

By the late 1950s something was alarmingly out of joint within the Wilsons' marriage, as Burgess acknowledged in a letter to Lynne's sister, written a few months after her death: 'It's a hard thing to say, but the last years – indeed, the whole period from leaving Borneo were pretty tough. I did my best but it wasn't good enough, I'm afraid.'† Would they have been any happier if Burgess had found work as a schoolteacher in Leicester, as Lynne had suggested? Probably not. Burgess, who was temperamentally too much of a free spirit to tolerate following other people's orders, had failed to get on with authority figures since the age of

* Margery Fishenden to author, 18 December 1998.
† Burgess, letter to Hazel Looker from Lija, Malta, 6 December 1968.

sixteen. His minor rebellions began with his initial falling-out with
the Jesuit priests at the Church of the Holy Name, continued
through his university career at Manchester (where he jeered, along
with his fellow students, at Professor Charlton's intellectual shortcomings), the Army (where he had regular shouting-matches with
Major Meldrum), his time at Banbury Grammar School (where he
libelled Gwen Bustin and Moyna Morris in *The Worm and the
Ring*), to the lessons at the Malay College in which he mocked
Jimmy Howell in front of the pupils. Later on, as a professional
writer, he embroiled himself in energetic disputes with literary
agents, literary editors, film producers, book reviewers, passport
offices, the Arts Council and the Inland Revenue. The image of
Burgess which emerges from these episodes is that of an unapologetic individualist who quickly became mutinous whenever he
found himself subject to authority in any of its forms. Yet his
apparent bloody-mindedness was almost invariably a matter of
defending a principle, or of making amends for an injustice that he
felt had been done to him. The 1940s and early 1950s represented
long years of poverty, boredom and creative disappointment for
Burgess and Lynne, and the spirit of optimism with which they had
gone to Malaya and Brunei was quickly modified by the knowledge
that they were still subject to arbitrary, inefficient bureaucracy and
to sub-standard housing, which was a more immediate cause of
grievance. Many of the complaints he voiced in his later years were
justified, too: Burgess *was* ripped off over the film rights to *A
Clockwork Orange*; his writing *was* undervalued by critics and
scholars in England; and the 90 per cent super-tax imposed by
Harold Wilson's government in the late 1960s drove Burgess out
of England along with other high-earning writers, actors and
musicians.

Towards the end of 1958, Burgess wrote scurrilous texts to fit
the music of seven well-known Christmas carols. He transcribed the
words and music (along with an original piece for piano, 'Interlude
for Small Organ') into an exercise book, which he decorated with
caricatures of his enemies:

> *Come all ye crawlers,*
> *Psychosycophantic,*
> *Purr and defer to the State Treasurer.*
> *Give him a parcel*
> *And then kiss his arcel.*
> *Pay homage at the Yacht Club,*
> *That snottier-than-snot club,*
> *Give pleasure to your treasure,*
> *The treaaas-ur-er.* *

This is a desperate piece of frivolity, written when he was at one of his lowest points. He was also drinking heavily – at least a bottle of whisky per day, according to one of his colleagues at the school. Sheila Spicer, another English expatriate who knew him in Brunei, says:

> He was a bit of an embarrassment to the education department and they wanted him out. He managed to offend a large number of the community, including the higher-ups. He was drinking and his wife was drinking. He wasn't happy, and the authorities weren't happy with him. But one didn't get the sack unless one had done something dreadful.

Finally, one morning in September 1959, Burgess collapsed on the floor of his classroom in the middle of a lesson and refused to move. He was stretchered off to Brunei Hospital, where he was examined by a redheaded Scottish doctor. This episode was to mark the end of his teaching career, and the beginning of his more productive life as a full-time professional writer.

---

* From Burgess's Brunei songbook (archive of the International Anthony Burgess Foundation, Manchester). This version of 'O Come, All Ye Faithful' also appears in *Beard's Roman Women* (London: Hutchinson, 1977), p. 81.

6

No End to Anthony

When Burgess flew back to England with Lynne in September 1959, he had no clear idea of the provisional diagnosis that his doctor in Brunei had made. Lynne made a characteristic impression on the aircrew on this homeward flight. According to Sheila Spicer, who knew the Wilsons in Brunei and took the same plane back to London shortly afterwards, the air hostesses remembered that Lynne had exhausted their supply of gin. She had also managed to be copiously airsick.

Lynne had been entrusted with a sealed envelope containing X-rays of her husband's head and a confidential letter addressed to the specialists at the Hospital for Tropical Diseases in London. This letter is now lost. According to Burgess's account of it in *Little Wilson and Big God*, Lynne secretly unsealed the envelope and read it, disclosing its contents to him three months later. If Burgess's second-hand reconstruction of the letter is to be trusted – and he claimed never to have set eyes on it himself – it diagnosed a possible brain tumour and ended with the words 'His wife is a chronic alcoholic.'*

The Wilsons' movements over the next couple of months are

---

* See *Little Wilson and Big God: Being the First Part of the Confessions of Anthony Burgess* (London: Heinemann, 1987), p. 443.

difficult to reconstruct with any precision. Shortly after their arrival in London, Lynne rented a room in a cheap London hotel while Burgess underwent a series of medical tests at the Hospital for Tropical Diseases, which referred him on to the Neurological Institute on Queen Square in Bloomsbury. He remained under observation in these hospitals for about eight weeks. Remembering this period in the 1980s, Burgess claimed that the consultant in charge of his case at the Neurological Institute was Sir Alexander Abercrombie, and that he was also seen by a junior neurologist named Roger Bannister, who had entered the record books in 1954 as the first athlete to run a mile in less than four minutes. More than forty years after the event, Dr (now Sir Roger) Bannister retains some memories of treating Burgess, but he is reluctant to disclose what he knows: 'Of course you know that there is a code that prevents any doctor from divulging details of former patients, living or dead.'[*] Nevertheless, he rejects the suggestion that he 'trepanned the Burgess cranium'. Sir Roger writes: 'I am not a surgeon and so have never trepanned anyone's head.'[†] He also points out there there was no doctor named Alexander Abercrombie (the consultant named in Burgess's memoirs) working at Queen Square while he was there.[‡] A couple of years after he had been examined at the Neurological Institute, Burgess boasted to the playwright and novelist Julian Mitchell that on one occasion he had 'run away from hospital and been chased down the street and caught by Roger Bannister'. Mitchell, to his credit, maintains that he didn't believe a word of this story.[§]

While Burgess was confined to his bed at the Neurological

---

[*] Sir Roger Bannister to author, 8 December 2002.

[†] Sir Roger Bannister to author, 27 July 2003. For the trepanning story, see Roger Lewis, *Anthony Burgess* (London: Faber, 2002), p. 258.

[‡] Did Burgess change the name in his memoirs because he was worried about a possible libel action? Or is 'Alexander Abercrombie' merely an element in the fictionalization of his own life's story, an imaginary doctor conjured into being for the autobiography?

[§] Julian Mitchell to author, 2 November 2001.

Institute, letters arrived from Brunei informing him that his teaching contract with the Crown Agents for the Colonies had been terminated, and that his Oldsmobile had been seized by one of his creditors. James Michie, his editor at Heinemann, remembers visiting him at the Queen Square hospital, where he was surprised to find Burgess sitting up in bed and looking suspiciously healthy. Michie remembers: 'I visited him late in 1959 when I heard that he was ill. But he didn't seem particularly unwell. There was no evidence of any intensive care. If anything he seemed rather talkative.'*

Lynne, who was supposed to be residing at a boarding house, succeeded in engineering a temporary disappearing act. She was spending most of her time in pubs and semi-criminal drinking clubs in Bloomsbury and Soho. In one of these she picked up a gargantuan man who shifted scenery at the Royal Opera House in Covent Garden, and she soon began to spend afternoons getting plastered with him rather than visiting her apparently sick husband. 'You know how I hate hospitals,' she told Burgess defensively, thinking back to the weeks she had spent recovering from her miscarriage after she was robbed and beaten up by GI deserters during the blackout in 1944. In the absence of any consolations beyond eating hospital meals, reading the downmarket newspapers and looking forward to Lynne's erratic visits, Burgess surrendered himself to 'the heartless machine' of an institution devised to treat the sick and the dying in minimal comfort, 'a one-sexed club where the only qualification is disease and there is always disease to talk about'. Confined to his bed on doctor's orders, he was obliged to urinate and defecate into what he termed 'impossible vessels', often soiling his sheets and pyjamas while aiming inexpertly at the bedpan. Thinking back to this period of humiliating confinement, he said in 1982: 'I remember once being made to get up in black London December and go out to a newsagent not yet open, there to wait shivering so that I could buy the ward's copies of the *Daily Mirror*. The following day I was

---

* James Michie to author, 15 November 2000.

to be investigated for a possible cerebral tumour.'* This memory cannot be strictly accurate, since he had in fact been discharged from hospital by the middle of November.

Some of the tests that he underwent were alarming. In the cellars of the Neurological Institute he was comprehensively scanned by arteriogram and electro-encephalogram machines. His head was pumped full of air, which left him bedridden with a pounding two-day headache. On two or three occasions, quantities of cerebro-spinal fluid, whose yellowish colour reminded him of superior neat gin, were syringed out of his spine. 'This is pretty unpleasant,' he said later. 'You feel the whole vertebral structure collapsing.' According to the first volume of Burgess's memoirs, Dr Bannister told him that the protein content of his cerebro-spinal fluid was unusually high. This abnormality, he was later informed, might indicate the presence of a brain tumour. Burgess commented, in an interview with Samuel Coale,

> What the norm is I don't know. How can we tell what the norm is? We can only tell what the norm is if everybody has a spinal tap [. . .] They said there's probably a tumour or some kind of growth which we can't see, which the instruments themselves aren't able to show us. It may be masked by living tissue or something. So the thing to do is to discharge you and give you a year to live.†

The diagnosis seems to have been an ambiguous one: nobody was certain that a tumour was present, but nobody was willing to declare that it was absent either. Burgess himself made matters more complicated after he had been discharged from hospital by failing to turn up for subsequent appointments at the Neurological Institute. Had he by this point stopped believing in the competence of the medical establishment, or was he simply afraid of submitting himself to further undignified medical probings? Remembering Moyna Mor-

---

* Burgess, *On Going to Bed* (New York: Abbeville Press, 1982), pp. 70–71.
† Burgess, interview with Samuel Coale in Monaco, 7 and 11 July 1978.

ris's account of the conversation in the Banbury school staff room, it may be that he simply wished to be allowed to get on with the business of dying, intending to write as much as he could before the cancer killed him.

Once again, the real difficulty with trying to establish what was actually going on is that other accounts he gave of the brain tumour story differ in significant respects from the 'official' version which appears in the autobiography. Burgess was unable to tell the story in the same way twice, and four of these variants are worth looking at in detail. The first comes from Dick Adler's *Sunday Times* profile of Burgess, published in 1967, which contains the earliest printed references to the medical tests and the 'death sentence'. Burgess told Adler that a brain tumour had been tentatively diagnosed by the doctors in Brunei, and that two (unnamed) London hospitals had confirmed these initial suspicions. 'They said that if I lived a year, I might make it. But I had to stay in a cold climate. I could never return to the East.' He was nevertheless convinced that there was more to his repatriation and sudden sacking than met the eye. 'They wanted me out of the way,' he said, and went on to suggest that the diagnosis was in some way connected to his unpopularity with the Crown Agents for the Colonies, who (he believed) were colluding with the doctors at three different hospitals in London and Brunei to get him dismissed from his schoolteaching job.*

The second version of the story comes from his 1988 radio interview with Dr Anthony Clare:

BURGESS: I found the life there [in Brunei] very frustrating [. . .] One day in the classroom I decided that I'd had enough. Let others take over. I just lay down on the floor out of a kind of interest, to see what would happen. Then I was picked up and shoved into the local hospital and various elementary tests were given, and then I was flown home. And then, eventually, my wife was told: 'There is evidence of a cerebral tumour, but it is

* Dick Adler, 'Inside Mr Burgess', *Sunday Times Magazine*, 2 April 1967, pp. 47–50, 49.

inoperable'. And – I don't know whether this is common – but she told me that they gave me a year to live.

CLARE: Did you believe it?

BURGESS: Well, not altogether. I mean, I felt too well. I'd come back from a torrid climate and uneatable food to pleasant, autumn England with a mild climate . . .

CLARE (interrupting): Would they have asked you about life out in Brunei, and the extent to which it was getting you down?

BURGESS: No, they were very interested in what they thought of as a failure of the libido. Which had happened. That was probably the heat.

CLARE: Had you been drinking a lot at the time?

BURGESS: Oh, a great deal, a great deal.

CLARE: How much?

BURGESS: Well, my wife was drinking far more than I . . . Let me tell you how much. Let's be totally honest about it. I was drinking, in the house itself, about a bottle of gin a day, and about half a bottle of gin in bars or on the town. I was drinking far too much.*

Gone is the conspiracy: instead he presents a *willed* collapse ('I just lay down on the floor out of a kind of interest'), and the loss of his libido, which is unlikely to be a symptom of cancer, but might be an indication of some other psychological distress. Nor is Clare's diplomatic suggestion that clinical depression or drinking might have been the true cause of his physical breakdown entirely rejected by Burgess.

The interview with Clare follows *Little Wilson and Big God* in suggesting that the news that he would die within the year was communicated not directly to Burgess but to Lynne, who kept it to

---

* *In the Psychiatrist's Chair*, BBC Radio 4, 27 July 1988.

herself for several weeks after she had heard it from the neurologists, and didn't finally confess it (because 'women do not like keeping secrets') until the last days of December 1959, between Christmas and New Year.* Yet it is hard to believe that Burgess himself would have been kept in the dark about the apparent gravity of his condition, unless – and it is worth keeping an open mind about this – he is quietly suggesting that the brain tumour and the terminal twelve months were only ever malicious inventions of Lynne's. This implication is certainly present in both the autobiography and the Clare interview, and it offers one possible way of unlocking the riddle of his terminal diagnosis.†

In his *Face to Face* television interview with Jeremy Isaacs in 1989, Burgess described his exit from Brunei and subsequent hospitalization in different terms again. He told Isaacs that he had been 'driven out of the Colonial Service, possibly for political reasons which were disguised as medical reasons'.‡ Although he did not specify the nature of the 'political reasons' – an uncharacteristic moment of reticence on his part – he was probably thinking of his friendship with Azahari, the leader of the revolutionary People's Party in Brunei, and of the occasion when Lynne had sworn at the Duke of Edinburgh at an official garden party. ('Welsh, is she?' was the Duke's response to his diplomatic hosts.) As with his interview with Adler in 1967, Burgess's remarks to Isaacs look like an admission that there was nothing wrong with him from a medical point of view, and that the authorities in Brunei were simply anxious to get rid of him.

Burgess's radio interview with John Dunn, broadcast in October

---

* See Burgess, *Little Wilson and Big God*, p. 447.
† It is difficult to say whether or not this is a sustainable interpretation, since it is sometimes present and sometimes absent in Burgess's oral narrations about his brain tumour. The suggestion that Lynne made the whole thing up was first put forward by Michael Ratcliffe in his article 'Inside Mister Burgess', *Observer*, Review section, 9 December 2001, p. 6.
‡ *Face to Face* (television interview with Jeremy Isaacs), BBC 2, 21 March 1989.

1990, casts further doubts on what the specialists actually told Lynne:

> I was sent home with a suspected tumour on the brain from Brunei, where I was working, and I think it was a diagnosis that the doctors made to cover themselves. There were various symptoms which they couldn't ascribe to anything but a cerebral tumour [. . .] My wife had a great deal to put up with, I think, having to keep the secret of my impending death. They told her without telling me.*

From this account it would appear that no reference to the suspected brain tumour was ever written down or communicated directly to Burgess himself. Could Lynne have misunderstood what she had been told, or even deliberately misrepresented what she'd heard? Burgess adds: 'Eventually she broke the secret, but she was already well on the way to dissolution.' Lynne's alcoholic decline had already reached a catastrophic stage, with her own life seriously disorganized since 1954 by drink, prescription drugs and random sexual pick-ups. How credible is it, in the circumstances, that Burgess would have made no effort to go back to a doctor to verify what Lynne had told him about his illness? Yet that is what he asks us to believe.

The tangle of stories that he wove around his hospital experiences is mystifying, not least because we have no independent medical evidence that would promise to solve the puzzle definitively.† In the years after 1959, the events which he referred to as his 'medical death-sentence' and 'terminal year' became part of the performance that he could be relied on to deploy for the benefit of interviewers – but the details of what he said on these subjects are

---

* *The John Dunn Show*, BBC Radio 2, 31 October 1990.
† The Public Records Act of 1958 decrees that English medical records are sealed for 100 years after the death of the patient, and the doctors who treated Burgess are bound by the Hippocratic Oath not to disclose the details of his case. The precise nature of his condition is therefore likely to remain a mystery until his doctors' notes are made available for inspection in 2094.

far from consistent. The disappearing tumour was simply absorbed into Burgess's extensive series of half-reliable anecdotes, and the process of its fictionalization would bear comparison with the wildly conflicting accounts that he gave of his family history.

A few facts are beyond dispute. We know that he collapsed in the classroom in Brunei, because two other teachers who were at the school (Mr Arshad and Mrs Fishenden) remember the incident taking place. We also know that he did not die, as predicted, from a brain tumour in the year 1959–60, and that he went on to enjoy another thirty-three years of vigorous life. If a suspected brain tumour was indeed the official diagnosis, then it must have been made in error. Yet *something* was wrong with Burgess in 1959, and – while his illness may have been brought on by heavy drinking, malaria or depression, none of which were uncommon among white Europeans who spent time in the former colonies, or a recurrence of the migraines which had troubled him throughout his Army career, or even a mild and undiagnosed form of epilepsy, a condition which is known to have occurred elsewhere in his immediate family – it clearly wasn't the inoperable cancer that he claimed it was.

One of the paradoxes of his joyless two-month detention in hospital is that it led him to write, almost immediately, one of his liveliest and most energetic comic novels. *The Doctor Is Sick*, which appeared on 21 November 1960 in an edition of 5,000 copies, follows the picaresque adventures of Dr Edwin Spindrift, a middle-aged linguist who has collapsed in the classroom while lecturing abroad, in Burma. Edwin is flown home to London and shoved into hospital, where he undergoes the same tests that Burgess had experienced at the Neurological Institute. A few hours before Edwin is due to undergo an operation to excise a genuine brain tumour, he escapes from hospital – penniless, shaven-headed, and in his pyjamas – in pursuit of his unreliable wife, Sheila, who has absconded with a shabby bearded painter called Nigel, taking all of their joint savings with her. While searching frantically for his wife, Edwin is himself pursued across London by Bob Courage, a queer Cockney gangster who has taken a fancy to him ('You're kinky, the same as what I am. I can see it in your eyes').* Armed with counterfeit money, stolen clothes and fake hair, Edwin is absorbed into London's criminal underworld with little difficulty. He has become a fake, but his new life as a rogue and con-artist seems more excitingly real to him than his former career as a chalky pedagogue.

Burgess dedicated the novel to Lynne, and it is clear that the marriage described in the book mirrors his own experience:

> He and Sheila had long ago agreed that sexual infidelity was not really infidelity at all. You could accept a drink or a cigarette from somebody, why not also an hour or two in bed? It was the same sort of thing. Even when she had not been able, for some obscure reason of fancy, to reciprocate a stranger's desire for her body, she had always been willing to lie still, be the passive food for that appetite [. . .] To prefer just to *be* with somebody else, to engage of one's own free will in spiritual intimacy with another, that was true adultery.†

Burgess claimed that Lynne had fallen out of the habit of reading his fiction after the early volumes of the Malayan trilogy, so it is unlikely that she ever discovered how many of her foibles had been catalogued in the novel.

Not that the book is single-mindedly cruel or vengeful in its intentions. What is truly surprising is the self-critical way in which Burgess satirizes his own unquenchable lust for linguistic abstractions through the character of Edwin Spindrift. Sheila taunts him, woundingly and unmercifully, with his all-consuming passion for 'bilabial fricatives', and towards the end of the book he comes to realize that his cerebral love affair with language has left him utterly disconnected from the solid, experiential world of objects and people: 'He had lived too much with words and not what the words stood for [. . .] Let him loose in the real world, where words are glued to things, and see what he did: stole, swore, lied, committed

---

* Burgess, *The Doctor Is Sick* (London: Heinemann, 1960), p. 145.
† Ibid., p. 13.

acts of violence [...] He'd treated words as things, things to be analysed and classified, and not as part of the warm current of life.'* The intensity of self-accusation that Burgess achieves in such passages is remarkable. Caricaturing his own linguistic obsessions through Edwin, he demonstrates a sharp awareness of his own responsibility for the disappointments and failures of his marriage to Lynne. It is clear that Sheila is not solely to blame for the mutual incomprehension and loathing which characterize the Spindrifts' married life. As the story approaches its conclusion, Edwin lists his failings in an improvised alliterative poem:

> *Ineffectual fornicator,*
> *Purge of poor publicans,*
> *Kettle-mob catamite,*
> *Cheater of Chasper,*
> *Furniture-fracturer,*
> *Light-hearted liar,*
> *Counterfeit-cashman,*
> *Free meal filcher.*†

Nonetheless, Burgess's implicit self-criticism, which blows like a scourging wind throughout this confessional novel, is modified by the bawdy levity of the lowlife chapters, which are populated by an engaging collection of whores, thieves, con-artists and gangsters – the grotesque habitués of subterranean Soho. The overall effect is something like a comic rewrite of Graham Greene's *Brighton Rock*, but the extravagant wordplay and verbal wit are recognizable Burgessian signatures.‡ As with the central figures of Edwin and

---

* Ibid., pp. 152–3.
† Ibid., p. 188.
‡ Burgess's invented criminal slang in *The Doctor Is Sick* is pretty impenetrable. One conversation between two of the gangsters goes like this: 'Witch the narnoth and cretch the giripull.' 'Vearl pearnies under the weirdnick and crafter the linelow until the vopplesnock.' 'Worch?' 'Partock mainly at finniberg entering. Word fallpray when chock veers garters home' (p. 148). Whatever is supposed to be going on here – and no Burgess critic has yet succeeded in unravelling its meaning – it is

Sheila, many of the criminal and bohemian characters are transcriptions from real life. Several of Lynne's boyfriends appear under thin disguise – their names have been changed, but their physical characteristics and habits of speech are accurately recorded – and the Stone brothers, a pair of Cockney-Jewish identical twins called Harry and Leo, are modelled on the owners of an illegal drinking club in Bloomsbury where Lynne was a regular customer in 1959. (The Wilsons remained in contact with the brothers for a few months after they had left London, and one of them gave Burgess the plot for a short story, 'The Great Christmas Train Mystery'. He sold the story to *Argosy*, an upmarket literary magazine, for the handsome sum of £30.)*

Reviewers on both sides of the Atlantic were generally baffled by *The Doctor Is Sick,* and one or two of the responses were openly hostile. Walter Keir wrote anonymously in the *Times Literary Supplement* that it was 'very much a picaresque romp [. . .] full of crooks and aberrations and cafés and "kinkys",' but he found the book's presentation of contemporary London merely 'gimmicky'. Denis Donoghue of the *New York Review of Books* said: 'Mr

---

clearly the work of a writer who was already warming up to do this sort of thing at novel-length in *A Clockwork Orange.*

* Burgess summarized the story in a lecture he gave at the University of Angers on 22 January 1983: 'I'd been in a pub in London, and a man – a real rogue – told me that he had worked for a time as a steward on British Railways, serving meals in the dining car. And the previous Christmas Day [1958] he had been on duty and they were serving Christmas dinner in the dining car of a train travelling from London to Penzance. And when the dinner had been served – it was a very good dinner, in so far as British Rail could serve a good dinner – he came in to the tables and presented the bills, and was surprised that nobody tipped him nor his fellow steward. Later on he discovered that a man had stood up while the two stewards were back in the galley and said, "Ladies and Gentlemen, I think you will agree that we have had a most admirable meal, and I think that we ought to reward our stewards and our cook as much as we can this Christmas Day." So he went round with a hat and took the money and got off at the next stop.' See 'Anthony Burgess on the Short Story' in *Les Cahiers de la Nouvelle,* no. 2 (January 1984), pp. 31–47, 33.

Burgess is a lively writer, though the quality of the life is not the highest. One of the more innocent pleasures of the book consists in spotting the sources, other novels invoked for imitation. Basically it is a *Lucky Jim* book, with comic incidents sometimes indebted to *Our Man in Havana*. And there is the inevitable touch of *Ulysses*.' Maurice Richardson wrote in the *New Statesman*: 'Part of the trouble, I think, is that a cerebral tumour is not a subject that a novelist can monkey about with.' The least sympathetic response was Geoffrey Grigson's brief review in the *Spectator*: 'The words this novelist employs just don't produce things, or cohere, or make credible, in a sub-smart funniness (quotations from Webster, Eliot, Auden) I found not at all funny.' Christopher Ricks was the only critic intelligent enough to notice Burgess's indecent allusions to Gerard Manley Hopkins in chapter 12, where *Valour*, *Act*, *Pride*, *Plume* and *Brute Beauty* are the titles of pornographic magazines glimpsed through a newsagent's window. Ricks commented: 'Anyone who has had enough of "The Windhover" will think that Hopkins has had that coming to him for a long time.'*

What most of these early reviewers overlooked was the significance of Edwin's conversation with Sheila in the penultimate chapter, which is intended to throw the reality of the foregoing action into serious doubt. She tells him that he has been 'wandering in imaginary worlds' for three days while recovering from his brain operation, with the implication that his escape from hospital and peregrinations around London are a protracted series of delusions and fantasies.† Two interpretations of the novel are possible:

---

* Walter Keir, 'Portents and Symbols', *Times Literary Supplement*, 23 December 1960, p. 825; Denis Donoghue, 'Experiments in Folly', *New York Review of Books*, 9 June 1966, pp. 20–22; Maurice Richardson, 'New Novels', *New Statesman*, 3 December 1960, pp. 888–90; Geoffrey Grigson, 'Four Fantasies', *Spectator*, 25 November 1960, p. 860; Christopher Ricks, 'The Epicene', *New Statesman*, 5 April 1963, p. 496.

† The possibility of Edwin's madness is spelt out much more clearly in the script that Burgess wrote for a proposed film adaptation in the early 1960s, which is now in the Texas archive. The film never went into production.

'hallucinationist', in which the nightmarish underworld of criminal vice and polymorphous sexuality that Edwin claims to have witnessed exists purely within his head; and 'realist', in which Sheila may be lying to Edwin about his operation, in which case his journey around London must have taken place exactly as he remembers it. In a curious and vexing way, *The Doctor Is Sick* reflects the narrative ambiguities of Burgess's own illness and hospitalization.*

*

Burgess's sudden dismissal from the Colonial Service had left him with no obvious means of support except schoolmastering in England (a retrograde step, and precisely what he had gone to Malaya to avoid) or fiction-writing. Later in life, when his polished routine of cover-stories threatened to displace his memories of actual events, he claimed that he had been driven to become a full-time writer by the possibility – at best remote, if not actually imagined, fabricated by Lynne, or non-existent – that he was going to die before October 1960. As usual, the sequence of causes and effects was rather less exotic than the melodramatic fantasies he put into circulation. He had simply grown tired of a life of schoolteaching and adultery in remote places, and the critical success of the Malayan trilogy had persuaded him that it might now be possible to make a modest living out of fiction, literary journalism, translating and radio broadcasting. Although he and Lynne could not afford to live in London and did not wish to return to Lancashire or Leicestershire, rents on the south coast of England – which would still put them within an hour's commuting distance of Heinemann's offices and the BBC's television and radio studios – were reasonably low.

While they searched for somewhere permanent to live, Lynne

---

* Burgess gave a first edition of *The Doctor Is Sick* to his friend Olivia Manning, inscribed 'To Olivia – Much psychosomatic affection from John (Anthony Burgess)'. Was the dedication a joke, or a veiled confession about the true source of his 'brain tumour'?

found a one-bedroomed furnished flat to rent in Hove, a reasonably upmarket suburb of Brighton, and a place that Burgess remembered as being chiefly populated by grasping landladies, dipsomaniac widows, bag ladies and retired army majors, any of whom were likely, without warning, to recite their drink-impaired autobiographies to captive audiences in grotty saloon bars ('I have had part of my stomach removed [. . .] Six hours on the table. Nobody here can't beat that').* The exact address of Burgess and Lynne's flat in Hove is unknown, since he had forgotten it by the time he wrote his autobiography, and no correspondence from the few months they spent there has so far come to light.† Nevertheless, there is a physical description of the flat's interior in *Inside Mr Enderby*, where it doubles up as the poet Enderby's seedy rented lodgings (at a fictional address – 81 Fitzherbert Avenue). Enderby's kitchen cupboards are crammed with tinned sardines and pickled onions, and his bath is full of abandoned poetic drafts, which are slowly being eroded by a colony of hungry mice.‡ He is constantly searching for shillings to feed the coin-operated electric meter, and three-bar electric fires provide the flat's only heating. We are told that Enderby has converted the lavatory into a study, with a makeshift desk near the toilet

---

* Joseph Kell [i.e. Anthony Burgess], *Inside Mr Enderby* (London: Heinemann, 1963), p. 22.

† We are still waiting for a complete edition of Burgess's letters, of which I have a few hundred examples in my files. He was always diligent about dating them, sometimes eccentrically: 'Mohammed's birthday' [16 October 1956] and 'Dayafterbloomsday' [17 June 1965] are characteristic examples. Was it linguistic playfulness or an alcoholic trance that caused him to type his address as 'htragelppA, etchingham, xessuS tsaE' in a letter to Bill Holden of Heinemann on 25 February 1963, which was also the date of his forty-sixth birthday?

‡ One thing we can be sure of is that our man is not the same Anthony Burgess who (according to *Kelly's Directory*) was living at 39A Sloane Street, East Brighton, in 1960, since all of the available records show that John Burgess Wilson was known, for all purposes except the publishing of fiction, by his real name until he left England in October 1968. If the Wilsons' actual place of residence in Hove remains mysterious, this is partly because they did not stay there long enough to show up on the local Register of Electors.

and an electric fire to warm his bare legs as he goes about his interconnected tasks of creation and purgation. Thinking of the prologue to Shakespeare's *Henry V*, he conceives of his lavatory seat as a 'wooden O' to be brandished against the hateful outside world of prose, which wishes him nothing but harm.

Asked in an interview about his source for this flatulent, misanthropic poet, Burgess said:

> When I was working in Borneo in the late 1950s, I was suffering from malaria, had a slight delirium, and I went into the toilet and thought I saw a man sitting on the toilet seat writing poetry. I suppose the vision lasted a mere microsecond but the character remained, and I wrote four books about this character whom I called Enderby – a poet, very squalid, masturbatory [. . .] This I can't explain. The character has nothing to do with me, but his talent for writing poetry must be to some extent my own.*

Despite these protestations, Enderby's biography is a mirror-image of Burgess's early years: both are renegade Catholics from the north-west of England; both are the sons of unhappy tobacconists; both bear vicious grudges against their illiterate stepmothers; both have miserable, unheroic Army careers during the Second World War; and in later life both are the victims of film adaptations, in which a famous director misrepresents their original creative work. The texts of Enderby's poems presented in the novels are Burgess's own early poems, dating back as far as his teenage years, which speak of identical romantic entanglements and theological crises. However, Enderby is a virgin, a bachelor in love with his Muse, and timorous of flesh-and-blood women, whereas Burgess was a married man who was involved throughout his life with women to whom he was not married. More importantly, Burgess does not share Enderby's pronounced misogyny and misanthropy, which reach their most savage intensity in the third volume of his adventures, *The Clock-work Testament* (1974).

The masturbating poet seems in many ways to represent the roads that Burgess had not taken: if he had not married Lynne in 1942; if he had allowed his joyless childhood to develop into a full-scale neurosis; if he had clung to his early ambition to make a reputation for himself as a poet; if he had allowed himself to grow into a less tactful, a less intelligent, a less forgiving, a less generous man than he was – then it is possible that he might have come to resemble Francis Xavier Enderby. Enderby is more than merely Burgess's shadow: he is a demonic, monastic, spermatic worst-self, a brutal auto-caricature, an anarchic anti-Anthony. Although Enderby is by no means incapable of charm and sensitivity, he seems to represent a greatly inflated version of what Burgess recognized as his own flaws and shortcomings. Yet the character's extravagant hatreds and prejudices are emphatically not those of the ironic author who stands behind him, quietly mocking all of Enderby's desperate, picaresque, self-destructive follies. Enderby is to Burgess what Humbert Humbert is to Vladimir Nabokov: a grotesque, autonomous figure who shares little of the author's true personality, but who possesses a broadly similar linguistic talent.

Burgess drew extensively on his knowledge of Hove for the first Enderby book. A passing reference to an uphill journey along Goldstone Villas to the station indicates that he must have been familiar with the territory immediately to the south of the railway line. The internal geography of the novel, which mentions pubs such as the Neptune on Kingsway and the Freemason's Arms on Western Road ('haunt of all local lesbians over fifty'), suggests that Enderby's flat is probably located in the part of Hove known locally as Poets' Corner, where the streets are named after famous writers (Shake-speare Street, Byron Street, Sheridan Terrace, Coleridge Street and Cowper Street).*

---

* Burgess, *Inside Mr Enderby*, p. 30. See also Douglas Milton, 'Enderby's Hove', *Anthony Burgess Newsletter*, no. 4 (August 2001), pp. 30–32.

In spite of the plethora of 'brain tumour' stories, there is nothing to suggest that Burgess genuinely thought he was going to die while he was writing *Inside Mr Enderby*, which was completed in 1960 but unpublished until 1963. Looking back on his time in Hove, he said: 'I felt well. I felt vigorous. I was writing heavily. Two thousand words a day.'* ('Writing heavily' is characteristically playful formulation, writing as an addiction or a compulsion, cognate with smoking or drinking.) In the novels he produced between October 1959 and the middle of 1961, Burgess began to think in earnest about contemporary England, his viewpoint being very much that of a man who wished to present himself as an outsider. Passing through London on home leave in April 1959, he had said that coming back from Brunei made him feel more than ever like a foreigner. He was struck, for instance, by the 'ingratitude' of English people who complained about the price of meat and fresh vegetables. 'I'm going back to incessant heat, no variety, no change of season, and all of these things are laid on here like a free show, in England. And yet all people can do, it seems, is to watch the television.'† In another interview with *The Times*, he said: 'Of course the time abroad helped: things change so rapidly nowadays that even a very short time away means that one experiences the real shock of strangeness on coming back to places and things one thought one knew.' He added that his intention in the novels he wrote next would be 'to look at England as an unusually knowledgeable foreigner might, to study its scene, its people, its way of life from the outside, at a certain ironic distance'.‡ As usual, Burgess was keen to make himself sound like an alien in the country of his birth and upbringing. It suited the purposes of his fiction to encourage readers to believe that he was an internationalist writer of the

* *In the Psychiatrist's Chair* interview.
† Burgess, radio interview with Patricia Brent (*The World of Books*, 9 May 1959).
‡ Anon., 'Anthony Burgess: From Our Special Correspondent', *The Times*, 16 January 1964, p. 13.

Somerset Maugham kind, who merely happened to be spending time in England in between journeys to more exotic places.

He reflected, in a long article for the *Listener*, on the new direction his novels would take after his return from the East. 'The exotic,' he wrote, 'is a dangerous and corrupting thing for the novelist to write about,' because the 'strangeness' and 'glamour' of remote places encouraged a journalistic style of fiction (in which 'the content is more important than the technique') that was opposed to the more careful aesthetic patterning he associated with the genuinely literary novel. Having discarded the accoutrements of the so-called 'exotic novel' after *Devil of a State*, what was Burgess now trying to accomplish? 'The answer, I would say, lies in the related fields of myth and language. [The novelist] must either revivify old myths or create new ones [. . .] The more banal, commonplace, everyday, the subject-matter of the novel is, the more the novelist is compelled to work hard at his craft.' He admitted that this was a 'puritanical view' to be taking, but he affirmed his newly discovered commitment to the fictional 'here and now'. He concluded – although this was a view that he would later revise – 'One wonders how much true devotion to his art is shown by the novelist who expatriates himself because of income tax, disillusionment with English society, climate, or in search of greater sexual tolerance. It is the novelist's duty to stay here and suffer with the rest of us. He can, through his art, lessen that suffering.'* He had

---

* Burgess, 'The Corruption of the Exotic', *Listener*, 26 September 1963, pp. 465–7. This article began life as a radio talk commissioned by P. H. Newby, the controller of the BBC Third Programme, who wrote in an internal memo (dated 5 April 1963): 'Burgess must be conscious of the difficulty of writing about situations which readers cannot measure against their own experience. There are all sorts of dangers in this situation – charlatanry, the exploitation of local colour and so on. What kind of relationship to his readers does he envisage when he is treating exotic material?' Burgess's article, which takes in both the Malayan trilogy and his early English novels, is therefore a direct reply to the questions posed in Newby's memorandum.

made a firm decision in favour of domestic social realism, and was proposing to take a hard look at the condition of England.

One of the central preoccupations in the novels he wrote around this time (*The Doctor Is Sick*, *The Right to an Answer*, *One Hand Clapping* and *Inside Mr Enderby*), is the extent to which England had altered – and not, apparently, for the better – between 1954 and 1959. The successive Conservative governments of Winston Churchill, Anthony Eden and Harold Macmillan had coincided with the end of wartime rationing and a sharp rise in economic prosperity, which manifested itself in a new spirit of consumerism (cheap cars, refrigerators and televisions), the emergence of a youth culture, a revival of the sexual permissiveness that had flourished during the war, and a gradual falling-away of religious belief. Burgess was appalled by these developments, but he reserved his most savage wrath for the apparent menace of creeping Americanization, particularly in films, television and popular music. England, he complained, had fallen under a 'Deadly Transatlantic Influence'; and the English people, seduced by the 'Big American Glamour', were in danger of being 'absorbed' into the 'American Museum'.*

He mocked this new Americanized England unmercifully in *One Hand Clapping* (1961), which is one of his bitterest statements about secular consumerism and the approaching collapse of English high culture. Janet Shirley, the novel's twenty-three-year-old narrator, is the empty-headed product of a secondary modern school in 'Bradcaster' – an imaginary northern town which seems to be an amalgam of Bradford and Manchester. Janet works as a shelf-stacker in the Hastings Road supermarket, and her husband Howard deals in used cars. Their life consists of betting on horses, eating reheated food out of tins and watching quiz shows on commercial television. Burgess makes no attempt to conceal his contempt for such activities. He uses the English of the *Daily Mirror*, the most popular working-class newspaper of the late 1950s, as his template for the novel's deliberately impoverished prose style:

* See Burgess, *Honey for the Bears* (London: Heinemann, 1963), p. 201.

Sometimes in the evening when we sat looking at the TV [. . .] the feeling would come over me that it would be nice to have a little child upstairs calling down 'Mummy'. This was especially during the commercials, showing mother and daughter both protected by the same soap, or the mother loving her children so much that she washed all their clothes in Blink or whatever it was (they're all the same, really) or the mother and father and little children sitting down to a good nourishing dinner of Somebody-or-other's Fish Fingers.*

When Howard puts his photographic memory to profitable use by entering a big-money television quiz show called *Over and Over* – based on a real ITV programme called *Double Your Money*, hosted by an energetic Canadian called Hughie Green – he and Janet are suddenly able to afford 'the best of everything'. They eat at expensive restaurants (where they are sneered at by waiters because of their proletarian manners), stay in posh hotels, visit the theatre (which they decide is less exciting than the telly) and travel to the United States – a country that, by the early 1960s, looks and feels exactly like the Americanized post-war England they have left behind.† Janet says of New York:

Some of the buildings were very high and very new, but they have those in London now. I got the idea that wherever you went all that would matter would be the people, and they seem to be all pretty much the same. I suppose the only real reason for travelling is to learn that people are the same. I tell

---

* Joseph Kell [i.e. Anthony Burgess], *One Hand Clapping* (London: Peter Davies, 1961), p. 12.

† Not that Burgess had any first-hand experience of America at this stage in his career. He first went there in 1966, five years after *One Hand Clapping* had been published. The novel, incidentally, was warmly appreciated in Communist Eastern Europe. It was translated into Polish in 1973, under the title *Klaskac jedna reka*, and was later adapted as a popular stage musical in Warsaw. The Soviets interpreted the novel as an ideological fable about the evils of capitalism – a jaw-dropping failure to understand its point and purpose. They didn't pay out any royalties either, to Burgess's considerable chagrin.

you that now, so you've no need to waste your money on travelling.*

Burgess – who is loading the dice throughout the book with regard to his moral arguments about consumerism – is anxious to demonstrate that Howard and Janet's pile of money has failed to make them any happier. What they lack, the novel proposes, is an informed awareness of their own culture and history. They are presented as victims of an egalitarian school system which has declined to give them anything resembling a proper education:

> There was young Mr Slessor with the beard who said he was a beatnik and called us cats and chicks. He was supposed to teach us English but said he didn't dig the king's jive. Crazy, man, real cool. It was pathetic. Mr Thornton, who taught history, said he knew we wouldn't be interested in all those old kings and queens so he just played his guitar and sang very dull songs, so we weren't allowed to have any history.†

This is Burgess writing in apocalyptic mode, convinced that the pre-war system of grammar schools and scholarships (from which he had benefited) had at least given intelligent students from working-class areas like Moss Side the opportunity of a proper education.

Measuring the early 1960s against his memories of the 1930s, he judged Harold Macmillan's Britain to be a place on the edge of cultural annihilation, where even literature seemed powerless to halt the rising tide of vulgarity and degeneration. His own literary novels were selling poorly. Despite the minor success of *Devil of a State* (which was a Book Society choice in 1961), Heinemann had decided to reduce the print-run of Burgess's first editions, from 6,000 copies of *Beds in the East* in 1959 to 4,250 copies of *The Worm and the Ring* in 1961. The first edition of *Inside Mr Enderby* in 1963 amounted to just 2,500 copies, of which 950

---

* *One Hand Clapping*, pp. 143–4.
† Ibid., p. 8.

were still in the warehouse, unsold, in April 1967.* At this point none of Burgess's new novels were generating the level of excitement which had greeted the Malayan trilogy, and the English novels were a lot slower to find an audience than his earlier works had been.

One Hand Clapping implies that some mystical and indefinable core of traditional Englishness has been lost in the generation that came to maturity after the Second World War. The other books that Burgess wrote immediately after his return to England are equally nostalgic for a golden age of social stability and high culture, when wives knew how to cook proper food and everybody made their own entertainment around the piano, or recited poetry (from memory) for pleasure. In *The Right to an Answer*, Denham's forcefully expressed opinions ('I can feel damnation being broken in like a pair of shoes') are indistinguishable from those of Burgess himself. 'The post-war English mess,' he declares, during a monologue on the sins of the modern world, is 'made by having too much freedom [. . .] You suffer from the mess, the great democratic mess in which there's no hierarchy, everything's as good – and therefore as bad – as everything else.'† As in *One Hand Clapping*, blandness and homogeneity are the recurring motifs in Denham's description of the 'rather large smug Midland city' in which the novel is set, where all of the houses (and, it's suggested, the lives that are lived within them) are said to be identical: 'I don't suppose it would matter which one you went in, really. I suppose they're all the same inside. Pot ducks flying up the wall. And the telly.'‡

Yet it would be misleading to conclude that Burgess's fictional presentation of the Midlands and the industrial North is unremittingly splenetic and pessimistic. As with *Inside Mr Enderby*, each of these English novels contains a poet character whose art promises to redeem the otherwise gloomy surroundings where it is practised.

---

* Unsigned sales memoranda, no date [but probably 1968] (Heinemann archive).
† *The Right to an Answer* (London: Heinemann, 1960), p. 3.
‡ Ibid., p. 30.

In *The Right to an Answer* it is Everett, a hack journalist by day but
a poet by night, who writes the verse which stands at the novel's
centre.* And in *One Hand Clapping* we meet Redvers Glass, a
shabby bohemian poet probably modelled on Dylan Thomas, whose
long poem provides a commentary on Janet's artless narrative at the
same time as possessing a force and eloquence that lie far beyond
her limited verbal powers:

> *But shall I say there was a sort of hopelessness, a sort of*
> *Sickness which further living could not cure,*
> *Aggravate, rather. We started off with those certain loves*
> *Or desires for love which men have, such as,*
> *Being English, a desire to love England.*
> *But we saw England delivered over to the hands of*
> *The sneerers and sniggerers, the thugs and grinners,*
> *England become a feeble-lighted*
> *Moon of America, our very language defiled*
> *And become slick and gum-chewing.*†

It is characteristic of Burgess that he invariably looks to the
elegant manipulation of the written word as a source of consolation and possible deliverance from the 'mess' of late twentieth-
century culture. 'Mr Burgess is convinced,' he once wrote, sliding
rather grandly into the third person to make his point, 'that our
salvation lies in understanding ourselves, [and] that such understanding depends on a concern with language.'‡ It is a purely

---

* Everett's 'Epitaph on a Printer', for example, consoles Denham shortly after his
father has dropped dead: 'He, who did not originate the Word, / Yet brought the
Word to man when man was ripe / To read the Word. But that ill-bound, absurd /
Book of his body's gone. A mess of type / That death broke up reads greater
nonsense now. / Now God re-writes him, prints him, binds him, never / To fail or
be forgotten: God knows how / To make one copy that is read for ever' (ibid.,
p. 211). This is a representative example of what Burgess's poetical Muse could
turn out on a good day.
† *One Hand Clapping*, p. 165.
‡ Burgess, *Moses: A Narrative* (London: Dempsey & Squires, 1976), p. 192.

secular form of 'salvation' that Burgess is interested in (although those references to 'damnation' and 'salvation' indicate that here is a writer who finds it impossible to avoid interpreting the world in broadly Catholic terms), and one to be arrived at through the aesthetic transport that only words and literature can bring. From a purely artistic point of view, his fiction about England is defiantly affirmative, and the industrial decay he delineates asks to be understood as a sooty backdrop to the transcendent music of poetry. This limited promise of salvation through language is a recurring motif throughout Burgess's published writing. If his fictional England is still capable of producing poets – and, presumably, novelists and musicians – then its indigenous culture cannot yet be said to have been completely suppressed, absorbed or Americanized. His English novels admit a cautious and heavily qualified optimism, despite the misleading grimness of first appearances.

Burgess and Lynne left their flat in Hove in the early spring of 1960, moving to a rather grander house called 'Applegarth' in Etchingham, East Sussex, which was to be Burgess's principal home and workshop for the next eight years. The village of Etchingham takes its name from Sir William de Echyngham, who died in 1389, shortly after he had finished paying for the construction of the Church of the Assumption and St Nicholas. This church held few excitements for Burgess, especially since it had been expropriated by Protestants. He was more interested in the literary history of Sussex. His new residence was a short walk away from Rudyard Kipling's house, Batemans, and in the early years of the twentieth century Henry James, Joseph Conrad and Ford Madox Ford had all lived in the district around Rye, a few miles away. Etchingham itself is not far from Hastings and Battle – Burgess regularly visited a dentist in Battle, which is the home town of Kenneth Toomey, the fictional son of a dentist, in *Earthly Powers* – and in 1965 he proposed to Dwye Evans at Heinemann that he should write what he called 'a sort of novel-travel-diary, very original' to celebrate the Norman Conquest of 1066, under

the title 'With Strod and Trug Through Darkest Sussex'.* This
ambitious-sounding Sussex novel (enigmatic-sounding, too: who or
what were 'Strod' and 'Trug'?) has not surfaced in any of the
Burgess manuscript collections, and it seems likely that it was
never properly begun.

At some indeterminate point in the early 1960s, while living in
Etchingham, he sketched out an Elgarian orchestral piece called
'Song of the Southern Downs', a tone-poem in a recognizably early
twentieth-century idiom, intended to present in musical form the
landscape of the Sussex hills. It is an ambitious composition, with
parts scored for flutes, oboes, clarinets in A, two bassoons, four
horns in F, three trumpets in C, trombones, tuba, kettle-drums,
large percussion section, pianoforte, violins, violas, cellos and
basses. The Song (dedicated 'To Jake') has never been performed.
Apart from a Christmas carol – a setting of the anonymous text 'I
sing of a maiden', which he sent to literary friends in December
1961 – this is the only substantial musical work that Burgess is
known to have composed between his 'Merdeka' symphony (1957)
and the Shakespeare songs that he wrote for the Hollywood musical
Will! (or 'The Bawdy Bard') in 1968.†

He described the geography of Etchingham in an article for the
Hudson Review:

---

* Burgess, letter to Dwye Evans, 17 June 1965 (Heinemann archive). Among the
other plans for future novels outlined in this letter were: *Enderby Outside* (the
'completion' of the Enderby story); 'Something in the Blood' (a saga-style story
about a Eurasian dentist); 'The Smell of Fish' (a parody of Dante's *Divine Comedy*
with a fishmonger hero, which metamorphosed into *Any Old Iron* in 1989); 'It Is
the Miller's Daughter' (a novel with a French setting, which survives in the form of
two long fragments); 'Ragday' (a memoir of his student days in Manchester in
1939); and an untitled novel about a composer. Roland Gant, the senior fiction
editor at Heinemann, noted in the margin: 'ADE [Dwye Evans] says he never
mentions any of these projects now'.
† 'I sing of a maiden', scored for voice and piano in C major, notated in ballpoint
pen on twelve-stave quarto manuscript paper. The manuscript is in the collection
of Mrs Diana Gillon.

The village is more primitive than my readers may be willing to believe. I live on the select side of the street, and here we have cesspools. On the other side they have nothing. They defecate into buckets and bury the ordure in their gardens. This is very difficult in the winter when the earth is frozen [. . .] At last, though, after half a century of rural council dithering, the drains are coming through. At the bottom of my garden there are noisy engines with claws and teenage labourers with transistors. I have to do most of my writing at night.*

The importance of drink within the Wilson ménage is confirmed by the writer and translator Peter Green, who was an occasional guest at their Etchingham house in the early 1960s. Green describes his visits to 'this unbelievably characterless little box of a house' as 'not to be forgotten'.

One took the train down, and John would meet one at the station, and there would always be a call in to the pub, using it both as a pub and an off-licence, and a bottle of gin for Lynne, and a bottle of whatever took his visitor's fancy, which in my case was Scotch, and the beer which simply went with every-thing. And then one went back, and his idea of an evening at home was to sit and drink and go on drinking until you simply had to go to bed [. . .] He had a sort of harmonium-cum-small-organ upstairs on the landing, which he used to go and play at intervals. I don't know if this was to settle his drink, or what. I sometimes think he was commenting on what was going on downstairs [. . .] I remember one evening when the talk was getting very dismal, he went upstairs and played 'Nearer My God Than Thee'. Finally, either when the bottles were empty or when everybody was absolutely incapable, we'd all reel off to bed.†

* Burgess, 'Letter from England', *Hudson Review*, vol. XX, no. 3 (Autumn 1967), pp. 454–8, 454.
† Peter Green, unpublished interview with David Thompson (1998). Transcript in Angers archive.

Although Peter Green enjoyed Burgess's company and conversation, his view of Lynne was on the whole unsympathetic. 'The thing that really fascinated me was [Burgess's] Henry V hairdo. And then I met Lynne as well and, to my astonishment, she had a Henry V hairdo as well. The two of them together were a knock-out.' Attempting to sum up Lynne's character, he says: 'I really do think, allowing for everything, Lynne was one of the most awful women I've ever met. She was bloody-minded. She urged him on to all sorts of excesses of anger and vengeance that I don't think he would ever have considered on his own.' The extent of her alcoholism was by now difficult to overlook.

> She drank like the proverbial fish. I watched her work her way
> through an entire half bottle of gin in the course of an evening
> on her own. I wish I'd ever known what made Lynne tick. Or,
> for that matter, why they got married. Except that perhaps they
> needed to, as it were, be a hone and a knife – just sharpen each
> other, or suffer from each other [. . .] This was, to everybody
> outside, an impossible marriage which he persisted in as a kind
> of alcoholic *Sherston's Progress*. Because he drank as much as
> she did, and lasted considerably longer.

Green remembers Lynne as an aggressive drunk, whereas Burgess was more of 'a sad drinker'. 'It stimulated him, in the way that it made him talk more, but it did not make him happy [. . .] He did tend to be more articulate, but more articulate in a curiously depressed sort of way.' The scruffy, boozy, bohemian life they had built for themselves in Sussex was reflected in Burgess's appearance: 'I never saw Burgess dressed smart in my life [. . .] He was what you might call journalist/prep-school casual. Old worn jackets, tatty pullovers, crummy grey pants, generally with food marks on them somewhere.'

According to Burgess's early Etchingham letters, the village was a place of hostility and suspicion. In April 1961, just over a year after he and Lynne had moved into Applegarth, he complained to his step-sister: 'Living as we do, surrounded by mean, thin-lipped

Sussex people, we often think nostalgically of Lancashire which is, when all's said and done, sufficiently honest and robust. Sussex people are unamiable, to say the least.'* A month later, on 11 May 1961, when Lynne was in the middle of another of her 'nervous collapses', he had modified his opinion of these 'unamiable', 'mean, thin-lipped' villagers. In the second letter, Lynne is reported to be 'quite ill', but the neighbours are said to be 'kind'. One of these neighbours was Gordon Sears, a London-based doctor who kept a country cottage in Etchingham. Dr Sears's daughter, whom he introduced to the Wilsons, was the actress Heather Sears. Burgess enjoyed their company, and told Agnes Tollitt: 'This makes a change and puts us into contact with the great world again, but it's amazing and frightening how one gets out of the habit of *wanting* to see people. This cutting-off from life is terribly dangerous, I suppose, but more and more we tend to want it that way.'†

Lynne's precarious mental state had become a source of anxiety to her doctor in Etchingham. Towards the end of 1960, she had made two suicide attempts within the space of a few weeks, swallowing a potentially lethal dose of Nembutal sleeping tablets on both occasions. As with her earlier pill-swallowing episode in Malaya, Burgess discovered her and was able to make her vomit up the tablets before they could do any serious damage. The general practitioner in Etchingham was John McMichael (the same 'J. McMichael, M.B., Ch.B.' to whom Burgess dedicated *Tremor of Intent*, 'gratefully', in 1966), and he made efforts to have Lynne admitted to an asylum. Burgess, however, refused to sign the necessary papers for her committal.

He had health problems of his own in the spring of 1961. His wisdom teeth were extracted, and he went into hospital for an operation to remove a cyst from his back. He was worried about perishing under the anaesthetic, and consoled himself on the eve of the operation by re-reading two of his favourite books of literary

---

* Burgess, letter to Agnes Tollitt, 3 April 1961.
† Ibid.

essays, *Axel's Castle* by Edmund Wilson and Cyril Connolly's *Enemies of Promise*. Not long after he had emerged from hospital, the Inland Revenue wrote to him with an unexpected tax demand for £260. Pleading lack of money, Burgess and Lynne cancelled a proposed visit to his relations in Manchester. Burgess then settled down to what he called a 'mysterious chronic session of trigeminal neuralgia'. The cyst in his back gave him the starting-point for an implausible short story, in which a man who has grown fat on rich food discovers that valuable black pearls are growing under his skin.*

Even as Burgess was protesting his poverty, his hard work at the typewriter since 1959 was beginning to pay off. A speculative letter to P. H. Newby, the Controller of BBC Radio 3, had resulted in commissions to write and deliver a series of radio talks (on music and literature, Malayan women and James Joyce). The publishing house W. W. Norton began to issue his novels in America, starting with *The Right to an Answer* in 1961, which gave Burgess another source of advances and royalties. In London he had acquired a literary agent, Peter Janson-Smith, who had negotiated a £200 advance with Heinemann for the UK rights to *The Worm and the Ring*, overseas and translation rights to be sold separately.† And in January 1961 he was invited to write a regular weekly column on new fiction for the *Yorkshire Post*, which added another £50 to his yearly income until 1963. As the parcels of books arrived at the house in Etchingham, Lynne did the initial job of sifting through them to decide which novels should be reviewed.‡

By the summer of 1961 they both felt in need of a holiday abroad. Leningrad was an unusual choice of destination for English tourists during the Cold War (unless they were members of the Communist

* Burgess, 'A Benignant Growth', *Transatlantic Review*, no. 32 (Summer 1969), pp. 10–15.
† Peter Janson-Smith to author, 19 February 2002.
‡ Dick Adler, 'Inside Mr Burgess', *Sunday Times Magazine*, 2 April 1967, pp. 47–50.

Party), but Nikita Khrushchev's regime was well disposed towards casual tourism. The Soviet Union promised to provide Burgess with good copy for his journalism and radio work. Politically naive at the best of times, he knew nothing of the USSR beyond what he had read in the newspapers. He wrote that 'One expects to find a totalitarian state full of soft-booted, white-helmeted military police, conspicuously armed, [. . .] a certain coldness, a thinness of blood, all emotion channelled into love of Big Brother.'* What he found there confounded his expectations, and led directly to the composition of two of his most striking novels, *Honey for the Bears* and *A Clockwork Orange*.

---

* Burgess, 'The Human Russians', *Listener*, 28 December 1961, pp. 1107–8.

7

Tolchocking and Sheer Vandalism

If anyone had asked Burgess why he and Lynne were proposing to visit Leningrad in the summer of 1961, he would have found it difficult to formulate a straightforward reply. A number of motives seem to have drawn him there, the strongest of which was curiosity. He told Agnes, his stepsister, that he was going at the suggestion of his publisher, who hoped that a saleable Russian novel might come out of the journey ('It was almost inevitable,' said Maire Lynd, the chief reader at Heinemann, 'that, having christened him Burgess, we should send him to Russia').* The wish to gather material for a Cold War fiction was clearly a strong incentive, especially since Heinemann had offered to advance Burgess's travel expenses, which they were willing to offset against future royalties. Beyond the financial appeal of a book commission, there was also the likelihood of being able to exploit his journey by writing articles and radio features about it. Having accepted Heinemann's offer, he was left with the immediate problem of finding enough money to pay for Lynne's passage to Leningrad, since she refused to be left behind in Etchingham. As it turned out, her presence as his unpredictable companion was to provide a focus for his Russian travel narratives, both fictional and journalistic.

---

* Maire Lynd, reader's report on *Honey for the Bears*, 2 May 1962 (Heinemann archive).

Literary curiosity provided another important reason for wanting to visit Russia. Burgess had been impressed by Alexander Pushkin's verse-novel *Eugene Onegin*, parts of which he had memorized in the original Russian, and he read Fyodor Dostoyevsky's *Crime and Punishment* in English translation shortly before he sailed.* He later recalled a conversation about Dostoyevsky's novel with a waiter in a Leningrad restaurant, who told him that it was 'a crime to write it and a punishment to read it'. He was curious to see how accurately the city, known in pre-revolutionary days as St Petersburg, was represented in the novel, and how far Dostoyevsky had succeeded in describing the mindset of ordinary Russians.

Burgess began teaching himself Russian early in 1961, armed with copies of *Getting Along in Russian* by Mario Pei, *The Penguin Russian Course* by J. L. I. Fennell, and Waldemar Schapiro's *Collins Russian Gem Dictionary*.† As he began to study the language, it occurred to him that it might be possible to write a novel narrated in an invented slang which would be a hybrid of English and Russian, with elements of Romany, Lancashire dialect and Cockney rhyming slang. He set about the task of compiling a modified Russian vocabulary of about 200 words, with the intention of brainwashing the reader into learning the basics of Russian. The first sixty pages of this new novel, which he proposed to call *A Clockwork Orange*, were complete before he left England at the end of June. A letter from 1961 confirms that Dostoyevsky was at the front of his mind as he was at work on the early section of the novel. Shortly after he had finished the first seven chapters, he wrote to Diana and Meir Gillon:

---

* For Burgess on Pushkin, see 'Pushkin and Kinbote' (review of Vladimir Nabokov's four-volume translation of *Eugene Onegin*), *Encounter*, May 1965, pp. 74–8.
† These books are in the Burgess collection at the University of Angers. His copy of the Collins Russian dictionary is inscribed (in Cyrillic characters) 'Ivan Wilson'. For Burgess on the Russian language, see *A Mouthful of Air* (London: Hutchinson, 1993), pp. 136–7, 163–7.

I'm writing this to you before trying to push on with my Clockwork Orange book. I've just completed Part I – which is just sheer crime. Now comes punishment. The whole thing's making me rather sick. My horrible juvenile delinquent hero is emerging as too sympathetic a character – almost Christ-like, set upon by the scourging police. You see what I mean by moral deterioration.*

Language was also an important part of Burgess's decision to visit the Soviet Union. He wanted to hear Russian being spoken by Russians, to practise speaking it himself, and to refine a simple yet plausible Slavic vocabulary that could be deployed when he came to revise and complete A Clockwork Orange. There is no foundation to the rumour, originally put forward by a downmarket London newspaper in 2002, that he went to Russia for reasons of Cold War espionage. When I asked a former diplomat from the Moscow embassy about the possibility that Burgess was secretly employed by British intelligence, he told me that a volubly indiscreet drunk such as Burgess, who also happened to be married to a suicidal alcoholic, would have been solidly at the bottom of the list when it came to recruiting potential secret agents, in spite of his considerable linguistic talents. No official papers confirming the espionage rumour have so far come to light, and there is nothing among Burgess's private diaries or financial papers to suggest that he was paid to spy on the Russians.

The possibility of making money by offloading Western luxury goods on the black market was certainly appealing to Burgess, who suggests in his autobiography that he sold a suitcase-load of smuggled nylon dresses at a high profit in a subterranean lavatory beneath the Astoria Hotel. Yet he does not mention this episode, which is exactly the kind of risky enterprise that he would have been likely to boast about to his English friends, in any surviving letters from

* Burgess, letter to Diana and Meir Gillon (no date, but early 1961). Quoted in Books, Maps, Photographs and Manuscipts, Phillips auction catalogue, no. 13,132 (London: Phillips, 2001), pp. 104–5.

1961, and his recollection of how much he was paid for each dress varies between his different published accounts (the price is said to be anywhere between 6 roubles 50 kopeks and 15 roubles).* Paul Hussey, the bisexual hero of *Honey For the Bears* (1963), goes to Leningrad intending to gather black-market roubles by selling suit-cases full of dresses that he has smuggled from England. The details of the episode are so similar to the later account in *You've Had Your Time* that, in writing his later 'non-fiction' account, Burgess appears to have plundered his fictionalized version of the Leningrad trip. But this is far from being a unique example of Burgess's tendency to fictionalize the past. As with the sections of the auto-biography which deal with the Malayan trilogy, *The Doctor Is Sick* and the phantom brain tumour, elements of published fiction have bled into his memoirs, distorting the actual into recognizably novel-istic shapes.

Honey for the Bears gives every appearance of having been written up out of a diary (perhaps compiled purely as an aide-memoire for the novel and then discarded) that Burgess kept while he was in Russia in the summer of 1961. It is hard to believe that his memory alone would have been sufficient to retain such a substantial mental picture of Leningrad for six months between returning to England and beginning work on the book, especially given that in the second half of 1961 he also completed *A Clock-work Orange* and translated two novels out of French, before settling down to write *Honey for the Bears* in January and February 1962. His picaresque Russian novel is densely loaded with topo-graphical detail, recorded conversations, food, drink, odours and the general life of Leningrad – and the inflated, comically distorted account of the city which he set out in fictional form later merged completely with his actual recollections.

Burgess's early impressions of Leningrad are recorded in the

* See, for example, *Honey for the Bears* (London: Heinemann, 1963), p. 19, and *You've Had Your Time: Being the Second Part of the Confessions of Anthony Burgess* (London: Heinemann, 1990), p. 43.

journalism he wrote shortly after he had returned to England. He recalled, in an article published late in 1961, that 'The city is terribly shabby and slummy-looking despite the Byzantine gold of the cathedral, despite the unbelievable splendour of the Winter Palace.'* Everywhere he and Lynne went, there were feculently reeking blocked-up drains and the smell of borscht, 'that omnipresent soup, coarse and delicious', whose unpredictable ingredients might include 'ragged gobbets of beef, veal, chicken, with sometimes the after-thought of a pale frankfurter peeping out of the wrack of cabbage and shredded meat'. He felt no particular animus towards a waiter who told him that all the restaurant tables were full when he could see for himself that they were empty, because 'perhaps what I call lying is only a Russian unwillingness to face reality'. At the Metropol Restaurant, he and Lynne ordered a beef stroganoff which arrived, stone cold, after no more than four hours had elapsed. Among the other customers he observed 'plenty of weeping and ineffable de-pression', which he regarded as symptomatic of the manic-depressive Russian temperament. Thirstily waiting to be served, and having failed to catch the attention of waiters dressed in white tuxedos and tennis-shoes, Burgess and Lynne helped themselves to bottles of Czech beer from an unattended refrigerator. Nobody objected. Around them, other customers who had fallen asleep through bore-dom or drunkenness were violently awakened and ejected by a grim-looking Soviet matron armed with a pair of tongs, who shoved balls of cotton wool soaked in ammonia into nostrils and eyes. Burgess fell into conversation with an amiable drunk whose perfect com-mand of idiomatic English suggested that he was probably a KGB agent. In spite of public rowdiness, drunken disorderliness and obvious soliciting on street corners, there was no evidence of a uniformed police force ('Perhaps all the police are secret police, and perhaps the only crimes are political crimes.') 'What I loved most about the Russians,' he wrote, cheered and surprised by the absence of the grim Orwellian dystopia that he had been expecting to find,

* Burgess, 'The Human Russians', *Listener*, 28 December 1961, pp. 1107–8.

'was their inefficiency [. . .] The painted girls solicited and the teddy-boys raged and romped, but no police came. It is my honest opinion that there are no police in Leningrad.'*

As he and Lynne tried to leave the Metropol at three in the morning, 'A hellish noise of bawling and banging and smashed glass came from the street; there was a frenzied hammering on the front door.'† The hammerers were *stilyagi*, young Russian teddy-boys, armed with coshes and broken bottles. The door was opened, and the *stilyagi* politely stepped back to make way for Burgess and Lynne. Once the door had been safely bolted again, they resumed their shouting and hammering. What struck him about this incident was the internationalism of well-dressed, violent youth. To the eye of the novelist, these Russian thugs, dressed in the height of Soviet summer fashion, were indistinguishable from their quiffed, suited, knuckle-duster-wielding counterparts in England. The enactment outside the Metropol of ritualistic, dandified violence provided a solid rationale for Alex and his three droogs (*drugi* being the Russian word for 'friends'), about whom Burgess had already begun to write in *A Clockwork Orange*:

> We wore waisty jackets without lapels but with these very big built-up shoulders ('pletchoes' we called them) which were a kind of mockery of having real shoulders like that. Then, my brothers, we had these off-white cravats which looked like whipped-up kartoffel or spud with a sort of a design made on it with a fork. We wore our hair not too long and we had flip horrorshow boots for kicking.‡

The episode outside the Metropol helps to explain why the precise location of *A Clockwork Orange* is never specified. The novel consistently refuses to make it clear whether the action is supposed to take place in England, mainland Europe, or somewhere in the

---

* Ibid., p. 1108.
† *Honey for the Bears*, p. 97.
‡ Burgess, *A Clockwork Orange* (London: Heinemann, 1962), p. 2.

former Union of Soviet Socialist Republics. The important point is that Alex's story might happen anywhere. The ambiguous setting allows Burgess to present teenage aggression as a universal phenomenon, and this idea of youth carries more significance, according to the book's internal logic, than either politics or geography.

The apolitical futurism of the novel, in which the visceral excitements of music and ultra-violence have displaced ideology, is consistent with Burgess's own lack of real interest in the Soviet system. His involvement as a tourist was purely aesthetic and linguistic. He regarded Sovietism as an anomaly, and he frequently reiterated his belief that the spirit of the Russian people would prevail over their political masters. His opinion of Communism – a naive and under-informed judgement, perhaps, but one that was nevertheless founded on sincere theological convictions – was that, like the American consumer capitalism which opposed it, the Soviet Union was a manifestation of the Pelagian heresy, a temporary nuisance which was inevitably heading towards self-destruction under the haphazard leadership of Nikita Khrushchev, the Secretary-General of the Communist Party between 1958 and 1964. The Cold War, Burgess declared, was merely a game of chess which had reached a temporary stalemate, symbolized by the East/West division of Berlin.* Even so, it was prescient of him to have recognized that Communism was merely a passing phase. He regarded it as no more or less contemptible than capitalism, or Western European syndicalist socialism. Looking at politics from a position of distance and detachment was a convenient way of not having to think about it at all. For Burgess, going to Leningrad was primarily a matter of

---

* For Burgess on East and West Berlin, see 'A Metaphysical City', *Listener*, 18 July 1963, p. 30. For his views on Chairman Mao and Chinese Communism, see 'Thoughts on the Thoughts', *Spectator*, 15 September 1967, p. 322. See also his wider reflections on the 'evil and incompetence' of socialist governments ('Socialism is based on a tangle of false premises: human beings are totally different from what Socialists think they are. But Socialism can at least modify the human make-up: we are all becoming bitter, disillusioned, obsessed by politics – which should be as unobtrusive as drains') in 'Spectator Symposium', *Spectator*, 29 July 1966, p. 138.

wanting to speak Russian and to marvel decadently at the surviving splendours of pre-revolutionary Tsarist architecture on Nevsky Prospekt.*

Lynne's health had gradually improved under the care of her doctor in Sussex. Burgess told Agnes Tollitt in May 1961 that 'Lynne is eating and sleeping better but she has to continue treatment [for bursitis] for at least the next three months.' However, she tended to become fragile and unpredictable whenever she was away from home. Following the sea voyage out from London, she had collapsed in the Tivoli Gardens in Copenhagen. She then took to her ship's bunk with a 'strange rich-coloured rash' on her neck, emerging occasionally from her cabin to stir up political trouble by loudly demanding why the Soviets had banned *Doctor Zhivago*.†
Her condition deteriorated considerably a few days after they had arrived in Leningrad. Still suffering from the rash, and hobbling around the city on a badly swollen ankle, she oscillated between states of energetic animation (dancing, drinking, fist-fighting in the street) and sudden exhaustion followed by spectacular collapses.

At some point early in July – the talk at dinner the previous evening had been of Ernest Hemingway's suicide on 2 July 1961 – Lynne downed a mixture of beer, vodka and cognac and lay down in the street outside a 'low tavern'. It was two-thirty in the morning

---

* For a selection of Burgess's reviews of Russian literature, see *Homage to Qwert Yuiop: Selected Journalism 1978–1985* (London: Hutchinson, 1985), pp. 448–60, and 'One Very Well-Buttered Parsnip' (review of Peter Levi, *Boris Pasternak: A Biography*; Christopher Barnes, *Boris Pasternak: A Literary Biography*; Eugeny Pasternak, *Boris Pasternak: The Tragic Years 1930–60*; Boris Pasternak, *Poems 1955–59* and *An Essay in Autobiography*), *Observer*, 7 January 1990, p. 41.

† Burgess claims, in his *Observer* review-article on Pasternak, that 'In 1960 [i.e. 1961], on my first visit to Russia, I had my copy of *Doctor Zhivago* confiscated by customs and, at a ridiculous literary conference, had to hear Pasternak reviled for misrepresenting the October Revolution.' But he writes in *You've Had Your Time*, published later the same year: 'we had no trouble with the fatherly customs officer [. . .] My copy of *Doctor Zhivago* he ignored' (p. 42). Another conundrum, then, and a further example of Burgess's reluctance to tell a story the same way twice.

and there were no taxis to be found. An ambulance was summoned, but it took an hour to arrive, and there was nothing to do except admire the 'white Leningrad summer night that Pushkin describes so beautifully'.* She was taken to a hospital – either to the Petrogradskaya Instituta or the Pavlovskaya Bolnitsa (Burgess's Russian travelogues mention both these places) – where the rash was diagnosed as a symptom of capitalist malnutrition and an allergy to vodka. Lynne submitted doubtfully to the care of a lesbian nurse, who greeted her with the words '*Aaaaah, Anglichanka*'. The function of Soviet nurses, Burgess reflected, was 'less clinical than maternal'. One of them rocked his suffering wife in her arms and crooned Russian lullabies. He acted as translator while the hospital forms were filled in, for Lynne spoke hardly any Russian (although in an earlier account he writes that his 'tiny bit of Russian had burst at the seams', and a friendly Anglo-Polish fur merchant did the translating). 'Were we members of the British Communist Party, they wanted to know. We said we weren't. They seemed pleased for some reason.'

He gave three contradictory accounts of what he was up to during the ten days when Lynne was incapacitated. In a BBC radio talk broadcast in September 1961, he claimed that, while she was resting at the Astoria (she was not required to stay at the hospital in this version of the story), he wandered the streets radiating out from St Isaac's square, carrying a prescription given to him by a bearded doctor, and looking in vain for an *aptyeka* or state druggist to dispense penicillin.

> In my best Russian I said to various Dostoevsky characters: 'Where, comrade, is the nearest *aptyeka*?' They were all evidently healthy people, well-fed on Soviet food, for they did not know. I walked miles and miles and miles, past canals and tinsmiths, state-butchers and watch-repairers, but I could find

---

* Burgess, 'A Rash in Russia', *Woman's Hour*, BBC Home Service, broadcast 18 September 1961.

no *aptyeka* [. . .] In tears and with difficulty I found my way
back to the hotel.*

In the autobiography (1990) he claims that Lynne was detained in
hospital for 'over a week'. Unable to afford the extortionate tourist
rates at the Astoria, he befriended a beatnik Russian, Sasha (or
Alexei) Ivanovich Kornilov, who worked as a guide at the Hermit-
age, and went to stay at his flat, not far from the Ninth of January
Park and the Kirov Works metro station. This was on the ninth
floor of 'a hideous flatblock with a rain-striated bas-relief image of
a worker in heroic overalls'.† This description of the flatblock, with
its Stalinist murals, has a good deal in common with Alex's home in
A Clockwork Orange:

> In the hallway was the good old municipal painting on the
> walls – vecks and ptitsas very well developed, stern in the
> dignity of labour, at workbench and machine with not one
> stitch of platties on their well-developed plotts. But of course
> some of the malchicks living in 18A had, as was to be expected,
> embellished and decorated the said big painting with handy
> pencil and ballpoint, adding hair and stiff rods and dirty
> ballooning slovos out of the dignified rots of these nagoy (bare,
> that is) cheenas and vecks.‡

In Comrade Kornilov's flat, he claimed to have made love to a thin,
blonde woman – Finnish, not Russian – called Helvi, who had been,
until recently, Sasha's temporary mistress. Apparently she transferred her affections to Burgess because 'She needed someone
maturer, gentler, more experienced.'§

An earlier article, 'The Human Russians', published in the
Listener three months after the radio talk, casts doubt on this
version of events. In his memoirs Burgess states that his reason for

---

* Burgess, 'A Rash in Russia'.
† Burgess, *You've Had Your Time*, p. 50.
‡ Burgess, *A Clockwork Orange*, p. 31.
§ Burgess, *You've Had Your Time*, p. 51.

moving into Sasha's flat was that he could not afford to stay on at the Astoria. 'The Human Russians' tells a rather different story: 'An Intourist man told me I would have to pay £25 for a single night in a double room in the Astoria Hotel. What I actually paid was something under 30s.; I have the bill to prove it'.* Thirty shillings was slightly less than the price of two hardback novels in the early 1960s (the first edition of *A Clockwork Orange* was priced at 16s.) – the equivalent of about £30 in today's currency – and easily affordable to Burgess, who had been paid his travel expenses in advance by Heinemann. If he did remain at the Astoria for a week or ten days until he took the ship back to London, then the details of the 1990 version of the trip to Leningrad must be fabricated. Did Helvi exist, or did he call her into being at the typewriter in order to make himself appear to be more of a Don Juan than he was? The answer may lie in *Honey for the Bears*, in which the English hero, Paul Hussey, has a series of erotic encounters with Russians of both sexes in a seedy Leningrad flat ('He had her flat on the bed in no time. "Be persistent," he told himself, "and every woman must soften; it is in the nature of every woman to yield." Gasping, he released her mouth and swallowed a chestful of Russian air. He and the creaking bed had her sandwiched beautifully').† Meanwhile, Paul's American wife is discovering her lesbianism with a female doctor in a Soviet hospital. When Burgess came to write the Helvi episode in *You've Had Your Time*, he seems to have lifted the sex scene from the pages of his novel, claiming it as part of his personal experience.

*

As Burgess and Lynne sailed back to London, he was already making notes towards *Honey for the Bears*, and contemplating the hard task of finishing *A Clockwork Orange*. The ending of the novel was an area of particular difficulty. He was still revising and

* Burgess, 'The Human Russians', p. 1107.
† Burgess, *Honey for the Bears*, p. 145.

reworking it more than thirty years later. Critics agree that the ending represents a large area of contention.* Briefly stated, the problem is that the earliest published editions, the UK Heinemann edition of 1962 and the US Norton edition of 1963, have different endings. Subsequent paperback editions compound the problem: depending on their place of publication, they follow either the Heinemann text (twenty-one chapters) or the Norton text (twenty chapters).

Although Burgess believed that the presence or absence of this twenty-first chapter made a significant difference to the meaning of the novel, it is evident from his writings on the subject that he held different opinions at different times as to which ending was 'correct'. The difference in emphasis between the two versions is best explained with reference to the theological contention that under-pins so much of Burgess's thinking: between Augustinianism and Pelagianism, as first expressed in *A Vision of Battlements*.

The Norton text of *A Clockwork Orange* ends at part three, chapter 6 (the twentieth chapter) and shows us Alex recovering in hospital from his suicide attempt, now apparently unbrainwashed or deprogrammed. He is given a series of psychological tests, and his responses are evidently those of an unconditioned thug. Towards the end of this chapter, he proposes to return to his former ultra-violent ways: 'I could viddy myself very clear running and running on like very light and mysterious nogas, carving the whole litso of the creeching world with my cut-throat britva [. . .] I was cured all right.' He has been restored to the unrepentant criminal Alex whom we encounter at the beginning of the novel. There is an artful and uncompromising circularity about this ending, and an emphatic

---

* See A. A. DeVitis, *Anthony Burgess*, Twayne's English Authors series (New York: Twayne, 1972), pp. 110–12; Geoffrey Aggeler, *Anthony Burgess: The Artist as Novelist* (Albama: University of Alabama Press, 1979), pp. 178–82; Samuel Coale, *Anthony Burgess* (New York: Frederick Ungar, 1981), pp. 96–8; John J. Stinson, *Anthony Burgess Revisited*, Twayne's English Authors series (Boston, MA: Twayne, 1991), pp. 59–60.

rejection of the notion that novels should concern themselves with the moral progress of their protagonists. By emphasizing the unreformed sinfulness of Alex, the twentieth chapter reveals itself to be an Augustinian conclusion. Alex has been 'cured', but not saved.

The Heinemann text ends at part three, chapter 7 (the twenty-first chapter), and admits the possibility of regeneration. Alex, who has recovered from the Ludovico conditioning, returns to the streets and forms another gang of droogs – Len, Rick and Bully. The opening paragraph refers us back to the novel's opening page by repeating the sentence 'We were sitting in the Korova Milkbar making up our rassoodocks what to do with the evening, a flip dark chill winter bastard, though dry.' But the echo is not sustained, and there are indications that Alex, now aged eighteen ('not a young age'), is maturing. He is now listening to lieder as well as symphonic music, 'just a goloss and a piano, very quiet and like yearny', and we learn that he has begun to think about mortality:

> I got a sudden like picture of me sitting before a bolshy fire in an armchair peeting away at this chai, and what was very funny and very very strange was that I seemed to have turned into a very starry chelloveck, about seventy years old.*

Deciding not to take part in a proposed evening of ultra-violence, he goes alone to a café where he meets Pete, one of his former droogs, who is now married and has settled down to a life of 'harmless' bourgeois domesticity, 'little parties, [. . .] wine-cup and word-games'. Alex begins to think in terms of finding a wife and having a child. As he contemplates a future that is likely to involve fatherhood, his narrative ends with a clearly stated farewell to teenage outrages:

> Yes yes yes, there it was. Youth must go, ah yes. But youth is only being in a way like it might be an animal. No, it is not like being an animal so much as being like one of those malenky toys you viddy being sold in the streets, like little chellovecks

* *A Clockwork Orange*, p. 191.

made of tin and with a spring inside and then a winding handle
on the outside and you wind it up grrr grrr grrr and off it itties,
like walking, O my brothers. But it itties in a straight line and
bangs straight into things bang bang and it cannot help what it
is doing. Being young is like being like one of these malenky
machines.*

This turning away from ultra-violence may be interpreted as
Pelagian, in the sense that Alex acknowledges his potential for
goodness autonomously, without the direct intervention of divine
grace. At no point does he express remorse for his former wickedness, yet the position he articulates here is a willed and reasoned
turning away from his former criminality. For this reason, the
twenty-first chapter is a Pelagian conclusion. These theological
resonances are everywhere present, though nowhere stated, in the
novel's two possible endings.

The margins of the typescript record one half of a long conver-
sation between Burgess and his editor at Heinemann, James Michie.
The overwhelming majority of the marginal comments relate to
Burgess's hesitations about Nadsat. He writes next to certain words
'Don't like this' (with reference to the verb 'filly' on page 5) or
'Don't like this much' (referring to 'lubbilubbing' on page 16). He
seems to have marked up the first seven chapters of the typescript
for his editor, indicating areas of uncertainty and possible revision.
There are fewer alterations after Alex's incarceration at the end of
part one. According to James Michie, Burgess sent the first section
of the book to Heinemann and proceeded with the rest of the book
after receiving editorial advice.†

---

* Ibid., p. 195.
† James Michie to author, 15 November 2000. Michie states: 'The only thing I
remember is giving some advice about the rate at which the reader is expected to
learn the new language. I was saying, "Make it gently *accelerando*. You can't throw
too much of it at them too quickly because otherwise the dumber ones among them
will think this is too difficult." I think that's one of the great successes of the book:
you can read it and you learn a new vocabulary without pain.'

A few examples from the typescript illustrate how the novel took shape over the course of the four months when Burgess was composing and revising it, between April and August 1961. In the margin of page 20, next to the word 'zheena' (meaning 'wife'), Burgess asks whether there might be a 'better word'. Later he circles the word 'droog' and writes in the margin, 'Should [it] be drook?' He writes that he is 'Not too happy' about the word 'drencrom', which is one of the drugs sold with the old moloko plus at the Korova Milkbar. Elsewhere he alters 'smeeking' (meaning 'laughing') to 'smecking'. These hesitations and revisions suggest that Nadsat, rather than being an argot that was carefully planned out in advance, acquired its real shape as the novel was being written and revised. Burgess also frequently uses the left-hand margin to provide Cyrillic transliterations of Nadsat words. The general tendency of these revisions seems to be towards a thickening or enriching of Nadsat at the expense of Standard English. When Alex is about to seduce the two ptitsas from the disc-bootick, Burgess alters the line, 'Aha, I know what you want, I think', to rakish mock-Elizabethan: 'Aha, I know what thou wantest, I thinkest'. *A Clockwork Orange* reveals itself to be a text which became steadily more complex, from a linguistic point of view, during the process of revision. Indicating one possible cut ('Now they would take sleep-pills. Perhaps, knowing the joy I had in my night music, they had already taken them'), Burgess writes in the margin that these words are 'Too ordinary'.

One comment on the typescript raises a point about cultural history. When Alex and his gang put on their 'maskies' or disguises, one of the masks shows the face of Elvis Presley. Next to the words 'Elvis Presley', Burgess writes, 'Will this name be known when [the] book appears?' Burgess worried that Elvis was a passing fashion, unlike the upmarket literary writers whose names became streetnames in the novel: 'Amis Avenue', 'Priestley Place', 'Marghanita Boulevard'.* The typescript also contains four bars of music, which

---

* For more detail on Burgess's dismissive response to the popular music of the

accompany the prisoners' hymn ('Weak tea are we new brewed / But stirring make all strong. / We eat no angel's food, / Our times of trial are long') in part two, chapter 1. Burgess's music is in the key of G minor, and it is approximately in the style of one of J. S. Bach's Chorales. The likely reason for the absence of music in the Heinemann edition is that the printing cost of inserting these four bars would have been prohibitive. The 1962 edition was published a couple of years before cheap offset lithography became widely available.*

The other significant feature of the typescript is the presence of illustrations. Burgess provides a series of seven line-drawings, very similar in style to his character sketches for *The Eve of Saint Venus.*† One of the 'millicents' or policemen who arrests Alex is depicted as an ill-shaven, ape-like thug, and throughout the text we find other images of exploding clockwork oranges, disgorging their cogs. The most interesting drawing is the one which shows our friend and narrator Alex. Burgess sketches him dressed in what he would call 'the heighth of fashion', with a dangling quiff of hair, large padded shoulders and an extravagant cravat. These pictures are slapdash pen-and-ink affairs drawn at high speed: it may be that Burgess was at one time thinking of *A Clockwork Orange* as an illustrated novel; it is also possible that the drawings were included merely for the sake of whimsical decoration, perhaps as a private joke between the author and his editor.

Finally, the most revealing annotation on the typescript is a handwritten query referring to the disputed twenty-first chapter. At the end of part three, chapter 6, there is a note in Burgess's hand:

1960s, see (for example) 'Critic on the Hearth', *Listener*, 12 September 1963, pp. 398–9; 'The Arts', *Listener*, 11 March 1965, p. 381; 'The Antis: The Weasels of Pop', *Punch*, 20 September 1967, pp. 430–31.

* For this information I must thank Dr Adriaan van der Weel from the Centre for the History of the Book at Leiden University.

† The *Eve of Saint Venus* sketches are in a notebook in the archive of the Anthony Burgess Center at the University of Angers.

'Should we end here? An optional "epilogue" follows.' The implication of this question is that Burgess genuinely did not know how
the novel should conclude when it left his typewriter in August
1961; and it is obvious from the published texts that his editors,
James Michie at Heinemann and Eric Swenson at Norton, arrived
at very different answers. In a preface to the 1987 Norton edition,
Burgess stated, long after the event, that 'Those twenty-one chapters
were important to me', and he went on to formulate a retrospective
argument that the novel had been planned and written as a unified
twenty-one-chapter entity.* But his original query ('Should we end
here?') is obviously at variance with this later claim.

Burgess expresses serious hesitations about *A Clockwork
Orange* in his long *Paris Review* interview with John Cullinan.† This
interview, first published in 1973, was recorded in Wisconsin on
2 December 1972, less than a year after the film had been released
in New York, but long enough after the premiere for Burgess to
have begun to have his doubts about it. The question of the optional
epilogue emerges as a point of unresolved doubt. He told Cullinan:
'I don't know what to think now. After all, it's twelve years since I
wrote the thing'. These uncertainties are amplified in his response to
a later question:

> I was very dubious about the book itself [. . .] So when the
> American publisher made this objection to the final chapter, I
> didn't feel myself to be in a very strong position. I was a little
> hesitant to judge the book; I was a little too close to it. I
> thought: Well, they might be right. Because authors do tend to
> be (especially after the completion of a book) very uncertain

---

* Burgess, 'Introduction: A Clockwork Orange Resucked' in *A Clockwork Orange*
(New York: Norton, 1987), pp. v–xi, vi; reprinted in *One Man's Chorus: The
Uncollected Writings*, ed. by Ben Forkner (New York: Carroll & Graf, 1998),
pp. 226–30.
† John Cullinan, 'Anthony Burgess' in *Writers at Work: The Paris Review Interviews: Fourth Series*, ed. by George Plimpton (Secker & Warburg, 1977),
pp. 323–58.

about the value of the book; and perhaps I gave in a little too weakly.

These remarks seem to suggest that Burgess favoured the Heinemann ending. Yet a couple of sentences later he says: 'I've been persuaded by so many critics that the book is better in its American form that I say "All right, they know best."'* Having talked inconclusively around the question of the two endings, he ends the discussion with a refusal to make a definitive pronouncement in favour of either. On his decision to allow the novel to appear with its twenty-first chapter excised in 1963, he says: 'I'm not able to judge myself now as to whether I was right or wrong.'

The account of the novel's history that Burgess gave to Cullinan was repeated in a letter to the editor of the *Times Literary Supplement*, published on 11 January 1980. 'When, in 1961, the typescript of the novel was offered to Messrs W. W. Norton in New York,' Burgess writes, 'the managing editor was unwilling to publish without the excision of the final chapter [. . .] I was told that American readers would prefer unregenerability and thuggishness stretching to the crack of the doom [sic].'† According to this letter, the dropping of the twenty-first chapter, to which the author 'weakly agreed', was a pre-condition of publication in the United States. Burgess fails to mention that he already had doubts about it himself. On reading Burgess's letter, the Vice Chairman and Executive Editor at Norton, Eric Swenson, disagreed with the statements it contained about the editorial process, and he wrote a letter of his own to the *TLS*:

---

* It is likely that Burgess was thinking, in particular, of A. A. DeVitis's critical book, which had been published a few months earlier. DeVitis writes: 'The William Heinemann 1962 edition of *A Clockwork Orange* includes a chapter wisely omitted from the American editions.' He goes on to describe the Heinemann ending as a 'failure' which 'contradicts the rationale that animates the novel.' See DeVitis, *Anthony Burgess*, p. 110.
† Burgess, 'Letters to the Editor', *Times Literary Supplement*, 11 January 1980, p. 38.

Anthony Burgess's letter to you of January 11 has come to my attention. I am the editor of the American edition of CLOCK-WORK ORANGE to which he refers. His claim that we refused to publish unless the last (up-beat) chapter of the published, British edition were dropped is hereby denied. We did tell him that the Polyanna ending left us unconvinced; he replied that he agreed, that he had added it only to mollify his *British* publisher, and that he would be pleased if we dropped it. As I have written him, we seem to have diametrically opposed memories of the matter. I, however, claim to have supporting documents and witnesses.*

Burgess sold the annotated typescript of *A Clockwork Orange* to McMaster University in Ontario in 1967. By the time he recorded his conversation with Cullinan in 1972, he was no longer able to refer to the marginal notes he had made during the process of composition. Like much of Burgess's journalistic and autobiographical writing, this interview shows an author who is at some level engaged in creatively reimagining the history of his own work.

Burgess's most detailed statement on the editing of the American *Clockwork Orange* is in 'A Clockwork Orange Resucked', his introduction to the revised 1987 Norton edition. Once again he claims that the initial suggestion to cut the twenty-first chapter came from Eric Swenson, and that he allowed himself to be talked into omitting it for financial reasons: 'I needed money back in 1961 [. . .] and if the condition of the book's acceptance was also its truncation – well, so be it.'† This implies, contrary to Swenson's account, that there was no discussion between author and editor of which ending was more satisfactory from a moral or aesthetic point of view. The analogy Burgess proposes here is that the Heinemann version is

---

* Eric Swenson, letter to the editor, *Times Literary Supplement*, 20 February 1980 (Norton archive).
† Burgess, 'Introduction: A Clockwork Orange Resucked', p. vi. This introduction is reprinted in Burgess, *One Man's Chorus*, pp. 226–30.

'Kennedyan' (accepting 'the notion of moral progress'), whereas the shorter Norton text is 'Nixonian' ('with no shred of optimism in it'), and he indicates a distinct bias in favour of the Heinemann ending. Alex, we are told, is finally able to exercise, in the twenty-first chapter, the freedom of choice that Brodsky and the Minister of the Interior had tried to suppress using aversion therapy. (That he is also exercising this freedom at the end of the twentieth chapter, where he proposes to resume his criminal activities, is not a point that Burgess cares to acknowledge.) He also elaborates on what he sees, twenty-five years after the event, as one of the book's major shortcomings: 'I tend to disparage *A Clockwork Orange* as a work too didactic to be artistic. It is not the novelist's job to preach; it is his duty to show.'* The particular criticism he makes in the preface is that the novel's sermon on free will is spelt out too plainly by the prison chaplain, rather than being implied or dramatized in a less direct way.

Eric Swenson, once again dismayed by the imputation that he had acted in a draconian fashion when editing the novel, wrote a short essay in reply to Burgess, which he proposed to include, along with Burgess's introduction, in the 1987 Norton edition. This unpublished document gives a valuable second perspective on the editorial process:

> What I remember is that he responded to my comments by telling me that I was right, that he had added the twenty-first, upbeat chapter because his British publisher wanted a happy ending. My memory also claims that he urged me to publish an American edition without that last chapter, which was, again as I remember it, how he had originally ended the novel. We did just that. It may or may not prove anything that the truncated American edition has been far more successful than the British version. Be that as it may, the dropping of chapter twenty-one was never a condition of publication.†

---

* Burgess, 'Introduction: A Clockwork Orange Resucked', pp. v–xi, x.
† Eric Swenson, '*A Clockwork Orange*, Rewound'. Unpublished typescript.

A letter of 7 July 1986 from Swenson to Burgess explains the circumstances in which Swenson's essay was suppressed:

> I gather [. . .] that you do not want my contribution to the debate in the new edition of CLOCKWORK ORANGE – which I understand and more than half expected. My only wistful wish is that somewhere in your Introduction you might introduce the thought that your publisher has a different memory of events [. . .] One of the principles of my editorial life is that the author is indeed the author [. . .] We would never have excised the last chapter over your objections.*

In the light of these documents from the Norton archive, it seems likely that Burgess's memory of events is at fault. But the original exchange of letters between Burgess and Swenson from the early 1960s, which would settle the issue decisively, is missing from the files.

Burgess has a good deal to say about the composition of *A Clockwork Orange* in his private letters. The earliest references to the novel occur in a series of twenty-seven letters and postcards that he sent to his friends Diana and Meir Gillon between April 1961 and February 1962. He began his correspondence with the Gillons after he had reviewed their collaboratively written novel, *The Unsleep*, for the *Yorkshire Post*.† These letters provide a detailed account of his anxieties and hesitations about the novel while he was in the process of composing it. In the first surviving letter, written in April 1961, Burgess writes:

> I'm in the early stages of a novel about juvenile delinquents in the future (I'm fabricating with difficulty a teenage dialect compounded equally of American and Russian roots). There's a lot, I think, to be done in this field.‡

---

* Eric Swenson, letter to Burgess, 7 July 1986 (Norton archive).
† See Burgess, 'Another Brave New World', *Yorkshire Post*, 6 April 1961, p. 4.
‡ Burgess, letter to Diana and Meir Gillon. Quoted in *Books, Maps, Photographs and Manuscripts*, Phillips auction catalogue, p. 104.

The futuristic element noted here is clearly visible in the novel. The references to satellite television 'worldcasts' and to 1960 as a distant historical date are two indications that the events of the book take place at some point late in the twentieth century or early in the twenty-first. However, while his Nadsat language was originally planned as a fusion of Russian and American (rather than British) English, the American element seems to have been dropped at some point before he completed the 1961 typescript, which shows little evidence of Americanisms.* The one exception is Alex's American-sounding use of 'like' as a syntactical filler, as in 'We had four of these lomticks of like Prison Religion this morning.'

Other letters from the Gillon correspondence reveal Burgess's uncertainty about how readers of the novel will respond to Nadsat, and he voices a particular anxiety (both in the letters and in the margins of the typescript) about the difficulty of his invented argot from the reader's point of view. He quotes a sample passage from the novel-in-progress for the attention of the Gillons' son, who was learning Russian in 1961:

> To revert to this question of inventing a slang to be used by juvenile delinquents in the future. I wonder if your son could make anything of this? (From my tentatively titled *A Clockwork Orange*) – '. . . He was creeching out loud and waving his rookers and making real horrorshow with the slovos, only the odd blurp blurp coming from his keeshkas, like some very rude sort of interrupting sort of a moodge making a shoom . . .' I also have malchicks smecking away and lewdies getting razdraz and dratsing with nozhes and britvas and a length of the old oozy from round the tally. I wonder if this sort of thing will work. One can read the reviews before one's started writing, but it doesn't help, does it? One does what one has to do.†

---

* Later, in the 1987 Norton introduction, Burgess refers to Nadsat as 'a Russified version of English'. See 'Introduction: A Clockwork Orange Resucked', p. x.
† Burgess, letter to Diana and Meir Gillon. Quoted in *Books, Maps, Photographs and Manuscripts*, p. 105.

A *Clockwork Orange* is unique among Burgess's works in that he sought editorial advice, both from his editor at Heinemann and from the Gillons, while the book was underway. None of his other typescripts are marked up with possible cuts to a comparable extent. Nor are there any letters relating to other novels which speak of similar doubts as to whether 'this sort of thing will work'.

In a later letter, it is the novel's violence that concerns him. Burgess writes that he has been 'pushing on desperately' with *A Clockwork Orange*, 'which nears its climax and quick denouement', but adds that 'because of its language and boring violence people may hate it (violence is meant to be boring, but some critics won't see that)'. The tone of anxious pessimism comes through again as he approaches the novel's conclusion:

> I just plod on and this week hope to bring *A Clockwork Orange* to its bitter end – about 70,000 words only or even less; I don't think readers will be able to take all that much of it. I'm not at all satisfied, but I obviously can't scrap it now.

*

A Clockwork Orange was published on 14 May 1962 in an edition of 6,000 copies. Burgess was frustrated by the disappointing early reviews, especially John Garrett's short notice in the *Times Literary Supplement* and Robert Taubman's 250-word review in the *New Statesman*.* Garrett's review quotes Lord Hailsham's dictum that 'English is being slowly killed by her practitioners' and seeks to relate this to Burgess's linguistic innovations. He goes on to complain, with a veiled imputation of blasphemy, about 'the author's language and questionable taste', concluding that Burgess 'seems content to use a serious social challenge for frivolous purposes, but himself to stay neutral'. Taubman also expresses reservations about Nadsat, which is said to be 'a great strain to read'. His final

* Anon. [i.e. John Walter Percy Garrett], 'Other New Novels', *Times Literary Supplement*, 25 May 1962, p. 277; Robert Taubman, 'Djunaesque', *New Statesman*, 18 May 1962, pp. 717–18.

judgement is that, in spite of the book's futuristic content, 'There's not much fantasy here; Mr Burgess works by keeping close to the way things are now, and the novel can be read, for instance, as straight satire on the indulgence of a good many current writers to their teenage heroes.' This does not allow for the possibility that the reader might be seduced by the novel's language to the extent of becoming desensitized to the horrors of droogish ultra-violence, and the claim that the novel aims at 'straight satire' looks like a misreading, if only because it underestimates the likely degree of collusion between reader and narrator.

A longer and more considered review, published in the *Spectator*, gives a more favourable account of the book. In 'Horrorshow on Amis Avenue', Julian Mitchell writes:

> If Mr Burgess is, in some ways, a pupil of Mr Waugh, he yet has an originality of manner and subject which place him, to my mind, among the best writers in England. Yet he has never received the critical attention granted to Angus Wilson and Kingsley Amis, with whom at least he deserves to rank. Certainly his prose is more attractive than either's, and he is prepared to take risks which they are not.*

While noting 'a certain arbitrariness about the plot', Mitchell praises Nadsat as 'an extraordinary technical feat'. Defending the 'experimental' qualities of the novel, he writes that 'the whole conception vigorously exhibits Mr Burgess's great imaginative gifts [. . .] Mr Burgess is far too good and important a writer not to go in any direction he chooses.'† Mitchell's article is important because it indicates that the initial response to the novel was not universally

---

* Julian Mitchell, 'Horrorshow on Amis Avenue', *Spectator*, 18 May 1962, pp. 661–62, 661.
† See also Julian Mitchell, 'Wracks of Empire' (review of *Devil of a State*), *Spectator*, 3 November 1961, p. 636. For Burgess on Mitchell, see *The Novel Now* (London: Faber, 1971), pp. 118, 212.

hostile, as Burgess later claimed in *You've Had Your Time*.* A novelist, screenwriter and fiction reviewer for the *Sunday Times*, Mitchell was a prominent literary figure in the early 1960s, and his judgements carried a certain amount of critical weight. His role in the formation of Burgess's reputation did not end with this review: his later piece for the *London Magazine* was the first attempt to discuss Burgess's fiction at essay length.†

After Stanley Kubrick's film adaptation was released in 1971, Burgess was often asked about violence in interviews, and he was keen to make the point that he did not regard *A Clockwork Orange* as representative of his larger body of fiction. He developed this line of argument in a conversation with Robert Louit, published in the French *Magazine Littéraire* in 1974: 'Actually, the success of *A Clockwork Orange* has given me a rather false reputation, since you'll find very little violence and very little direct representation of sex in my other novels. I've always been slightly reserved, even timid, in my treatment of these subjects.'‡ The emphasis on the lack of violent episodes in his other novels is misleading, given the *crime passionnel* which forms the climax to *The Right to an Answer*, or the killing of Howard Shirley with a coal hammer in *One Hand*

---

* See also Stanley Edgar Hyman's untitled review of the American edition, *New Leader*, 7 January 1963, p. 13. Hyman compares *A Clockwork Orange* with George Orwell's *Nineteen Eighty-Four*. The review welcomes the novel's linguistic inventiveness, but deplores the absence of a Nadsat glossary.

† Burgess's letters to Julian Mitchell indicate how closely the two writers worked to bolster each other's reputations. In a postcard dated 4 July 1963, Burgess joked: '*I'll* write the article and then we can split the dibs. Libel me as much as you like (official).' Mitchell sent Burgess a draft of the *London Magazine* piece before publication, which was returned on 30 July with a long letter of corrections and suggestions for expansion. In a third letter, dated 2 February 1964, Burgess thanked Mitchell for the article (now published), and offered to review his next novel. Three months later (on 25 April) Burgess and Mitchell appeared together on BBC radio to comment favourably on each other's new books. The transcript of their broadcast is in the BBC Written Archives.

‡ Robert Louit, 'Entretien avec Anthony Burgess', *Magazine Littéraire*, April 1974, pp. 26–8, 26.

Clapping, or the protracted drugging and drowning of Mr Theodorescu in *Tremor of Intent*. On the other hand, the point about there
being 'very little *direct* [my italics] representation of sex' elsewhere
in his fiction is a fair one. The significant moments of reticence in
A Clockwork Orange are usually overlooked in discussions of the
novel's violence. When Alex is on the point of molesting the two
ten-year-old ptitsas, he says, 'What was actually done that afternoon
there is no need to describe, brothers, as you may easily guess all.'
Later, while he is being forced to watch scenes of sexual violence
during the Ludovico brainwashing, we are told: 'I do not wish to
describe, brothers, what other horrible veshches I was like forced to
viddy that afternoon.' After his discharge from prison, when he is
beaten up by Billyboy and two of his former droogs who have been
recruited into the police force, he says, 'I will not go into what they
did.' Unlike its later film adaptation, the book pointedly declines, at
such moments, to titillate or to excite. Instead of 'our dear old droog
the red-red vino on tap' starting to flow, as in the first seven
chapters, the novel retreats, particularly in its concluding third
section, into a carefully judged not-showing.

Late in life, Burgess came to regard *A Clockwork Orange* as a
burden and an embarrassment. Although he acknowledged that the
fame he enjoyed was to a large extent bound up with the public's
awareness of Kubrick's film, it disappointed him that this short and
uncharacteristic novel was better known than other works which
pleased him more. When he was asked in 1983 to name his favourite
books, he replied that he was proud to have written parts of *The
Right to an Answer*, all of *MF* and the fourth chapter of *Napoleon
Symphony*.* But he continued to write *Clockwork Orange* articles
until the end of his life, to speak about the book and the film in
interviews, to write prefaces to new editions of the novel, and to
make new stage adaptations with music. *A Clockwork Orange* was
unfinished business, and Burgess's commentaries on it disclose an
ongoing anxiousness to limit the ways in which it was understood.

* Burgess, letter to Anthony LoProto, 6 March 1983.

One of his pronouncements is particularly surprising, since it speaks of Alex's adult life beyond the end of the novel. In a 1985 television interview with Isaac Bashevis Singer, he said:

> In my version, the English version, [Alex] grows up, he understands that violence is an aspect of youth. He has energy. He'll be able to use it to create. He will become a great musician [. . .] I wanted to show that violence is in our nature. We can't ignore it. We can't pretend it doesn't exist.*

In making this statement, he was gesturing towards an area of experience that the novel itself leaves unclear. In imagining a life for his fictional hero beyond the end of the book, Burgess was demonstrating that *A Clockwork Orange* was still imaginatively alive for him. He was unsure how the book should end when he delivered it to Heinemann in 1961, and this uncertainty about endings persisted. There was a sense in which the story, with its disturbing riot of aggressive energies, was never fully finished.

---

* Quoted in Anthony Burgess and Isaac Bashevis Singer, *Rencontre au Sommet* (Paris: Arte/Mille et Une Nuits, 1998), p. 52.

8

The Bawdy Bard

This was the order of a typical Burgess day in Etchingham in the 1960s. He would get up between seven and eight in the morning – 'grudgingly', he said – and bring himself to full wakefulness by blasting out William Walton's *Portsmouth Point Overture* or the *Crown Imperial March* on the record-player downstairs. Then he would kick his dog, a border collie named Haji, and call him a lazy bastard. Breakfast would be followed by an hour or two of jokes and conversation with Lynne. She would open the morning's post while he went through the newspapers (*The Times* and the *Daily Mirror*).* Around ten o'clock he would go upstairs to his study, a large room with a south-facing window, looking out on to a long garden where caged guinea-pigs chewed the grass to save the trouble of having to mow it. He would settle down at the typewriter with a pint-mug of strong tea – 'stepmother's tea' is what F. X. Enderby calls it – made with 'no fewer than five Twinings Irish Breakfast tea-bags'.† He would

---

* Some of the details of Burgess's daily routine are taken from Paul Boytinck's biographical essay in *Anthony Burgess: An Annotated Bibliography and Reference Guide* (New York: Garland, 1985), pp. vi–xxxv. See also Geoffrey Aggeler, 'Anthony Burgess' in *Dictionary of Literary Biography*, vol. 194, ed. by Merritt Moseley (New York: Gale, 1998), pp. 49–72.

† 'Lowering the Steaks' (interview with Thomas Bridgstock), *Evening Standard*, 26 May 1989, p. 31.

remain at his desk for at least eight hours every day, weekends included, smoking excessively (his regular intake was eighty cigarettes per day) and rising occasionally – because he suffered from haemorrhoids, which he called the Writer's Evil – to pace around the study. 'I'm a very slow writer,' he told Thomas Churchill in 1968.

> I have a lot of energy. I'm fairly strong. I can stay at the table for a long stretch, smoking a lot. Get a fair amount done that way. I get a thousand words a day down, you see, in good conditions. Which is all right. Ideally you get an 80,000 word book done in eighty days, two and a half months, about three months. I have written a novel in four weeks.*

When his concentration failed, he would take three dexedrine tablets, washing them down with a pint of iced gin and tonic before returning to the typewriter. Piles of books for review – sent by the *Yorkshire Post*, the *Listener*, the *Observer*, the *Times Literary Supplement* and the *Spectator* – covered the floor of his study and overflowed, like lava from a volcano, onto the landing and down the stairs. (He reviewed more than 350 novels in just over two years for the *Yorkshire Post*, and there were always other freelance writing jobs on the go. Peter Green says: 'He was very professional in the sense that, like George Orwell, he knew exactly how much he had to read of a book in order not to fall flat on his face when reviewing it.') In the early evening, usually between five and six o'clock, Lynne would cook a meal in the traditional Welsh manner, with everything fried in lard. The rest of the evening was spent reading and watching the television – often for money rather than for pleasure, because Burgess wrote a weekly column of television criticism for the *Listener* between May 1963 and July 1968. Apart from work, of which there was obviously a great deal, there was also the drinking to get done. Burgess and Lynne would get through a couple of bottles of wine over dinner, and a dozen bottles of Gordon's gin were delivered to the house every

---

* Thomas Churchill, 'An Interview with Anthony Burgess', *Malahat Review*, January 1971, pp. 103–27, 127.

week – an astonishing amount considering that they hardly ever entertained visitors. Burgess's rate of gin consumption was not measurably lower than his wife's. When he wasn't drinking gin in the house, or downing pints of beer with double-whisky chasers at the Etchingham Arms – his habitual den in the village, from which Lynne had been barred after a fist-fight with the landlord – he was devising life-threatening cocktails, such as the Hangman's Blood ('I recommend this for a quick, though expensive, lift'), which he described to readers of the *Guardian* in 1966: 'Into a pint beer-glass doubles of the following are poured: gin, whisky, rum, port, and brandy. A small bottle of stout is added, and the whole topped up with champagne or champagne-surrogate. It tastes very smooth, induces a somehow metaphysical elation, and rarely leaves a hangover.'*

Once a week Burgess would load two suitcases with books and take the train from Etchingham to London, where he offloaded his unwanted review copies at Louis Simmonds's bookshop near Chancery Lane. Simmonds paid him half the cover price for each book in cash. 'This,' wrote Burgess in 1966, in one of his regular articles about the evils of taxation, 'is the one segment of my income that escapes the scrutiny and penal impost of Her Majesty's Department of Inland Revenue.'† Armed with a pocketful of banknotes, he would take his lunch at the Café Royal, leaving a generous tip ('Anthony Burgess is frightened of waiters and tips them extravagantly,' V. S. Naipaul told Paul Theroux. 'Taxi drivers, too').‡ Then he would go shopping for cigars and Cordon Bleu cognac before returning to Etchingham on the 4.20 train from Charing Cross. As he said of Enderby, this was 'a quiet way of life which harmed no one'.§

Joyce Sweetman, a woman from Etchingham who came in twice

---

* Burgess, 'Rationality in Drinks', *Guardian*, 23 November 1966, p. 16.
† Burgess, 'Letter from England', *Hudson Review*, vol. 19, no. 3 (Autumn 1966), p. 456.
‡ Paul Theroux, *Sir Vidia's Shadow: A Friendship Across Five Continents* (London: Hamish Hamilton, 1998), p. 191.
§ *Inside Mr Enderby* (London: Heinemann, 1963), p. 76.

a week to clean the house, was well placed to observe the domestic habits of Mr and Mrs Wilson. She told me:

> I knew John and Lynne Wilson very well, as I did the cleaning for them the time they lived here, and we became very good friends. I am also living in their house which John sold me when he moved to Malta [. . .] Mostly he did his writing during the day, but he used to stop up all night sometimes. Lynne used to hide empty gin bottles everywhere. All the years I knew them, I never knew her drink a cup of tea or coffee. I don't think she realized she was so ill. John said to me, 'If Lynne tries to pick a fight with you, just agree with everything she says.' I never had any trouble with her, but when she got drunk she could be very loud and nasty. She did the proof-reading and sorted out the new books. The only time she ever went out was when she was drinking. The three of us took the bus to the Bear Hotel in Burwash. She was very nice to me. John said, 'If I ever make a fortune from selling a book, I will leave you this house.' I rented the house after he left, and he let me have it rent-free for the first six months. Then I remarried in 1972 and bought the house from him for three thousand pounds.*

Mrs Sweetman, who first met the Wilsons in 1960 and regularly spent time in their house for the next eight years, is disinclined to believe the rumour (which she had never heard before I mentioned it during my interview with her) that Burgess was recovering from a suspected brain tumour. 'He was in very good health,' she says. 'I never knew him to be ill.'

He returned to one of his persistent themes, the conflict between 'Augustinian' authoritarianism and 'neo-Pelagian' liberalism, in a dystopian novel, *The Wanting Seed*, published by Heinemann on 1 October 1962 in an edition of 7,000 copies. Taking a futuristic perspective similar to that of *A Clockwork Orange*, Burgess predicts an England in which Christianity, fertility and heterosexuality will have been outlawed. His heroine, Beatrice-Joanna (her name is taken from

* Joyce Sweetman to author, 25 and 29 June 2003.

Thomas Middleton's seventeenth-century play *The Changeling*), is a dissident earth-mother who runs away to Wales to give birth in the house of her brother-in-law, who is a sort of recusant priest. Working in a comic-apocalyptic style, the book brings together many of Burgess's obsessions and preoccupations: homosexuality, the tyranny of the state, over-population, perpetual war, spontaneous orgies, the persistence of religious feeling in an age of ideological secularism, and cannibalism. 'So long as we have genuine cannibalism, we may have a return to Catholic Christianity with its sacrificial elements,' he said in an interview published in *Playboy*.* When the producer Carlo Ponti proposed to turn the novel into a film in the 1970s, Burgess suggested Ponti's wife, Sophia Loren, for the part of Beatrice-Joanna. But the film project failed because, as Burgess put it, 'the theme of the script I wrote (it ends with organized cannibalism) was considered too daring by potential backers'.† Like most of his fiction, the novel turns out to be broadly Catholic in its thinking about morality and sin. He told John Cullinan: 'We English take our Catholicism seriously, which the Italians and French don't, and that makes us earnest and obsessed about sin. We really absorbed hell [...] I believe the wrong God is temporarily ruling the world and that the true God has gone under.'‡ This was wildly unorthodox, but Burgess's belief in the ubiquity of Original Sin had survived his apostasy in an undiminished state, as his novels clearly demonstrated.

Kingsley Amis, who had been sent an early copy of *The Wanting Seed* by James Michie in the hope that he would provide 'a kindly quotable phrase', promptly sent it back with a handwritten note: 'Yes, I got it – but I don't want it, well hell, I mean it had its points

---

* C. Robert Jennings, 'Playboy Interview: Anthony Burgess', *Playboy*, September 1974, pp. 69–86, 86.
† Burgess, 'Sophia' in *Homage to Qwert Yuiop: Selected Journalism 1978–1985* (London: Hutchinson, 1986), pp. 127–31, 131.
‡ John Cullinan, 'Anthony Burgess' in *Writers at Work: The Paris Review Interviews: Fourth Series*, ed. by George Plimpton (London: Secker & Warburg, 1976), pp. 346–7.

– I read about 2/3 – but not enough. I caught a kind of facetious seriousness in it that got me down [. . .] (You know, he hasn't read enough science fiction, either.)'* Other reviewers were less curmudgeonly. In the *New Statesman*, Robert Taubman said: 'Mr Burgess is unfailingly inventive and apposite; a tough-minded Augustinian himself, to judge from his horror at the way people and governments behave, but an Augustinian with a sense of fun [. . .] He bears it all lightly, and this is both a serious novel and unusually engaging.'†
Walter Keir wrote in the *Times Literary Supplement*, 'Here too is all the usual rich exuberance of Mr Burgess's vocabulary, his love of quotations and literary allusions [. . .] This, then, is a remarkable and brilliantly imaginative novel, vital and inventive.'‡

Earlier that year, on 5 January, the *Worm and the Ring* libel case had begun, when Gwendoline Stella Bustin of Banbury instructed her lawyers to issue a claim for damages against John Burgess Wilson and William Heinemann Limited. Identifying herself in her statement of claim as the real-life original of the character Alice (the fictional school secretary), she alleged that certain 'false and malicious' passages in *The Worm and the Ring* had caused her to be held in ridicule, contempt and derision by right-thinking people in Oxfordshire. The writ contains fourteen closely-typed pages of quotations which are said to be libellous. For instance:

'I thought you might know something about this woman [. . .] She seems definitely unbalanced, the sort who might shout out dirty words under an anaesthetic. Not that her complaint is operable.'
'What seems to be the matter with her?'
'Frustration. Hypochondria. Hysteria. One of these days she may be really dangerous. Sex does queer things to people,

* Kingsley Amis, letter to James Michie, 9 January 1962, in *The Letters of Kingsley Amis*, ed. by Zachary Leader (London: HarperCollins, 2000), p. 596.
† Robert Taubman, 'Prospects', *New Statesman*, 5 October 1962, pp. 460–61.
‡ Walter Keir, 'The Hungry Sheep', *Times Literary Supplement*, 5 October 1962, p. 773.

especially when it's leaving them. It rends them like a departing devil. I've seen her type before. The poison-pen spinsters, the dried-up duennas who advance and retreat at the same time, lure a man on and then call for the police'.*

This libel writ was a disaster for Burgess and Heinemann as prospective co-defendants. Once Miss Bustin's lawyers had established that the internal geography of the novel referred to Banbury and to Banbury Grammar School (where she had worked since 1920, like Alice in the novel), she had no difficulty in proving her case. When Burgess was interviewed about her libel allegation in the *Banbury Guardian*, he blustered unconvincingly about his benevolence and good intentions: 'I was deeply hurt when I heard that Miss Bustin had taken exception to certain passages [. . .] Of course, there was no intention whatsoever on my part to link her or anyone else in Banbury with the characters in *The Worm and the Ring*. I would not be such a fool as to do such a thing. The book was completely fictitious – the characters, the theme and the setting.'[†] But it was too late to protest his innocence. Heinemann (who, after all, had a lot more to lose financially than Burgess did) had already agreed to a generous out-of-court settlement of £100, and to withdraw and destroy the entire first edition. James Michie recalls that Burgess 'couldn't see that he hadn't done sufficient to disguise [Miss Bustin], or he couldn't see that there was anything wrong in saying *that*'.[‡] So *The Worm and the Ring* was suppressed, and has never been reprinted in its original form. Roland Gant, the editorial director at Heinemann, oversaw the production of a sanitized second edition in 1970, with Burgess's consent but without his active participation in the editorial process.[§]

---

* Burgess, *The Worm and the Ring* (London: Heinemann, 1961), pp. 263–4.
[†] Anon., 'Why I Wrote "The Worm and the Ring" – Anthony Burgess', *Banbury Guardian*, 16 August 1962, p. 3.
[‡] James Michie to author, 15 November 2000.
[§] There is no reason from a legal point of view why Burgess's 1961 version should not now be republished, since Gwendoline Bustin died in 1974.

Heinemann had had a bad decade with several other incidences of libel and obscenity, hence the swift and expensive out of court settlement. James Michie remembers:

> In the 1950s a man called Walter Baxter published a book called *The Image and the Search*, which had a homosexual theme, and Alexander Frere [the chairman of Heinemann] had to go to court. It shook him considerably. That's not libel, but it did contribute to nervousness on Frere's part. And then *Lolita* came in and Frere didn't want to touch it because he'd got his fingers burnt with Walter Baxter.
>
> I can remember another libel case – a book about D. H. Lawrence, *The Intelligent Heart*, by a man called Harry T. Moore. He said that Lawrence had slept with some English aristocrat. And she wrote in, threatening libel. I offered to write back saying, 'Come on, be a sport. Does anybody care?' I wrote this letter which was approved of by [Harold] Rubinstein, who was our libel lawyer, and it succeeded. I was rather proud of that.
>
> Then Michael Campbell [i.e. the Honourable Michael Mussen] wrote a novel and it was just about to come out when he said, 'I forgot to tell you. The main character is a portrait of my aunt.' I said, 'Good God. Why didn't you say so before?' So I said, 'Get a taxi. Go to Heathrow. Fly to Dublin. Get her to read it in 48 hours and get her to sign something saying that she sees the humour of it.' He went off looking absolutely ashen-faced, because she was quite a dragon as portrayed in the book. And he came back with the letter. Otherwise we'd have had to pulp five thousand copies.*

Yet Burgess's frequent protests about the timidity of his publishers (which may be found in his journalism, in both volumes of autobiography, and in his long *Encyclopædia Britannica* article on

* James Michie to author. For more detail on the Walter Baxter obscenity trial, see John St John, *William Heinemann: A Century of Publishing 1890–1990* (London: Heinemann, 1990), pp. 405–12.

'The Novel') were rooted in his ignorance of the punitive damages and further bad publicity that Heinemann would have risked if the *Worm and the Ring* case had gone to court.* Michie believes that such innocence is characteristic of the generation of novelists to which Burgess belonged: 'Ask any author if they based a character on X or Y or Z, and they'll say no, because they based their character on X *and* Y *and* Z. They think they've made a mélange which is impenetrable, but they haven't. They put in something like a withered hand which gives the whole show away.'

Burgess devoted much of the second half of 1962 to a lucrative sub-literary endeavour, 'London and the CLRP: A Centennial Tribute to the City of London Real Property Company Ltd, 1864–1964'. It was commissioned for £3,000 by an agency which specialized in the production of such volumes. Lynne brought her training in economics to bear on the project, and redacted many of the crucial documents, which Burgess assembled into a lively historical narrative. Diana and Meir Gillon carried out additional research in the CLRP's files. Most company histories lack the excitements associated with novels or journalism, but in Burgess's hands the City of London Real Property Company comes to life in unexpected ways. The chapter dealing with the Second World War draws on Burgess's first-hand memories of the Blitz, and he connects the destruction of large sections of the city by Nazi bombs with the Great Fire of 1666:

> The City was now being seriously hit. It was then that the habit of sleeping in Underground stations began – a habit that the Government had no wish to encourage, for it was believed that a troglodyte mentality might develop: Londoners might take to these dens, setts and warrens permanently, never wanting to come up again. The feeling of security that came from going

---

* Burgess, 'The Novel' in *New Encyclopædia Britannica*, 15th edition, vol. 13 (Chicago: Encyclopædia Britannica, 1974), pp. 276–98. The unedited 100-page typescript of Burgess's article is in the archive of the International Anthony Burgess Foundation in Manchester.

underground was often quite illusory. Many of the tubes were
insufficiently deep for real safety, but the psychology of the
ostrich was hard to break. It was this kind of thinking that led
to the crowding of the ill-fated Café de Paris: it seemed safe
because it was under the ground, but all that lay above it was
its own roof and that of the Rialto Cinema.*

He had often visited the Café de Paris during the war, and a number
of his friends had died there when it was bombed. There are fictional
interludes, too, such as when he imagines the life of a typical City
clerk before the war, and reconstructs his journey to work. Even
when engaged in hackwork, Burgess finds it hard to write a dull
sentence. This is probably why the City of London Real Property
Company rejected the typescript when Burgess submitted it to them
in October 1962. The officers of the company judged it to be 'too
literary'.

Burgess was in hot water again in 1963, when *Inside Mr
Enderby* was published (on 16 April, in an edition of 2,500 copies).
This book, written three years earlier, was the second of his 'Joseph
Kell' novels, of which *One Hand Clapping* had been the first. John
Wilson had adopted this second *nom de plume* at the suggestion of
James Michie, who wanted to disguise the fact that 'Anthony
Burgess' had written six novels between 1959 and 1961. Michie was
worried that reviewers might accuse Burgess of writing too quickly
or carelessly.† Although few of the book's reviewers were aware
that Burgess was behind *Inside Mr Enderby*, they nevertheless

---

* Burgess, 'London and CLRP' (unpublished typescript), pp. 73–4.
† It was a source of regret to Burgess that Kell's novels sold badly, and he killed
him off in 1968 when he composed the dust-jacket copy for *Enderby Outside*:
'Before he died, Joseph Kell bequeathed to Anthony Burgess not merely his
copyrights and royalties, but also his identity. His dying wish was that Mr Burgess
should conclude the story about Enderby, the poet, already half-told in *Inside Mr
Enderby* [. . .] Mr Burgess's talent is revealed, on the evidence of this sequel, as not
inferior to that of the late Joseph Kell.'

recognized it as an important comic novel. David Lodge wrote in the *Spectator*:

> The eponymous hero is a middle-aged poet of distinction. The author convinces us of the distinction not only through the quality of his casual observation ('A lone midget cauliflower swam like a doll's brain in dense pickle') but through poems which are liberally quoted and very attractive [. . .] A sad story, but from first page to last it is absurdly, outrageously funny.*

In the *Listener*, Jocelyn Brooke said:

> Mr Kell writes with a sustained poetic brilliance which strikes me as quite masterly. His prose is subtle and allusive yet muscular, and his command of language never flags. In most contemporary writing the pattern of the syntax is more or less predictable: given the first half of the sentence, one can guess, approximately, how it will end [. . .] Mr Kell, however, is constantly springing syntactical surprises: the expected phrase suddenly modulates, as it were, into another key, or is varied by some wayward *appoggiatura* or adroit syncopation.†

This review speaks perceptively about the excitements of reading Mr Kell, and 'JBWABJK' (as he called himself in a letter to Julian Mitchell) must have been pleased by the musical analogy with which Brooke concludes his piece.

Exploiting his pseudonymous publication, Burgess wrote his own review of *Inside Mr Enderby* for the *Yorkshire Post*. According to his own version of events, he had forewarned Kenneth Young, his editor in Leeds, that the novel was about to appear. When a copy arrived in the post, he decided that Young was secretly asking him to review his own book as a joke, but without wanting to make the request directly. The prank backfired catastrophically when news of the deception leaked out, and Young appeared on Granada television's news programme to sack Burgess from his lucrative

* David Lodge, 'Home Run', *Spectator*, 10 May 1963, pp. 6038–11.
† Jocelyn Brooke, 'New Novels', *Listener*, 25 April 1963, p. 723.

reviewing job. The following week, the *Yorkshire Post* printed an apology to its readers, in which Burgess was sourly denounced: 'It now appears that Joseph Kell is none other than Anthony Burgess [. . .] We apologize to those readers who may have been under the impression, as we were, that they were being given a disinterested appreciation of the novel.'* In his defence, Burgess pointed out that Sir Walter Scott had pulled a similar stunt with the first volume of *Waverley*, and that as the author of *Inside Mr Enderby* he knew its flaws better than anyone, and hadn't been shy about cataloguing them. The story of Burgess having reviewed his own book was the stuff of easy journalistic copy. Almost immediately, it entered the 'shithead factfile' on Burgess (to borrow Martin Amis's phrase), which is to say that it was repeated in most of the subsequent newspaper profiles and in all of the obituaries published in November 1993.

However, *Inside Mr Enderby* was merely one of eight novels discussed in Burgess's fiction round-up of 16 May 1963, the others being *The Natural* by Bernard Malamud, *A Penny for the Guy* by Teo Savory, *Travelling People* by B. S. Johnson, *The Unconquered Son* by Ralph Dulin, *The Glass-Blowers* by Daphne du Maurier, *Daughter of the House* by Evelyn Ames and *Wolf Willow* by Wallace Stegner. With characteristic generosity and enthusiasm, Burgess described Malamud as 'a ferocious literary talent', claimed that Savory was 'one of this year's undoubted originals', and said that Johnson's first novel is 'original [. . .] in the way that *Tristram Shandy* and *Ulysses* are original'.† He adopted a more ambivalent tone in his assessment of Joseph Kell:

> Joseph Kell's first novel, *One Hand Clapping*, was a quiet and cunning female monologue that fell from the presses almost unnoticed. One Australian periodical acclaimed its virtues in a two-page review that, giving a thorough synopsis of the plot, must have made purchase of the book seem supererogatory. For

---

* Anon., 'Burgess and – Kell', *Yorkshire Post*, 20 May 1963, p. 6.
† Burgess, 'Poetry For a Tiny Room', *Yorkshire Post*, 16 May 1963, p. 4.

the rest, reviewers had other things to think about. That little book now thinly stalks the bookstalls as a paperback, its bright eyes quietly watching the reception of its successor.

Whatever readers may think of the content of *Inside Mr Enderby*, they are hardly likely to ignore the cover. This shows a lavatory seat (wood, not plastic) entwined with ivy. It is Mr Enderby's lavatory seat, wherefrom he blasts his poetry at the world. (Mr Eliot said recently – and in the *Yorkshire Post*, too – that poetry is a lavatorial or purgative art.)

If the world takes no notice, Mr Enderby will not worry. He has rejected the world; he has retreated into the smallest room in the house; there, scratching bared knees, he writes the verse that his Muse dictates to him.

But the world will not leave him alone altogether. It drags him out of his lavatory to receive a poetry prize and a proposal of marriage from Vesta Bainbridge, a *chic* vision from a woman's magazine. Soon, Enderby is on his honeymoon in Rome.

This eternal city is the antithesis of the toilet: here is the Church, here is the State, here, in lapidary form well-preserved, is the meanest history known to man. Here, too, is treachery, for Rawcliffe, a jealous fellow-poet, has stolen a poetic plot from Enderby and persuaded Cinecitta to turn it into a bosomy horror-film. Enderby, appalled, flees.

But his Muse flees also. He can no longer write. He attempts – unhandily, as with everything except his craft – a suicide which the State tut-tuts over. He is turned into a useful citizen, normal and unpoetic. There is a middle way between greatest Rome and the smallest room – the way of the decent job and the decent life. Enderby is cured.

This is, in many ways, a dirty book. It is full of bowel-blasts and flatulent borborygms, emetic meals ('thin but over-savoury stews,' Enderby calls them) and halitosis. It may well make some people sick, and those of my readers with tender stomachs are advised to let it alone.

It turns sex, religion, the State into a series of laughing-stocks. The book itself is a laughing-stock.

> And yet and yet and yet. How thin and under-savoury every-
> thing seems after Enderby's gross richness.

Did anyone think that this was a selling review? Not even
Kenneth Young could have accused Burgess of abusing his position
to puff his own goods. But the other crucial piece in the puzzle is
Peter Green's review of *Inside Mr Enderby*, which was the first to
unmask Burgess as the novel's true author. This appeared in the
Daily Telegraph on 19 April 1963 – nearly a month before Burgess's
review was published in the *Yorkshire Post*. It is likely that Kenneth
Young would have seen Green's piece in the books pages of the
Telegraph, because Young was also a regular *Telegraph* contributor
(and had reviewed *The Right to an Answer* for the same paper in
1960). Peter Green suggests that Young set the whole thing up
because he was looking for an excuse to get rid of Burgess, and that
Burgess was the innocent party in someone else's Byzantine game of
literary politics. Although latterly he became fond of detecting
conspiracies against him where none existed, on this occasion he
had good cause to feel aggrieved. Undeterred, he increased his rate
of production of book reviews for other publications. But sales of
Inside Mr Enderby were slow (950 copies of the first edition were
still in the warehouse in 1967) and Burgess cursed his editors at
'William Hangman' for having talked him into adopting a second
nom de plume.

As his reputation and notoriety grew, Burgess often found
himself in the company of readers and fellow writers when he was
invited to book-launches, public debates, parties at the BBC, and
formal dinners in London, Leeds, Wakefield and Manchester. In
September 1961 he went on a lecture tour of public libraries and
literary societies in the north of England. While lecturing in West
Yorkshire, he stayed with George Patrick Dwyer, 'a kind of stepcousin', who had been ordained as the Bishop of Leeds in 1957 (in
a letter to Agnes and Jack Tollitt, Burgess said that Leeds, though
presumably not the Bishop's Palace, reminded him of Leningrad).
Bishop Dwyer was promoted to the rank of Archbishop of Birming-

ham in 1965, and he remained in the city until his death in 1987. As a student in Rome, he had written a doctoral thesis on the problem of evil in Charles Baudelaire's poetry, and his interest in literature meant that, of all the Manchester Dwyers, his company was the most congenial as far as Burgess was concerned. When the *Independent* asked Burgess to name his hero in 1989, he nominated Archbishop Dwyer ('a Roman Catholic prelate in the Rabelaisian tradition'). 'George always understood precisely what my novels were about,' he wrote. 'He knew all about evil, and not just as the poetic theme of Baudelaire [. . .] George knew that the good-evil dichotomy was the real thing and the right-wrong one a mere expedient sham [. . .] He left me to struggle with my soul in my own way, knowing that my intellectual engine was in order; what it lacked was the fuel of conviction.'*

Gore Vidal remembers meeting Burgess and Lynne at a party organized by Heinemann to launch his novel *Julian*, a Book Society Choice, in October 1964. As Vidal recollects the encounter, 'He was tall, pale, eyes narrowed from cigarette smoke of his own making [. . .]; she was small, round faced, somewhat bloated.'† At fortissimo volume, and in an accent which he found difficult to comprehend, Lynne accosted Vidal with the information that he was too young to have been honoured by the Book Society, who had previously selected *Devil of a State* as their book of the month in October 1961, when Burgess was forty-four. Vidal, who was a mere thirty-nine years old, antagonized her further by voicing his suspicion that the Book Society was a collection of 'aged flappers reciting Dorothy Richardson over sugary tea'. 'I have written more novels than Mr Burgess,' he declared, 'and over a greater length of time.' Rapid

* 'My Hero: Anthony Burgess on George Patrick O'Dwyer' [sic], *Independent Magazine*, 11 March 1989, p. 70.
† Gore Vidal, 'Obsession', *New York Review of Books*, 7 May 1987, pp. 3–8. For Burgess on Vidal, see 'Patriotic Gore' (review of *Lincoln*) in *Homage to Qwert Yuiop*, pp. 522–5; and *Ninety-Nine Novels: The Best in English Since 1939* (London: Allison & Busby, 1984), p. 129.

calculations were made over a greasy finger-buffet of sausage rolls. 'Anyway,' said Burgess, 'I'm actually a composer.' Vidal, having no symphonies of his own to add to the tally, thought this was an excellent come-back. 'I ceded the high ground to him. Lynne did not. She rounded on him: you are *not* a composer. Pussy-whipped, he winced and muttered.'

Kingsley Amis provides further glimpses of Burgess and Lynne. She appears fleetingly in his novel about the 1960s, *Difficulties with Girls*, as a collapsed writer's wife who is seen at a party, legless and 'trying to heave herself upright from a sofa by hauling at a curtain'.* Burgess seems not to have recognized this caricature when he reviewed *Difficulties with Girls* for the *Observer* in 1988. 'The future,' he wrote, 'will learn about the state of English today not from the linguists but from the novels of Amis. To say nothing of the customs and morality that go along with the language.' Amis's other memories of Lynne follow the same pattern. He remembers that at another party Burgess had to placate her when she tried to start a fight with Terence Kilmartin, the literary editor of the *Observer* (and also, therefore, one of the people who was helping to pay for her weekly crate of Gordon's gin). When the Amises and the Wilsons met for lunch at the Café Royal in London, she was 'a bit pissed and rather spoiling an occasion [Burgess] had clearly very much wanted to be a success'.† Martin Amis, too, remembers Burgess and Lynne visiting his parents at home when he was a boy: 'I have a faint image of a jovial, talkative man, consistently out-decibelled by his wife'.‡ Shortly after the Café Royal meeting,

---

* Kingsley Amis, *Difficulties with Girls* (London: Penguin, 1989), p. 230.
† Kingsley Amis, 'Anthony Burgess' in *Memoirs* (London: Hutchinson, 1991), pp. 274–8. For Burgess on Amis, see 'The Great Gangster' (review of *The Anti-Death League*), *Listener*, 17 March 1966, p. 401; 'Amis and Enemies' (review of *I Want It Now*), *Listener*, 10 October 1968, p. 475; *The Novel Now*, pp. 143–7; and 'Misogyny?' (review of *Stanley and the Women*) in *Homage to Qwert Yuiop*, pp. 514–16.
‡ Martin Amis, *Visiting Mrs Nabokov and Other Excursions* (London: Jonathan Cape, 1993), p. 244.

Kingsley Amis and Burgess went out drinking, minus wives, at a pub in Kilburn or Hammersmith. According to Amis's version of the story,

> He proved, though amiable enough, to have little in the way of small-talk. It was as though he was so far above the hurly-burly that he habitually occupied some private stratosphere. But he did tell me something about his wife's rape by some GIs during the war, and went on to say that he was on the look-out for a sword-stick – he had with him a stout but conventional walk-ing-stick – from which if ever menaced by ruffians he would draw and brandish the blade, shouting (and he shouted in illustration), 'Fuck off, I've got cancer!' Yes, I thought uneasily, seeing the look in his eye, you bloody mean it.

Burgess's mission to find a sword-stick had certainly been accomplished by March 1966, when he visited the United States on a lecture tour. He withdrew his weapon from its cherrywood case and waved it at a gang of youths who threatened to rob him in New York. The would-be robbers fled. Burgess translated the experience into an elaborate fantasy of an American woman being seduced by an English swordsman ('At least it was unsheathed, at last it was unsheathed') in a long poem, 'The Sword', which he published later that year in the *Transatlantic Review*.* This theme continues through his works of the 1970s and 1980s: numerous translations of Edmond Rostand's swashbuckling play *Cyrano de Bergerac*; *The Clockwork Testament*, in which Enderby prevents a rape by flour-ishing his sword-stick and drawing blood on the New York subway; the *Attila* filmscript, where the conquering Hun fences energetically (like Marlowe's Tamburlaine before him) with words and sabres; and *Any Old Iron*, in which the principal characters ultimately rediscover the sword Excalibur and wonder how its legendary

---

* 'The Sword', *Transatlantic Review*, vol. 21 (Summer 1966), pp. 30–32; reprinted in Burgess, *Revolutionary Sonnets and Other Poems*, ed. by Kevin Jackson (Man-chester: Carcanet, 2002), pp. 32–3.

powers should be put to use in the modern world.* In each of these works, Burgess's swords and sword-carriers stand for truth, integrity and high rhetoric – 'sword' being an anagram of 'words', as Burgess, who was fascinated by swords, words and anagrams, must have realized. Armed with their collection of blades, Enderby and the others ask to be understood as versions of Cyrano (who is Burgess's archetype of the hyper-literate soldier-poet), cultivated warriors unafraid to raise their swords against the barbarian armies of yobs and philistines. The idea finds its strongest expression in *A Clockwork Orange*, where Mr F. Alexander writes: 'Whoever heard of a clockwork orange? [. . .] The attempt to impose upon man, a creature of growth and capable of sweetness, to ooze juicily at the last round the bearded lips of God, to attempt to impose, I say, laws and conditions appropriate to a mechanical creation, against this I raise my sword-pen.'†

*

To a limited extent Lynne was Burgess's collaborator in his literary work, as the legal partnership agreement they drew up in 1964 acknowledges. She carried out much of the primary research for his London book, and provided advice on couture for the female characters in his novels. Making use of her degree-level French, she also worked with him in translating three novels into English: *The Olive-Trees of Justice* by Jean Pelegri (1962), *The New Aristocrats* by Michel de Saint-Pierre (1962), and *The Man Who Robbed Poor Boxes* by Jean Servin (1965). Claiming full credit for what was not wholly his work, Burgess said of these translations in 1985:

> I have done three French novels for money, such as it was, and only one was worth doing – Servin's *Deo Gratias*, which became *The Man Who Robbed Poor Boxes* [. . .] Another

---

* Stanley Kubrick equips Alex with a sword-stick in the film version of *A Clockwork Orange*, although no such object appears in the book. Perhaps Burgess had mentioned the sword-stick in his conversations with the director?
† Burgess, *A Clockwork Orange* (London: Heinemann, 1962), pp. 21–2.

novel, whose name I refuse to remember, was so indifferent in
the original that I tried to transform as well as translate, and I
gained wry satisfaction from seeing my own felicities ascribed
by reviewers to the original author and praised as the sort of
thing English novelists could not do.*

We can date the beginning of Lynne's terminal decline from the last
of these collaborations in 1965. Peter Green tells the story of an
overnight visit to the house in Etchingham, which developed in
unexpected and alarming ways.

> Lynne was not exactly your attractive young thing. She was a
> bit witchlike, if you can imagine an overweight witch. I had
> gone to bed and had passed out like a light, only to be woken
> at three in the morning by the realization that I had my hostess
> on top of me, *with intent* [. . .] So I figured the only thing to do
> was to leave her to it, and eventually – probably – she would
> go away. And in fact both of these things happened. And next
> morning [. . .] everybody was exactly the same as always at
> breakfast. And I thought to myself: Does John know that she
> gets up to these games? And I think probably yes. He had this
> enormous weight of guilt about her. And since I had this feeling
> that sex didn't interest him all that much, when I read all this
> stuff in the first volume of his autobiography about his sexual
> exploits, I thought: I wonder if he invented them partly to give
> himself a good reason for excusing Lynne.†

The artist Edward Pagram, who provided the illustrations for
A Vision of Battlements and *The Eve of Saint Venus*, was another
overnight guest at Applegarth in the mid-1960s. When he arrived at
the house, Lynne scolded him for having forgotten to bring her any
flowers. Like Peter Green, he was worried that she would try to
assault him during the night. Pagram writes: 'After much drinking

* Quoted in Paul Boytinck, *Anthony Burgess: An Annotated Bibliography and
Reference Guide* (New York: Garland, 1985), p. 152.
† Interview with Peter Green, summer 1998 (transcript in Angers University
Library).

[. . .] I went up to bed, incapable and exhausted, convinced that I would be molested in some way and looking for something to protect myself. I found a small statuette, which I slept with under the covers.'* Pagram is one of the few witnesses who took the trouble to talk to Lynne at length, and his memories of their conversations are illuminating: 'Lynne Burgess told me on various occasions that John felt he had a great book within him that would one day emerge. She said he had a dread of getting lung cancer (although they both continued to smoke). She told me of an Italian teacher who she feared was after her husband.' His abiding memory of her is as 'a warm, bubbly and friendly woman who ideally should have been somebody's mum'. Deborah Rogers, who became Burgess's literary agent in the mid-1960s – working at first for Peter Janson-Smith, and then at her own newly established agency – remembers Lynne as difficult and ill-tempered. 'She was a bit angry and aggrieved,' says Rogers.

> The only times I met her she was usually somewhat the worse for the bottle. You'd go round for a drink. They were living in this grotty little house, and the living-room was dominated by the bar. She would sit on her bar-stool, but she'd always started falling off by about six in the evening. And then she'd get quite abusive. You'd occasionally see her at a party with him, but she didn't come out much [. . .] It was very difficult to work out what she had become, and what she had been originally.†

Burgess writes in his memoirs that, towards the end of her life, Lynne retreated into her own past, and was only really happy when she was remembering the minor triumphs of her childhood in Wales, where she'd been the head girl at Bedwellty Grammar School and captain of the hockey team. According to Lynne's niece, her life had started to go wrong when Burgess had sentenced her to three years as a colonial housewife in Malaya. Her letters give very little away.

---

* Edward Pagram to author, 24 April 2003.
† Deborah Rogers to author, 17 February 1997.

On paper, she is usually on her best behaviour, thanking friends and family rather stiffly for sending presents. These letters betray no signs of the fierce, unpredictable Mrs Wilson who is commemorated in other people's anecdotes. Yet Burgess had never been an easy man to be married to. In Banbury, she had grown tired of listening to his boasting about the quality of his music (she could never stand to be in the room when he was performing it, and would feign a coughing fit to excuse herself) and his monologues about the bone-headedness of radio people who refused to broadcast his amateurish compositions. Later on, in Etchingham and Chiswick, one of the reasons why he spent so many hours in the study was that writing was a bomb-proof way of avoiding her company. The American writer Leslie Fiedler, who knew Burgess and both his wives, comments: 'I don't think he had a real talent for marriage, but he kept trying.'*

Burgess himself conceded in 1990 that he had been married to Lynne for twenty-six years without particularly liking her. He suspected that one of the reasons why their marriage had come to resemble a civil war was that he had been suffering from thwarted paternity-lust. When he was asked, in 1966, to write his entry for *Who's Who*, he listed 'wife' as one of his hobbies. He was attacked for this, and tried to explain himself in the pages of *Vogue*, where he argued that the most important aspect of a marriage was the evolution of a private language, a system of codes and signals which would be incomprehensible to outsiders: 'I think I have a vocation for gaining the maximal fulfillment, which means communicative fulfillment, which means even a kind of spiritual fulfillment, out of living with a particular woman. But, frightened of the big words, and also incurably facetious, I have to talk of my wife as a hobby.'†
Later on, when he was raging against the custom of multiple divorce in America ('It stems from the desperate fear of fornication'), he spoke about the difficulties of his first marriage and said that he had

---

* Leslie Fiedler, interview with Tess Crebbin, 15 October 1996.
† Burgess, 'Private Dialect of Husbands and Wives', *Vogue*, June 1968, pp. 118–19.

never seriously considered leaving Lynne, even though they had both been carrying on affairs since 1942:

> If I could manage to sustain marriage for 26 years with a person who wasn't necessarily the best person for me in the world, I don't see why the hell other people can't [. . .] I mean, if you fornicate quietly, it's just something quite transient. It's nothing to do with the major issue of marriage, which is about an immense complex intimacy with another person; sex is neither here nor there.*

He would not let go of the traditional Catholic notion of marriage as an indissoluble sacrament. If a couple were married in the sight of God and the Church, what went on in divorce courts had no bearing on the matter. This attitude is characteristic of Burgess's Catholicism: although he called himself an unbeliever, he still felt constrained by the rules he claimed to have abandoned in his teens. His intellect had rejected a system of faith on rational grounds, but he was still very much connected to it emotionally. Beyond this, it is possible – as another friend, D. J. Enright, has suggested – that he secretly relished the guilt, misery and embarrassment which were inevitable consequences of being married to Lynne. Quoting T. S. Eliot, Enright says of Burgess: 'He could not escape suffering and could not transcend it, so he *attracted* pain to himself.'†

*

Burgess's decision to write a novel about Shakespeare's love-life, to be narrated wholly in mock-Elizabethan English, was motivated by an urge to celebrate the 400th anniversary of the playwright's birth on 23 April 1964. The novel's title – *Nothing Like the Sun*, which refers to the sonnet beginning 'My mistress's eyes are nothing like the sun' – is intended as a warning. It implies, with a fair degree of

* C. Robert Jennings, 'Playboy Interview: Anthony Burgess', p. 78.
† D. J. Enright, *Interplay: A Kind of Commonplace Book* (Oxford: Oxford University Press, 1995), p. 233.

humility, that the fakeries of Burgess's language are a dim candle in comparison with the brighter Shakespearean sun, and that reading a fictionalized biography is a poor substitute for immersing ourselves in the deeper waters of the original plays and poems. Work on this novel began while the snow was still on the ground in January 1963, and Burgess struggled with it intermittently for ten-and-a-half months. Not long after it had been published, he wrote that the process of composition had been 'almost haemorrhoidally agonizing'. He estimated that this book, which was revised more extensively than anything he had written before, 'must have consumed yards of paper and thousands of cigarettes' (more than 25,000, assuming that he was smoking his usual eighty per day for a period of 315 days).* Every page was typed and retyped at least six times. The opening chapter went through so many drafts that he despaired of ever finishing, and a letter to his editor at Heinemann indicates that he was still revising the first section as he approached the end of the book.† His early preparations had included compiling a chronological table of historical events, annotating his edition of Shakespeare's plays, and filling a notebook with information about 'the *morbus Gallicus* – the French pox, or syphilis'.‡

As with *A Clockwork Orange*, Burgess's speculative account of Shakespeare's life in *Nothing Like the Sun* is largely a pretext for exhibiting his own enormous talents as a manipulator of language.

---

* He gives a detailed account of the composition of *Nothing Like the Sun* in 'Genesis and Headache', an essay collected in *Afterwords: Novelists on Their Novels*, ed. by Thomas McCormack (New York: Harper & Row, 1969), pp. 28–47.

† Shortly after Burgess recorded this chapter for *Before Publication* on Radio 3, he wrote to Julian Mitchell: 'My BBC talk was about my Shakespeare novel, which I fear that a lot of people will regard as pisstaking, him being a great bard and all' (letter to Julian Mitchell, no date but early 1964). The programme was recorded on 31 October 1963 and broadcast on 2 February 1964.

‡ 'Genesis and Headache', p. 31. For Burgess on syphilis, see also 'A Pox on Literature' (review of Roger L. Williams, *The Horror of Life*) in *Homage to Qwert Yuiop*, pp. 476–8.

He was justifiably proud of the fact that – with one significant exception – the novel's text includes no word that would have been unfamiliar to Shakespeare, and to this end he carried out research into the vocabulary of the glove-maker's trade that Shakespeare's father had pursued in Stratford ('The cutting of the trank, the slitting of the slim fourchettes, the bitty gussets, the thumb, the slit binding').* The one deliberate anachronism is the word 'spurgeoning', which is an affectionate reference to the literary critic Caroline Spurgeon, author of *Shakespeare's Imagery and What It Tells Us* (1935), whose book was known to Burgess from his undergraduate days in Manchester. He paid tribute to her with: 'He kicked in youth's peevishness at the turves of the Avon's left bank, marking with storing-up spaniel's eye the spurgeoning of the black-eddy under the Clopton Bridge.'†

Burgess's novel takes its biographical arguments from a number of sources, some of them reliable but most of them clearly not. Like many of the literary detectives who had gone before him, he began by looking at internal evidence within Shakespeare's sonnets. There is no objective proof of the notion that Shakespeare was in love with a 'fair youth' (possibly 'Mr W. H.', who is said to be 'the onlie begetter of these ensuing sonnets' on the title-page of Thomas Thorpe's 1609 edition) and that he subsequently transferred his affections to an anonymous black or dark-skinned woman. The American critic Samuel Schoenbaum, who wrote about Burgess's Shakespeare, and whose books on Shakespeare were well known to Burgess, issued a valuable warning to would-be biographers: 'Because Shakespeare is, of all, the artist about whom curiosity is most intense, it is not surprising that many in search of revelations would delve into his works and find what is not there.'‡ But

---

* Burgess, *Nothing Like the Sun: A Story of Shakespeare's Love-Life* (London: Heinemann, 1964), p. 8.
† Ibid., p. 3.
‡ S. Schoenbaum, *Shakespeare's Lives* (2nd edition, Oxford: Clarendon Press, 1991), p. 36

Burgess was not delayed for long by scholarly considerations such as these. Shakespeare's erotic life, he maintained, demanded 'to be probed with the novelist's instruments', even if only in a speculative way.* Even so, he acknowledged in a 1964 radio interview with Julian Mitchell that, like any other Shakespearean biographer, he had spent most of his time writing in the dark:

> The impression I got as I worked, delved deeper into the character of Shakespeare, was that there was nothing there. It became rather frightening. I remembered the warning that is inscribed on Shakespeare's grave: 'GOOD FRIEND FOR IESVS SAKE FORBEARE / TO DIGG THE DVST ENCLOASED HEARE'. I thought a curse was coming through, but [. . .] the curse would be the discovery that there was nothing there.†

His second source of Shakespearean information was even less reliable than the love affairs described in the sonnets. In the 'Scylla and Charybdis' chapter of James Joyce's *Ulysses*, Burgess found the rumour, propounded by Stephen Dedalus in the reading room of the National Library in Dublin, that Shakespeare's wife, Anne Hathaway, had had sex with his brother, Richard.‡ The second section of *Nothing Like the Sun* develops Joyce's notion at length, and Burgess borrows several of Joyce's fictional devices – stream of consciousness, a journal, a mock-sermon, a discovered manuscript, verse disguised as prose, and *Finnegans Wake* dream-discourse – in order to make his case. Harold Bloom, who considers *Nothing Like the Sun* to be 'the only successful novel ever written about Shakespeare', comments: 'I long ago jumbled the library scene [from *Ulysses*] and Burgess's imaginings together in my mind and am startled always,

---

* 'Genesis and Headache', p. 30.
† *The World of Books* (interview with Julian Mitchell), BBC Home Service, 25 April 1964.
‡ See James Joyce, *Ulysses* (London: Bodley Head, 1960), pp. 235–80. For Burgess's detailed commentary on this chapter, see *Here Comes Everybody: An Introduction to James Joyce for the Ordinary Reader* (London: Faber, 1965), pp. 126–32.

rereading Joyce, not to find much that I wrongly expect to find, which is gorgeously present in Burgess.'*

Even as he was drafting the novel, Burgess was aware of the likelihood that scholars would disapprove of his fictional Shakespeare (who is always referred to in the text as 'WS'). Anxious to forestall hostile criticism, he decided to place the novel's main narrative within an ironic frame. We are told on the opening page that what follows is 'Mr Burgess's farewell lecture to his *special* students (Misses Alabaster, Ang Poh Gaik, Bacchus, Brochocki, Ishak, Kinipple, Shackles, Spottiswode and Messrs Ahmad bin Harun, Anguish, Balwant Singh, Lillington, Lympe, Raja Mokhtar, Prindable, Rosario, Spittal, Whitelegge etc) who complained that Shakespeare had nothing to give to the East'. This fictional 'Mr Burgess' thanks his students for their gift of three bottles of *samsu* or powerful rice-wine, which he is evidently drinking as he delivers the lecture: 'Another little drop. Delicious. Well, then'; 'I am near the end of the wine, sweet lords and lovely ladies.'† Any factual errors or passages of crazed speculation can therefore be attributed not to the author but to the intoxicated character who happens to share his name. This narrative device gives Burgess the freedom to move his story in any direction he chooses without having to worry

---

* Harold Bloom, *The Western Canon: The Books and School of the Ages* (London: Macmillan, 1995), p. 416. Apart from Joyce's novel, two other critical works, Frank Harris's *The Man Shakespeare and His Tragic Life-Story* (1909) and Ivor Brown's *Shakespeare* (1949), were also influential in shaping Burgess's thinking on matters of biography. For Burgess on Frank Harris, see his review of Harris's memoir, *My Life and Loves*, in *Listener*, 12 November 1964, p. 769: 'Even today there is a fair section of the submerged reading public that thinks highly of *The Man Shakespeare* and takes it as fine scholarship [. . .] He can still be an oracle to the half-educated. Perhaps sex has something to do with it: a man with such enormous phallic appetites can only be divine or diabolic; we listen to him as to the voice of the life-force. [. . .] This book is precisely what you think it is going to be – an enormously long parade (nearly a thousand dense pages, five volumes in one) of egomaniacal opinions, most of which turn out to be right.'
† *Nothing Like the Sun*, pp. 38, 224.

about strict accuracy.* Like *The Doctor Is Sick*, or Nabokov's *Pale Fire* (which Burgess reviewed in the *Yorkshire Post* just two months before he began *Nothing Like the Sun*), the novel takes care to map out the borders of its fictional world.†

A page from Burgess's *Nothing Like the Sun* notebook shows us exactly how the novel looked in its skeletal form. These are his notes for the scene in which Shakespeare first encounters Fatimah, the brown-skinned Eastern temptress who in Burgess's version of the story is the Dark Lady of the Sonnets ('If hairs be wires, black wires grow on her head'). These reveal his early attempts at finding a satisfactory narrative idiom:

> Drake returned from circumnavigation 1581. Could bring back Malay girl (Philippines?). When WS meets her she is, say, 19 yrs old.

> Syphilis: Incubation: 4 weeks, then primary sore or chancre. After 2 months fever, loss of appetite, vague pains, faint red rash on chest, hair falls out (cf. Shakespeare portrait), sores, enlargement of lymphatic glands.

> Sample dialogue:
> 'Who is she?'
> 'She? One of the Queen's Glories. A heathen born, now a Christian. When Sir Francis Drake returned from round the world in '81 he brought her from the Indies, an orphan, her parents being killed by Sir Francis' own men.'

> Shakespeare appraised her wide nose, the big lips, the bare brown bosom that showed her, in the fashion, a virgin still. (This will not bloody do at all. *Far* too pedestrian.)

---

* Burgess admired Christopher Isherwood's habit of giving his own name to fictional characters in novels such as *Goodbye to Berlin*, *Lions and Shadows* and *Down There on a Visit*. See Burgess, 'Character Called Isherwood', *Yorkshire Post*, 8 March 1962, p. 4.
† Burgess, 'Nabokov Masquerade' (review of Vladimir Nabokov, *Pale Fire*), *Yorkshire Post*, 15 November 1962, p. 4.

The floor was littered with fallen chestnut-leaves, like over-fried fillets of fish.

The shadow of fern in the vase passed over his hand, giving it the look of a skin disease.

Their garden was verminous with fallen apples.*

He planned *Nothing Like the Sun* to have two long sections: part one (1577 to 1587), in which 'Mr Burgess' lectures on Shakespeare as an adolescent, reluctant husband, schoolmaster and incipient playwright; and part two (1592 to 1599), with Shakespeare as the Earl of Southampton's homosexual lover, the professional man of the London theatre, the seducer of the Malayan Dark Lady, the wealthy gentleman with a coat of arms (motto: 'Non Sans Droict'), the discoverer of his wife's adultery back in Stratford, the brothel-haunting syphilitic, and the melancholic ranter against lechery in *King Lear* and *Troilus and Cressida*. The novel's ten-page epilogue contains the terminal hallucinations of the dying writer, his brain having been softened by tertiary syphilis. Shakespeare's voice merges in the epilogue with that of 'Mr Burgess', who is by now heavily drunk on *samsu*, and the concluding page is written as a mock-catechism which imitates the penultimate 'Ithaca' chapter of Joyce's *Ulysses*:

> *What is your great crime, then?*
> Love, love, and it is always love. Not wisely but too. Fatimah. I will distribute copies of that sonnet after the lecture. You can never win, for love is both an image of eternal order and at the same time the rebel and destructive spirochaete. Let us have no nonsensical talk about merging and melting souls, though, binary suns, two spheres in a single orbit. There is the flesh and the flesh makes all. Literature is an epiphenomenon of the action of the flesh.†

---

* Quoted in 'Genesis and Headache', pp. 44–5.
† *Nothing Like the Sun*, p. 233.

Burgess commented on the novel's ambiguous ending: 'The dying brain cracks, but its last words are "My Lord." Whether this means Jesus Christ or the Earl of Southampton I am not prepared to say.'*

The writing of *Nothing Like the Sun* was to occupy Burgess until November 1963, although his work on it was interrupted by two visits to Tangier, weekly reviewing assignments for the *Yorkshire Post* and the *Listener*, and the swift production in the summer of a book on linguistics, *Language Made Plain*. Peter Green, to whom the first edition of this book was dedicated, comments:

> [It] struck me as a fairly low-level general introduction to the subject, but also reminded me of the old canard about linguists – that they can theorize in about twenty languages, none of which they really know. The thing that always struck me about the non-fiction works was how shaky John was on the grammar and syntax of any language I happened to know. On Joyce, on the other hand, he was superb: understood exactly what JJ was about [...] Their minds ran along virtually identical lines. Linguistically, both were inspired amateurs.†

On 20 July 1963 Burgess wrote to David Machin at Heinemann: 'The ghost of sweet Master Shakespeare rides heavy on me [...] This slowness is, I fear, unlike me.' Minor corrections were still being made by letter on 30 November. Early on, Burgess had toyed with the idea of publishing the first section as a self-standing novella and returning to the project later, but he feared that he would lack the courage to return to Shakespeare's life and eventual death if he abandoned the story halfway through. He pushed on, then, and wrote a series of energetic vignettes: the bubonic plague outbreak of 1592; the horrific execution of Roderigo Lopez; epic bouts of sex (Shakespeare's wife buggers him with a dildo in one memorable

---

* 'Genesis and Headache', p. 43.

† Peter Green to author, 13 December 2000. For Simeon Potter's review of *Language Made Plain*, which includes a long list of errors, see 'Preaching Polyglottism', *Times Literary Supplement*, 23 April 1964, p. 337.

episode); and the final descent of the goddess who whispers deathless poetry into the ear of WS. Burgess confided to Julian Mitchell that Shakespeare's Muse as she is presented in the novel is not the true goddess he believes her to be, but a manifestation of tertiary syphilis. As he wrote this chapter he was surely thinking back to the patients whose symptoms he had observed when he worked as a medical orderly on the GPI ward at Winwick Hospital during the Second World War.

Nothing Like the Sun was published on 20 April 1964 in an edition of 8,500 copies. Most of the reviewers recognized that it represented an ambitious change of direction in Burgess's writing. D. J. Enright wrote in the *New Statesman*:

> *Nothing Like the Sun* is a clever and tightly constructed book, reminiscent in its smaller and more sensational way of Mann's *Doctor Faustus*, full of the author's old verbal ingenuity (with something of Shakespeare's to boot), and likely to be one of the most remarkable (though ambiguous) celebrations of the Bard's quartercentenary – although what it celebrates is clearly something other than the Bard [. . .] Mr Burgess has set himself so awesome a task that it seems hardly proper to complain at all. Only a gifted word-boy could have managed an Elizabethan-style idiom which most of the time strikes one as simply good lively English.*

Eric Partridge, the lexicographer whose pioneering *Dictionary of Slang and Unconventional English* (1937) was much admired by Burgess, wrote in *Books and Bookmen* that *Nothing Like the Sun* was 'at once profound and engrossing, torrential in its surging narrative, molten in its emotional impact, magistral in its employment of a style rich, vigorous and deeply moving: a book that,

---

* D. J. Enright, 'Mr W.S.', *New Statesman*, 24 April 1964, pp. 642–4; reprinted as 'A Modern Disease: Anthony Burgess's Shakespeare' in Enright, *Man Is an Onion: Reviews and Essays* (London: Chatto & Windus, 1972), pp. 39–43, 40.

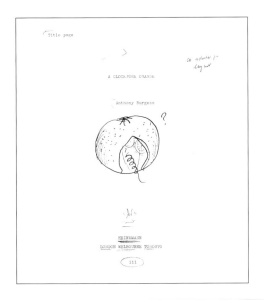

18. The title page from Burgess's 1961 typescript of *A Clockwork Orange*. (Copyright Liana Burgess)

19. Burgess's pen-and-ink sketch of Alex, the hero and narrator of *A Clockwork Orange*, from the 1961 typescript. (Copyright Liana Burgess)

some new torture for me, you bratchny?"

"It'll be your own torture," he said, serious. "I hope to God it'll torture you to madness."

And then, before he told me, I knew what it was. The old ptitsa who had all the kots and koshkas had passed on to a better world in one of the city hospitals. I'd cracked her a bit too hard, like. Well, well, that was everything. I thought of all those kots and koshkas mewing for moloko and getting none, not any more from their starry forella of a mistress. That was everything. I'd done the lot, now. And me still only fifteen.

60.

20. (*left*) Stanley Kubrick and Malcolm McDowell on the set of *A Clockwork Orange*. (From *Stanley Kubrick: A Life in Pictures*)

21. (*below*) 'A Crockwork Lemon': *Mad* magazine's parody of Kubrick's film, June 1973. (From *Mad About the Movies*)

22. (*right*) Filming *A Clockwork Orange*. Stanley Kubrick with camera, Malcolm McDowell with plaster phallus. (Kobal Collection)

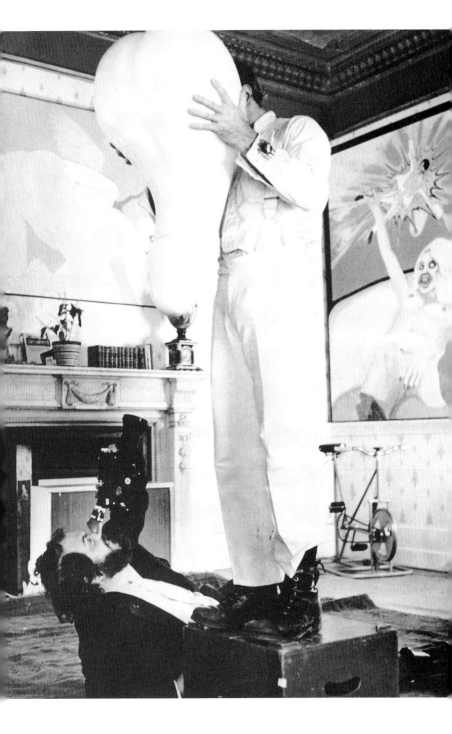

23. The last photograph of Lynne, taken at the Time/Life building on Bruton Street, London, 12 February 1968. (Collection of Ceridwen Berry)

24. (*left*) Burgess with his son Paolo Andrea – later known as Andrew Burgess Wilson. Piazza Santa Cecilia, Rome, early 1970s. (Liana Burgess/International Anthony Burgess Foundation)

Facing page

25. (*top left*) Burgess with his second wife, Liliana Macellari (the Contessa Pasi della Pergola), around the time of their marriage in 1968. (Liana Burgess/ International Anthony Burgess Foundation)

26. (*top right*) Burgess and Paolo Andrea. (Liana Burgess/International Anthony Burgess Foundation)

27. Liana and Paolo Andrea.
(Liana Burgess/International Anthony Burgess Foundation)

28. (*right*) Snapshot of Burgess in New York, early 1970s. (Liana Burgess)

29. (*left*) Burgess's self-caricature, first published in the *Paris Review* in 1973. (Copyright Liana Burgess)

Facing page

30. Burgess in playful mood with stuffed reptile, mid-1980s. (Magnum)

31. Milton Hebald's clay bust of Burgess, which appeared on the dust jackets of *Little Wilson and Big God* (1987) and *You've Had Your Time* (1990). Sculpted in Bracciano in the early 1970s, the bust is now at the International Anthony Burgess Foundation in Manchester. (Photograph by Milton Hebald)

32. Burgess as whisky priest. Caricature by William Rushton, from the *Independent* magazine, 11 March 1989. (Estate of William Rushton)

leaving us stunned and exhausted, also and more importantly leaves us wealthy'.*

The wealth of Burgess's responses to Shakespeare did not end with the publication of *Nothing Like the Sun*. Three years later, in the winter of 1967, he was approached by the actor William Conrad, who was then a producer at Warner Brothers/Seven Arts, to write a Hollywood musical based on Shakespeare's life, under the working title 'The Bawdy Bard'. The film was never made – it was shelved indefinitely after a reshuffle of senior management at the studio in 1970 – but Burgess got as far as writing a six-hour script and sketching out an overture and music for some of the songs. There was ambitious talk of casting Robert Stephens as Shakespeare, Maggie Smith as Anne Hathaway, David Hemmings as Christopher Marlowe, and James Mason as Philip Henslowe. An extract from this script, which remains the property of Warner Brothers, was published in *Show* magazine with a long commentary by Burgess. Ben Jonson's song, which he delivers after he has been branded on the thumb as punishment for stabbing a fellow playwright, is representative of the film as a whole:

> *Ale and Anacreon,*
> *Beer and Boethius,*
> *Sack and Sophocles, these*
> *Please my heart*
> *More than the farting littleness,*
> *Borborygmic brittleness,*
> *Jokes and japes*
> *Of the apes and jackanapes*
> *One sees*
> *Courting the great*

---

* Eric Partridge, 'Language at Work: Language at Play', *Books and Bookmen*, February 1976, p. 20. For Burgess on Partridge, see 'Slangfest', *Listener*, 2 March 1967, p. 299; 'Twixt Proverb and Quote', *Times Literary Supplement*, 26 August 1977, p. 1027; and 'Partridge in a Word Tree' in *Eric Partridge in His Own Words*, ed. by David Crystal (London: André Deutsch, 1980), pp. 26–30.

> *In court, on estate.*
> *Fleas!*
>
> *And women of course.* *

A number of Burgess's verbal signatures are here, particularly his ornate, archaic vocabulary and his fondness for internal rhymes ('apes' / 'jackanapes'). Yet it is difficult to imagine Peter Ustinov, the actor Burgess had in mind for the part of Ben Jonson, singing about 'Borborygmic brittleness' in a studio film intended to make money. One of the weaknesses of Burgess's lyrics, here and elsewhere, is that there are usually too many consonants and not enough open vowels. He was unpersuaded by the principle that, in the context of a Hollywood film, simplicity (or at least some words that could be sung) might be in order.

Burgess's 'Bawdy Bard' is substantially the same as the Shakespearean stage musical that Enderby writes in *Enderby's Dark Lady* (1984). In the novel, the actor who is supposed to be performing the part of WS is taken ill at the last moment, and, in the absence of an understudy, Enderby is persuaded to become the star of his own show. Naturally, he has already fallen in love with April Elgar, the black actress who plays the Dark Lady. Yet more is going on in this book than Burgess merely recycling a yellowing filmscript from his filing cabinet. *Enderby's Dark Lady* suggests identifications not just between Burgess and Enderby, as authors of the same Shakespearean musical, but also (more importantly) between Burgess/Enderby and Shakespeare. In the concluding section of the novel Enderby, wearing full Elizabethan costume, pauses to admire his reflection in the dressing room: 'Shakespeare looked at Enderby from the mirror and coldly nodded.'†

---

* Burgess, 'To Be Or Not To Be In Love With You', *Show: The Magazine of Film and the Arts*, January 1970, pp. 75–80.
† *Enderby's Dark Lady, or, No End to Enderby* (London: Hutchinson, 1984), p. 141. Enderby's performance as Shakespeare connects with one of Burgess's unpublished short stories, 'Double Saviour', in which 'Anthony Burgess' is called

In 1970 Jonathan Cape published Burgess's *Shakespeare*, a 250-page illustrated biography. 'I ought to be ashamed,' the author confessed not long before it came out, 'but I am doing it for the money.' Despite his hesitations, the book drew praise from Terry Eagleton, who wrote that it was 'raised above the usual standard of such productions by a bright, racy, neatly intelligent text which compensates for its occasional fancifulness and facetiousness by packing a good deal of out-of-the-way information into its prose'.* The picture research on the book was carried out by a bright and diligent editor named Yorke Crompton, who commented – with intelligence, tact, and immaculate copperplate handwriting – on Burgess's text, correcting a number of misquotations and factual errors. Further Shakespearean projects – literary, musical and dramatic – were to follow. A television series on Shakespeare's life was commissioned by ATV in 1973. Like 'The Bawdy Bard', this never went into production, but the scripts have recently come to light in the archive of the International Anthony Burgess Foundation in Manchester. *Love's Labour's Lost* provides both the melody and the text for Burgess's Symphony in C, first performed in Iowa City in October 1975. *Will and Testament*, an imaginative reworking of Rudyard Kipling's short story, 'Proofs of Holy Writ', was published in an edition of eighty-six copies, illustrated by Joe Tilson, by the Plain Wrapper Press in Verona in 1977.† Sticking fairly close to Kipling, the story puts

---

on to edit a silent film, and accompanies it with his own piano soundtrack at the first screening. This avant-garde film is then internationally praised and prized. 'Burgess got none of the credit,' the story tells us, 'nor did he desire it.' As in the Enderby novel, he is clearly projecting his thwarted artistic fantasies on to a fictional character.

* Terry Eagleton, 'Books: From Postcard-Length Data, A Wealth of Images and Legends', *Commonweal*, 30 October 1970, pp. 129–31.

† Kipling's story is discussed at some length in Burgess's *Shakespeare* (pp. 233–4), and again in *You've Had Your Time*: 'There is a short story by Kipling called 'Proofs of Holy Writ' which shows Shakespeare arguing with Ben Jonson about biblical *mots justes*, and from it I took the idea – not confirmed by any known documentation – that the Jacobean poets had been brought in to polish the proofs

forward the impossible theory that Shakespeare had a hand in revising the proofs of the King James Bible, and that he autographed his contribution by inserting the words 'shake' and 'speare' into the translation of Psalm 46. Burgess hadn't noticed that the same words also occur in the same positions in the Geneva Bible, published four years before Shakespeare was born, but there is still plenty of entertaining period detail in his unreliable version of the story.

Burgess's Shakespeare re-emerges in 1979, this time having metamorphosed into *Mr WS: A Ballet on the Career of William Shakespeare*, a suite for full orchestra. The score calls for an array of Elizabethan instruments, including pipes, shawms and tabors; the music itself is a mixture of galliards, sea shanties, court dances, death-marches and sarabandes. *Mr WS* was broadcast in full as part of Radio Scotland's programme *An Airful of Burgess* on 21 August 1994, and there is a recording of this performance in the BBC sound archive. In February 1979 Burgess's lecture on *Henry VIII* (or *All Is True*) was broadcast on BBC television. He filmed the programme in his Monaco apartment – a valve trumpet and Josephine Baker's piano are visible in the background – armed with a facsimile of the First Folio and a scale model of the Globe Theatre.* His undated settings of two Shakespeare songs, 'Under the Greenwood Tree' and 'Come Thou Monarch of the Vine' (from *Antony and Cleopatra*), have recently been performed at Brown University in Providence, Rhode Island. Finally, there are two whimsical Shakespearean short stories to be found in *The Devil's Mode*: 'A Meeting in Valladolid', which dramatizes an imaginary debate between Shakespeare and Cervantes; and 'The Most Beatified', in which Prince Hamlet attends a necromantic lecture on aesthetics delivered by Marlowe's Doctor

---

of the poetic books of the Bible' (p. 337). For a conclusive answer to these Shakespearean speculations in Kipling and Burgess, see John Sharpe, 'Myth of the Bible Bard', *Spectator*, 28 July 2001, p. 26.

* *Shakespeare in Perspective: Henry VIII*, BBC television, broadcast 25 February 1979. Transcript published in *Shakespeare in Perspective*, vol. 1, ed. by Roger Sales (London: BBC/Ariel, 1982), pp. 88–95.

Faustus at Wittenberg. This is to say nothing of the journalism, where Shakespeare and Joyce are frequently invoked as the touch-stones of unmatchable literary value.

Burgess was clearly deeply attracted to WS as a subject to be probed in fiction, short stories, songs, orchestral music and screen-plays. In the 1970 biography, he writes that Shakespeare 'is our-selves, ordinary suffering humanity, fired by moderate ambition, concerned with money, the victim of desire, all too mortal'.* The talent displayed in his plays and poems 'reconciles us to being human'. Shakespeare 'is the name of one of our redeemers'. This idea of arriving at redemption through music or literature is a common theme in Burgess's literary criticism ('Art,' he suggests in *Urgent Copy*, 'is the organization of base matter into an illusory image of universal order') but there is a particularly strong element of self-identification in his vision of Shakespeare as a highly produc-tive writer who shared his own devotion to paronomasia and the flashier kind of verbal pyrotechnics. When Jeremy Isaacs put it to Burgess in a television interview that there might be moments of 'showing-off' in his novels, his instant response was to ask Isaacs: 'Do I show off? Does Shakespeare show off?'[†] In his Shakespeare biography, he speculates at one point that the middle-aged play-wright might have suffered from 'Bürger's arterial blockage'. There is no evidence at all to support this suggestion, but Burgess happened to be afflicted by the same condition while he was writing the book, and simply transposed it on to his biographical subject.[‡] Speaking in another interview in 1973, he described Shakespeare as 'an ordinary man with an irrelevant talent – a talent he didn't really care a damn about'. He added: 'That's what I've always liked about him – the way he took the money and ran.'[§] This idea of

---

* Burgess, *Shakespeare* (London: Jonathan Cape, 1970), p. 261.

† *The Late Show: Face to Face*, BBC 2, 21 March 1989.

‡ *Shakespeare*, p. 259.

§ Sheridan Morley, 'Anthony Burgess Answers Back', *The Times*, 6 August 1973, p. 7.

professionalism, in the sense of being a pen or typewriter for hire, establishes one of the parallels between the burgess of Stratford and the Shakespeare of Manchester (a play on words that AB couldn't resist using whenever he was invited to lecture on WS). It also helps to explain why Burgess devoted so much enthusiastic labour to theatrical script-writing, literary journalism and film, all of these being activities in which the writer is given a clear sense of how much his words are worth. Moreover, he was aware of his ancestral roots in the clodhopping drama of Glasgow music halls and Manchester silent cinemas. The theatrical milieux in which his parents had made their living were not so far removed from the clowning, cross-dressing and melodrama of Elizabethan playhouses, and he drew extensively on these underworlds when he came to write *The Pianoplayers* in 1986.

It clearly mattered a good deal to Burgess that *his* Shakespeare – a reconstructed, semi-fictional Shakespeare, cobbled together from a variety of materials – should be a kind of outsider: a provincial writer, largely self-educated, who was emphatically not a graduate of the universities of Oxford or Cambridge. His own Mancunian prejudices against London, the effete south-east of England and the ancient universities were unshakeable, and he was not in any case inclined to examine or discard them. From Burgess's point of view, Shakespeare provided a cheering example of a writer who had infiltrated the establishment in spite of his unmetropolitan origins. Asked, as he frequently was, to defend *A Clockwork Orange* against the accusation that it was a work which might corrupt its readers, or even incite them to commit acts of violence, Burgess preferred to make the case for his own book obliquely, by drawing comparisons with Shakespeare's bloodthirsty tragedies: 'If I am going to be blamed [. . .] I must point to Shakespeare's *King Lear* or *Hamlet*. *Hamlet* may have been responsible for many a young man's killing his stepfather, or trying to.'* In an article for the *Observer* in 1993, he wrote: 'In *King Lear*, the tearing out of

* C. Robert Jennings, 'Playboy Interview: Anthony Burgess', p. 72.

the Earl of Gloucester's eyes seems a gratuitous sop to the corruption of the viewer ("Out, vile jelly") [. . .] If *A Clockwork Orange* can corrupt, why not Shakespeare and why not the Bible?'* These grandiose self-comparisons were part of Burgess's larger campaign to talk himself into the canon of English literature through sheer persistence and force of will. If they look and sound vain, it is vanity of an especially complicated kind, bound up with an acute awareness of the nature of his own gifts. Besides, Burgess was never alone in suggesting that the immodest range and variety of his literary oeuvre might have had things in common with the Elizabethan writers (Shakespeare, Marlowe, Thomas Kyd, Thomas Nashe, John Webster) whose works he felt closest to. Harold Bloom is one of many commentators who believe that Burgess's fictional heroes have the dimensions of Falstaff or Hamlet.† To make such claims for WS, or Victor Crabbe, or Enderby, or Kenneth Toomey in *Earthly Powers* (or even Alex in *A Clockwork Orange*, who has a Machiavellian appeal comparable with Shakespeare's Richard III), is to acknowledge the broad range of melancholy, introspection, wickedness and gallows humour that Burgess, at his best, is capable of creating.

* Burgess, 'Stop the Clock on Violence', *Observer*, 21 March 1993, p. 25.
† Harold Bloom (ed.), *Anthony Burgess: Modern Critical Views* (New York: Chelsea House, 1987), pp. 1–8. For John Bayley on Burgess and the Elizabethans, see 'From the Ridiculous to the Ridiculous', *New York Review of Books*, 19 September 1974, p. 32.

9

'I Wish My Wife was Dead'

When, in his seventies, Burgess secluded himself in Monaco and looked back on his earlier dealings with writers and publishers, he found it surprising that he had enjoyed relatively few close friendships with other novelists. Yet the archives in Angers, Texas and Manchester reveal him to have been an energetic correspondent, and he exchanged regular letters with (among others) Julian Mitchell, Eric Partridge, Rex Warner, Diana and Meir Gillon, Martin Bell, Geoffrey Aggeler, Olivia Manning, A. S. Byatt, Shirley Conran, Georges Belmont, Richard Ellmann and Graham Greene. One of the strangest of his involvements was with William Seward Burroughs, best known as the author of *Queer*, *Junky* and *Naked Lunch*. Burgess and Lynne first met him a few days after they set out from London to Tangier on 29 March 1963. Burroughs, who was three years older than Burgess, was the most talented member of the American 'Beat Generation', and his circle of friends included Jack Kerouac, Allen Ginsberg and the writer-composer Paul Bowles. A recovering heroin addict, Burroughs had already abandoned various careers as an anthropologist, bartender, journalist and cockroach exterminator. He was now writing in Tangier, often with a long row of joints lined up on his desk. His usual method of working was to type frenziedly for several days without sleep or interruption, following the dictation of the hallucinatory voices that he heard in his altered state. As the pages fell out of his typewriter and on to the floor, they were gathered up and assembled into books by friends such as Ginsberg, who acted as his agents and editors. His early novels were published in Paris by Maurice Girodias of the Olympia Press, who specialized in sensational and borderline pornographic writing that was likely to fall foul of the obscenity laws in Britain and the United States. At the time of his first meeting with Burgess, Burroughs had published *Naked Lunch* in a small French edition, and was waiting nervously for a mass-market edition to appear in England. Burgess, in his capacity as a literary journalist, was to be instrumental in engineering the successful reception of this novel among British readers.

Morocco in the early 1960s was famous for its plentiful cheap hashish and homosexual rough trade, as the diaries of Joe Orton (another regular visitor) illustrate. Bill Holden of Heinemann had supplied Burgess with letters of introduction to what he called 'various minor pansy writers', including Robin Maugham (nephew of the more famous W. Somerset Maugham) and Rupert Croft-Cooke (1903–79, writer of mystery stories). It was possibly John Calder, Burroughs's London publisher, who engineered Burgess's meeting with Burroughs. Certainly the two writers got on well enough to wish to keep in touch later. At Burroughs's apartment, Burgess would have observed his habit of working while listening to three radios at once, each tuned to a different station. It is an idea which returns in Burgess's *The End of the World News* (1982), a novel whose form attempts to mimic the experience of watching three television channels simultaneously. At this time Burroughs was in the process of writing his 'cut-up' trilogy, composed according to a collage technique he had devised with the painter Brion Gysin. As he explained in an interview in 1964, 'Pages of text are cut and rearranged to form new combinations of word and image, that is, the page is actually cut with scissors, usually into four sections, and the order rearranged.'*

---

* Quoted in Barry Miles, *William Burroughs: El Hombre Invisible* (London: Virgin, 1993), pp. 118–19.

He was willing to be distracted from his experimental labours to read extracts from Jane Austen aloud to Lynne, who had taken to her hotel bed following another of her nervous collapses. She returned to England without a tan, although it was only the prospect of sun that had persuaded her to travel.

Burgess's main purpose in visiting Tangier was to gather local colour that could be deployed in *Enderby Outside*, and the novel shows that he used his time profitably. The physical sense of Morocco comes across very powerfully in his descriptions of 'a soothing marijuana fag', 'thudded drums and weak pipe-skirls, fowl-squawks and ass-brays', 'blind men howling for baksheesh', 'rubbery gobs' of goatmeat roasted on skewers over a brazier, 'fruit-barrows, donkey-whippers, brown and black vociferators in pointed hoods', 'people in turbans, nightgowns with stripes, and what-you-call-them djebelas', pimping taxi-drivers who ask, according to taste, '*Tu veux une femme?*' or '*Tu veux un garçon?*' and 'a fezzed man outside a shop [. . .] showing rugs and saddles and firearms'.* Floating pungently above all this is the smell of mint tea. Enderby meets William Burroughs in an expatriate bar called the Fat White Doggy Wog: 'He looked like an undertaker, mortician rather; his suit was black and his spectacles had near-square black rims, like the frames of obituary notices in old volumes of *Punch* [. . .] He sounded not unkind, but his voice was tired and lacked nuances totally.'† This fictional Burroughs is seen cutting strips out of newspapers and sticking them at random on to another sheet of paper, which gives Burgess the opportunity to attempt a parody of Burroughs's cut-up prose: 'Balance of slow masturbate payments inquiries in opal spunk shapes notice of that question green ass penetration phantoms adjourn.' Burroughs's opinion of this doubtful homage is unrecorded.

Fascinated by the international community of Tangier, and wanting to make use of it in a novel, Burgess returned to Morocco

---

* Burgess, *Enderby Outside* (London: Heinemann, 1968), pp. 113–35.
† Ibid., p. 138.

on at least two further occasions, in November 1963 and October
1966. His friendship with Burroughs continued by letter, and the
two writers met again in London after Burroughs had moved to a
flat at 8 Duke Street, near Piccadilly, in 1967. Burroughs told his
biographer, Barry Miles:

> We went out to a number of pubs. I had been very much
> impressed with his novel *Clockwork Orange* and had written
> something for it ['I do not know of any other writer who has
> done as much with language as Mr Burgess has done here – the
> fact that this is also a very funny book may pass unnoticed'];
> that was the basis of the relationship. I found him extremely
> charming. Very much interested in my work, as I was in his.

When Burroughs asked Burgess if he knew any other writers in
London, he is said to have replied, 'No, they're all a bunch of
swine.'*

Burgess was unfailingly gracious in his public statements about
Burroughs's fiction. He reviewed *Naked Lunch* in the *Guardian* ('a
palimpsest of obscenity so emetic that no amount of casuistry will
be able to justify a charge of inflammation and corruption [. . .] It
is a picture of hell, and hell is not corrupting'), and defended it in
a long letter to the *Times Literary Supplement* when Dame Edith
Sitwell said it was the sort of thing one might expect to find written
on a lavatory wall.† Later on, when he reviewed *Nova Express* in
1966, he continued to argue, against the general tide of opinion,
that Burroughs was a 'courteous, hospitable, erudite, gifted and
dedicated writer'. This is not to say that Burgess over-estimated the
quality of Burroughs's writing, or was indifferent to its faults. In a
review of *Cities of the Red Night*, he said that Burroughs had 'opted
for a lack of intellectuality that makes his fantasies no more than

---

* Quoted in Victor Bockris, *With William Burroughs*, (revised edition, London:
Fourth Estate, 1997), p. 74.
† Burgess, 'On the End of Every Fork' (review of Burroughs, *Naked Lunch*),
Guardian, 20 November 1964, p. 9; 'Letters to the Editor', *Times Literary Sup-
plement*, 2 January 1964, p. 9.

loose collages in which the news is always the same – getting anally screwed with Bengal lights, attempting bizarre violence with an insufficient musculature, getting fixes [. . .] When we have pederastic thrusts on every page we soon start to yawn. There is much concern with catching the sperm of hanged men, and sexual strangulation is a recurrent, and soon boring, theme.'* For Burgess, as for the resolutely queer Burroughs, sex remained a problem both in literature and in life.

Almost without exception, Burgess's novels present marriage in terms of guilt and self-laceration. Julian Mitchell has commented that 'the typical Burgess protagonist is a teacher with a propensity towards infidelity, an impossible wife, and a capacity for suffering endless humiliation'.† There are no happy heterosexual couples in his fiction, and the possibility of erotic fulfilment rarely arises in his writing before 1968. Even in *Tremor of Intent*, Burgess's spy-thriller, energetic lust and satyriasis are followed by a total renunciation of sex: the reformed secret agent becomes a tranquilly celibate Catholic priest in the final chapter. Elsewhere in the novels, there is plenty of joyless adultery, unconsummated passion and grotesque syphilitic death. Only Burgess's gay and lesbian characters seem to be enjoying themselves, possibly because they are exempt from the strictures of marriage.

When *Honey for the Bears* was published in 1963, Christopher Ricks wrote a long article for the *New Statesman* in which he suggested that the author might have shared Paul Hussey's interest in homosexual relationships – a possibility which had also occurred to Lynne, as Burgess tells us in *You've Had Your Time*. She had caught him looking at German youths and naked Berber boys on the beach in Morocco, and started to ask awkward questions about

---

* Burgess, 'Burroughs's Bad Dreams' (review of *Cities of the Red Night*), *Saturday Review*, March 1981, p. 66. See also 'Yards and Yards of Entrails' (review of *Nova Express*), *Observer*, 13 February 1966, p. 27.
† Julian Mitchell, 'Anthony Burgess', *London Magazine*, February 1964, pp. 48–54.

his sexuality. In the *New Statesman*, Ricks presented his case diplomatically:

> Throughout the novels [Burgess] has apparently been trying to make up his mind about the epicene, and in the first one (*Time for a Tiger*) his prose took on a delighted and very uncensorious lilt as it observed androgynous Ibrahim [. . .] That homosexuality is not wicked, not ethereally spiritual, not incompatible with other things, but a rather pleasant virtuosity – if this is not subversive, then what would be?*

Lynne memorized the relevant paragraphs of this review and quoted them accusingly at Burgess. His reaction was one of vague surprise. 'Who is this *New Statesman* man who says I am epicene?' he asked Bill Holden at Heinemann.

James Michie, who edited Burgess's novels until 1963 and also knew him socially, found it difficult to arrive at any firm conclusions.

> Was he a homosexual who wanted to live a heterosexual life on the surface, or what? The first book, I remember, definitely had undertones. And when I met him I just assumed, in an unimportant way, that he was gay. On the other hand, then comes Lynne and then comes Liana – very curious associations, both of them, but nevertheless marital ones.†

Having met Lynne, Michie came to suspect that Burgess was 'perhaps mentally homosexual but not actively' – which is a fair assessment of what seems to be going on in the novels and what is known about the life. Peter Green, who knew Burgess better than Michie did, took a very different view of his sexuality: 'What struck me about JB [Wilson] was that he was *scared* of women. And no, despite his fascination with the subject, I don't think he was gay

---

* Christopher Ricks, 'The Epicene', *New Statesman*, 5 April 1963, p. 496.
† James Michie to author, 15 November 2000. With reference to Lynne's adulteries, Michie comments: 'If Lynne was sleeping with other men, I can't imagine John being anything other than acutely *interested*.'

either.'* Even so, he remained profoundly interested in exploring homosexuality in fiction, and it is thematically central to some of the later novels, such as *Earthly Powers* and *A Dead Man in Deptford*. Between 1959 and 1963, Burgess seems to have been almost entirely celibate, and he confessed to C. Robert Jennings that he had compensated for the absence of real-life sex in this period by channelling his desires and frustrations on to the page:

> In my own most creative period of writing, I had less sex than I'd ever had in my life before. During the four years when my wife was very ill and the period I was writing things like *Enderby* and *Tremor of Intent* and the Shakespeare book – highly sexed books, incidentally, which may have a lot to do with sublimation – I was sort of acting a lot of sex out in the books.†

Deborah Rogers, who was Burgess's literary agent from 1967, says: 'With his sexuality, I think, as with everything else, the distinction between life and fantasy was completely blurred [. . .] I think an awful lot of him was self-invented. If you have that sort of fertile mind, maybe self-invention is the most satisfactory way of being.'‡

The erotic solitude that had been a constant feature of Burgess's life since his return from Brunei was on the point of ending in December 1963. Lynne's father had died in the August of that year, and she had inherited a large portion of his estate, including property (the rental income from some flats in Leicester was divided

---

* Peter Green to author, 2 November 1999.
† C. Robert Jennings, 'Playboy Interview: Anthony Burgess', p. 78. Burgess claims in the same interview that the sexual activities of Dylan Thomas had more often than not taken place when he was alone in the bathroom. Once Burgess gets going on the subject of auto-eroticism, he isn't inclined to drop it in a hurry: 'Quite a number of artists masturbate, then they write. Our sexual energy has been aroused, now we come, now we're able to concentrate on the *other* aspect of this energy, which is the creative aspect. In other words, the sexual act becomes a kind of irrelevance, and rather a nuisance.'
‡ Deborah Rogers to author, 4 January 2002.

equally between Hazel and Llewela) and a £15,000 legacy from her grandfather Joseph Jones's patent fire extinguisher, the device on which her ancestral fortune had depended.* Lynne bought shares in Butlin's, ICI, Elliott Automation and United Newspapers with some of this inheritance, and she proposed to spend the rest on a small house in London. In December, Burgess and Lynne took possession of 24 Glebe Street, Chiswick, W4 (telephone number Chiswick 1411), which they had bought on a fifty-five-year lease for £3,000. It was in this newly acquired and nearly empty house that Burgess first met Liliana Macellari Johnson, the Italian translator of Thomas Pynchon and Lawrence Durrell.

Liliana was born on 25 September 1929 at Porto Civitanova on the Adriatic coast, famous as a fishing port and as the birthplace of the poet Annibal Caro. She was the only surviving daughter of Gilberto Macellari, an actor who had died young, and the Contessa Maria Lucrezia Pasi Piani della Pergola, who died in her nineties in 1983. Educated in Bologna, Rome and at the Sorbonne in Paris, Liliana was separated from her husband, a black Bostonian called Benjamin Johnson, who had translated Italo Svevo's short stories into English. She worked as a language teacher and lived on Elder Street in East London with Roy Lionel Halliday, a Geordie drifter of no fixed occupation. When she read *A Clockwork Orange* and *Inside Mr Enderby* in 1963, she sent Burgess a letter suggesting that they should meet for lunch to discuss an article she was writing. Liliana (who invariably shortens her name to Liana) remembers:

> I was beside myself with joy when I read both these works
> because my task was to write for the *Bompiani Literary Alman-
> ack* a panorama of the literary output covering a year in English
> language [. . .] The average number of titles appearing was
> 32,000, out of which I had to choose and discuss a handful.

---

* 'An improved chemical mixture or compound for extinguishing fires and destroying explosive fire damp in coal mines', according to the documents registered at
the Patent Office by the Bolton inventor Joseph Jones (father of Edward Jones) on
13 July 1867.

I had discovered two, so I thought, masters, comparatively unknown.*

Burgess said of their first encounter: 'She was dark-haired, beautiful, lively, and hated equally the Italian state and the Roman Church. I was powerfully attracted to her, she at least to my work.'†
He wrote in the *Confessions* that she had filled his heart 'at once and forever'. They made love on a December afternoon at 24 Glebe Street, and nine months later, on 9 August 1964, Liana gave birth to a son, Paolo Andrea Macellari (known in adult life as Andrew Burgess Wilson). Although the name John Burgess Wilson does not appear on the birth certificate, it is more than likely that this child was his. At the age of forty-seven, he had at last accomplished his ambition to become a father. Liana left London in 1967 to take up a teaching post in Cambridge, where she bought a house at 25 Victoria Road.‡ She and Burgess continued to meet occasionally, although always in secret. He told Samuel Coale: 'We had been consorting together since 1963. I had to have some sexual outlet, because I was having none with my wife. It was all guilt. This was

---

* Liana Burgess, 'Speech for the Anthony Burgess Symposium in Angers' in *Portraits of the Artist in A Clockwork Orange*, ed. by Emmanuel Vernadakis and Graham Woodroffe (Angers: Presses de l'Université d'Angers, 2004), pp. 261–5, 261.

† *You've Had Your Time: Being the Second Part of the Confessions of Anthony Burgess* (London: Heinemann, 1990), p. 88.

‡ The journalist Martin Cropper (who interviewed Burgess for the London *Evening Standard* in 1990) writes: 'In the early 1970s the Contessa owned a house in Victoria Road, Cambridge. When I lived there (summer 1972) the original furnished let had turned into a squat, sans furniture. The wooden panelling in the bathroom had been ripped out with meat hooks by the Mid-Anglia Drug Squad – an event I personally witnessed. When you walked in the garden you crunched over used hypodermics.' When Burgess and Liana arrived in Cambridge to inspect what remained of her property, 'the Contessa reached for her solicitor, a blameless old party who sincerely believed that I was called Robert Zimmerman (I spelt it for him), in which name I duly received a Notice to Quit. When I met Mr and Mrs Burgess 18 years later I thought it politic not to mention any of this' (Martin Cropper to author, 16 December 2002).

kept absolutely quiet. The liaison was not a regular one. It was very, very clandestine. And we didn't feel free to get away.'* Lynne must have known something, because she confided her suspicions to Edward Pagram and to her sister, Hazel. Yet Burgess went on living with her for another four years, and he told Anthony Clare that he took care to conceal from her the information that he had fathered a son by another woman: 'There are some things that one has to keep away from people who are vulnerable. There was also a sense that my future was going to go on, whereas the future of my first wife was not. It was evident that here was a woman who was not fit for normal life.'†

Between 1964 and 1968 Burgess and Lynne divided their time between Chiswick and Etchingham, spending most of the year in London but returning to Sussex for the summer months and at Christmas. When they went back to Etchingham, the journey usually took the form, at Lynne's insistence, of a lurching pub-crawl in a taxi. They were driven from pub to pub by Terry Sutton (the cab-driver mentioned by Kingsley Amis in his memoirs and in chapter 15 of *Difficulties with Girls*), who eventually bought 24 Glebe Street from Burgess in the 1970s. Interviewed for a French television documentary, Sutton claimed that, when Burgess was reviewing operas for *Queen* magazine in the mid-1960s, he would send Sutton to new productions to make notes about the costumes and scenery, and then write his articles using Sutton's notes and published opera scores, without ever having set foot in the theatre.‡

Another close friend in Chiswick was the poet Martin Bell, an engaging talker, drinker and metropolitan dandy. A schoolmaster by profession, Bell had made English translations of Laforgue and Apollinaire, and he wrote light verse about Lynne's collection of cats and dogs. One of his poems, 'A Vocation Possibly', is written in a persona very close to Enderby's: 'This tiny room, this cabin,

---

* Samuel Coale, interview with Anthony Burgess in Monaco, 7 and 11 July 1978.
† *In the Psychiatrist's Chair*, BBC Radio 4, 27 July 1988.
‡ Quoted in *Un Siècle d'Ecrivains: Anthony Burgess*, directed by Elisa Mantin, France 3, 1997.

this monk's cell / Pantaloon decrepit scholar's den / Shuffles me like a full pack of cards'.* Burgess repaid the compliment by composing the piano music which heralds the destruction of the world by nuclear war in Bell's apocalyptic 'Senilio's Broadcast Script' (which is itself a riposte to another poem, 'Your Attention Please', written by Bell's friend and editor Peter Porter).† Bell kept up a correspondence with Burgess for some years after he had left London to become the Arts Council's writer in residence at Leeds University. Their friendship depended on blunt speaking and the avoidance of euphemism. Burgess wrote to Bell from Rome in 1976: 'You poets are lazy buggers but more honoured than us novelists [. . .] Your bloody socialists have fucked things up pretty successfully, but Mrs fucking Thatcher won't do better. What a mess England is, and the price, god help us, of drink. Still, Italy's pretty bad. It's purgatory there but hell elsewhere.'‡ Burgess encouraged Bell to get on with his autobiography, and he published a laudatory review of Bell's *Collected Poems 1937–1966* in the *Spectator*, paying close attention to the poems dedicated to Lynne and himself. Bell's poetry is said to be 'totally unselfpitying, funny, sad, horribly exact, vindictive without rancour [. . .] It calls on every conceivable verse technique and even a page or so of pretentiously avant-garde music.'§ Burgess was aware that Bell desperately needed the royalties that a selling review might bring, and this wasn't an isolated example of talking up the reputations of literary friends. Later on, in August 1977, he wrote a similarly laudatory article for the *Times Literary Supplement* about Eric Partridge's *Dictionary of Catch Phrases*, because he knew that Partridge, who had no pension, was struggling to pay his wife's

---

* Martin Bell, *Complete Poems*, ed. by Peter Porter (Newcastle: Bloodaxe, 1988), p. 231.
† Martin Bell, 'Senilio's Broadcast Script' in *Complete Poems*, pp. 104–7. See also 'Your Attention Please' in Peter Porter, *Collected Poems*, vol. 1 (Oxford: Oxford University Press, 1999), p. 45.
‡ Burgess, letter to Martin Bell, dated St Bridget's Day [i.e. 1 February], 1976.
§ Burgess, 'Summoned by Bell', *Spectator*, 9 June 1967, p. 714.

nursing-home fees. And he went on saying polite things in print about Kenneth Young, Kingsley Amis and Graham Greene even after he had fallen out with them.

Burgess tried to exorcize some of his guilt about Lynne by burying himself in work. Two more novels were published by Heinemann: *Tremor of Intent*, a thriller which blends elements of Ian Fleming (gluttony, satyriasis, truth-serums, assassinations) and James Joyce (eschatology, coded messages, dream sequences, betrayals, faith lost and rediscovered); and *Enderby Outside*, in which the questing poet, pursued by the police for a crime of which he is innocent, retraces Burgess's own journey into the druggy beatnik labyrinth of Tangier, hoping to exact lethal vengeance on his enemy, Rawcliffe, who has stolen Enderby's idea for a long poem about the Minotaur, sold the story to a film producer, and run off to Morocco with the loot.* He was planning at least three other novels, but lacked the clear run of time that would have been necessary to complete them, mainly because his journalistic commitments for the *Listener*, *Spectator*, *Guardian* and other publications were becoming too burdensome. One of these abandoned novels, 'It Is the Miller's Daughter' (the title is taken from a Tennyson poem), survives in the form of two chapters published in the *Transatlantic Review* and *Partisan Review*. The second, about a composer named Charles Levey Clegg, was to have taken in his professional career of seventy years, 'from *L'Après Midi d'un Faune* to the Beatles'. Burgess promised readers of the *Hudson Review* that this would be a book about 'Love, work, travel, crime – I envisage half-a-million words, all in the first person singular. And there will be faked photographs and musical analyses, complete with music-type illustrations. Britain's answer to *Jean-Christophe* and [Thomas Mann's] *Doctor*

---

* For Frank Kermode's review of *Enderby Outside*, see 'Poetry and Borborygms', *Listener*, 6 June 1968, pp. 735–6; reprinted in Kermode, *Modern Essays* (London: Fontana, 1971), pp. 289–93. For Auberon Waugh on the same, see 'Seat of Pleasure', *Spectator*, 24 May 1968, p. 745. For John Willett on *Tremor of Intent*, see 'Spying for Laughs', *Times Literary Supplement*, 9 June 1966, p. 509.

Faustus.'* Heavily modified, and with its main character transformed from a musician into a man of letters, this chronicle-novel
emerged thirteen years later as *Earthly Powers*. Burgess outlined a
third unwritten novel in an article for *The Times*:

> I should also like to be publishing a [. . .] saga of the English
> theatre, beginning with mystery plays and ending with the Cruel
> and the Absurd, and it should feature a family that has always
> had greasepaint (or its earlier equivalents) in the blood.
> Throughout the history of the stage a member of the family has
> regularly fallen desperately in love with a member of another
> family – of the kind that provides audiences, not actors. Some
> accident always prevents the fulfilment of this love, but when,
> at the present day, there are no obstacles of an accidental
> nature, the rapprochement must be of a very frustrating kind,
> since one of the pair is homosexual.†

Burgess envisaged a book of 600 pages, to be published under the
Shakespearean title 'All the Men and Women', but in fact he wrote
no more than a fifteen-page opening chapter.

For the art publisher Paul Elek he wrote introductions to two
folio-sized illustrated coffee-table books, *The Age of the Grand
Tour* and *Coaching Days of England*. Although these were essentially well-paid pieces of hack-work, they gave him the opportunity
to indulge in parodic historical fiction. His contribution to the stage-
coach book is a nineteenth-century fantasy, full of boozing and
sybaritic meals in roadside taverns, composed in the vigorous style
of *The Pickwick Papers*:

> Surrounded by panels of old oak, under a smoky ceiling, you
> have eaten your early breakfast. It was served by a sniffing
> waiter smelling strongly of brandy (either a cold-cure or a

---

* Burgess, 'Letter from England', *Hudson Review*, vol. XX, no. 3 Autumn 1967,
pp. 454–8, 455.
† 'Books Wanted in 1976: A Dream of Publishing', *The Times*, 2 February 1967,
p. 16.

dawn-livener) and it consisted of three fried eggs, nearly a pound of local-cured ham, very hot toast soaked in butter, and almost a quart of coffee, well-laced with rum.*

He shows himself to be more than willing to deploy the techniques of novel-writing elsewhere in his journalism: his review of Nell Dunn's *Talking About Women* is written entirely as a dialogue between two imaginary working-class women ('A: But now you can have any man you want. I mean, you can, can't you? B: Any man I want? I suppose I can in a sort of way, but they're like animals some of them. I mean, giving you babies. That's not what sex is for really, is it?'); and he wrote a biographical essay about Samuel Johnson in which the language imitates Johnson's own *Lives of the English Poets*. When Stanley Kubrick published his illustrated *Clockwork Orange* screenplay (most of the dialogue is lifted directly from the novel, even though Kubrick is the sole author credited on the title page), Burgess reviewed it slashingly, in the voice of our droog and brother Alex:

> This Book will tolchock out into the darkmans the Book what there like previously was, the one by F. Alexander or Sturgess or some such eemya, because who would have slovos when he could viddy real jeezhny with his nagoy glazzies? And so it is like that. Righty right. And real horrorshow. And lashings of deng for the carmans of Zubrick. And for your malenky droog not none no more.†

---

* *Coaching Days of England, Containing An Account of Whatever Was Most Remarkable for GRANDEUR, ELEGANCE and CURIOSITY in the time of the COACHES of ENGLAND, Comprehending the Years 1750 until 1850, Together With an HISTORICAL COMMENTARY by ANTHONY BURGESS, and in addition decorated and illustrated with a great Number of drawings, prints and Views in Perspective gathered on purpose for this Work*, ed. by Francis Haskell (London: Paul Elek, 1966), pp. 9–26, 10.
† Burgess, 'Sisters Under the Skin', *Listener*, 2 December 1965, p. 914; 'Johnson (?) on Johnson', *Horizon*, Summer 1968, pp. 60–64; 'Burgess on Kubrick on Clockwork', *Library Journal*, 1 May 1973, p. 1506.

The hidden obscenity was probably lost on most readers, but it helps to know that 'zubrick' is the Arabic word for 'penis'.

Despite his fluency as a journalist and cultural commentator, Burgess grew uneasy with his success as a contributor to newspapers, magazines, radio and television programmes. He was too much in demand, he felt, and he worried that his reluctance to decline any reasonable commission might also involve spreading his talent too thinly. Above all, he feared that the main job of novel-writing was being squeezed out by squandering his energies on book-reviewing. Acutely aware that, as a freelance, he was rarely given enough time or space to offer a considered critique of the work under review, he confessed some of his doubts about the journalistic marketplace in a letter to Julian Mitchell:

> I have hardly read a book, except those I've reviewed, since I started writing. The SPECTATOR wanted, or want, I don't know which, me to write something long about a writer called Elizabeth Bowen. I must, if I do it, erect a shameful façade of with-science-blinding with-it references, going on about Henry James and Edith Wharton and so on. It's all a bloody sham, and criticism will never flourish in such circumstances.*

Many of the freelancer's common anxieties are visible in Burgess's letter: the worrying about deadlines; the nagging suspicion that he is underqualified to assess the book under review (shamming it, in other words); the conviction that whatever he is doing cannot properly be called 'criticism'. And the letter goes on to complain about the meanness of publishers (Faber in this case), which is, Burgess believes, what forces novelists to involve themselves in this kind of 'shameful' enterprise.

Journalism was an activity that Burgess went on disparaging and feeling guiltily ambivalent about, in spite of his deep immersion in

---

* Letter to Julian Mitchell, no date but probably January or February 1964. The review (of Elizabeth Bowen's *The Little Girls*) was published as 'Treasures and Fetters', *Spectator*, 21 February 1964, p. 254.

it. He underestimated his proficiency and undervalued the importance of his contribution to larger discussions about contemporary
fiction and poetry. His complaints that journalism was an ephemeral
business were often beside the point, especially considering the high
quality of the articles he reprinted in the two volumes of selected
journalism which appeared in his lifetime, *Urgent Copy* (1968) and
Homage to Qwert Yuiop (1986). One of the incidental pleasures of
these books is that they chart the evolution of Burgess's opinions
on other twentieth-century writers, such as Graham Greene, Saul
Bellow, Vladimir Nabokov, Robert Graves, Kingsley Amis, John
Updike, George Steiner, Marshall McLuhan and Claude Lévi-
Strauss. His guiding principle as a critic was to draw attention to
whatever was good and admirable in the books that came his way,
with the aim of providing encouragement to fellow authors. This
wasn't so much a refusal to make discriminations as a recognition
that expressions of hostility would have been pointlessly destructive.
He was not greatly interested in demolishing established reputations,
and left this task to other reviewers. As he writes in the introduction
to *Urgent Copy*, 'Behind the new bad book one is asked to review
lie untold misery and a very little hope. One's heart, stomach and
anal tract go out to the doomed aspirant.'*

In spite of his private anxieties, he was a more gifted and
conscientious critic than he gave himself credit for – 'a natural',
according to Peter Green. As Clive James has said, 'if Burgess's
literary journalism was meant to be such an inherently inferior
activity he might have done us the grace of being worse at it, so that

---

* Burgess, *Urgent Copy: Literary Studies* (London: Jonathan Cape, 1970), p. 11.
Not everyone was delighted by Burgess's journalism. The poet Geoffrey Grigson
complained: 'The words exhibit the quality of mind, a quality that no one will find
other than coarse and unattractive, I should think, or hope [. . .] I suspect this
reviewer's anxiety to convince himself (perhaps more than others?) that an insatiable liking for words amounts to an ability to use them well and to distinct purpose.
Only some such literary anxiousness coupled with energy could explain the way
Mr Burgess throws about in such a mode references to the obscurity of his own
scholarship' ('Insatiable Liking?', *Listener*, 7 November 1968, pp. 618–19).

we could have saved the money it cost to buy *Urgent Copy* and the
time it took to enjoy it. I have that excellent collection of pieces in
front of me now, almost falling to bits from being read in the bath.'*
What distinguishes Burgess's journalism is the unusual degree of
care that he took with it. His imagination is often seen to be
working at full capacity, as it is in the novels. Commenting, in the
Spectator, on the prospect of Britain's entry into the European
Common Market, he proposed that the British Prime Minister,
Harold Wilson, should speak to other heads of state in a single
European language, a kind of Esperanto which Burgess went on to
outline in the article: 'Vu Savvy, winju in Grobritannia av, post de
frichtful en terrible tempo de tory reglierung, wirklich en actual-
mento shlekt en cattivo en mal reglierung, moltifeel bocoop de gross
ding en shoze en cosay registrato. Nu, nun, actually, winju begin en
commence en initiate un novo tempo.'† Showing off, again? Not
entirely. The playfulness of this (which owes a clear debt to Joyce's
pan-European narrative idiolect in *Finnegans Wake*) is underpinned
by a serious concern with the common roots of languages, and the
possible ways in which they might converge if Europe were to be
unified.

On other occasions, he found it hard to conceal his lack of
sympathy for the youth culture of the 1960s, and the tone of his
articles became apocalyptic. He said of the Beatles that 'The words
of their songs, pathetic when compared with Cole Porter, are so
vapid that psychedelic meanings have to be imposed on them', but
he found their influence less harmful than that of disc-jockeys
('tanned and teethed, voltaic with manic enthusiasm, spurting their
vacuous encomia') and critics such as Kenneth Tynan who claimed
that the 'twanging nonsense' of *Juke Box Jury* was better than
Wagner and the Choral Symphony. 'Do they merit vitriol,' he asked,
'even a drop of it? Yes, because they corrupt the young, persuading

---

* Clive James, *The Metropolitan Critic: Non-Fiction 1968–1973*, (new edition,
London: Jonathan Cape, 1994), p. 274.
† 'Here Parla Man Marcommunish', *Spectator*, 25 November 1966, pp. 674–5.

them that the mature world, which produced Beethoven and Schweitzer, sets an even higher value on the transient anodynes of youth than does youth itself. For this they stink to heaven.' He devised a Hieronymous Bosch damnation for these corrupters of youth (or 'electronic lice'), a special circle of hell where they would be bound to 'a white-hot turntable (45 rpm for ever and ever), stuck all over with blunt and rusty acoustic needles, each tooth hollowed to the raw nerve and filled with a micro-transistor (thirty-two several pop-stations blaring through all eternity thirty-two worn flip-sides into their sinuses), an eternal Ringo battering the tympanic membrane.'*

He found time, amongst the production of other books and articles, to repay his large debt to James Joyce. A commission from Peter du Sautoy at Faber to write a non-fiction book called 'James Joyce and the Common Man' (written between January and August 1964 and published as *Here Comes Everybody*) coincided with an invitation from the television director Christopher Burstall to make a Joyce documentary for the BBC's *Monitor* series. Burstall and Burgess made two visits to Dublin for the programme, scouting locations in January 1965 and filming in February. Burgess conflates these two trips in the autobiography, where he also claims that he improvised an unscripted monologue on Joyce while the cameras rolled. In fact the BBC Written Archive holds three drafts of the script, titled 'Silence, Exile and Cunning', which indicate a slow and careful process of revision.† Burgess's second draft is outrageously ambitious for a television film: the stage-directions call for thunderstorms, jet planes, detonating atomic bombs, race-riots, and a large chorus of Dublin prostitutes. Burstall intended the documentary to be a personal commentary by one novelist on another, and it succeeds in this aim to such an extent that, watching the film, it is almost impossible to separate them. Burgess visits the ruins of the

---

* 'The Antis: The Weasels of Pop', *Punch*, 20 September 1967, pp. 430–31.
† An edited transcript of Burgess's *Monitor* film was published as 'Silence, Exile and Cunning', *Listener*, 6 May 1965, pp. 661–3.

Bloom residence at 7 Eccles Street (the house was being demolished
in February 1965) and stands beside Molly Bloom's iron bedstead
while an actress reads her monologue in voice-over. Most of what
Burgess says about Joyce in his commentary has a direct bearing on
his own writing:

> So many things draw me to Joyce: the dignity of the exile, the
> silence that won't complain or explain. Most of all, the miracle
> of the language. And I also admire, more than I can say, the
> manner in which Joyce has transmuted the ordinary stuff of
> life, the lowly, to something glorious and eternal. A stale bit of
> bread becomes the divine body [. . .] What every artist can still
> learn from Joyce is this need to look at the ring of a Guinness
> glass on a pub table, the sawdust on the floor, the ordinary
> trivial details of ordinary living.*

Burgess considered Joyce's loss of faith at some length in the
film and in the Faber book, which is dedicated to Christopher
Burstall. These reflections were prompted by his troubled awareness
of having set foot in Ireland, the birthplace of Manchester's Jesuit
priests and many of the Xaverian Brothers, for the first time. As he
retraced Joyce's footsteps around Dublin, he remembered his own
teenage traumas at the Church of the Holy Name in Manchester,
and thought about the extent to which reading Joyce had shaped his
development as a writer:

> I was drawn to a great Irish Catholic writer when he'd ceased
> to be either truly Irish or truly Catholic [. . .] He'd made his
> world out of the materials of the world he'd rejected. I wanted
> confirmation that the agonies and elation I knew as a renegade
> had some sort of artistic significance, meant something.

How much of a renegade the adult Burgess actually was remained
an open question. Defiantly Catholic in his fictional world-view,
though agnostic in everyday life, he told his stepsister that Graham

* *Monitor: Silence, Exile and Cunning*, directed by Christopher Burstall, BBC 1,
broadcast 20 April 1965.

Greene had been urging him by letter to return to the Church. Reconsidering Joyce's apostasy and measuring it against his own, he examined what it meant to be an apostate writer:

> The creation of a human community in fiction is the closest the novelist can get to the creation of a cosmos, but Joyce is ambitious enough to want to create a human body (chapter by chapter, organ by organ) which is a sort of configuration [. . .] of the ultimate celestial order. This is perhaps less blasphemous than it looks: it may even be taken as a gesture of piety. It may certainly be taken as Joyce's attempt to build for himself an order which is a substitute for the order he had abandoned when he abandoned the Church.*

When the Irish novelist William Trevor reviewed the Joyce documentary, he was not at all taken in by Burgess's dubious claim to be Irish: 'Mr Anthony Burgess, serious to the point of severity, spoke his own narration in the kind of academic English voice that Dublin street urchins delight in imitating [. . .] Rather more notably than in other circumstances and with other weapons, Englishmen and their cameras have a way of being successful when they strike the Irish scene.'† Burgess wrote later that his two heavily whiskied visits to Dublin had triggered another of his spiritual crises, and had almost sent him back to the faith of his fathers. Yet these doubts did not persist for long. He wrote another, less sensational, account of his apostasy less than two years afterwards: 'Strictly speaking, I have no right to feel anything at all about the way the Church is going, and no right either to remember as much ecclesiastical history as I do or to buy and read paperbacks on theology. I am an unbeliever.'‡

There were problems more immediate than the contemplation of his eternal soul. A sudden worsening of Lynne's health coincided

---

* Burgess, *Here Comes Everybody: an Introduction to James Joyce for the Ordinary Reader* (London: Faber, 1965), p. 87.
† William Trevor, 'Television – The Arts', *Listener*, 22 April 1965, p. 611.
‡ Burgess, 'On Being A Lapsed Catholic', *Triumph*, February 1967, p. 31.

with various physical deteriorations on Burgess's part. They were on their way back from a short visit to Gibraltar in October 1966 when she vomited blood in a hotel bedroom in Seville. After they had got back to England, she suffered a full hepatic portal haemorrhage: the vein feeding the remains of her wasted liver burst, discharging pints of blood into her stomach cavity. She was ambulanced off to the hospital in Hastings with what Burgess misleadingly referred to at the time as an 'escalated duodenal ulcer'. If he had looked up her symptoms in his *Illustrated Family Doctor*, he would have discovered that she was exhibiting all the usual signs of cirrhosis of the liver: fibrosis, destruction of the hepatic architecture, progressing to liver failure, portal hypertension, jaundice and ascites. She was given a blood transfusion and seemed to be making a slow recovery.

With Lynne temporarily out of the way, Burgess's teeth started playing up again. He wrote the third chapter of *Enderby Outside* with a cotton-wool swab soaked in hydrogen peroxide jammed into his upper left gum, the site of a suspected abscess. He consoled himself with an occasional brown bottle of light ale and worked on, bashing out freewheeling autobiographical articles for the *Hudson Review* and the *American Scholar*. Every afternoon he travelled fifteen miles by bus and train from Etchingham to visit Lynne at the hospital, where the nurses ('immigrants from the liberated British colonies') told her, 'You have bled too much' and 'You have damaged your liver'. Then he returned home to cook himself a solitary meal of rump steak, or a stew made from corned beef, potatoes and onions, or Welsh rarebit with poached eggs.*

A few weeks later he found that he was having difficulty in walking. A doctor in Tunbridge Wells told him that long years of heavy drinking and smoking had probably resulted in Bürger's disease or *thrombo-angiitis obliterans* in the arteries of his right leg. A Harley Street specialist, to whom Burgess went for a second opinion, said that it was 'premature arteriosclerosis, that it would

---

* Burgess, 'Letter from England', *Hudson Review*, Autumn 1967, p. 454–8, 454.

get worse, and that there would be no remission'.* The major symptoms were 'toothache in the right calf, and a sudden accession of pins and needles, like a monstrous toilet flush, in the right foot'; he developed an intermittent limp ('claudication', sounding more distinguished, was his preferred way of putting it), found it impossible to walk for long distances, and was forced to acquire a walking stick. A letter from Lynne to Agnes Tollitt tells us that his mobility was so badly impaired that it was painful for him to get around on buses and trains. Surrendering to the inevitable, he started using taxis instead. At the age of fifty, he began to look and feel like an ancient man. Matters were not improved by the loss of four lower incisors in a pub-fight in Chiswick with a bald Irishman who had insulted his dog. Burgess (who had already made low comedy out of Enderby's unreliable dentures) got himself a set of prosthetic teeth, but these could not be trusted to remain in place without a fixing agent. He and Lynne were both falling apart.

A change of diet relieved some of the symptoms in his leg – he was advised to drink spirits and to cut down on fatty foods – but the limp remained with him for the rest of his life. Following the medical wisdom of the day, he stopped smoking cigarettes and took up cigars. Whether this new regime of cheroots, panatelas and schimmelpennincks did him any good is open to question: he once said that he liked to smoke as many of these as he could without actually being sick. If anyone suggested that he should stop smoking altogether, he told the story of a bookseller friend of his who had

---

* Burgess, 'Views', Listener, 31 August 1967, p. 261. There is a minor puzzle here. This article gives us the earliest references to an arterial problem in his right leg. Later on, in an Observer article (16 March 1980, p. 33), in Homage to Qwert Yuiop (p. 20) and in You've Had Your Time (p. 364), he clearly refers to arterial pains in his left leg. Were both legs affected, separately or simultaneously? And were these 'monstrous' cramps and aches caused by Bürger's disease (which, according to the Hudson Review article, 'strikes most male Jews over 40 who smoke too many cigarettes') or by arteriosclerosis? Burgess's published accounts and Liana's letters inconsistently mention both.

tried to give up and had been afflicted by 'brown sweats'.* Burgess, who regarded himself as a martyr to nothing except literature, preferred slow suicide by smoking. 'Cancer of the lung,' he wrote, 'was probably only there to kill other people.'† The memory of having watched his father, a heavy-smoking tobacconist, die from pleurisy at the age of fifty-five was an inconvenient detail that he preferred to overlook.

He prepared for Lynne's death by writing a remarkable trio of short stories, published once only in obscure periodicals and anthologies of cheap horror. Burgess never allowed these stories to be collected, and they have disappeared from sight almost entirely. All three share a common theme: the murder of a hated wife by her long-suffering husband. The first to appear in print was 'A Pair of Gloves', a cleverly constructed series of monologues (possibly intended as a radio play) narrated by the remorselessly nagging murderee, who is never named.‡ This hysterical wife is devoted to the memory of her dead father – 'a fine handsome man and upright and smart and real proud of him my mother was' – and she is persistent in turning down the lascivious advances of Harry, her husband: 'Love? That's not love, that's sheer dirt and nastiness [. . .] Unnatural lust, that's what it is [. . .] You and your lustful desires [. . .] Degradation and unwholesomeness, that's what I let myself in for. My father would turn in his grave [. . .] I will not have that sort of nasty remark. That's an unclean and uncalled-for remark. That is blast feemy talking that way about my poor dead father.' It ends nastily, of course: the sexually frustrated Harry buys a pair of gloves and puts an end to the nagging by strangling his wife. She dies with the word 'Dad' on her lips.

Some of the same motifs recur in 'An American Organ', which,

---

* Lorna Sage, 'Still Angry After All These Years', *Observer*, 23 February 1992, p. 51.

† Burgess, *Shakespeare* (London: Jonathan Cape, 1970), p. 111.

‡ 'A Pair of Gloves' in *Lie Ten Nights Awake*, ed. by Herbert Van Thal (Hodder & Stoughton, 1967), pp. 9–17.

like 'A Pair of Gloves', was published in a paperback collection of
horror stories.* Once again, the murdered wife is unnamed, and she
accuses her husband of 'blasphemy' when he speaks out against her
beloved dead mother, whose assortment of furniture, china dogs
and Sèvres dinner-plates is cluttering up their small house in Oxfordshire. (The story's location resembles the Wilsons' former cottage on
Water Lane in Adderbury; and Lynne, as Burgess tells us in his
memoirs, was devoted to both of her parents.) The husband, who
narrates the story, is an amateur pianist who can't afford a piano;
his fingers 'itched for a keyboard of some kind'. While his wife is
out of the house, he takes his late mother-in-law's objects to an
antique shop, where he successfully exchanges them for a pedal-
operated American organ ('I treadled the pedals, feeding it wind, as
I lifted the lid. Yellow keys. Hungrily I fingered them'). This he
installs on the upstairs landing at home, just outside the bathroom.
His wife returns from work, is distressed at the loss of her treasured
maternal knick-knacks, and is persuaded to take a bath to calm
down. He dresses up in a dark suit and black shoes, as if for a
formal recital or funeral. He recalls the story of Smith, the notorious
bride-in-the-bath murderer, who played 'Nearer, my God, to Thee'
on the organ while his wife was drowning. After a short blast of
Wagner – the wedding march from Act III of *Lohengrin* – he goes
into the bathroom. 'She splashed away happily [. . .] Holding it firm,
I cracked her head quite hard against the head of the bath. This
wasn't quite enough, so I cracked it again. Then I let her slide into
the water so that her head was covered. She was not a very tall
woman and, even in that small bath, there was plenty of room.'
While her bubbling lungs fill with water, he pedals more air into
'the organ's lungs', warming up for the slow movement of Tchaikov-
sky's Fifth Symphony and Beethoven's 'Pathétique' sonata. He plays
on until the bath-water turns cold.

   A good deal of 'An American Organ' eventually found its way

---

* Burgess, 'An American Organ' in *Splinters*, ed. by Alex Hamilton (London:
Hutchinson, 1968), pp. 76–82.

into the thirteenth chapter of *The Pianoplayers*, but Burgess altered the story in one crucial respect when he revised it for inclusion in the novel: the sadistic killing has been removed. When Robert tries to drown Edna, having smashed down the bathroom door with an axe, they both become aroused, and this Lawrentian ritual of watery wrestling saves their marriage: 'It was the first time they'd either of them got anything out of Sex, he said, and from then on they had the water heater on all the time. Edna, as you might expect, couldn't get enough of it now, and they were the cleanest couple in Hammersmith [. . .] All this shows you the importance of Sex in people's lives, which I've never doubted and have spent a lot of my time trying to make people see.'* Burgess altered the story's tone entirely, from black melodrama to bathroom farce; and to some extent he covered his earlier tracks.† Yet he could never unwrite the fact that the wife is murdered in the original version, which he published while his own wife was dying.

The third of these stories is called, bluntly and simply, 'I Wish My Wife Was Dead'.‡ The central character is John Sturges, who has a despised 'nagging' wife, of whom he says: 'I wouldn't want to bear the knife myself, as the schoolbook says. But if she were to

---

* Burgess, *The Pianoplayers* (London: Hutchinson, 1986), p. 205.
† He was severe in his criticism of Evelyn Waugh for having spliced a short story, 'The Man Who Liked Dickens' (1933), into the text of *A Handful of Dust* (1934): 'This frightful ending (where Tony Last spends all his time reading Dickens to this half-breed in the jungle) appeared previously as a short story; and, knowing the short story, one has a strange attitude to the book. Which makes us feel that here is a deliberate pasting together, where this giant figure at the end that turns up does not spring automatically out of the book but is just taken arbitrarily from another work' (John Cullinan, 'Anthony Burgess', p. 339). The dates are important here. The interview was published in 1973, and if Burgess had changed his mind by 1986, this was partly because finding an ending for *The Pianoplayers* (which he'd been revising, on and off, since April 1977) had been a hellishly difficult business.
‡ Burgess, 'I Wish My Wife Was Dead', *Transatlantic Review*, Winter 1969–1970, pp. 40–44. A letter from Deborah Rogers to Burgess, dated 17 April 1969, indicates that this story was 'written some time ago', presumably before Lynne's death in March 1968.

cease upon the midnight with no pain, with her testatory arrangements unchanged, well – I guess that would be a great deal more convenient.' He also has a mistress considerably younger than himself, the grateful recipient of extra-marital cunnilingus ('a most profane and unprayerlike act'). Sturges is the manager of a prospering supermarket, and his wife – who, like Lynne, has a small private income – is taken hostage in her own home by a hit-man called Alvin, 'a stupid but tough gentleman with no talent for compassion or remorse'. Another man, identifying himself as 'Mr Schultz', arrives at Sturges's office and demands to be given the contents of the safe; he will then telephone the house and instruct Alvin to release the wife. If Sturges refuses, she will be killed. Sturges knocks out Schultz with a glass paperweight and picks up the telephone. In a perfect imitation of Schultz's upper-class English voice, he tells Alvin: 'Let her hev it [. . .] Shoot to kill, blahhhst you. I want to hear thet shot.' There are screams, followed by the noise of a gun being fired. Sturges, freed from his long burden of being nagged, and generously rewarded by his employer for heroically thwarting the robbery, leaves for Florida with his mistress.

Although Burgess's stories belong within a tradition of wife-murdering fiction and film, which includes works such as Alfred Hitchcock's *Dial 'M' for Murder*, Patricia Highsmith's *Strangers on a Train* and Evelyn Waugh's *Tactical Exercise*, he also knew his Freud well enough to write a novel and a television series about him – he once claimed that Freud and Jung made regular appearances in his dreams, interpreting the action as it unfolded – and would have been familiar with Freud's notion of the 'suppressed and unsuspected wish'. When Anthony Clare asked him, 'Did you want [Lynne] to live?', he saw at once which way the question was heading and nervously snapped back, 'I didn't want her to die.' Yet all three of these short stories were written between Lynne's first portal haemorrhage and her death less than two years later. Working within the frame of fiction, and speaking obliquely through imaginary voices, Burgess was able to acknowledge a number of possibilities that he later denied in the interview: that Lynne's life was nearing its end, and that her survival was an obstacle to his future happiness. For her part, she flatly refused to discuss her drinking and its effects on her health and appearance. These were the only conversational taboos between the Wilsons, but it was clear to most observers that she would not last long. Christopher Burstall, who got to know Lynne well in the mid-1960s, says: 'I felt regard for her, and I could see as an outsider that she was self-destructive. There's usually a reason for that. And I obviously felt sad.'* The literary agent Ed Victor, who met Lynne shortly before her death, puts the case more bluntly: 'She was a pathetic drunk. She was just sozzled all the time. There are certain people you meet and you know you can't deal with them. They're too far gone. She was terrifying.'†

Burgess's account of Lynne's decline and final illness is filtered through his intimate familiarity with the text of Joyce's *Ulysses*. In the autobiography he writes: 'I could take no pleasure in a body that had once been sweet as cinnamon but was now being wrecked through drink.'‡ In the 'Scylla and Charybdis' chapter of *Ulysses*, there is a corresponding sentence which refers to Anne Shakespeare: 'And in New Place a slack dishonoured body that once was comely, once as sweet, as fresh as cinnamon, now her leaves falling, all, bare, frighted of the narrow grave and unforgiven.'§ Perhaps he wanted to make another grandiose self-comparison with Shakespeare, whose wife is also said to be unfaithful in the novel (or between himself and Stephen Dedalus, who speaks these words). Or perhaps Burgess found it too painful to write about Lynne in a direct way, and fell back on Joyce's phrase as a defence against having to explore his own feelings in detail. The same thing happens in *Little Wilson and Big God* when he describes the death of his father. Instead of examining his own emotional condition, he

---

* Christopher Burstall to author, 7 June 2000.
† Ed Victor to author, 22 May, 2003.
‡ Burgess, *You've Had Your Time*, p. 111.
§ James Joyce, *Ulysses* (London: Bodley Head, 1960), p. 247.

reaches for a line from his favourite novel. Such moments in the *Confessions* reveal Burgess at his most evasive.

Lynne's end came, not unexpectedly, on the first day of spring. After a second and more serious haemorrhage in Chiswick ('there were not enough pots and pans in the kitchen to hold the tides of blood'), her specialist had warned Burgess that if she took another drink she would die.* According to Deborah Rogers, 'She was told that she must never drink again. Burgess dourly reported this' – although he said afterwards that he had considered the warning too melodramatic to be taken seriously. Discharged from hospital, Lynne drank ginless Schweppes tonic water zested with lemon-peel. But it was not long before she was demanding dry white wine and chilled lager (because, as she said, 'chilled things are good for the stomach'). Heavily jaundiced, and wearing a wig to conceal the fact that her hair was falling out, she attended a party with Burgess at the Time-Life building on Bruton Street in London on 12 February 1968. This was her final appearance in public, and she wore a long, embroidered Chinese silk jacket. A photograph taken at this party shows her looking bloated and wrinkled. They celebrated Burgess's fifty-first birthday at Glebe Street on 25 February. A few days later she collapsed at home and was sent by ambulance to the hospital in Ealing. Nothing more could be done for her. It took her nearly a month to die, and she was already in a coma when Burgess was summoned to the hospital to witness her final breath at 5.30 in the morning on Wednesday, 20 March. The cause of death was recorded as 'cardiac and liver failure'. He went home in a taxi in the rain, unconsoled by the noise of The Grateful Dead, who were singing away on the cab-driver's radio.

Everyone who knew Burgess at this time agrees that he was genuinely grief-stricken immediately after Lynne's death. She was cremated at Mortlake – not buried, at her own request, because she'd had an unreasonable fear of waking up underground in a coffin. Her niece, Ceridwen Looker, who travelled down from

---

* Burgess, *You've Had Your Time*, p. 150.

Leicester for the funeral with her parents, says: 'I was left in the house in Chiswick. I can remember they had a bar, which I thought was rather crass, in the living-room. I remember [Burgess] saying, "Help yourself to cigarettes and stuff. Drink what you want." I was only sixteen. I remember thinking, "I don't want these cigarettes." They were untipped Embassy. I helped myself to the green char-treuse.' Ceridwen disputes Burgess's suggestion that she went through Lynne's wardrobe on the day of her funeral and made off with a pair of leather boots: 'Absolutely no way would I want to try a dead woman's clothes on. Bear in mind that Llewela had bal-looned to a huge size by this time, and there I am, a sixteen-year-old, a size eight, very fit, a very healthy hockey-player. None of her stuff would have fitted me. Why make up a lie like that? That really incensed me. It still makes me mad after all these years.'*
Ceridwen regards Burgess's other anecdotes about her family as equally untrustworthy, especially his account of her parents' court-ship in Wales – of which he evidently had no first-hand knowledge, because Hazel Jones had already married William Looker before Lynne met Burgess in Manchester in 1938. Ceridwen listed various other factual errors and distortions in an article, 'Burgess the Betrayer', published in April 1993.†

Burgess's thirty-year relationship with Lynne has become so entangled in his web of fictions that it is almost impossible by now to distinguish her true character from his carefully polished reci-tations about her. He told Anthony Clare that she had been 'almost philosophically unfaithful' to him, and that her early infidelities had established the pattern of their marriage. Part of the problem was that the Second World War forced them to live apart for six years between 1940 and 1946, with the result that they had both looked for sexual comfort elsewhere. Burgess was enough of a Catholic to believe that divorce was out of the question, and Lynne, who attached no theological sense of sin to adultery, knew that their

---

* Ceridwen Berry (née Looker) to author, 12 October 1999.
† See Richard Heller, 'Burgess the Betrayer', *Mail on Sunday*, 11 April 1993.

marriage would hold regardless of how well or how badly she behaved. ('Lynne was nominally Anglican,' according to one of her neighbours from Adderbury, 'but I don't think she had much time for any sort of religion.')* Burgess remarked that she was fond of quoting a maxim from La Rochefoucauld: 'Ça vous donne tant de plaisir et moi si peu de peine.' 'Ça' in this context refers to the offer of her sexual favours.

Yet there was more to their marriage than playing away. Lynne was a loyal companion, a fellow drinker willing to match Burgess pint for pint and shot for shot. She cooked for him, cleaned their houses, invested shrewdly on the Stock Exchange, brought in extra money through teaching jobs, played the diplomatic wife in the East, and encouraged his literary ambitions. Lynne was highly educated and a capable intellectual sparring-partner. The legal partnership agreement they drew up in 1964 acknowledges that the literary life was one they had embarked on jointly. Without Lynne Wilson, perhaps there would have been no Anthony Burgess. Their marriage was a source of shared jokes and secret codes, a small civilization of two. Why, then, did Burgess vilify Lynne to the extent that he did in his autobiography? Ceridwen, her niece, believes that he simply resented her large and stable middle-class family: 'My mother told me that [Lynne] came home from Manchester one vacation [in 1938] and said that she'd met a man with a terrible home life. She felt sorry for him. He'd had a rotten childhood.'†

Ed Victor remembers Burgess 'howling at the moon' in the weeks immediately following Lynne's death, and Burgess himself describes the extent of his guilt and grief in You've Had Your Time: 'I had murdered a woman and had to be punished for it [. . .] What nonsense I had preached about free will: I should have snatched tumblers from her hand, emptied bottles down the sink [. . .] I hugged the blame. It was right for me to feel like a murderer.'‡

---

* Anthony Froggatt to author, 20 July 2000.
† Ceridwen Berry to author, 12 October 1999.
‡ Burgess, You've Had Your Time, pp. 180, 151.

Deborah Rogers confirms that he was in a state of great distress and recalls that his guilt was intensified by the relief he had felt when Lynne was sent off to hospital at the end of February. She says:

> Their routine was that he would get up at seven or seven-thirty in the morning and go down to this damp, lean-to kitchen. He'd let the dog out and the cat in. Then he'd get the ice out of the fridge and take it up to Lynne for her first gin of the day. When she was in hospital, he'd lie in bed rejoicing that he didn't have to get up for her morning gin. And then when she died he was consumed.[*]

Rogers also remembers driving Burgess down to Etchingham to help him sort out Lynne's clothes. 'It was haunting. Everything was as she'd left it. Her bedroom slippers were at an angle, as she'd got out of them. He insisted on giving me a lynx jacket and a ring.' The rest of Lynne's personal effects – everything except her books, which are now in the university library at Angers – were disposed of by the cleaning lady, Mrs Sweetman, who was instructed by Burgess to get them out of the house as quickly as possible.

The precise order of what happened next is uncertain. Burgess returned to Chiswick, where he spent time with the novelist Olivia Manning and her husband Reggie Smith, a BBC producer who had helped Burgess to find television work. It was common knowledge that the marriage between Manning and Smith had broken down, partly as a result of Smith's persistent philandering, although they continued to live together in a very modest house in St John's Wood. Not long before her death in 1980, Manning spoke to Francis King about Burgess. As King records in his autobiography, *Yesterday Came Suddenly*, 'Olivia told me that, only a week or two after the death of his first wife, Burgess suggested that she should marry him. She objected that she was already married to Reggie; to which he replied, "Well, divorce him!" Whether this is true or not I have

---

[*] Deborah Rogers to author, 4 January 2002.

never been able to confirm.'* King himself is sceptical about the anecdote, pointing out that, late in life, Olivia Manning often invented malicious stories about her friends.

Burgess himself said, in his interview with Samuel Coale in 1978, that he and Liana had been 'consorting together' since 1963, and that they were living together in Chiswick from April 1968, which is to say the month after Lynne had died. One of the few surviving documents from this time is a postcard to Julian Mitchell, dated 2 July 1968, in which Burgess announces that he is 'courting' and intends shortly to marry again because, as he puts it, 'I'm used to being married.' Liana is not mentioned by name in the postcard, but she is surely the woman he has in mind. Deborah Rogers remembers that 'About six weeks after Lynne had died I suddenly got a phone call from Burgess. He said: I'm getting married. Somebody I've known for some time.'† Their engagement was announced in the newspapers, and they finally married at Hounslow Registry Office on 9 September 1968. Burgess was fifty-one years old. Liana was thirty-eight. Paolo Andrea had just turned four.

Burgess talks at length about Paolo Andrea in a 1968 essay for the *Spectator*, published under the title 'Thoughts of a Belated Father'. 'I have just married again,' he writes, 'and my wife's dowry consists mainly of a four year old boy called Paolo Andrea [. . .] me being fifty and never till now having had any experience of father-hood, whether true, spiritual, step or foster.'‡ Burgess has shaved a year off his age here, and the article actually appeared three days before the date of his second marriage. The most interesting distor-tion, though, is that Paolo Andrea is referred to throughout the piece as Burgess's stepson rather than as his biological son. The wish to avoid upsetting Lynne's surviving family would have been a good and sufficient reason for this, and from Burgess's point of view there

---

* Francis King, *Yesterday Came Suddenly* (London: Constable, 1993), pp. 241–2.
† Deborah Rogers to author, 4 January 2002.
‡ Burgess, 'Personal Column: Thoughts of a Belated Father', *Spectator*, 6 September 1968, p. 322.

was also the knowledge that Archbishop Dwyer might see the article and take offence if it contained any suggestion of impropriety. The archbishop had telephoned the house in Chiswick when he heard about the engagement to Liana. 'Glory be to God,' he declared, on being told that Burgess was planning to marry an Italian woman, although a discreet veil was drawn over her anti-clerical and fiercely Leftist political views.*

Burgess's early dealings with Paolo Andrea were certainly paternal, but there were also elements of eccentricity and mutual incomprehension. Their relationship, as he said in the *Spectator* article, involved a good deal of nonsense-talk and 'mutual exhibition, mostly of posteriors'. The four-year-old Paolo Andrea was a creature of florescent 'bare ego' – inevitably, perhaps, since he was still engaged in what Burgess called 'the long barbarity of childhood'. He would wet the bed, steal cigars, smear treacle in his hair, and make loud demands for ice-cream or money. On one occasion he mixed a kind of improvised concrete out of yoghurt and shit. Burgess worried that an energetic four-year-old might be inclined to use his typewriter as a toy, or to urinate over the typescript and carbons of a half-finished novel. Uncharmed by the irrational roaring ego of this child, Burgess wished that the boy was ten years older. Yet he realized that by the time Paolo Andrea was fourteen, he would himself be sixty. 'When he is ready to earn a living,' he concluded, 'I shall probably be dead.' This isn't to say that affection was altogether missing from his feelings for his son – the charmingly inventive books Burgess wrote for him (*A Long Trip to Tea-Time* and *The Land Where The Ice-Cream Grows*) are evidence enough of that – but it is clear that he had a limited amount of patience with children. He tended to regard them as unformed beings who should be moulded into adults with the shortest possible delay. 'Burgess simply didn't understand children,' Deborah Rogers says.

---

* See Thomas Churchill, 'An Interview with Anthony Burgess', *Malahat Review*, January 1971, pp. 103–27.

'As far as he was concerned, a child was simply a small person. No concession was made to childhood or childishness.'

The long process of establishing the value of Lynne's estate and calculating what proportion of it should be paid to the Inland Revenue in the form of death duties began in 1968, but it was an argument which had still not been fully resolved when Burgess and Liana settled in Monaco in 1975. There were other disputes about his substantial income from writing film scripts. Deborah Rogers proposed that Burgess's minimum fee as a screenwriter should be US $25,000 per script. This was good news in principle, but between 1966 and 1968 Burgess received a series of unexpected tax demands for thousands of pounds. In his 'Letter to a Tax Man', he complained that it would be impossible to raise the large sums demanded at short notice, because it would involve selling his shares at a loss. His sense of panic and incomprehension about money is made clear in the article itself: 'I don't really know how all this came about. I do not live extravagantly. I smoke a lot (but that's a patriotic duty to the Exchequer) and very occasionally take a taxi, but I don't run a car. I have three suits. I try to drink only beer. I work seven days a week. The real answer is to work less.'*

Not true, or not entirely. The real answer was to clear out of Britain – where the Labour government had established a regime of punitive super-tax for the wealthy – and to push on with the job of writing in a low-tax haven elsewhere in Europe. Malta seemed to be the obvious destination: it was still within the sterling zone, and it was already the home of other expatriate writers, such as Desmond Morris (the best-selling author of *The Naked Ape*) and the minor English novelist Nigel Dennis. In the summer of 1968 Burgess visited Malta with Liana and bought a large white-marble *palazzo* on the Main Street in Lija. They returned to England, crated up their possessions to be shipped to Malta, and paid cash for a new Bedford Dormobile. This was to be their travelling home and office as they peregrinated from house to house around Europe for the next seven

---

* Burgess, 'Letter to a Tax Man', *Guardian*, 28 December 1966, p. 12.

years. Burgess was leaving England yet again, and this time there seemed to be no realistic prospect of coming back. On the eve of his departure, in November 1968, he described the Bedford van ('a miracle of British design, although much let down by slipshod British execution – screws missing, bad wood-planing and so on') and connected it with his reasons for wanting to get out of England in an article for the *Listener*:

> The van was delivered by a moron who could tell me nothing of how the thing worked. How to change a wheel? You'd better go and find out from a garage, mate. But, damn it all, I bought it from *you*. Not from me, you didn't, mate. I only got took on yesterday. Well, there it is – the British refusal to recover economically through interest in the act of selling [. . .] Take it or leave it, mate.*

He denied that he was scuttling off to Malta because of excessive taxation, claiming instead that his failing eyesight demanded stronger light than the British climate could provide. 'I find that my true reason is a desire to see words on a page with some clarity. English days are so dark [. . .] I hunger for the reading lamp of the sun. He left England to seek the light – let those be my last words.'

---

* Burgess, 'Views', *Listener*, 14 November 1968, p. 634.

10

Real Horrorshow

On the way to their decaying palazzo in Malta, Burgess, Liana and
Paolo Andrea wandered circuitously through France and Italy
between October and December 1968. They broke their journey in
Avignon, where they were robbed of passports and other valuables,
and in Rome, where they stayed with a friendly lawyer called
Andrew de Gasperis. The Dormobile served a variety of purposes: it
was a travelling office, part of a self-proclaimed 'struggle against
bourgeois conformity', a way of avoiding letters of demand from
the taxman, and a convenient vehicle for slipping across borders in
disguise as an innocent family of holidaymakers.* Twenty years
later, Burgess said that he looked back on the autumn of 1968 as
a period of hard work and healthy, rootless liberation: 'I was not
wholly free, for I had the duty of hammering away at my typewriter
every day, but what I wrote carried the breath of the open road.'
In San Severino, he met his new mother-in-law, Maria Lucrezia
Macellari, otherwise known as the Contessa Pasi della Pergola, an
aristocratic widow in her seventies ('a handsome old lady with fine
feet and ankles', as he put it), who was an enthusiastic amateur poet

---

* Burgess, 'The World Doesn't Like Gipsies' in *One Man's Chorus: The Uncollected Writings*, ed. by Ben Forkner (New York: Carroll & Graf, 1998),
pp. 138–40.

and abstract watercolourist. The Contessa was charmed by her four-year-old grandson, who spoke to her in an eccentric blend of Cambridge English, Italian and London street-slang. The Dormobile and its occupants continued south, heading for Malta. With Liana at the wheel, Burgess sat in the rear with a portable typewriter, working on a film adaptation of the first two Enderby novels for Warner Brothers.

From Brindisi they caught the ferry to Valletta. By 19 December they had arrived at 168 Main Street in Lija. Deborah Rogers wrote from London with the news that the Maltese authorities had accepted Burgess's application for residency, and that a balance of £14,479 6s. 4d. had been transferred to his account at Barclay's Bank in Valletta. He and Liana soon discovered that Malta was full of vexations. There was no electricity at the house, and Maltese bureaucracy seemed to be designed to prevent its swift connection. When Burgess asked a functionary at the Electricity Department how soon the power could be turned on, his request was met with mystical evasions and the words 'Let us consider the nature of electricity'.* An elderly neighbour used hairpins and screwdrivers to activate the supply. A telephone was promised in about three years. 'You have no conception,' Burgess was told, 'of the length of the waiting list, although we could spend a profitable morning considering why this is so. To start with, we have to be reborn after so many decades of stultifying colonial rule.' He decided that these episodes were symptomatic of a more general Maltese hostility towards foreign settlers, especially the British. A few months after arriving on the island, he wrote: 'Behind the smile and the beckoning hand lie the little bureaucrats whose lives depend on delay, quibbling and the accumulation of paper [. . .] The Maltese week is capable of stretching to a fortnight, and promises made by carpenters and plumbers are like the Church's promises of eventual beatitude.' He complained about the food, and was disappointed

---

* Burgess, 'Letter From Europe', *American Scholar*, vol. 38, no. 2 (Spring 1969), pp. 297–9.

by the winter weather: 'A dull or cold day on the Middle Sea depresses far more than a whole wretched December in London or New York: one recognizes that one isn't getting what one came for – sun – and that there's very little else one could conceivably come for.'

His catalogue of minor dissatisfactions grew longer. Copies of the French edition of *Tremor of Intent* were seized by the Maltese Office of State Censorship, which suspected that the book might contravene the strictly enforced obscenity laws. (The Danish translation slipped through the censors' net, probably because of its religious-sounding title, *Martyrenes Blod*, meaning 'the blood of the martyrs'.) In the spring of 1969, Burgess found that he was 'pustular and squamous' with chickenpox, which left him too feeble to work. He spent several weeks in bed with swollen glands, depression and thoughts of mortality. After the vomiting phase had passed, he found that he could not read or listen to music without experiencing 'changes in mental tone, and even in the process of mental apprehension'. When he tried to play Debussy's two *Arabesques*, piano pieces that he had known for years, his disorganized mind persuaded him that the music was somehow transmitting 'a quality of evil' to him: 'I mean that the music is an unclean and nasty substance, evil as the smell of bacon given to a dying man.'* Reading Ezra Pound's *Hugh Selwyn Mauberley*, he found that certain images from the poem 'were capable of moving out of the figurative world and approaching, if not actually reaching, the status of literal, tangible, visible brooches and enamels'. This was a new kind of synaesthetic reality, unassisted by drink or drugs. The frequency of the hallucinations diminished as he recovered from his illness.

Just before the chickenpox struck, in January 1969, Deborah Rogers wrote to inform Burgess that a pair of film producers, Si Litvinoff and Max Raab, who had bought the film rights to *A Clockwork Orange*, were now offering him $25,000 to write a script based on his own novel, to be directed by Nicholas Roeg. He

---

* Burgess, 'Views', *Listener*, 22 May 1969, p. 709.

eventually agreed, but only after Rogers had succeeded in doubling the fee. Burgess's film script, which was rediscovered in 2004 in his abandoned house in Bracciano, is an elaborate reworking and reimagining of *A Clockwork Orange* rather than a straightforward adaptation. It introduces a number of new Nadsat words not present in the original, as well as a series of extravagantly bloodthirsty dream-visions. Armed with a razor and a bicycle chain, Alex slashes, swishes and dances his way through a gaudy fantasy world, sexually aroused by the screams and moans of his enemies, and urged on to further atrocities by the classical soundtrack which plays constantly inside his head. His bedroom cupboard is full of horrors: chemicals, syringes, weapons, sadistic instruments, human bones and the skull of a small child. Burgess's stage-directions make it clear that this cinematic Alex is intended to represent the suppressed violent desires of the audience. As in the novel, the true villain of the film is the authoritarian, technological society which seeks to 'cure' him of the impulse to do evil. Disregarding the redemptive twenty-first chapter entirely, the ending of Burgess's film script follows the American edition of the novel. 'I'm cured all right,' says the deconditioned, post-clockwork Alex. In the final shot, he turns defiantly to the camera and asks, 'What's it going to be then, eh?' before running towards us with his cut-throat razor poised to draw blood. Although this script was discarded before the film was made, it has an intensity of violence which is largely missing from Stanley Kubrick's more euphemistic interpretation. Burgess's version is also much livelier than Kubrick's script from a linguistic point of view, and it is clear that the vocabulary of Nadsat was still expanding seven years after the first publication of the novel.

One of his visitors in Lija was the novelist Brian Aldiss, who, partly because he had also spent time in Malaya, had been an admirer of Burgess's work since the publication of *Time for a Tiger*. Aldiss first met Burgess and Lynne in London in the early 1960s, and he remembers that Burgess was 'extremely patient with a wife whose eccentricity readily turned into tipsiness'. Thinking back to his Maltese holiday with Burgess and Liana, Aldiss recalls:

He invited us to his palazzo. I went alone. The building was quite modest, set unobtrusively behind large double carriage doors in a steep street. Anthony was there with his new Italian wife. They were most welcoming. We sat on a balcony which overlooked the palazzo's central square, in one corner of which a lemon tree flourished. We were both smoking in those days; both of us have had to give up that agreeable habit, death being Anthony's motivation, survival being mine. Liana wheeled over a drink trolley and we started in on Cinzano, then into red wine. Anthony embarked on a long tale of his difficulties in getting to Rome, and then on to Malta to claim his palazzo. It was a pretty melancholy tale [. . .] Terrible transport problems met them in Valletta harbour. There were more terrible set-backs.*

Burgess spent much of 1969 working on highly paid film and television projects, none of which went into production. Litvinoff and Raab demanded scripts for *The Doctor Is Sick* and *The Wanting Seed*; Warner Brothers asked for a second draft of 'The Bawdy Bard'; Universal Studios wanted a film about Mary, Queen of Scots; Michael Holden commissioned a screenplay about the Black Prince. For the BBC, Burgess wrote a television play about wife-swapping called 'Somebody's Got to Pay the Rent' and an episode of *Quiller* ('Murder to Music'), but both of these were rejected. It was not until the autumn that he was able to get down to the beginning of a new novel. This was *MF* (or *M.F.* or *M/F*), written in response to a suggestion by William Conrad that somebody should update the Oedipus story and retitle it 'Motherfucker'. Burgess was on his travels again as soon as the first chapter had been completed and sent off to London. In September he was teaching at the Mediterranean Institute of Dowling College in Mallorca, where he found Robert Graves surrounded by a collection of stoned and bearded poets. Unimpressed by the hippies, Burgess insisted on lecturing in a jacket and tie. He flew on to North Carolina in November to take

* Brian Aldiss to author, 23 January 2003.

up a month-long post as a visiting professor at the University of
Chapel Hill. Here he met Ben Forkner, then a graduate student and
later a university teacher in France, who went on to edit *One Man's
Chorus*, a volume of Burgess's uncollected writings, in 1998. The
faculty and students at Chapel Hill were delighted by Burgess's
energy and erudition. Ben Forkner remembers:

> He held forth throughout the hand-shakings, receptions, official
> dinners, and late-night drinking sessions that followed. The
> holding forth lasted not for a few days only, but during the
> entire month of the stay [. . .] Here was the inspired eloquence
> his novels are filled with, the immense culture, the outrageous
> wit, the oddity and pithiness of phrase, the effortless impro-
> visation on any theme under the sun and moon.

On one particular day which is still a legend at Chapel Hill, Burgess
was asked to teach five different classes on subjects ranging from
Chaucer to James Joyce. Forkner witnessed 'a one-man parade of
spectacular virtuosity' as he followed Burgess from one lecture to
the next.

> After five hours of uninterrupted brilliance, without a hesitation
> or false note to mar the performance, no professor or student
> dared or desired to say a word [. . .] The explosive shock of
> these displays might have left his increasingly captive audience
> not only filled with awe and envy, but stunned into silence for
> good. Whenever he lectured in a classroom this was in fact
> often the case.*

Nevertheless, some of the senior professors had their doubts about
Burgess and his crowd-pleasing monologues. When he proposed that
the university should award him a doctorate in recognition of his
published work, he was told that, if he wanted a degree from Chapel
Hill, he was welcome to register as a postgraduate student and to sit
the examinations in the normal way.

---

* Ben Forkner, 'Introduction' to *One Man's Chorus*, pp. xiii–xx.

In December 1969 Professor Thomas Stumpf gave a public lecture on Burgess's novels at Chapel Hill. Pleased that his writing was being taken seriously for once, Burgess decided to attend. He was surprised to learn from Stumpf that the name of the main character in *A Vision of Battlements*, Richard Ennis or R. Ennis, could be reversed to form the word 'sinner'. Although Burgess liked to believe that he was, as he'd said in 1967, 'an unbeliever', he took this anagram as an indication that his conscious mind did not always know what was going on when he was at the typewriter. Catholicism always seemed to be creeping into his fiction through the back door.

When he returned to Lija in 1970, he was invited to give a lecture on censorship and obscenity at the Science Lecture Theatre of the University of Malta. He prepared a text in which he quoted from *Areopagitica*, John Milton's polemic to the English parliament in defence of unlicensed printing. Shakespeare and the Bible were at the heart of his argument against censorship. If these canonical works could be said to be violent or pornographic, then should they not join *Tremor of Intent* on the long list of books which were officially banned in Malta? He argued his case forcefully:

When I was a small boy, I saw another boy masturbating vigorously in front of a copy of the Holy Bible. It was one of those Victorian editions with the most lavish engravings. He was masturbating happily before an engraving of 'The Dance Round the Golden Calf'. Rather an inflammatory picture, I must admit. What do we do? Ban illustrated Bibles? Then how about non-illustrated Bibles, with the case in New York State of a man who murdered many children. When he was eventually found, he was asked why he murdered them and he said he was a great reader of the Bible and he was always most interested in the sacrifices perpetrated to make a sweet smell in the nostrils of the Lord by the patriarch Abraham. He was merely trying to do in his own life what a typical patriarch would have done. So with Haigh in England, who murdered many women and drank their blood. He said he was, from an early age, obsessed by the Sacrament of the Eucharist.*

Nobody had warned Burgess that he would be lecturing to an audience of three hundred Catholic nuns and priests. There were no questions afterwards, but 'a fat Franciscan made a throat-cutting gesture'.† One of his neighbours on Malta, the anthropologist and broadcaster Desmond Morris, wrote about Burgess's lecture in his diary:

> Common courtesy is considered to be a major attribute in these small, heavily populated islands and, despite his best intentions, Burgess's abrasive remarks are deeply offensive to his cultured audience. He keeps saying 'we', assuming that his known Catholicism will enable him to treat them as 'family', but to them he is a revered visitor, a famous, foreign exotic, and the last thing they expect from him is a public 'family row' [. . .] His brilliant literary and linguistic brain, which as a writer fills me with awe, is matched by an almost laughable unworldliness. He is like a genius child who hasn't yet learnt the social niceties. Whatever the opposite of street-wise is, he is it. He is library-wise and street-foolish.‡

In the course of a one-hour lecture, Burgess had transformed himself in the eyes of the Maltese from a distinguished guest into an undesirable alien. When he and Liana went away to Italy for a few days, they returned to find that their house had been padlocked and confiscated by the government. Burgess took the story to the London and New York newspapers, and the Maltese authorities were soon persuaded to deconfiscate the house. But clearly it was time to be moving on.

---

* Burgess, *Obscenity and the Arts* (Valletta: Library Association of Malta, 1973), pp. 13–14.
† Burgess, *You've Had Your Time: Being the Second Part of the Confessions of Anthony Burgess* (London: Heinemann, 1990), p. 194.
‡ Desmond Morris, *The Naked Eye: My Travels in Search of the Human Species* (London: Ebury, 2000), pp. 11–12.

They moved on to Italy, to the shore of Lake Bracciano a few miles north of Rome, where they bought a small fifteenth-century fortified house under the walls of the castello. Their new address was 1 and 2 Piazza Padella, Bracciano. Here Burgess completed *MF*, the first novel he had written since *Enderby Outside* in 1967. The final chapter contains a detailed account of Burgess's new environment:

> Lake Bracciano breaks on its shores like the North Sea, and from the cleared dining table on which I write I can watch the heads of foam racing in. All last night an unsecured window-shutter kept crashing, and though I got up three times to force it back to the wall and hold it with the iron *cicogna*, the gust freed it twenty minutes or so after I got back into bed [. . .] This morning Lupo Sassone, the garbage collector and oddjobman who lives next door, climbed out onto the parapet to make more acute the angle of the jut of the *cicogna* while the *tramontana* tore at him. I gave him a five-thousand-lire note, one thousand for each second of his work. Prices are high here in Bracciano, but I get a good rate of exchange for my dollars.*

This was to be his main home and workshop for the next four years, although there would be frequent excursions to the United States and Canada. Having settled in Bracciano and declared himself to be a kind of Italian – 'I had married into the Continent,' as he said on more than one occasion – Burgess wrote about Anglo-Italian literary relations in the preface to a new edition of three travel books by D. H. Lawrence (*Twilight in Italy*, *Sea and Sardinia* and *Etruscan Places*).

> It is of less importance that we should be able to pencil an ellipse around Italy and her dependencies and neighbors, saying 'D. H. Lawrence was here,' than that we should take pleasure in the response of a highly idiosyncratic temperament to the impact of new places [. . .] This was a period of

---

* Burgess, *MF* (London: Jonathan Cape, 1971), p. 216.

THE REAL LIFE OF ANTHONY BURGESS

immense creative activity for Lawrence, and that liveliness of
the sensorium and the imagination, given primarily to fiction,
is manifested also in these essays, with their relish and humor
and immense capacity for rapport with the mountains and the
lakeside and the people.*

Much of what Burgess has to say about Lawrence in this introduction, and elsewhere in his journalism, could also be applied to his
own literary career and reputation:

He ran away with a foreign woman [. . .] He put the members
of various local families in his novels and showed them up in a
bad light. He preached the importance of the erotic life; could
anything be more reprehensible? The Bloomsbury group that
for so long ruled English taste disliked him intensely. He was a
working man who had not been to Oxford or Cambridge: what
right had he to turn himself into one of England's most important novelists and poets?†

With *MF* completed, Burgess resumed his script-writing duties,
which left him with almost no time to think about another novel.
Nat Shapiro, the Broadway producer of *Hair*, asked him to write
the lyrics for a musical based on *Les Enfants du Paradis*. In August
1971 he completed the words and music for a theatrical version of
Joyce's *Ulysses*. There was talk of a biographical film about Harry
Houdini, for which Burgess agreed to write an outline. The composer Stephen Schwartz proposed to collaborate with him on a
musical version of *The Transposed Heads*, the magical Orientalist
novella by Thomas Mann. An American theatre requested a stage
play about Christopher Marlowe. Lord Birkett asked for a rewrite
of 'Uncle Ludwig', a proposed film about Beethoven, in which either
Richard Burton or Rod Steiger was supposed to have played the
composer. Another film producer paid Burgess for a script based on

---

* Burgess, 'Introduction' to *D. H. Lawrence and Italy* (New York: Viking, 1972;
Penguin, 1985), pp. vii–xiii.
† Burgess, 'Lorenzo' in *One Man's Chorus*, pp. 299–303.

Alec Waugh's novel, *A Spy in the House*. He worked hard on these screenplays, but the frustration of seeing them disappear into the chasm of non-production was intense. He also felt guilty about neglecting his primary trade of novel-writing. Three years elapsed between *MF* and his next novel, *Napoleon Symphony*, even though he was writing harder than ever.

There were occasional consolations. Warner Brothers paid him $25,000 (minus his agent's 10 per cent) for the film rights to *Nothing Like the Sun*. Then a commission arrived from Michael Langham at the Tyrone Guthrie Theater in Minneapolis for a new English translation of *Oedipus the King*. Burgess was keen to do it, not least because the incest theme of *MF* had compounded an interest in Freud and Oedipus, which he later developed in his novel about the life of Freud, *The End of the World News* (1982). When the fictional Freud family goes to the theatre in Vienna to watch Sophocles' play, it is of course Burgess's own translation that they are hearing:

> OEDIPUS: *Here he is,*
> *Sons and daughters of Thebes, your shame,*
> *The author of your pestilence – Oedipus,*
> *Killer of his father, defiler of*
> *His mother. Now let me be*
> *Hidden from all eyes.*
>
> *[Oedipus puts out his eyes. The Chorus screams.]*
> OEDIPUS: *Dark, dark. The sun has burst there*
> *For the last time.**

This is a characteristically bold reworking of a classical original, in which Burgess deviates from Sophocles and the ancient Greek theatrical tradition by making Oedipus pluck out his eyes onstage. The performances in Minneapolis were accompanied by a series of primitive-sounding Indo-European chants, composed by Stanley

---

* Burgess, *The End of the World News: An Entertainment* (London: Hutchinson, 1982), p. 97.

Silverman to a text by Burgess. In a letter to Michael Langham, the director of *Oedipus the King*, Burgess wrote: 'I think you're absolutely and brilliantly right to think of a kind of inspired anachronistic approach, a synoptic gospel of all ancient cultures. If this will inspire Stanley to produce music of a strangeness very remote from baroque oratorio, so much the better.'*

Burgess's association with Langham and the Tyrone Guthrie Theater led to two other theatre projects in the early 1970s: a brilliant verse translation of Edmond Rostand's *Cyrano de Bergerac* (later revived by the Royal Shakespeare Company at the Barbican Theatre in 1983), and the award-winning Broadway musical *Cyrano* in 1973. Michael Langham, who directed both these productions, befriended Burgess when he visited the theatre during rehearsals. He speaks illuminatingly about Burgess's self-identification with Rostand's heroic soldier-poet:

> I loved his drunkenness with language. I loved his capacity to reel with the delight of simply creating things that could express himself and what he felt through words [. . .] Anthony was a master of it and, of course, so was Cyrano. And Anthony's seeming refusal to accept the easy way to commercial success and to go his own way, to be true to himself about what he wrote [. . .] enormously appealed to me because [it's] the essence of Cyrano, who says: 'No, thank you. No, thank you. No, thank you.' It's a great aria, and that's his creed, his philosophy of life. And Anthony had that, I thought, himself.†

Langham is thinking of Cyrano's speech in Act Two of Burgess's translation, in which he refuses to join the retinue of Cardinal Richelieu and the Comte de Guiche:

---

* Burgess, letter to Michael Langham, 22 April 1972. Quoted in Burgess, *Oedipus the King*, ed. by Michael Langham (Minneapolis: University of Minnesota Press, 1972), p. 87.
† Interview with Michael Langham, 2 November 1996.

CYRANO: *What would you have me do?*
Seek out a powerful protector, pursue
A potent patron? Cling like a leeching vine
To a tree? Crawl my way up? Fawn, whine
For all that sticky candy called success?
No, thank you. Be a sycophant and dress
In sickly rhymes a prayer to a moneylender?
Play the buffoon, desperate to engender
A smirk on a refrigerated jowl?
No, thank you. Slake my morning mouth with foul
Lees and leavings, breakfast off a toad?
Wiggle and grovel on the dirty road
To advancement and wear the skin of my belly through?
Get grimy calluses on my kneecaps? Do
A daily dozen to soften up my spine?
No, thank you.*

Burgess was in his element when he was asked to turn the heroic couplets of his verse translation into songs for the musical version of *Cyrano*. The Welsh composer Michael Lewis provided the music, and Christopher Plummer (who won a Tony award for his performance) took the title role when the show opened at the Palace Theater in New York on 13 May 1973. The ingenious libretto was the true star of the show. The 'Nose Song', performed at high speed and with great vigour by Plummer in the original cast recording, showcases Burgess's ability to write dextrous, witty lyrics:

There are fifty score varieties of insult you could find:
The lyrical, satirical, commercial, controversial,
And quite frequently the kind kind,
If you possessed a minimal amount of mind.

If you, sir, had a molecule of spunk inside your head
And not the folly and fatuity you wear instead,
Or could be a man of letters,

* Edmond Rostand, *Cyrano de Bergerac*, translated and adapted by Anthony Burgess (London: Hutchinson, 1985), pp. 69–70.

Not just I-D-I-O-T,
You'd be equipped to best your betters,
Meaning me, me, me. *

While Christopher Plummer and the rest of the cast were rehearsing *Cyrano*, Burgess had taken up another teaching post as Visiting Professor of English Literature and Creative Writing at City College, New York. He is possibly the only person ever to have been both a university professor and a Broadway lyricist at the same time – a typically Burgessian fusion of 'high' and 'low' culture, and not one that he would have seen as in any way contradictory. The idea of having a temporary academic job pleased him more than the tiresome business of actually having to carry out his teaching duties. He began to sign his letters 'Professor Anthony Burgess', apparently unaware that this title was purely honorific. His students were on the whole unimpressed by his regular appearances on late-night television talk shows and in the pages of the *New York Times*. They'd never heard of Burgess before, and they saw no particular reason to treat him with the respect and deference that he'd been expecting. To them he represented little more than a middle-aged authority-figure with a funny foreign accent.

One of his colleagues at City College was the writer Joseph Heller, whose first novel, *Catch-22*, Burgess had reviewed admiringly for the *Yorkshire Post* in 1961. When Heller spoke about Burgess in 1996, he was still angry about the attitude of students at the college, which drew most of its intake from the poorer neighbourhoods in New York. At that time City College was operating an open-access policy, and there was no expectation that students should possess any previous qualifications. As Heller remembers it, many of them were inclined to vent their disaffection on to their teachers:

* *Cyrano*, A & M Records, 1973. Lyrics by Anthony Burgess based on his adaptation of Cyrano de Bergerac by Edmond Rostand. Music by Michael J. Lewis.

The kids were unruly, to put it mildly. Many of them were not even willing to study and they certainly didn't care about two well-known writers, like Burgess and I, being there [. . .] You have to keep in mind that many of these students came from poor and rough backgrounds. A lot of them were also black. So Burgess had two problems to deal with. One was the black and white problem. There was a lot of mutual racism between blacks and whites and he was a white man teaching black students. The other problem was that, to the students, Anthony Burgess, being a professor, represented the establishment and a lot of them hated the establishment and everything it stood for, even though the establishment had just given them access to free education and used its money to pay their teachers [. . .] They were capable of being very rude, very hurtfully so. They'd walk out in the middle of his class, or call him names, or talk back at him constantly, interrupt him while he was speaking, argue with him about even the most petty matters, talk among each other and ignore his requests to be quiet so he could continue teaching. They made fun of his British accent, the way he walked, his enthusiasm for literature.*

Heller, who experienced similar difficulties in the classroom, quickly became disillusioned with the experiment in free education and social inclusion that was going on at City College. 'It wasted our resources,' he said, 'not just the financial ones.' He refused to have any dealings with his students beyond the minimum amount of teaching he was required to do. But Burgess took another view, as Heller remembered:

His desire to teach, to bring about a positive change in what were sometimes rather deranged minds, exceeded by far his need for self-preservation. He made himself available to them, and the students made enormous demands on his time, excessively so, but then wasted his time because they had only come to him for another anti-establishment raving session. I admired

* Interview with Joseph Heller, 1996.

the way Burgess could take even the most hostile of these students seriously. He knew and remembered their names. He gave serious thought to even their most absurd statements. He wanted to know their backgrounds [. . .] to figure out where he might find a hook to reach them and bring about a positive change. I admired that, but I didn't like it.

Summing up his memories of having taught with Burgess in 1972–3, Heller, who had been given a terminal diagnosis shortly before he gave this interview, said:

I'm going to die soon and, like any dying man, I am now at the stage where I look back on my life. And I have to say that in all my life, even at its most compassionate moments, I have not even come close to reaching that enormous inner generosity that characterized Anthony Burgess. A lot of writers can be haughty, or irritable, or downright insane, but Burgess was one of the most modest, the kindest, people you'd ever meet. His greatest fault, I think, was that he cared too much about others, even insignificant others [. . .] This often rendered him unhappy because he cared about people who were not even worth caring about. I mean, what other writer of his standing would get emotionally hurt, really hurt, by some rubbish that a rebellious, angry student with a broken life throws at him? He was incapable of looking down on people, I think. It simply was not in his make-up. He could not see that some people mattered more than others. To him, everyone mattered.

An interview from 1973 gives another perspective on Burgess's time at City College. Jeremy Campbell found him 'puffing uneasily on a long, thin cigar' in his subterranean office at the college, where he held forth on the shortcomings of American university education: 'The students I know are terribly ignorant. I don't know how much they take in. They tend to abominate the past as the source of all hypocrisy, humbug and evil. All they want is a quick message [. . .] A university degree in this country may soon be worth no more than a high school diploma.'* America in the 1970s struck him as a country 'full of lies', and suffering from 'a ghastly inability to develop any kind of reasonable human culture'. Burgess also said that he was worried by the xenophobia of New York: 'A Cherokee Indian keeps sending me long, frightening, anti-British letters threatening to come after me with a tomahawk. Hoarse male voices abuse me on the telephone, telling me to eff off back to effing Russia just because I suggested that America would be better with a national health service.'

In New York, the Burgess family lived with their Ethiopian maid at Apartment 10-D, 670 West End Avenue, NY 10025. This is also Enderby's apartment in *The Clockwork Testament*, Burgess's bittersweet novel about the traumas of living and teaching and dying in New York in the early 1970s. The book – which was written flat-out in just three weeks, under the provisional title 'Death in New York' – draws directly on Burgess's memories of City College, although the details are grotesquely distorted for comic purposes. Enderby's response to his creative writing students is measurably less tolerant and humanistic than Burgess's own attitude as Heller describes it. One of these fictional students, the poet Lloyd Utterage (who exists in a state of utter rage), is 'very ugly [. . .] with a cannibal-style wire-wool hairshock'. He is represented to us as a 'melanoid' or 'black bastard' who sulks and sneers and guffaws 'in a way that Enderby could only think of as *niggerish*'.† Utterage's poetry is 'a litany of anatomic vilification'. It catalogues vengeful acts of sexual violence against the white man:

> *It will be your prick next, whitey,*
> *A loving chopping segmentally*
> *With an already bloodstained meat hatchet,*

---

* Jeremy Campbell, 'Burgess Quits the "Land of Lies and Ignorance"', *Evening Standard*, 14 March 1973, p. 21.
† Burgess, *The Complete Enderby* (London: Penguin, 1995), p. 430.

352 THE REAL LIFE OF ANTHONY BURGESS

> And it will lie with the dog-turds
> To be squashed squash squash.*

The Clockwork Testament comments sceptically on the racism which underpins the ideology of Black Power. 'Imagine a period,' Enderby tells his students, 'when this kind of race hate stupidity is all over.' They reply that he is unable to understand 'the ethnic agony' because he is a white male, and hence part of the system they have rejected. Between Enderby and his students there is no common language, no possibility of reconciliation. They insist that poetry is built out of strong emotions; he maintains that it is purely a matter of form and verbal structures. In setting up a confrontation between white racists and black racists, the novel seems to be entirely symmetrical in its prejudices. Yet it is Utterage, not Enderby, who is given the final word in the argument. After Enderby has declaimed a lyric by Ben Jonson ('Queen and huntress, chaste and fair') as an example of what poetry ought to be, Utterage tells him that he is a 'misleading reactionary *evil* bastard'.† Later on in *The Clockwork Testament*, another of Enderby's students, seemingly driven insane by feminism and lesbianism, bursts into his apartment with a loaded gun, determined to kill him because she believes that his poems have been raping her mind. Burgess's New York is a city of menace and randomness, but his novel challenges a few of the standard clichés about race and violence. When Enderby rides on the subway, he feels threatened by 'noisy ethnic people', 'gangs of black and brown louts' who wear swastikas and other 'symbols of destruction' on their jackets. On closer inspection, the loud youths turn out to be having a discussion about literature, and when a nun is nearly raped on the train – an episode which knowingly echoes the assault on F. Alexander's wife in Kubrick's version of *A Clockwork Orange* – it is three well-dressed white university students who are responsible for the attack. 'You did not educate people out of aggression,'

---

* Ibid., p. 425.
† Ibid., p. 431.

Enderby reflects, in a fit of Augustinian pessimism. 'Great liberal fallacy that.'*

Burgess's one-year appointment at City College was partly connected to the international fame that the film of *A Clockwork Orange* had brought him. Kubrick had persuaded Warner Brothers to buy the film rights to the novel for $200,000 in 1969.† Burgess saw very little of this money. His agent had sold an option to the producers Si Litvinoff and Max Raab for $5,000 a couple of years before Kubrick became interested. When it became clear that Kubrick's adaptation was making hundreds of thousands of dollars for Litvinoff and Raab, Burgess successfully sued them in 1974 for a 10 per cent share of the profits. Although he often complained in interviews that the film had earned him 'a few hundred dollars' or 'the laughable sum of five hundred dollars', the actual figure was much larger.‡ According to a royalty statement, Warner Brothers had paid Burgess $713,081 by June 1985. His substantial book royalties must also be added to this sum. The novel has been translated into French, German, Italian, Japanese, Russian, Spanish, Swedish, Norwegian, Turkish, Polish and Ukrainian; and the English-language editions have been continuously in print since 1972.

An unpublished letter to Burgess from Deborah Rogers confirms that Stanley Kubrick confronted the problem of the novel's two possible endings in the course of preparing the script for his film adaptation. On 27 February 1970 Rogers wrote:

---

* Ibid., p. 455.
† Kevin Jackson writes that Andy Warhol had previously paid $3,000 for the film rights to *A Clockwork Orange*. Warhol's loose adaptation is *Vinyl* (1965), which 'shows the Factory regular Gerard Malanga as a captured juvenile delinquent named Victor [. . .] being tortured with hot wax and force-fed with (probably) amyl nitrate. The action was not faked'. See Jackson, *Letters of Introduction* (Manchester: Carcanet, 2004), p. 220.
‡ See Vincent LoBrutto, *Stanley Kubrick: A Biography* (London: Faber, 1998), p. 365, and Paul Boytinck, *Anthony Burgess: An Annotated Bibliography and Reference Guide* (New York: Garland, 1985), p. xxx.

354   THE REAL LIFE OF ANTHONY BURGESS

I spoke to Stanley Kubrick the other day and he is most anxious to know which the correct ending is from your point of view – whether the extra chapter in the original English edition was added at an editor's suggestion and dropped in America at your own wish – or what. I am ashamed to say that I had not realised that there was any discrepancy between the two [. . .] I had been brought up on the English edition which was the one that I had read first. If you prefer the book without the final chapter (which Kubrick does), as in the American editions, I will instantly make sure that the Penguin edition conforms with that – so please do solve the riddle for us. Mr Kubrick is writing the script himself – and is hard at work.

Burgess's reply to this letter appears not to have survived, but the 1972 Penguin edition to which Rogers refers does indeed omit the twenty-first chapter. Kubrick's decision to follow the Norton version, having first sought Burgess's permission to do so through his agent, therefore emerges as a carefully considered aesthetic choice.

Stanley Kubrick's *A Clockwork Orange* was released by Warner Brothers in New York on 1 December 1971 and in London on 13 January 1972. The film immediately generated a series of hostile reviews, articles and letters to the newspapers on both sides of the Atlantic. Pauline Kael, the film critic of the *New Yorker*, compared the film unfavourably with Burgess's novel, arguing that the book's urgent and prophetic anxiousness about the death of humanism had been 'turned around' and misunderstood by Kubrick as screenwriter and director: 'The numerous rapes and beatings have no ferocity and no sensuality; they're frigidly, pedantically calculated [. . .] The "straight" people are far more twisted than Alex; they seem inhuman and incapable of suffering. He alone suffers.'* The problem with the film, as Kael defines it, is primarily one of style: 'gloating closeups, bright, hard-edge, third-degree lighting, and abnormally loud voices'. Whereas the novel was characterized by 'slangy Nad-

---

* Pauline Kael, 'Stanley Strangelove', *New Yorker*, 1 January 1972, pp. 50–53, 51.

sat' and 'the fast rhythms of Burgess's prose', the film is 'a stupor of inactivity [. . .] infatuated with the hypnotic possibilities of static setups'. Kael concludes with an argument about cinematic (as opposed to merely literary) violence:

> Practically no-one raises the issue of the possible cumulative effects of movie brutality. Yet surely, when night after night atrocities are served up to us as entertainment, it's worth some anxiety. We become clockwork oranges if we accept all this pop culture without asking what's in it. How can people go on talking about the dazzling brilliance of movies and not notice that the directors are sucking up to the thugs in the audience?

Yet Kael overlooks the film's prolonged engagement with the problem of free will, which is clearly articulated by the prison chaplain in his various sermons and lectures. This material, like most of Kubrick's dialogue, is taken directly from the novel.*

Vincent Canby's review, published in the *New York Times*, identifies Kubrick's adaptation as part of a wider trend of blood-thirsty films which includes Roman Polanski's *Macbeth* and Sam Peckinpah's *Straw Dogs*. Canby registers his disgust at the scene in which Alex 'cheerily kicks the guts and genitals of a man whose wife he is about to rape'.† He concedes that one of Kubrick's purposes is 'to analyze the meaning of violence and the social climate that tolerates it', and that the film seeks to aestheticize its ultra-violence, with a 'distancing' effect achieved by means of the

---

* See, for example, the chaplain's interjection in Part Two, chapter 7: ' "Choice," rumbled a rich deep goloss. I viddied it belonged to the prison charlie. "He has no real choice, has he? Self-interest, fear of physical pain, drove him to that grotesque act of self-abasement. Its insincerity was clearly to be seen. He ceases to be a wrongdoer. He ceases also to be a creature capable of moral choice" ' (Burgess, *A Clockwork Orange* (London: Heinemann, 1962), p. 128). This passage is spoken in the film with no alterations.

† Vincent Canby, 'Has Movie Violence Gone Too Far', *New York Times*, 6 January 1972, section 2, p. 1; reprinted in *Film 72/73: An Anthology by the National Society of Film Critics* (New York: Bobbs-Merrill, 1973), pp. 121–4, 121.

pervasive soundtrack (Rossini, Purcell, Elgar and Beethoven) and
the eccentric cinematography, notably the forty-second orgy scene,
corresponding, rather loosely, to the fourth chapter of the novel,
which was shot at two frames per second. (The resulting high-speed
orgy therefore reverses the standard slow-motion convention of
pornography by accelerating the action.) Canby's conclusion echoes
the unease that is also present in Kael's response: 'The shootings
had to become more vivid to impress us, to excite us and – whether
we like to believe it or not – to give us pleasure. Now that the
explicitness has gone almost as far as it can go, it may be that the
margins of pleasure have been exceeded.' Although the review
expresses admiration for Kubrick's visual artistry, it pointedly
reserves judgement on the question of how audiences will respond
to the 'tolchocking and Sheer Vandalism' (Burgess's phrase) that are
inescapably present in the adaptation.*

The British reception of A Clockwork Orange began more
cautiously, but it soon accelerated, following the appearance of
articles in the Sun and the Daily Mail, into something approaching
moral panic.† Penelope Houston's long article for The Times, 'Tolchocked by Kubrick', looks in detail at Kubrick's problem of finding
filmic equivalents for 'Burgess's baroque and spectacular word
patterns'.‡ As in 2001: A Space Odyssey, Kubrick achieves this
through music. Houston suggests a connection between Kubrick's
blackly comic use of Gene Kelly's 'Singin' in the Rain' in A Clockwork Orange and the closing sequence in Doctor Strangelove, in
which Vera Lynn sings 'We'll Meet Again' as the world is destroyed
by nuclear warheads. She describes Malcolm McDowell's screen
version of Alex as 'an articulate fragmentation bomb ticking

* Burgess, A Clockwork Orange, p. 78.
† See Anthony Shrimsley, 'Violence: Maudling Will See Shock Film', Sun, 10
January 1972, p. 1; Cecil Wilson, 'Brilliant . . . But Why All the Violence?', Daily
Mail, 11 January 1972, p. 7.
‡ Penelope Houston, 'Tolchocked by Kubrick', The Times, 8 January 1972, Satur-
day Review section, p. 8.

tirelessly at the film's centre'. However, she also predicts that *A Clockwork Orange* will be 'the season's banker bet for controversy, poised to jab at a public nerve'. This prophecy was at least partly fulfilled on the letters page of *The Times* four days later, when the artist Bernard Dunstan wrote, with reference to the film, that he was 'appalled at the atmosphere of calm acceptance with which such spectacles are discussed'.* Arguing against what he saw as a rising tide of 'cinematic sadism', Dunstan claimed in his letter that critics such as Houston were neglecting their duty to the wider public in failing to condemn sexually sadistic films:

> As one cinematic assault succeeds another our critics blandly tell us that the horrors of the past seem like milk and water now, and that a few years ago this couldn't possibly have been shown. I don't know which I find more unpleasant – the aesthetic attitude to 'choreographed violence', or the way we are often told that the film maker is, of course, dead against rape and shooting, but has to show us, in detail, what he doesn't like about it.

Another letter to the editor of *The Times*, published on 15 January 1972, complained about the wording of the press advertisements for *A Clockwork Orange* ('Being the adventures of a young man whose principal interests are rape, ultra violence and Beethoven'), as symptomatic of the 'forms of pollution which are downgrading life in this country today'.†

Lord Longford, a prominent Catholic political commentator who was much concerned with prison conditions and the rehabilitation of delinquents, made an ambiguous defence of the film in the diary column of *The Times* on the same day: 'I would certainly not describe it as a pornographic film. But [. . .] I wonder whether the apparent hopelessness of treating delinquents might be discouraging to those

---

* Bernard Dunstan, 'Violence Shown in Clockwork Orange' (letter to the editor), *The Times*, 12 January 1972, p. 11.
† R. W. Plenderleith, 'Crime in Advertising' (letter to the editor), *The Times*, 15 January 1972, p. 15.

concerned with reform, and encouraging to delinquents. I am not happy about the moral of the film, but I do not doubt that there is a moral purpose behind it.'* Longford's remarks are evidently a considered response to the 'hopelessness' of the film's concluding scenes, but he seems to have been unaware that a rather different 'moral' (namely Alex's autonomous choice of 'goodness' and domesticity) is offered in the final chapter of the Heinemann edition.

Early in 1972, the news pages of *The Times* reported that Reginald Maudling, the Home Secretary, had ordered a private viewing of *A Clockwork Orange* on 17 January, which was also attended by Stephen Murphy, the director of the British Board of Film Censors.† Maudling's press spokesman explained that the minister wished to see the film 'because of his concern about the current rise in violence', but the fact of Murphy's presence at the screening suggests that he was also anxious to ensure that the BBFC was exercising its powers in a politically acceptable way.‡ Nothing seems to have come of this meeting (there was no suggestion, for example, that the film should be cut or recertified), but the intervention of the Home Secretary on a question of classification after a film had been passed for cinema release was unprecedented, and an indication of the scandalous reputation that the Kubrick version of *A Clockwork Orange* had acquired within a few weeks of its first showing in New York.

It's been suggested, in Paul Joyce's Channel Four documentary, *The Return of A Clockwork Orange* (2000), that the British release of the film played a part in exacerbating the instability of Edward Heath's Conservative government early in 1972.§ Unemployment

---

* 'PHS', 'The Times Diary: Like Clockwork', *The Times*, 15 January 1972, p. 14.
† Anon., 'Mr Maudling Sees Film With Censor', *The Times*, 18 January 1972, p. 4.
‡ See John Trevelyan, *What the Censor Saw* (London: Michael Joseph, 1973), pp. 217–19.
§ *The Return of A Clockwork Orange* (produced and directed by Paul Joyce), broadcast on Channel Four, 18 March 2000.

was climbing towards one million, which was the highest level it had reached since 1945. A six-week miners' strike had begun on 9 January, and the blockade of power stations by striking mineworkers had resulted in a series of power cuts. Factories, deprived of electricity, sent workers home. Heath declared a temporary state of emergency, which did little to resolve the immediate crisis. Meanwhile, the sectarian and military violence in Northern Ireland was escalating: 173 soldiers and civilians had died as a result of political terrorism in 1971, and the Paratroop Regiment shot and killed thirteen Catholic demonstrators during a civil rights march on Sunday 30 January 1972 (the killings which have come to be known as 'Bloody Sunday'). The British release of Kubrick's film coincided with a moment when politicians and the public were much preoccupied by the idea of lawlessness, which goes some way towards accounting for the political nervousness that the adaptation gave rise to.* The Home Secretary's request to see *A Clockwork Orange* occurred at a time when the possibility of ultra-violence breaking out, whether on English picket-lines or in the militarized six counties of Northern Ireland, seemed particularly acute. Maudling's reaction was apparently that of a politician who was already under pressure to take action against what he had termed 'the current rise in violence', and he was not the only politician who expressed concern about Kubrick's film. Maurice Edelman, the Labour MP for Coventry West who chaired the all-party Parliamentary Film Committee, organized another screening of the film for MPs on 26 January 1972.† Edelman, himself a novelist, and also the dedicatee of *Honey for the Bears*, coined the phrase 'the pornography of violence', and he denounced Kubrick in a letter published in the London *Evening Standard*.‡

Burgess's review-essay on Kubrick's *A Clockwork Orange*,

---

* See Martin Gilbert, *Challenge to Civilization: A History of the Twentieth Century 1952–1999* (London: HarperCollins, 1999), pp. 431–9.

† 'PHS', 'The Times Diary', *The Times*, 25 January 1972, p. 14.

‡ See Burgess, *You've Had Your Time*, p. 246.

published in the *Listener* on 17 February 1972, was a response to this generally unfavourable climate of opinion. His defence of Kubrick is also a defence of his novel against what he regards as a series of journalistic misreadings. The film, described here as a 'radical reworking' of the novel (seeming to concede that a certain amount has been lost or altered in translation), is said to be 'very much a Kubrick movie, technically brilliant, thoughtful, relevant, poetic, mind-opening'.* Burgess's short account of the background to the novel takes in the wartime attack on his first wife by American deserters, his memory of overhearing the expression 'as queer as a clockwork orange' in a London pub in 1945, his frenzied production of five novels in the space of fourteen months after returning from Brunei, and the contemporaneous rise of an aggressive youth culture in the late 1950s.† Having sketched the circumstances of the novel's composition, he moves to an assessment of the film, and makes a long response to the charge that it is, or might be, 'sucking up to the thugs in the audience'. He is careful to distinguish his libertarian approach to the issue of free will from the behaviourist psychological theories of B. F. Skinner, the author of *Beyond Freedom and Dignity*:

> What my, and Kubrick's, parable tries to state is that it is preferable to have a world of violence undertaken in full awareness – violence chosen as an act of will – than a world conditioned to be good and harmless [. . .] B. F. Skinner, with his ability to believe that that there is something *beyond* freedom and dignity, wants to see the death of autonomous man.

---

* Burgess, 'Clockwork Marmalade', *Listener*, 17 February 1972, pp. 197–9, 197.
† 'The youth of the late Fifties were restless and naughty, dissatisfied with the postwar world, violent and destructive, and they – being more conspicuous than mere old-time crooks and hoods – were what many people meant when they talked about growing criminality [. . .] How to deal with them? Prison or reform school made them worse: why not save the taxpayer's money by subjecting them to an easy course in conditioning, some kind of aversion therapy which should make them associate the act of violence with discomfort, nausea, or even intimations of mortality? Many heads nodded at this proposal' (p. 198).

He may or may not be right, but in terms of the Judaeo-Christian ethic that *A Clockwork Orange* tries to express, he is perpetrating a gross heresy [. . .] The wish to diminish free will is, I should think, the sin against the Holy Ghost.

As an attempt to summarize the free-will argument of the book, this seems reductive, and the two possible futures that Burgess proposes (thuggish, marauding youth or conditioned, harmless zombies) are in many ways untrue to the complexity of his novel. The article says nothing about Alex as an intelligent, articulate figure who is capable of responding to the 'high' culture of orchestral music. Here, as elsewhere, an unshakable belief in the 'Judaeo-Christian ethic' (by which he clearly means an Augustinian Catholic ethic) lies at the heart of Burgess's defence of *A Clockwork Orange*:

It was certainly no pleasure to me to describe acts of violence when writing the novel: I indulged in excess, in caricature, even in an invented dialect with the purpose of making the violence more symbolic than realistic, and Kubrick found remarkable cinematic equivalents for my own literary devices.

Clearly, these references to pleasureless writing and to the level of linguistic complication in the novel say nothing about the visceral thrill that a cinema audience might derive from watching scenes of droogish ultra-violence in the first half of the film. Moreover, Burgess's attempt to equate the intentions of the novel with those of the film sits awkwardly with his earlier statement that the screen adaptation is a substantial 'reworking' of the book. Although Burgess seeks to have it both ways, it is difficult to be fully persuaded that the film is, at the same time, a faithful adaptation, a 'radical reworking' and 'very much a Kubrick movie'.*

Christopher Ricks responded to Burgess's *Listener* article a few weeks later, in a sceptical essay for the *New York Review of Books*,

* Burgess repeats his claim that the novel and the film are 'very much like each other' and 'painfully close' in 'Juice from a Clockwork Orange', *Rolling Stone*, 8 June 1972, p. 52.

which assessed the film and some of the criticism that it had generated.* Of all the commentators who attempted to identify points of difference between Burgess's novel and Kubrick's film version, Ricks gives the most valuable account of what had been altered in translation and why these changes were significant. He is also willing to take issue with Burgess's defence of the film. Ricks contends that the film is evasive in its dramatization of the ethical problems of brainwashing and free will. He argues that the 1962 edition of the novel 'compacted much of what was in the air' at the time of its publication, especially the widespread enthusiasm, even among *soi-disant* liberal journalists, for aversion therapy as a possible 'cure' for homosexuals, drug-abusers and alcoholics. With detailed quotations from Burgess's text, Ricks shows that the element of gleefully narrated, unapologetic ultra-violence in the novel, which he sees as one of its strengths, is seriously diminished in Kubrick's version. Hence there are fewer examples of petty crime than in the novel: Burgess's accounts of the shop-crasting and the tolchocking of the old man outside the public library are both excised. Furthermore, Kubrick elects not to show Alex's murder of 'Pedofil', the homosexual prisoner in State Jail 84F, preferring instead to concentrate on the sadism of the prison warders and Dr Brodsky. 'The real accusation against the film,' writes Ricks, 'is certainly not that it is too violent, but that it is not violent enough; more specifically, that with a cunning selectivity it sets itself to minimize both Alex's violence and his delight in it.' The film removes some of the novel's most repellent scenes, thereby presenting its protagonist as a more attractive or seductive figure than Burgess's Alex. Furthermore, although the novel makes a number of references to Alex's habitual use of hallucinogens and intravenous drugs, these are entirely missing from the film.† Most of Kubrick's interpolations

---

* Christopher Ricks, 'Horror Show', *New York Review of Books*, 6 April 1972, pp. 28–31; reprinted as 'Stanley Kubrick: *A Clockwork Orange*' in Christopher Ricks, *Reviewery* (London: Penguin, 2003), pp. 348–58.

† On the subject of drugs (or 'the old moloko plus', in Nadsat), Burgess writes that

tend to distort the meaning of the novel. The writer-director's original scenes either distract attention away from Alex's thuggishness by introducing crude, grotesque comedy – as with Mr Deltoid's predatory sexual advances and the incident when he drinks water from a glass containing false teeth – or else present Alex as the helpless recipient of institutional oppression, as in the scene where the chief warder leeringly inspects Alex's anus with a pencil-torch during his induction into the prison.

Ricks notices that Kubrick has adapted the brainwashing chapters with 'cunning selectivity'. In particular, the director has passed over several references in the text to the films which Alex is forced to watch after the Ludovico drug has been injected into his bloodstream. Burgess writes: 'It was a very good like professional piece of sinny, and there were none of those blobs you get, say, when you viddy one of these dirty films in somebody's house in a back street.' It is evident that Alex's response to the Ludovico films is bound up with his prior awareness of visual culture, but in excluding any comparable discussion of the techniques of film-making from his script, Kubrick ignores the awkward fact that the 'sinny' is one of the objects of explicit criticism in Burgess's version. Cinematic violence is confronted both implicitly and explicitly within the novel, yet Kubrick chooses to disregard the relevant passages, 'righteously unaware', as Ricks puts it, 'that any of [his] own techniques or practices could for a moment be asked to subject themselves to that same scrutiny as they project'. Burgess's novel, on the other hand, is willing to engage in 'some thinking and feeling which Kubrick should not have thought that he could merely cut'.

A Clockwork Orange 'merely describes certain tendencies I observed in Anglo-American society in 1961 (and even earlier) [. . .] True, there was not much drug-taking then, and my novel presents a milk-bar where you can freely ingest hallucinogens and stimulants, but I had only just come back from living in the Far East, where I smoked opium regularly (and without apparent ill effects), and drug-taking was so much part of my scene that it automatically went into the book'. See Burgess, 'Juice from a Clockwork Orange', p. 53.

364 OF ANTHONY BURGESS

Ricks brings a similar degree of intelligence to his reading of
'Clockwork Marmalade', the review-article from the *Listener*. He
takes issue with two aspects of Burgess's defence. First, on the
question of whether the author derived any gratification from
composing scenes of ultra-violence, Ricks counter-insists that 'on
such a matter no writer's say-so can simply be accepted, since a
writer mustn't be assumed to know so – the sincerity in question
is of the deepest and most taxing kind'. Responding to Burgess's
protestations that the theological content of his novel has been
misinterpreted, Ricks quotes a sentence from Dr Johnson's biographical essay on Jonathan Swift: 'The greatest difficulty that
occurs, in analyzing his character, is to discover by what depravity
of intellect he took delight in revolving ideas, from which almost
every other mind shrinks with disgust.' This suggests that the
novel was playing with fire from the start, and that no amount of
theological talk was going to diminish the ultra-violent content of
Burgess's text. Ricks claims that the novel itself is 'simply pleased'
with its raping, drugging and tolchocking. Finally, he raises the
question of what happens if readers of the novel or spectators of
the film do not happen to share Burgess's Christian frame of reference. How much weight is carried by Burgess's indignant claim
that 'the wish to diminish free will' is 'a sin against the Holy Ghost'
if we don't believe in the Holy Ghost? The large questions that
Ricks asks about the novel and the film are as pertinent now as
they were in 1972. Do the novel and the film demand that we take
for granted their ethical standpoint with regard to free will? Might
Burgess's novel be saying something entirely different to an atheist
or agnostic reader, for whom the terms 'good' and 'evil' do not
necessarily represent eternal verities? And is the book being recklessly simplistic when it presents its readers with a stark choice
between chemically lobotomized clockwork oranges and murderous
droogs?

Burgess's position with regard to the film's authorship was an
awkward one. Having identified himself, in the *Listener* article, as
'the fountain and origin' of the film, he left himself badly placed to

avoid subsequent accusations that he was indirectly responsible for the episodes of street violence that Kubrick's adaptation was said to have provoked. The most serious incident associated with the film was the murder of a homeless man in Fenny Stratford, Buckinghamshire, in April 1973. When the case came to court, the prosecuting lawyer, Mr John Owen, said: 'If this was robbery, it was all for 1½p or it may have been carried out for excitement as a result of the film. If so, the makers of the film have much to answer for.' The juvenile convicted of the killing, who was not named in press reports, pleaded guilty, and was sentenced to be detained during Her Majesty's pleasure.*

*

The year 1974 was a turning point for Burgess in more ways than one. The publication of *Napoleon Symphony*, which was translated into French and Italian shortly after the English edition had appeared, did much to reinforce his credentials as a genuinely European writer with an acute interest in formal experimentation. In the same year he decided to cut his few remaining ties with England. He wrote to Deborah Rogers to announce that Liana proposed to set up her own European literary agency which would represent his work. Income tax had been a constant problem since 1968, the chief difficulty being that of getting money to Italy from Great Britain without having to pay tax in both countries. This was the primary reason behind Burgess's decision to abandon his house in Bracciano and to move to Monaco, where there was no income tax, and widows did not have to pay death duties on their husbands'

---

* For a contemporary report on the trial, see '"Clockwork Orange" Link with Boy's Crime', *The Times*, 4 July 1973, p. 2. For subsequent responses by Burgess and others, see Sheridan Morley, 'Anthony Burgess Answers Back', *The Times*, 6 August 1973, p. 7; and Marcel Berlins, 'Lawyers Reject Author's Attack', *The Times*, 7 August 1973, p. 2. For an account of other violent crimes allegedly provoked by Kubrick's film, see Ali Catterall and Simon Wells, *Your Face Here: British Cult Movies Since the Sixties* (London: Fourth Estate, 2001), pp. 102–21.

estates. He and Liana bought a large top-floor apartment at 44 rue
Grimaldi in Monaco, and Burgess got down to the completion of
Abba Abba, his novel about an imaginary meeting in Rome between
the dying John Keats and Giuseppe Gioacchino Belli, the author of
3,000 obscene and blasphemous sonnets in the Roman dialect. The
second half of the book, originally titled 'Belli's Blasphemous Bible',
contains Burgess's translations of seventy-one of these sonnets.
Working from literal translations prepared by Liana, he took care
to preserve the coarse bawdiness and irreverence of Belli's Roman
originals:

> *One day the bakers God & Son set to*
> *And baked, to show their pasta-master's skill,*
> *This loaf the world, though the odd imbecile*
> *Swears it's a melon, and the thing just grew.*
> *They made a sun, a moon, a green and blue*
> *Atlas, chucked stars like money from a till,*
> *Set birds high, beasts low, fishes lower still,*
> *Planted their plants, then yawned: 'Aye, that'll do.'*

> *No, wait. The old man baked two bits of bread*
> *Called Folk – I quite forgot to mention it –*
> *So he could shout: 'Don't bite that round ripe red*
> *Pie-filling there.' Of course the buggers bit.*
> *Though mad at them, he turned on us instead*
> *And said: 'Posterity, you're in the shit'.* *

ABBA ABBA is the ryhme-scheme of the octave in a Petrarchan
sonnet and, because 'abba' is the Aramaic word for 'father', these
are also the last words of the dying Jesus Christ on the cross. The
same phrase is engraved on Burgess's tombstone in Monaco. The
novelist A. S. Byatt comments: 'It is a phrase out of the Bible which
any man might say at the moment of death. It has the immortality
of the circle. It's a beginning which doesn't have an ending. It's a

---

* Burgess, *Abba Abba* (London: Faber, 1977), p. 92.

good tombstone, I think.'* Writing in *Encounter*, the poet Tom
Paulin said that Burgess 'justifies his title which isn't an example of
merely tricksy punning, but an absolutely appropriate naming of his
subject'. He added that *Abba Abba* was 'the work of a wise and
subtle visionary'. Edwin Morgan commented, with reference to the
Belli translations, that 'They are coarser than the Scots versions of
Robert Garioch, and one word is so fucking pervasive as to be
wearisome.'†

We can catch a glimpse of Burgess and Liana at home in
Monaco from the journals of Sam Coale, a young American college
professor who called on them at 44 rue Grimaldi while he was
researching a book about Burgess. This is what Coale observed on
Friday 7 July 1978:

> He opened the door of the apartment at the top of the stairs
> on the top floor in the old sandstone-colored building, shops
> on the ground floor, black-iron grilled balconies, 44 Rue Gri-
> maldi, a busy hectic street in the middle of other plush shops,
> sparkling wide windows piled with shoes, draped with clothes,
> winking with jewelry in the bright morning light. I'd taken the
> 9.30 train from Villefranche. There he was, immediately
> friendly and easy-going, a swirl of bushy long grayish-brown
> hair like some mad painter, his features blurred in a pink pale
> puffy face as if he'd been asleep, heavy-lidded eyes, dressed in
> black loafers with no socks, slacks and some kind of reddish
> checkered shirt. His appearance seemed blurred, almost sloth-
> ful, entirely relaxed as he led me into his workshop or his
> 'atelier', one long open room the length of the balcony in
> front, complete with a musical score he was writing at the old
> upright piano, table with typewriter and strewn papers, book-
> cases crammed and books piled at random on the floor, a

---

* A. S. Byatt in *The Burgess Variations: Part Two*, BBC 2, 27 December 1999.
† Tom Paulin, 'Incorrigibly Plural: Recent Fiction', *Encounter*, vol. 49, no. 4
(October 1977), pp. 82–5; Edwin Morgan, 'The Thing's the Thing', *Times Literary
Supplement*, 3 June 1977, p. 669.

carpetless wooden expanse, a television. He got me the biggest cup of tea I'd ever seen, a pool of tea, and we sat in chairs by the piano, the tape recorder between us on a third chair. Liliana burst in in a ruffled green-flowery low-cut 'peasant' dress, jet black hair, full bosom bursting at the ruffles, also completely at ease and chatting away. In the hall, a xerox machine. She xeroxed for me the missing last chapter of *A Clockwork Orange* and gave to me a new Burgess book on Jesus translated into French to carry to Warsaw and get translated into Polish there, *L'Homme de Nazareth* [*Man of Nazareth*]. Something about Knopf offering only $45,000 for it in New York. Much chatter about 'stupid' publishers, things out of print, taxes and contracts: isolated in Monaco to write, more or less friendless here, an outpost from their house outside Rome. Everywhere bookcases and odd piles, his complete works on the way to the kitchen where we lunched on a cold chicken dish and red wine [. . .] Later he showed me 150 typescript pages of the new novel on Somerset Maugham and Pope John, *The Instruments of Darkness*, 2 or 3 pages a day, each perfected before moving on to the next; film scores to write and edit and narrate. We listened to his 'Iowa' symphony on tape in his study, a small cluttered room off the main hall with an autographed picture of Sophia Loren above his desk and a picture of Stonehenge. He closed his eyes, caught every beat of the modern, 12-tone-sounding cacophony blasted over the tape, followed by a film score from a film on Italians in New York, delightfully light with flutes and piano: he said he'd write me a two-page piece for piano. Amid the disarray, the apparent careless appearance, the mind never faltered, quickly articulate, the eyes opened and rivetting as he nearly chain-smoked on little cigars, and the tapes went on. One failed to record; he assured me all was well; we summarized our remarks on a new tape and began again.

The novel about Somerset Maugham and the Pope that Coale saw in Monaco underwent many changes of title during the six years it had taken Burgess to write it. It began as 'The Prince of the

Powers of the Air'. In the late 1970s it was known as 'The Instruments of Darkness'. In Burgess's letters it is also referred to as 'Eternal Power' or 'Absolute Power'. The English-speaking world knows it as *Earthly Powers*.

11

Anthony's End

Speaking about *Earthly Powers* to Georges Belmont, one of the novel's French translators, Burgess described it aphoristically as 'a book about a homosexual novelist and his brother-in-law, the Pope'.* Spanning more than eighty years of narrative and 650 closely printed pages, *Earthly Powers* is a grim catalogue of the horrors of the twentieth century, projected on to a panoramic canvas which takes in England, America, Malta, Italy, France, Germany, Monaco, Malaya, Australia and Africa. Among other matters, this vast, energetic novel addresses the rise and fall of literary modernism, the failure of orthodox religion, suicide cults, blasphemy, pornography, apostasy, theology, miracles, the Holocaust, cannibalism, and the persistent problem of evil. These weighty historical abstractions are dramatized through the figures of Kenneth Marchal Toomey – an elderly writer who has been an eye-witness to many of the events that he narrates – and Father Carlo Campanati, better known as Pope Gregory XVII, who is probably, if Toomey's account of his life is to be believed, also an agent of the Devil.

Burgess had been promising to write a big novel about the papacy ever since he completed *Napoleon Symphony* in 1973, and the idea of a book which would feature a 'papal villain' was first

* Georges Belmont to author, 1 July 1997.

mentioned in a letter dated 11 December 1970. He told the readers
of the *Times Literary Supplement* in March 1973 that the first forty
pages of this novel were filed away in a sun-bleached folder, but he
cursed Broadway and *Cyrano* for preventing him from getting down
to a prolonged stretch of work on it.* His progress was inevitably
slowed down over the next eight years by a deluge of other commitments. Less ambitious writing projects, some of which were
distinctly sub-literary, kept getting in the way. Apart from film and
television scripts (*Jesus of Nazareth*, *The Spy Who Loved Me*,
Schreber, *Freud*, *The Sexual Habits of the English Middle Class*),
he published two children's books (*A Long Trip to Tea-Time*, *The
Land Where the Ice-Cream Grows*), a long poem of nearly 200
pages (*Moses: A Narrative*), and four other novels (*Beard's Roman
Women*, *Abba Abba*, *1985* and *Man of Nazareth*) while *Earthly
Powers* was underway.

He devoted much of 1978 and 1979 to the hard task of wrestling
his 'Pope novel' to its conclusion. In a letter to Wolfgang Krege, his
German publisher at Klett-Cotta in Stuttgart, he argued the case for
the importance of this particular book within his oeuvre:

> EARTHLY POWERS – An attempt to show that I could write
> a novel as long as one of those nineteenth-century blockbusters
> (although Dickens and Tolstoy were long because they wrote
> for serial publication – no longer, alas, an available outlet for
> the novelist), this is a panoramic survey of the twentieth century
> as told by the brother-in-law of the fictional pope Gregory, and
> an attempt to deal with the damnable mystery of good and evil
> as manifested in the worst century that history has ever known.
> It is also meant to be funny.†

Although this is a fair summary of what *Earthly Powers* is
about, it falls short of giving an accurate sense of what Martin
Amis has called the novel's 'manic erudition', 'garlicky puns' and

* Burgess, 'Viewpoint', *Times Literary Supplement*, 23 March 1973, p. 322.
† Burgess, letter to Wolfgang Krege, 2 April 1986.

'omnilingual jokes'.* If the style is the man where the novel's narrator, Kenneth Toomey, is concerned, this is also the case for his
mercurial creator. Considered purely in terms of the variety and
inventiveness of Burgess's prose, there is a strong case for saying –
as Henry Fielding said of *The History of Tom Jones, A Foundling* –
that *Earthly Powers* contains 'a hint of what [he] can do in the
sublime'.† Burgess did his best to sum up the complexities of the
novel's plot in an article for the *Washington Post*:

> The narrator is an aging homosexual writer modelled on Wil-
> liam Somerset Maugham. His sister married an Italian musician
> whose brother was a priest. This priest rose to be Cardinal
> Archbishop of Milan and eventually, in 1958, Pope Gregory
> XVII. He can, if the reader wishes, be identified with Pope John
> XXIII. The homosexual writer narrator is asked by the Vatican
> to confirm that he witnessed a miracle performed by Pope
> Gregory, when he was still only Monsignor Campanati, in a
> Chicago hospital in 1929. The narrator, whose fictional trade
> leads him to confuse the imagined with the actual, is forced to
> look back over his long life, assemble the undoubted historical
> and biographical and separate them from what is fabled by the
> daughters of memory. He sees the miracle clearly; a small boy
> dying of meningitis is restored to life by the laying on of hands
> and a simple prayer.
>
> But what happened to this boy in later life? Surely God, in
> subverting the processes of nature, had some special intention
> for him? In discovering this special intention we come face to
> face with the great mystery of good and evil. Perhaps it is too
> easy to think in terms of a perpetual war going on between
> God and the Devil: the universe is not sustained by so simplistic

---

* Martin Amis, 'Burgess at His Best', *New York Times*, Book Review section, 7
December 1980, pp. 1, 24; reprinted in Amis, *The War Against Cliché* (London:
Jonathan Cape, 2001), pp. 121–3.
† For Burgess on Fielding ('the man who is, conceivably, England's greatest
novelist'), see his review of Martin Battestin's biography, *Observer*, 29 October
1989.

a dichotomy. Perhaps God, if he exists, is beyond good and evil and is merely an ultimate power to whom human morality is of no interest. He is on nobody's side.*

Burgess made the same identification between Carlo Campanati and Pope John XXIII in an interview with Geoffrey Aggeler, in which he referred to Pope John as 'a Pelagian heretic' and 'an emissary of the Devil'.† The nature of Pope John's offence was that he had altered the doctrines of the Church, encouraged an ecumenical dialogue with other sects and religions, and (worst of all, in Burgess's view) vernacularized the traditional Latin Mass. To non-Catholics, Burgess's anger at the reforms within a community of believers that he had voluntarily left more than forty years earlier might seem weirdly out of proportion, as well as being hard to reconcile with his status as a renegade. Yet his sense of himself as a Catholic outsider becomes more comprehensible in the light of his deeply felt homesickness and nostalgia. In old age, he found it impossible to contemplate returning to a Church whose forms of worship no longer resembled those he had known when he took the decision to renounce them in 1933.‡

The shape of Toomey's career as a writer owes a good deal to W. Somerset Maugham, as Burgess points out in his *Washington Post* article, but substantial autobiographical elements are also present in the text. Toomey's house in Malta, for example, is Burgess's house at 168 Main Street, Lija, and their neighbours (the Borgs and the Grimas) have the same names. In Monaco, the

---

* Burgess, 'The Genesis of "Earthly Powers"', *Washington Post*, Book World section, 23 November 1980, pp. 1–2, 13.
† Quoted in Geoffrey Aggeler, *Anthony Burgess: The Artist as Novelist* (Alabama: University of Alabama Press), p. 24.
‡ John J. Stinson comments on the vexed and vexing nature of Burgess's religious views: 'Burgess castigates the Church for what he sees as its capitulation to dissolute modernizing forces [and] tells the Church, which he no longer believes in, what its practices and beliefs should be.' See John J. Stinson, *Anthony Burgess Revisited* (Boston, MA: Twayne, 1991), p. 19.

narrator and his sister take an apartment on the rue Grimaldi where, in real life, most of *Earthly Powers* was written. One of Toomey's early lovers dies in the same Spanish influenza epidemic which killed Burgess's mother and sister in 1918. Some of Burgess's undergraduate poems are reattributed to Valentine Wrigley, another of Toomey's boyfriends, whose name suggests slippery unreliability and chewing gum. The pope's half-brother, Domenico Campanati, writes a Burgessian stage musical called *Blooms of Dublin*, adapted from James Joyce's *Ulysses*. Toomey's nephew, the anthropologist John Campion, gives a lecture whose text is directly lifted from one of the essays that Burgess collected in *Urgent Copy*.* 'Professor Borghese' is cited as a learned authority in the field of linguistics. A digression on the English translations of Psalm 23 draws on another of Burgess's book reviews.† There are sniping references to an illiterate film director, whose name is variously given as 'Labrick' and 'Lubrick'. Burgess's French translators, Georges Belmont and Hortense Chabrier, are commemorated as the fictional 'Dr Belmont' and 'Father Chabrier'. The surnames of Lynne's old boyfriends, 'Currie' and 'Pécriaux', are given to two other minor characters.

These encoded autobiographical references have a resonance which goes beyond the simple notion of an artist wanting to conceal his signature within the work. Burgess wrote himself into the text of *Earthly Powers* because the novel's subject matter was deeply felt as well as imagined. One of the charges levelled against Pope Gregory is that he is a Pelagian heretic, and the novel's theological chapters allow Burgess to revisit his theory about Augustine and Pelagius, resuming a line of argument that he'd pursued in *A Vision of*

---

* See Burgess, 'Word, World and Meaning', *Times Literary Supplement*, 6 May 1965, p. 350; reprinted in *Urgent Copy: Literary Studies* (London: Jonathan Cape, 1969), pp. 221–7.
† Burgess, 'The Lord Is My, Etc.: Psalm 23' (review of *Psalm Twenty-Three: An Anthology*, ed. by K. H. Strange and R. G. E. Sandbach), *Times Literary Supplement*, 7 July 1978, p. 760; reprinted as 'Quiet Waters' in *Homage to Qwert Yuiop: Selected Journalism 1978–1985* (London: Hutchinson, 1986), pp. 39–41.

Battlements, *The Worm and the Ring*, *A Clockwork Orange*, *The Wanting Seed*, *Tremor of Intent*, *Jesus of Nazareth* and *1985*. In chapter 44 of *Earthly Powers*, Toomey is asked to read the typescript of a theological tract written by the future Pope, who gives himself away as a Pelagian heretic:

> The responsibility for sin could not be placed wholly on the shoulders of the human sinner, and God, knowing the strength of his enemy, was infinitely merciful to the dupes of that enemy, but man was not free of the necessity to develop judgement, the capacity to recognize evil when it masqueraded as the highest good. Why did God allow evil to exist? A question not to be asked. Without evil there could be no freedom of choice. But so pervasive is that original good, that it can inhere in evil as a potential consequence [. . .] You could blame yourself for lack of moral judgement, but not for the dynamic which animated your acts of evil. Original sin was original weakness, not being sufficiently clever, or Godlike, to spot the machinations of the fiend. I was not surprised to find, in one of the appendices, a rehabilitation of the heretic Pelagius.*

As the novel neared its completion, Burgess struggled to clarify its main theme. He knew that Domenico and Toomey had to collaborate on an opera, and that the libretto of the opera must somehow comment on Toomey's life in ways that would be apparent to the reader but not to the first-person narrator. What he lacked was a suitable story for the opera. As his deadline approached in the winter of 1979, a journalistic commission from the *Times Literary Supplement* came to his aid. He was asked to review a book by Charles W. Jones about the life of St Nicholas of Bari.† From Jones he learned of a short story by Anatole France, in which St Nicholas rescues three boys from drowning in a pickle barrel. He

---

* Burgess, *Earthly Powers* (London: Hutchinson, 1980), p. 344.
† See Burgess, 'The Santa Claus Story' (review of Charles W. Jones, *Saint Nicholas of Myra, Bari and Manhattan*), *Times Literary Supplement*, 21 December 1979, p. 149.

takes them into his house and raises them as his adopted sons. The
first boy grows up to become a brothel-keeper, and Nicholas is
tempted into unchaste acts at the brothel. The second boy denounces
him to the Church for the heresy of Arianism, which he has never in
fact preached. The third becomes a soldier, and is responsible for
the indiscriminate killing of women and children. This story forms
the basis of the opera within the novel.

Like St Nicholas, Toomey is betrayed by three of his homosexual
partners, vicious and untrustworthy whores who rob him, humiliate
him and vilify him in the pages of the *Daily Mail*. His fictional
biography is a mirror of Nicholas's life, and it is suggested at the
end of the book that he is a kind of secular saint, a martyr to
literature. It is typical of Burgess that he allowed the final shape of
Earthly Powers to be determined by a book which had arrived,
almost at random, for review. Yet this improvised quality might
also be regarded as one of the novel's strengths: the broad ideas of
evil and betrayal, which perhaps represent the novel's only structur-
ing principle, leave him with enough freedom to assemble his story
from a range of disparate materials, including music, literary history
and autobiography. Watching the energetic improvisation proceed
from page to page is one of the novel's many satisfactions.

Burgess's large investment of time and energy brought him
impressive financial rewards. Michael Korda at the New York
publishing house Simon and Schuster bought the American edition
of *Earthly Powers* for $275,000 and printed 100,000 copies of the
first hardback edition. In London, James Cochrane of Hutchinson
offered a more modest advance of £40,000. When the novel was
published in October 1980, Bernard Levin wrote in the *Sunday
Times*:

> The historical sweep, the range of the enquiry, the immense
> wealth of illustrative allusion, the explosive energy with which
> the book is crammed, the giant appetite for event and descrip-
> tion, the brilliance of the parodies, the iron control over at any
> rate nine-tenths of the material, the colour and daring, the relish

of the true creative artist for his creation – all these combine with the theme to make *Earthly Powers* an achievement which any living writer would be proud of, and no dead one ashamed [. . .] Mind you, Mr Burgess's prose, as always, boils over from time to time: 'Carlo was busy sucking an orange as a weasel might suck a brain' and 'The moon was like a round of Breton butter with fromatical veins' [. . .] Mr Burgess is so anxious to demonstrate that he knows more words than we do that he trips himself up: a 'mephitic hogo' is a tautology, meaning only a stinking stink. It can't be helped; with this author it is always necessary to take the hispid with the glabrous, and the credit balance is overwhelming.*

George Steiner wrote in the *New Yorker*: 'The whole landscape is the brighter for [*Earthly Powers*], a feat of imaginative breadth and intelligence which lifts fiction high.'† In another review in the *Times Literary Supplement*, Jeremy Treglown commented: '*Earthly Powers* is a big, grippingly readable, extraordinarily rich and moving fiction by one of the most ambitiously creative writers working in English.'‡

The highest praise of all came from Georges Belmont, the fiction editor at Editions Laffont in Paris, who had known James Joyce in the 1930s and made translations of his poems. He sent Burgess and Liana a congratulatory telegram: 'ALWAYS KNEW IT WOULD BE ANTHONY'S ULYSSES'.§ Translated into French by Belmont and Hortense Chabrier, *Earthly Powers* won the Charles Baudelaire Prize and the Prix du Meilleur Livre Etranger in 1981. In Britain it was shortlisted for the Booker Prize, but the panel of judges (chaired by Professor David Daiches, who had reviewed Burgess's *Moses*

---

* Bernard Levin, 'By His Works Ye Shall Know Him', *Sunday Times*, 12 October 1980, p. 42.
† George Steiner, 'Scrolls and Keys', *New Yorker*, 13 April 1981, pp. 156–62.
‡ Jeremy Treglown, 'The Knowledge of Good and Evil', *Times Literary Supplement*, 24 October 1980, p. 1189.
§ Georges Belmont, telegram to Anthony Burgess, 22 October 1980.

dismissively for the *Times Literary Supplement* in January 1977) awarded the prize to William Golding for *Rites of Passage*.*

The *Saturday Review*, to which Burgess had contributed an occasional diary column since 1978, sent Rhoda Koenig to Monaco to interview him. She remembers this meeting as one of the most unusual encounters in her career as a writer:

> After all the stately, snotty grandeur [of Monte Carlo], chez Burgess was a bit of a shock. It looked like a student squat. Very drab, very messy, papers everywhere. His wife, Liana, said, 'It is the cat. He likes to ski (whooshing gesture with the arm) on the papers.' I didn't actually see the cat, but he certainly manifested his presence – the cloakroom to which I was sent when I asked for the lavatory did double duty as a cat box and hadn't been changed for some time [. . .] Burgess himself was terribly nice, rather like a friendly crumpled paper bag (I mean his looks).†

When Koenig mentioned Noël Coward, he turned to the piano and started to play 'Mad Dogs and Englishmen'. She sang along, and she taught Burgess how to play 'Mene Mene Tekel', a song by Harold Rome from the musical *Pins and Needles*. 'He was a very good pickup pianist, which I told him, and which pleased him very much [. . .] During the interview Shirley Conran dropped by and was very amused that he was playing and I was singing and said this isn't like any kind of interview I'm familiar with.'‡

---

* According to Martyn Goff of the Booker Prize Foundation, 'Burgess was at the Savoy Hotel in London. He did say to me that there was "no way I'm putting on evening dress and coming unless I know I've won". When the judging was over I rang him from the Guildhall and told him that Golding (for *Rites of Passage*) had won, and he said, "Right, Martyn, I'm not coming."' Quoted in *The Man Booker Prize: 35 Years of the Best in Contemporary Fiction* (Booker Prize Foundation, 2003), p. 27.

† Rhoda Koenig to author, 18 May 2003. See also Koenig, 'The Unearthly Powers of Anthony Burgess', *Saturday Review*, December 1980, pp. 34–7.

‡ Shirley Conran, the author of *Superwoman*, was Burgess's neighbour in Monaco. He read the typescript of her best-selling novel, *Lace* (1982), and suggested

Liana seemed to Koenig 'to be taking vagueness to the point of an art form', although 'like all vague people she would abruptly come out of her coma at odd moments, to firmly grasp the wrong end of the stick'. But what struck Koenig above all about Burgess was his generosity.

> He asked me how I was going to write the article and I said I guess in longhand and he said no, you can't write a whole article in longhand, and insisted on lending me his typewriter, which I found astonishingly nice [. . .] He was rather keen on me. He wrote across one review he sent me, 'To Miss Koenig, who persistently refuses to become my adopted daughter,' which rather took me aback.

She was not the only woman for whom Burgess expressed paternal feelings: he told at least three other young female friends in Monaco that he regarded them as the daughter he'd never had. Yet this was never said in a predatory way. According to Koenig, 'There was nothing remotely improper about anything he said – he was just being cute, and his wife was in the next room.' Burgess liked the company of women, especially if they happened to be young and attractive, and he enjoyed showering them with flattery and charm.

*

From Monaco it was a short train journey to Antibes, where Graham Greene had been living since the early 1960s. Burgess had resumed his association with Greene after 1975, partly on the basis of the generous reviews and longer critical assessments of Greene's work that he had been writing. These articles (which are invariably

---

revisions. This led to the rumour that he was Conran's ghost-writer. When she asked for his permission to name him in the acknowledgements, Burgess wrote to her from his country house in the Var (6 rue des Muets, Callian), on 10 November 1981: 'I don't think it's in order to express this putative help or encouragement publicly [. . .] I think it might even be considered indiscreet to mention help. So please don't bring me into it.' For the ghost-writing story, see 'Not So Dainty Lace-Making', *Evening Standard*, 13 May 1985, p. 6.

confessional as well as critical) reveal much about Burgess's sense of what the responsibilities of a Catholic novelist should be.* His responses to Greene's work often articulate strong disagreement with the moral basis of novels such as *Brighton Rock* and *The Heart of the Matter*: 'Greene is obsessed with evil-doing as a means of asserting identity. Only God is good, therefore all that man does is not-good. But men ought to make their not-good acts pretty definite – by committing adultery, for instance.' Greene's fiction is said to be informed by a 'heterodox' deterministic view of mankind as unregenerably wicked, and by denying the possibility of moral progress or human perfectibility (the will towards the good, in other words), he appears to go well beyond Burgess's Augustinian definition of Original Sin. Yet in spite of these objections to the theology of Greene's books, Burgess admired the aesthetic qualities of the

---

* For Burgess on Greene, see 'The Novelist's Agony' (review of *In Search of a Character*), *Yorkshire Post*, 23 November 1961, p. 7; 'New Fiction' (review of *The Comedians*), *Listener*, 3 February 1966, p. 181; 'The Manicheans', *Times Literary Supplement*, 3 March 1966, pp. 153–4; 'The Wearing of the Greene' (review of John Atkins, *Graham Greene*), *Guardian*, 11 November 1966, p. 8; 'More Comedians' (review of *May We Borrow Your Husband?*), *Spectator*, 21 April 1967, p. 454; 'Politics in the Novels of Graham Greene', *Journal of Contemporary History*, no. 2 (April 1967), pp. 93–9; *The Novel Now: A Student's Guide to Contemporary Fiction* (London: Faber, 1967; revised edition, 1971), pp. 61–4; 'Graham Greene as Monsieur Vert', *Tablet*, 15 March 1975, pp. 259–60; 'God and Literature and So Forth', *Observer*, 16 March 1980, p. 40; reprinted as 'Monsieur Greene of Antibes' in *Homage to Qwert Yuiop*, pp. 20–25; 'Travels with Graham Greene' (review of *Ways of Escape*), *Saturday Review*, January 1981, pp. 64–5; 'How to Defect' (review of *The Human Factor*) in *Homage to Qwert Yuiop*, pp. 26–8; 'Hidalgo Ingenioso' (review of *Monsignor Quixote*), ibid., pp. 28–30; 'A Seeker of Pain' (review of Norman Sherry, *The Life of Graham Greene*, vol. 1), *Daily Telegraph*, 8 April 1989, Weekend section, p. 13; 'The Sinner at the Heart of the Matter', *Daily Telegraph*, 4 April 1991, p. 13; 'Graham Greene' (unsigned obituary), *Daily Telegraph*, 4 April 1991, p. 21. Burgess also contributed to *Graham Greene at 75* (BBC Radio 4, broadcast 20 September 1979) and the three-part television documentary, *Arena: The Graham Greene Trilogy*, BBC 2, 8–10 January 1993.

writing itself: 'As for Greene's mastery of a highly contemporary and very economical sinewy prose style, one can be in no doubt there. No word otiose, and every word full of flavour. And the Greene world [. . .] remains rich, recognisable, idiosyncratic.'

On 16 March 1980 the *Observer* published Burgess's long interview with Greene, who was eager to refute Burgess's charge that his novels were preoccupied by evil to an unhealthy degree. He claimed that 'nobody in my books is damned – not even Pinkie in *Brighton Rock*. Scobie in *The Heart of the Matter* tries to damn himself, but the possibility of his salvation is left open [. . .] Nobody, not even the Church, knows enough about divine love and judgement to be sure that anyone's in hell.'* Yet Greene revealed his unorthodoxy when he claimed that 'Hell may be necessary, but I don't think there's anybody in it.'

This interview allowed Burgess to develop and to reiterate ideas first put forward in his reviews of Greene's fiction, particularly the notion of the 'seedy' as a metaphor for mankind's predicament after the Fall. Having identified the thematic hallmarks of Greene's novels ('joyless sex', 'hopeless, empty men in exile', 'evil as something palpable'), he is able to query the philosophy and theology which seem to stand behind them. Greene replies, not entirely politely, that only 'Superficial readers say that I'm fascinated by damnation'. In other respects the interview is remarkable for the extent to which it evades religious questions. For the most part, the two novelists speak about writing as a branch of aesthetics: a neutral activity whose primary purpose is 'the desire to divert', as Greene puts it.

The thirty-year friendship between the two writers, which (according to Burgess) had always been qualified by a 'coolness' on Greene's part, came to an end in 1988. The circumstances of their

---

* Burgess, 'Monsieur Greene of Antibes' in *Homage to Qwert Yuiop*, pp. 20–25, 24. Greene is paraphrasing the words of the anonymous old priest in the concluding pages of *Brighton Rock*: 'You can't conceive, my child, nor can I or anyone – the . . . appalling . . . strangeness of the mercy of God.' See Greene, *Brighton Rock* (London: Heinemann, 1938; reprinted 1947), p. 331.

falling-out are outlined in two personal letters from Greene, written from his apartment on the Avenue Pasteur in Antibes, both of which were sent on 17 June 1988. In the first letter Greene writes:

> I hear you have been attacking me rather severely on the French television programme Apostrophes because of my great age and in the French magazine *Lire*, because of my correspondence with my friend Kim Philby. I know how difficult it is to avoid inaccuracies when one becomes involved in journalism but as you thought it relevant to attack me because of my age (I don't see the point) you should have checked your facts. I happen to be 83 not 86 and I trust that you will safely reach that age too. In *Lire* you seem to have been quoted as writing that I had been in almost daily correspondence with Philby before his death. In fact I received ten letters from him in the course of nearly 20 years. You must be very naif if you believe our letters were clandestine on either side. Were you misinformed or have you caught the common disease in journalism of dramatizing at the cost of truth?*

Later the same day Greene sent a second letter, which ended the affair. He wrote: 'I have now received another cutting in which you claim I told you of an aggrieved husband shouting through my windows (difficult as I live on the fourth floor). You are either a liar or you are unbalanced and should see a doctor.'

Burgess's last words on Greene were published in the *Daily Telegraph* on 4 April 1991. In a personal memoir of their friendship, 'The Sinner at the Heart of the Matter', he explained that the involvement between the two writers had ended with vituperative letters from Greene, 'whose fury was not matched by the exquisite small handwriting in which it was couched'. The *Telegraph*'s unsigned 5,000-word obituary of Greene was also written by Burgess. This is his longest critical statement on Greene's life and works, although he has not previously been identified as the author. He sets

---

* Quoted in Graham Greene, *Yours Etc.: Letters to the Press, 1945–89* ed. by Christopher Hawtree (London: Reinhardt/Viking, 1989), pp. 175–6.

out his case robustly: '[Greene's] fictional Christianity began to be called Jansenist by the learned – unregenerate evil inhering in the natural creation as much as the man-made. Disgust excused extravagant imagery.'* Although much of the obituary is a fair-minded summary of Greene's literary career, a few of Burgess's judgements are grudging. 'Even [Greene's] admirers,' he writes, 'might balk at attributing greatness to him, and his achievements hardly measure up to those of Dickens or Tolstoy or Joyce.' The piece ends with Burgess elaborating on the theology of Greene's novels:

> He is a dangerous writer. His theology cannot often be trusted. English Catholics, even converts, are tempted by more heresies than are the children of baroque Mediterranean Christianity. The greatest temptation is provided by the British heresiarch Pelagius, a monk who denied original sin, doubted the need for divine grace, and believed that man could attain some sort of perfection by his own efforts. His doctrines, which flourish in Britain's mild air, are at the root of both the major political ideologies of the country, though they are more conspicuous in socialism [. . .] In Greene's fiction, however, there is little flavour of empiricism (which has something of Pelagianism about it). There are instead paradoxes and anomalies – the sinner who is really a saint, the philanthropist who is really a destroyer.

Burgess's final judgement on Greene is that, although he was attracted by the neo-Pelagianism of Communist regimes, particularly in South America (as described, for example, in his Panamanian memoir, *Getting to Know the General*), the novels are resolutely Augustinian in their insistence on the hopelessly flawed and fallen nature of man. Burgess's commentary is consistent in its theological points of reference, but it is also clear from his reviews that his

---

* Anon. [i.e. Anthony Burgess], 'Graham Greene', *Daily Telegraph*, 4 April 1991, p. 21.

enthusiasm for Greene's novels diminished sharply after the publication of *The Human Factor* in 1978.*

*

Burgess did not allow himself much leisure to enjoy the critical and
popular success of *Earthly Powers*. Other novels demanded to be
written, including the genre-breaking omnium gatherum, *The End
of the World News* (subtitled 'An Entertainment'), which appeared
in 1982. This apocalyptic narrative presents three simultaneous lines
of plot: Sigmund Freud's discovery of the unconscious; Leon Trot-
sky's visit to New York in 1917; and the final destruction of the
earth by an asteroid. All three of these stories had begun life as
commissions for film, television and theatre, but their fusion within
a single novel radically alters the meaning of the individual threads.
Burgess reached for a musical analogy, and he justified the counter-
pointing of narratives in an author's note on the dust-jacket of the
original Hutchinson edition: 'It is the new way of reading, derived
from the new way of watching television. To view one channel at a
time is no longer enough: we need three distinct yet simultaneous
imaginative stimuli: the family of the middle and late 1980s will
have to be a three-screen family.'

Michael Wood said of the book in the *New York Times*: 'This
is not the scorching apocalypse of Lawrence or Yeats but a love
song to what would be lost if the world went away: all its colors
and tastes and smells and finally forgivable mistakes. It is an old
song but a good one, made attractive not by its newness but by its
steady virtue and the liveliness of Mr Burgess's arrangement of it.'†
Steven Connor makes a persuasive case for the unity of the three
narratives in *The English Novel in History 1950–1995*, arguing that
questions of science, revolution and history are consistent features
of the novel. 'By taking us out beyond the end of the world and the

---

* See 'How to Defect' in *Homage to Qwert Yuiop*, pp. 26–8.
† Michael Wood, 'A Love Song to What Would Be Lost', *New York Times*, Book
Review section, 6 March 1983, pp. 3, 25.

end of historical narrative,' Connor writes, 'Burgess appears also [. . .] to be demonstrating the dangers of the historical forgetfulness of the present.'*

In 1984, shortly after he had completed *Enderby's Dark Lady* (the final volume of the quartet), Burgess began and abandoned a novel about the history of the English stage, 'All the Men and Women', of which a handful of pages survive in the Texas archive. A television series about the early history of Christianity, written by Burgess for the producer Vincenzo Labella under the title *A. D.*, was broadcast in that same year. His novelization of these scripts, *The Kingdom of the Wicked*, was published in 1985, as was *Flame into Being*, an eccentric critical study of D. H. Lawrence, which coincided with the centenary of Lawrence's birth. Burgess's musical settings of four poems by Lawrence ('End of Another Home Holiday', 'Song of a Man Who Has Come Through', 'Snake' and 'Bavarian Gentians') were performed in Nottingham, and he planned an opera based on Gustave Flaubert's *Bouvard et Pécuchet*.

His new version of Weber's opera *Oberon* was performed by Scottish Opera in Glasgow, and revived at La Fenice in Venice two years later. 'There might have been a fear,' wrote the opera critic of *The Times*, 'that Anthony Burgess's new libretto would destroy the essential character of the opera to which Weber gave his last weeks, but that is very far from being the case: *Oberon* remains a total mess.'† Burgess's new translation of Prosper Merimée's libretto for Bizet's *Carmen* was performed by the English National Opera in 1986. *Homage to Qwert Yuiop*, a selection of his essays and book reviews, and *The Pianoplayers* appeared in the same year.

Little Wilson and Big God: Being the First Part of the Confessions of Anthony Burgess was published, by Heinemann in London and Weidenfeld & Nicolson in New York, on Burgess's

---

* Steven Connor, *The English Novel in History 1950–1995* (London: Routledge, 1996), p. 215.
† 'Dynamitism Held Hostage to Modern Misdirection', *The Times*, 24 October 1985.

seventieth birthday, 25 February 1987. Before publication, the book was read by libel lawyers, who compiled an eleven-page list of potentially actionable passages. Burgess told his editor at Heinemann, Fanny Blake, that he would be unwilling to change the names of the people he had referred to unless the lawyers insisted. But many of his assertions, such as the statement that Lynne 'copulated in the Manche with a young man called Emile Pécriaux', would have been impossible to substantiate in court. His name was changed to 'Emile Sollers' (a reference to the French novelist Philippe Sollers, who'd included a character called 'Anthony Burgess' in his novel, *Femmes*, published three years earlier), although Monsieur Pécriaux appeared under his real name when the same story was repeated in *You've Had Your Time*. One of Burgess's Army colleagues was described as having 'the eyes of a murderer'. This was amended to 'eyes of mystique'. Major Meldrum, who was 'detested' in the typescript, is said to have been 'admired' in the published text. The name of Jack Davies, the man who had taken Lynne's virginity in Wales when she was below the age of consent, was changed to 'Rees Evans'. Fanny Blake agreed to check through the public records to find out whether the individuals who'd been defamed in the typescript were still alive. What emerges from this libel correspondence is Burgess's apparent concern that other people should be named and described accurately in his memoirs, even though much of what he has to say about himself is extravagantly distorted. The lawyers warned him that it would have been safer to say that a particular character was based on a real person rather than that he had merely been renamed in a novel. Burgess accepted this suggestion and revised his text accordingly. Yet 'renamed' was the word that he had originally wanted to use, and it reveals a good deal about how he viewed the equation between literature and life.

A second volume of autobiography, *You've Had Your Time*, was completed in 1988 and published in 1990. Although Burgess's health was beginning to fail, there was no falling-off in his industriousness at the typewriter as he claudicated towards his mid-seventies. In 1985 he and Liana had acquired a modern house with a nuclear shelter in its basement in Lugano, Switzerland, not far from the Italian border. This became their new centre of operations, and it was here that he completed two further novels, *Any Old Iron* (1989) and *Mozart and the Wolf Gang* (1991). He also translated and adapted Alexander Gribeyedov's Russian stage comedy *Woe Out of Wit* under a new title, *Chatsky (The Importance of Being Stupid)*, for the Almeida Theatre in London. The first production, directed by Jonathan Kent, was staged in March 1993.

When *A Mouthful of Air*, a revised and expanded edition of *Language Made Plain*, was published in 1992, Burgess appeared on *Start the Week* on BBC Radio 4 to promote it. The programme went out live from Broadcasting House in London. Melvyn Bragg was in the chair, and the other guests were Michael Palin, Harold Prince (director of the musical *Kiss of the Spiderwoman*), the journalist Rosie Boycott and the novelist Zoë Heller. The programme began with a round-table consideration of Madonna's illustrated book, *Sex*. Asked to comment on Madonna's status as a feminist icon, Burgess said: 'I would go back to the 1930s and say that we'd already reached the limit of sexual exploitation with Mae West, who saw that sex was fundamentally funny and was herself a kind of parody of a desirable object [. . .] It's a book for a sick age.' Casting around for a link to the next item, Bragg said: 'Your book is called *A Mouthful of Air*, Anthony Burgess. We see Madonna [in *Sex*] with a mouthful of turd.' As the other guests fell about laughing, Burgess muttered something mildly indecent but only half-audible about 'bilabial fricatives'.

He continued reviewing novels, dictionaries and literary biographies into his seventies, producing regular weekly pieces for the *Observer* and *Independent* (1989–1992), and occasional longer articles for the *Times Literary Supplement*, the *New York Times*, the *Corriere della Sera* and *Il Giornale*.* In an interview with Clare Boylan of the *Guardian*, Burgess announced that he had been

---

* Burgess's lecture on literary journalism, 'Confessions of the Hack Trade', was published in the *Observer* on 30 August 1992, pp. 41–2.

working intermittently since 1989 on a novel in verse.* This was *Byrne*, the last piece of fiction that he saw to completion. The narrative is composed in 600 stanzas of Byronic ottava rima, and the typescript indicates that the novel was finished on Ash Wednesday 1993, the day before his seventy-sixth birthday.

Burgess produced a number of other unpublished (and hitherto uncatalogued) literary and cinematic works during his last years in Switzerland and London. 'An Essay on Censorship' is a long poem in heroic couplets, composed as an immediate response to Ayatollah Khomeini's *fatwa* against the novelist Salman Rushdie on 14 February 1989. According to the typescript, Burgess completed his poem, whose verse-form and stately tone are borrowed from Alexander Pope's 'Essay on Man', a few weeks after the *fatwa*, on 10 April, when he was staying with his son at 8 King's Road in Twickenham.

'Eternal Life', a film adaptation of the French science fiction novel *La Vie éternelle* by Jacques Attali (1989), was completed in 1991.† He wrote a proposal for an unwritten non-fiction book, 'Modernism and Modern Man' (1992), which sets out his opinions on literary modernism in some detail; and that same year the Hollywood producer Dino de Laurentiis commissioned him to write a television version of 'Samson and Dalila'. Burgess's script, which draws heavily on Milton's dramatic poem *Samson Agonistes*, was judged to be too upmarket for American viewers.‡

---

* See Clare Boylan, 'While the Smoke Clouds Gather: Writers at Work', *Guardian*, 22 August 1991, p. 32.

† Jacques Attali, *La Vie éternelle: roman* (Paris: Fayard, 1989).

‡ Dino de Laurentiis wrote to Burgess on 21 August 1992: 'As you know, American network TV must answer to its commercial sponsors and to an audience which is much less sophisticated than the feature audience for which you are accustomed to writing. We're concerned that the present draft strays too far from what will be acceptable to the network [. . .] It's questionable how much interest the audience will have, for example, in the fine points of Hebrew law and theology. In addition, there are moments when Samson's extreme violence risks alienating the audience.' For Burgess on de Laurentiis ('He is pushing on with his filming of the whole Bible,

Death was much in his thoughts in the early 1990s, particularly since many of his friends and contemporaries (Graham Greene, Alberto Moravia, Lawrence Durrell, William Golding) were expiring. Attempting to make sense of death ('It's a good idea to take control of death while you're still alive,' he had said in an interview a decade earlier), he wrote a short piece of drama, 'The End of Things: Three Dialogues for Old Men', in April 1991. Three characters in their eighties, Aubrey, Nigel and William, meet for a series of lunches in a café on the rue Grimaldi in Monaco. All three are English expatriates. Their conversations take in death and the afterlife, beauty and truth, the nature of God and the abstract notions of good and evil. William, the central character, is an Augustinian lapsed Catholic, who complains (as Burgess had frequently done) about the vulgarity of the modern world and the corrosive power of television and youth culture. Nigel, though admitting God as the original cause of the Big Bang, tends towards a more or less rationalist position. He asks: 'Where was [God] at Auschwitz? Where was he when my poor mother screamed in terminal cancer?' Aubrey, a Pelagian, answers this by asserting the principle of free will: 'Man was free to create Auschwitz. It would have been wrong of God to stop him.' Burgess uses the voices of these three narrators to argue out large metaphysical questions. The dying William is given the last word in the dialogues: 'Montaigne taught the best religion – a humorous scepticism towards everything. With my bodily orifices sealed, my sins confessed and absolved, I hope to sink into my last sleep humorously sceptical.'

Burgess was diagnosed with lung cancer at the Sloane-Kettering Clinic in New York on 8 October 1992. The following day he had agreed to lecture on translation at the Cheltenham Festival of Literature. He began by telling his audience that he expected shortly to be translated himself. News of this illness was reported in the *Independent* by Kevin Jackson, who had directed the documentary

and he admits how much he likes being "the boss" '), see 'Takeover', *Listener*, 23 May 1963, p. 884.

Burgess at Seventy for the BBC in 1987.* Burgess had always maintained that he would come back to England to die, and with Liana he moved to a flat in London, just off Baker Street. This was 63 Bickenhall Mansions on Bickenhall Street, where, at the end of 1992, he resumed work on *Byrne*.

Even though he knew that he was dying, he continued to produce regular book reviews for the *Observer*, and the last of these were published on the three Sundays which followed his death. He gave his last interview, to Elvira Huelbes of *El Mundo*, Madrid, on 4 November 1993.† Burgess died a few minutes before midnight on Monday, 22 November 1993 at the Hospital of St John and Elizabeth in St John's Wood, London. He was seventy-six years old. At Liana's request, the news of his death was not announced by Leslie Gardner, his London literary agent (who had represented him since the early 1980s, and to whom he'd dedicated *The Devil's Mode*), until 25 November. Long obituaries appeared in the broadsheet newspapers the following day, and his death was reported on the front pages of (among others) *The Times*, the *Independent*, the *Guardian*, the *Daily Telegraph*, the *New York Times* and *Le Monde*. The anonymous obituarist in *The Times* described him as 'a powerful and mischievous novelist', 'a professional critic and polymath amateur *savant*' and 'a giant in his tattered humanity and his intolerable wrestle with words and meanings'.‡

Malcolm Bradbury's retrospective article on Burgess's fiction was published in the *Independent on Sunday* on 28 November. Bradbury claimed that Burgess was 'the great postmodern storehouse of British writing', 'an important experimentalist [. . .] an encyclopedic amasser'. The article identified six works as being

---

* Kevin Jackson, 'Traveller's Tales and Verbal Remedies', *Independent*, Weekend section, 17 October 1992, p. 28. See also Kevin Jackson, 'The Final Journey of a Working Writer', *Independent*, section 2, 29 November 1993, p. 19.
† Elvira Huelbes, 'The Last Words', reprinted in *Guardian*, section 2, 26 November 1993, p. 7.
‡ Anon., 'Anthony Burgess' (obituary), *The Times*, 26 November 1993, p. 23.

central to the Burgess canon: the Malayan trilogy, *A Clockwork Orange*, *Nothing Like the Sun*, *MF*, the Enderby novels and *Earthly Powers*. Bradbury concluded that these novels 'make a vast record of the second half of the 20th century, a collective pulling together of what a deeply engaged literary and linguistic mind might draw from what had already been written, what it was now time to write'.* Although most of the obituary notices took a favourable view of Burgess's energy and productivity, there were a few dissenting voices. The poet and biographer Andrew Motion wrote in the *Daily Telegraph*: 'I think his reputation has always been a rather uncertain one. This is partly because there's so much by him and no one reads it all and partly because, for all its brilliant technique, it is not always easy to see where the centre lies.'†

Where *does* the centre lie? Those who take an interest in Catholic fiction would argue that *The Worm and the Ring*, *Tremor of Intent*, *A Clockwork Orange* and *Earthly Powers* are novels which belong within the identifiably Catholic tradition of Graham Greene, Evelyn Waugh and David Lodge, although Burgess is more inclined than these other writers to ask hard questions about the conflict between his religious and national identities. Scholars of James Joyce prefer to play up Burgess's credentials as a modernist Anglo-Irish writer, and his critical commentaries on Joyce are still taken seriously by Joyceans. Other readers insist on the importance of the Malayan trilogy as a valuable documentary account of the last days of the British colonial presence in the East. Musicologists have argued the case for *Napoleon Symphony* as a bold fusion of orchestral music, poetry, parody and narrative prose. Freudians and structural anthropologists might be more inclined to agree with Burgess's own view that *MF* is his greatest work. Shakespeareans and Marlovians favour *Nothing Like the Sun* and *A Dead Man in*

---

* Malcolm Bradbury, 'Anthony Burgess: A Passion for Words', *Independent on Sunday*, 28 November 1993, p. 3.
† Quoted in David Holloway, 'Anthony Burgess, the Polymath, Dies at 76', *Daily Telegraph*, 26 November 1993, pp. 1–2.

Deptford; A. S. Byatt has written about her fondness for *Abba Abba*; William Boyd is passionate about Enderby and the two volumes of autobiography, which he describes as among the best novels that Burgess ever wrote.* Even from this brief survey of critical opinion, it is clear that his writing speaks to an unusual variety of readers, and for different reasons.

An appreciation of Burgess's full achievement must take in the large body of writing (and talking) that he did in areas other than the novel, including book reviews, cultural criticism, interviews, and his work for television, radio and film. He was one of the first literary writers who was also a television critic, performer and script-writer. He was also, of course, a great giver of interviews. His forays into the visual media are deeply connected to his more traditional literary activities, and many of his television and radio interviews offer useful ways of approaching the novels. Performing was an important aspect of Burgess's creativity, and theatre was, after all, in his blood. Audiences at literary festivals, the National Theatre and the Institute of Contemporary Arts were more than willing to pay to hear him hold forth on literary subjects. If they wished to be entertained, Burgess was always happy to give them what they wanted.

His reputation has been in a state of flux and uncertainty since 1993. *A Clockwork Orange* is a work which seems certain to outlive its author, but it would be a pity if Burgess were to be remembered for just one of his thirty-three novels. As yet there has been no collected edition of his works, and only a handful of his novels are currently available in Britain and America. The majority of his remarkable books are waiting to be reprinted and rediscovered by the generation of readers which has come to maturity since his death. He may yet have his time. The writer and broadcaster Melvyn Bragg puts the case like this: 'It's as if the ship has come home and on the dockside is this huge cargo. And nobody knows what to do

---

* William Boyd in *The Burgess Variations: Part One*, BBC 2, 26 December 1999.

with it. We're still in the process of sifting.'* One of the best tributes to Burgess's talent and achievement came from Auberon Waugh in a diary column published in November 1993:

> Always an admirer but never a close friend of Anthony Burgess, the novelist, musician and polymath, I found myself deeply saddened by news of his death. Although he was 76, I always thought of him as an unusually brilliant, *angst*-ridden young man who was destined to become a close friend as soon as he had resolved life's problems to the extent of settling in London and allowing those of us who loved him to burn incense at his feet [. . .] The prophetic element in *A Clockwork Orange* becomes more apparent with every month that passes. Now he is dead, perhaps we shall start paying him the attention he deserves.†

---

* Melvyn Bragg to author, 10 October 2001.
† Auberon Waugh, 'The Way of the World', *Daily Telegraph*, 27 November 1993, p. 19.

Acknowledgements

My largest debt of gratitude is to Peter Davidson and Jane Stevenson, without whose kindness, encouragement and good advice this book could not have been written. I would also like to acknowledge the support of the Department of English and Comparative Literary Studies at Warwick University, the School of English and Film at Aberdeen University, the Engelsk Institutt at the University of Trondheim, and the English Research Institute and Writing School at Manchester Metropolitan University.

Paul Goring, Peter Straus, Charlotte Greig and Derek Johns commented helpfully on a number of early drafts. I am particularly grateful to Kate Harvey for her tireless and perceptive editorial work as the manuscript approached completion.

Liana Burgess Wilson (the Contessa Pasi), Anthony Burgess's wife, Italian translator and executrix, has been a good friend to this book. Although this is not an official or authorized biography, Liana has very generously given me permission to consult publishers' archives. She has supported and encouraged my research since we began corresponding in 1998. Her unflagging commitment to scholarship has led to the creation of two major archives, the Anthony Burgess Center at the University of Angers and the International Anthony Burgess Foundation in Manchester.

Paul Boytinck, Burgess's bibliographer, sent me copies of Burgess's letters, as well as the six cubic feet of paper that he had accumulated in

the course of fifteen years of research. His annotated bibliography (New
York: Garland, 1985) was the key to this remarkable collection of
primary material. Everyone who studies Burgess owes him a large debt.

The following individuals have kindly submitted to interviews,
provided essential information, or sent copies of manuscripts, letters,
photographs, interviews, books, cassettes, compact discs and videos:
Jackie Adkins, Geoffrey Aggeler, Garrick Alder, Grace Allanson, Martin
Allitt (Banbury Public Library), Martin Amis, Bruce Arnold, Zainal
Arshad, David Ashbridge, Brian Bagnall, Sir Roger Bannister, Professor
Susan Bassnett, Dave Batchelor (BBC Radio Scotland), Reginald Bate,
Georges Belmont, David Benedictus, the late Ceridwen Berry (née
Looker), the late Martin Blinkhorn, Sonia Blinkhorn, Mark Bones,
Professor Brian Boyd, William Boyd, Baron Bragg of Wigton (Melvyn
Bragg), Mary Brian, Don Briddock, Professor Patricia Brückmann, Yves
Buelens, Christopher Burstall, Joan Bussingham, John Calder, Denis
Cartwright, Samuel Coale, Richard Cohen, John Coldstream, Shirley
Conran, Tess Crebbin, the late Arthur Crook, Martin Cropper, Molly
Currie, Patric Curwen, Brother Cyril (Xaverian Brothers, Manchester),
Peter Dance, Ron Daniels, Fr James Dwyer, Lucy Ellmann, Professor
Stephen Ellmann, the late D. J. Enright, Duncan Fallowell, Dr Akos
Farkas, the late Leslie Fiedler, Anne Field, Margery Fishenden, Professor
Ben Forkner, Simon Francis, Anthony Froggatt, Virginia Gallico, Leslie
Gardner (Artellus Ltd), Diana Gillon, Dr Nicholas Godlee, the late
Giles Gordon, Professor Peter Green, Dr Stella Halkyard (John Rylands
Library), Terry Hands, Jan Harlan (Estate of Stanley Kubrick), Oliver
Harris, Jeremy Hawthorn, Christopher Hawtree, the late Anna Hay-
craft ('Alice Thomas Ellis'), Greg Hayman, Arnold Hunt, Kevin Jack-
son, Howard Jacobson, Peter Janson-Smith, Evelyn Jones, Leslie Jones,
Jonathan Kent, Professor Sir Frank Kermode, Dr Jonathan Key, Francis
King, Wolfgang Krege, Christiane Kubrick, Professor Anne Laurence,
Lydia Levington, Michael J. Lewis, Nigel Lewis, Martin and Alison
Littleboy, Vincent LoBrutto, David Lodge, Professor Monty Losowsky,
Fr Thomas J. McCoog (Society of Jesus), Patrick McDonagh, Gus
MacDonald, Shiela McQuattie, Noël Makin, Carole Mansur, Douglas
Mason, Mrs Sheila Mather, Jonathan Meades, James Michie, Douglas
Milton, Julian Mitchell, Desmond Morris, the late Moyna Morris,
Blake Morrison, Valérie Neveu, Peter Nockles (John Rylands Library),

Richard Nutting, Charles Osborne, Edward Pagram, Gabriele Pantucci, Paul Phillips (Brown University), Peter Porter, Monica Powell, Felix Pryor, Dato' Yunus Raiss, Max Rambod, Michael Ratcliffe, Professor Christopher Ricks, Robert Robinson, Deborah Rogers (Rogers, Coleridge & White), Harvey Rose, Jean Rose, Dr Alan Roughley (International Anthony Burgess Foundation), George Sandulescu, Sir Jimmy Savile, Nicholas Shakespeare, Professor Ronald A. Sharp, Alison Shell, Carl Spadoni, Dame Muriel Spark, Sheila Spicer, Professor Thomas F. Staley, Dr Winifred Stevenson, John J. Stinson, Hugh Stoddart, Susie Stratford (née Kerridge), Professor Thomas A. Stumpf, Joyce Sweetman, the late Eric Swenson, David Thompson (BBC), Dr Laura Tosi (University of Venice), Ed Victor, the late Alexander Walker, Peter Walker, David Wallace, John Walton, the late Auberon Waugh, Anthony Whittome (Hutchinson), Graham Wilton, John Wilson, Vera Wood.

I am grateful for the assistance generously given by the following institutions and their staff: the International Anthony Burgess Foundation (Manchester); the Anthony Burgess Center (Angers); BBC Written Archives Centre; McMaster University Library, Hamilton, Ontario; Harry Ransom Humanities Research Center, University of Texas at Austin; William Heinemann Archive; Random House Archive; Columbia University Library, New York; Cambridge University Library; Warwick University Library; Brotherton Library (Leeds); Downside Abbey; University of East Anglia Library; Imperial War Museum; Leeds Central Library; Leicester University Library; National Library of Scotland; British Library National Sound Archive, Queen Mother Library (Aberdeen); John Rylands University Library (Manchester); Manchester Central Library.

I have received other kinds of help and encouragement from Ben Anderman, Sherry Ashworth, Jean Baxter, Alan Biswell, James Biswell, Valerie Biswell, Peter Blegvad, Lorna Bradbury, John Cassini, Wayne Clews, Jim Concannon, Ben Cottam, Jason Cowley, Andrew Crumey, Camilla Elworthy, Claire Ferguson, Giles Foden, Matthew Frost, Rick Greene, Flavio Gregori, David Haywood, Dominic Head, Jeremy Hoad, Kaarina Hollo, Martin Holmes, Mark Hutchings, Kath and Graham Hutton, Kathryne Jennings, Siobhàn Keenan, Mark Kilfoyle, Mark Le Fanu, Dominique Lemarchal, Andrew Losowsky, Steven Louth, David McCallum, Bernadette McConnell, Paul Magrs, David Mehegan, Rod

Mengham, Colin Midson, Matthew Mills, the late Dominic Montserrat, Debbie Moody, David Morley, Murrough O'Brien, Shane Murphy, Nigel Parke, Tom Payne, Richard Perrie, Mark Rawlinson, Simon Rees, David Robinson, Julian Robinson, Professor Michael Schmidt (FRSL), Dirk and Sabine Sinnewe, Nancy Sladek, Martin Stannard, Kate Summerscale, Libby Tempest, Neil Taylor, Matt Thorne, Russell Thorne, Euan Thorneycroft, Jeremy Treglown, Emmanuel Vernadakis, Andrew Weir, Graham Woodroffe and Professor Sue Zlosnik.

Bibliography

(1) Books by Anthony Burgess
(in order of publication)

Time for a Tiger (London: Heinemann, 1956)
The Enemy in the Blanket (London: Heinemann, 1958)
[As John Burgess Wilson] *English Literature: A Survey for Students* (London: Longman, 1958)
Beds in the East (London: Heinemann, 1959)
The Right to an Answer (London: Heinemann, 1960)
The Doctor Is Sick (London: Heinemann, 1960)
The Worm and the Ring (London: Heinemann, 1961)
[As Joseph Kell] *One Hand Clapping* (London: Peter Davies, 1961)
Devil of a State (London: Heinemann, 1961)
A Clockwork Orange (London: Heinemann, 1962)
The Wanting Seed (London: Heinemann, 1962)
[As Joseph Kell] *Inside Mr Enderby* (London: Heinemann, 1963)
Honey for the Bears (London: Heinemann, 1963)
The Novel To-Day (London: Longman/British Council/National Book League, 1963)
Nothing Like the Sun: A Story of Shakespeare's Love-Life (London: Heinemann, 1964)
The Eve of Saint Venus (London: Sidgwick & Jackson, 1964)
Language Made Plain (London: English Universities Press, 1964)

A Vision of Battlements (London: Sidgwick & Jackson, 1965)

Here Comes Everybody: An Introduction to James Joyce for the Ordinary Reader (London: Faber, 1965)

A Shorter Finnegans Wake (London: Faber, 1966)

Tremor of Intent (London: Heinemann, 1966)

Coaching Days of England (London: Paul Elek, 1966)

The Novel Now: A Student's Guide to Contemporary Fiction (London: Faber, 1967)

The Age of the Grand Tour (London: Paul Elek, 1967)

Enderby Outside (London: Heinemann, 1968)

Urgent Copy: Literary Studies (London: Jonathan Cape, 1968)

Shakespeare (London: Jonathan Cape, 1970)

MF (London: Jonathan Cape, 1971)

Joysprick: An Introduction to the Language of James Joyce (London: André Deutsch, 1973)

Obscenity and the Arts (Valletta: Malta Library Association, 1973)

The Clockwork Testament; or, Enderby's End (London: Hart-Davis, MacGibbon, 1974)

Napoleon Symphony (London: Jonathan Cape, 1974)

A Long Trip to Teatime (London: Dempsey & Squires, 1976)

Moses: A Narrative (London: Dempsey & Squires, 1976)

New York (Amsterdam: Time-Life International, 1976)

Abba Abba (London: Faber, 1977)

Beard's Roman Women (London: Hutchinson, 1977)

1985 (London: Hutchinson, 1978)

Ernest Hemingway and His World (London: Thames & Hudson, 1978)

Man of Nazareth (London: McGraw Hill, 1979)

The Land Where the Ice-Cream Grows (London: Ernest Benn, 1979)

They Wrote in English, 2 vols. (Milan: Tramontana, 1979)

Earthly Powers (London: Hutchinson, 1980)

The End of the World News: An Entertainment (London: Hutchinson, 1982)

This Man and Music (London: Hutchinson, 1982)

On Going to Bed (New York: Abbeville Press, 1982)

Enderby's Dark Lady; or, No End to Enderby (London: Hutchinson, 1984)

Ninety-Nine Novels: The Best in English Since 1939 (London: Allison & Busby, 1984)

The Kingdom of the Wicked (London: Hutchinson, 1985)

Flame into Being: The Life and Work of D. H. Lawrence (London: Heinemann, 1985)

The Pianoplayers (London: Hutchinson, 1986)

Homage to Qwert Yuiop: Selected Journalism 1978–1985 (London: Hutchinson, 1986)

Blooms of Dublin: A Musical Play Based on James Joyce's Ulysses (London: Hutchinson, 1986)

Little Wilson and Big God: Being the First Part of the Confessions of Anthony Burgess (London: Heinemann, 1987)

A Clockwork Orange: A Play with Music (London: Hutchinson, 1987)

Any Old Iron (London: Hutchinson, 1989)

The Devil's Mode and Other Stories (London: Hutchinson, 1989)

A Clockwork Orange 2004 (London: Arrow, 1990)

You've Had Your Time: Being the Second Part of the Confessions of Anthony Burgess (London: Heinemann, 1990)

Mozart and the Wolf Gang (London: Hutchinson, 1991)

A Mouthful of Air: Language and Languages, Especially English (London: Hutchinson, 1992)

A Dead Man in Deptford (London: Hutchinson, 1993)

Future Imperfect (London: Vintage, 1994)

Byrne: A Novel (London: Hutchinson, 1995)

A Clockwork Orange, with an introduction by Blake Morrison (London: Penguin Twentieth-Century Classics, 1996)

One Man's Chorus: The Uncollected Writings, ed. by Ben Forkner (New York: Carroll & Graf, 1998)

A Clockwork Orange: A Play with Music, (2nd edition, London: Methuen, 1998)

Revolutionary Sonnets and Other Poems, ed. by Kevin Jackson (Manchester: Carcanet, 2002)

(2) Translations by Anthony Burgess

Pelegri, Jean, *The Olive Trees of Justice*, trans. by Anthony Burgess and Lynne Wilson (London: Sidgwick & Jackson, 1962)

Saint-Pierre, Michel de, *The New Aristocrats*, trans. by Anthony Burgess and Lynne Wilson (London: Gollancz, 1962)

Servin, Jean, *The Man Who Robbed Poor Boxes* (London: Gollancz, 1965)

Rostand, Edmond, *Cyrano de Bergerac* (New York: Alfred A. Knopf, 1971)

Sophocles, *Oedipus the King*, ed. by Michael Langham (Minneapolis: University of Minnesota Press, 1972)

Oberon Old and New (London: Hutchinson, 1985)

Meilhac, Henri and Halévy, Ludovic, *Carmen: An Opera* (London: Hutchinson, 1986)

Griboyedov, Alexander Sergeyevich, *Chatsky (The Importance of Being Stupid): A Verse Comedy in Four Acts* (London: Almeida Theatre, 1993)

(3) Selected Articles and Reviews by Anthony Burgess

'After the Minotaur', *Yorkshire Post*, 22 March 1962, p. 4 (review of Mary Renault, *The Bull from the Sea*; John Wain, *Strike the Father Dead*; Clara Winston, *The Hours Together*; Norman R. Ford, *The Black, the Grey and the Gold*; Sheila Howarth, *Bogeyman's Plaything*)

'Angus Wilson's Best', *Yorkshire Post*, 5 October 1961, p. 4 (review of Angus Wilson, *The Old Men at the Zoo*; Richard Hughes, *The Fox in the Attic*; John O'Hara, *Sermons and Soda Water*; V. S. Naipaul, *A House for Mr Biswas*; Nicholas Monsarrat, *The White Rajah*; Julian Green, *Each in His Darkness*)

'Another Brave New World', *Yorkshire Post*, 6 April 1961, p. 4 (review of Diana and Meir Gillon, *The Unsleep*; Dorothy Whipple, *Wednesday and Other Stories*; Roald Dahl, *Someone Like You*; James Purdy, *Colour of Darkness*; Alec Waugh, *My Place in the Bazaar*; Lilian Halegua, *The Pearl Bastard*)

'Artless Chronicle of the Days of Youth', *Yorkshire Post*, 18 May 1961, p. 4 (review of Godfrey Smith, *The Business of Loving*; Pierre Sichel, *The Sapbucket Genius*; Louis de Wohl, *Lay Siege to Heaven*; Robert Shaw, *The Sun Doctor*)

'Bell Rings the Changes', *Yorkshire Post*, 23 August 1962, p. 3 (review of Lettice Cooper, *The Double Heart*; Edward Upward, *In the Thirties*; Thomas Hinde, *The Cage*; Robert Lund, *Daishi-San*)

'Best of the Spate: Looking Back at the Year's Fiction', *Yorkshire Post*, 28 December 1961, p. 3

'Black Agony', Yorkshire Post, 21 February 1963, p. 4 (review of James Baldwin, *Another Country*; George MacDonald, *Phantasies and Lilith*; Fletcher Knebel and Charles Bailey, *Seven Days in May*; Stefan Heym, *Shadows and Lights*; Jerome Weidman, *My Father Sits in the Dark*; Ralph Allen, *Ask the Name of the Lion*)

'Braine at the Top', *Yorkshire Post*, 4 October 1962, p. 5 (review of John Braine, *Life at the Top*)

'Brave and New', *Yorkshire Post*, 29 March 1962, p. 4 (review of Aldous Huxley, *Island*)

'Burgess on Kubrick and Clockwork', *Library Journal*, 1 May 1973, p. 1506

'Cain and Abel in Algeria', *Yorkshire Post*, 21 March 1963, p. 4 (review of Maurice Edelman, *The Fratricides*; Patrick Raymond, *A City of Scarlet and Gold*; Donald Jack, *Three Cheers for Me*; Alexander Cordell, *Race of the Tiger*; Ira J. Morris, *A Kingdom for a Song*; Angus Heriot, *The Island is Full of Strange Noises*)

'Celts in Conflict', *Yorkshire Post*, 13 July 1961, p. 4 (review of Bryher, *Ruan*; Jean Rikhoff, *Dear Ones All*; Herbert Lobsenz, *Vanguel Griffin*; Henry Treece, *Jason*)

'Character Called Isherwood', *Yorkshire Post*, 8 March 1962, p. 4 (review of Christopher Isherwood, *Down There on a Visit*; W. J. White, *The Devil You Know*; Camilla Carison, *You Are Mine*; John Harris, *The Spring of Malice*; Richard Matheson, *The Beardless Warriors*, Rachel Grieve, ed., *Best Doctor Stories*)

'Characters in Orbit', *Yorkshire Post*, 8 February 1962, p. 4 (review of Nathalie Sarraute, *The Planetarium*; Rayner Heppenstall, *The Connecting Door*; R. C. Sherriff, *The Wells of St Mary's*; Janet Frame, *Faces in the Water*; Claude Faux, *The Young Dogs*; Carlo Cassola, *Bebo's Girl*)

'Clockwork Marmalade', *Listener*, 17 February 1972, pp. 197–9

'The Corruption of the Exotic', *Listener*, 26 September 1963, pp. 465–7

'Crouchback Concluded', *Yorkshire Post*, 26 October 1961, p. 4
(review of Evelyn Waugh, *Unconditional Surrender*)

'Doctrine of the Diamond', *Observer*, 16 June 1991, p. 60 (review of
Octavio Paz, *Conjunctions and Disjunctions, Alternating Current*;
Octavio Paz, *Marcel Duchamp: Appearance Stripped Bare*)

'Essence and Appearance', *Yorkshire Post*, 25 January 1962, p. 4
(review of Storm Jameson, *The Road from the Monument*; Thomas
Hinde, *A Place Like Home*; Robert Holles, *The Siege of Battersea*;
Nigel Balchin, *Seen Dimly Before Dawn*; Arthur Roth, *The Shame
of Our Wounds*)

'First Citizen of Athens', *Yorkshire Post*, 7 February 1963, p. 4 (review
of Rex Warner, *Pericles the Athenian*; Alfred Grossman, *Many
Slippery Errors*; John Updike, *Pigeon Feathers*; William Butler, *The
House at Akiya*; Fausta Clalente, *The Levantines*; George Andrzey-
evski, *The Gates of Paradise*)

'Forger's Faith', *Yorkshire Post*, 20 September 1962, p. 4 (review of
William Gaddis, *The Recognitions*; Ian Brook, *The Black List*;
Frederic Raphael, *The Trouble with England*; Catherine Ross, *The
Colours of the Night*)

'From Angels to Angelique', *Yorkshire Post*, 24 August 1961, p. 4
(review of Richard Condon, *Some Angry Angel*; Laura Del-Rivo,
The Furnished Room; Junichiro Tanizaki, *The Key*; Benjamin
Siegel, *A Kind of Justice*; Sergeanne Golon, *Angelique and the
Sultan*)

'Gay Outsider in an Insider's Job', *Yorkshire Post*, 26 January 1961,
p. 4 (review of William Cooper, *Scenes from Married Life*; William
Faulkner, *The Mansion*; Zoë Oldenbourg, *Destiny of Fire*; Romain
Gary, *Nothing Important Ever Dies*)

'Gerald Kersh at His Peak', *Yorkshire Post*, 29 June 1961, p. 4 (review
of Gerald Kersh, *The Implacable Hunter*; John Steinbeck, *The
Winter of Our Discontent*; Muriel Spark, *Voices at Play*; Robert
Lait, *The Africans*)

'Goodbye to Berlin and Farewell to Arms', *Observer*, 6 May 1990,
p. 61 (review of Ian McEwan, *The Innocent*)

'Graham Greene', *Daily Telegraph*, 4 April 1991, p. 21

'Graham Greene as Monsieur Vert', *Tablet*, 15 March 1975,
pp. 259–60

'Great Expectations', Observer, 28 March 1993, Beginnings section, p. 4 (on A Vision of Battlements)

'Hatred Afloat', Yorkshire Post, 1 November 1962, p. 4 (review of Katherine Anne Porter, Ship of Fools; Ruth Prawer Jhabvala, Get Ready for Battle; Herman Wouk, Youngblood Hawke)

'Heady World of Lowry', Yorkshire Post, 3 May 1962, p. 4 (review of Malcolm Lowry, Hear Us O Lord from Heaven Thy Dwelling Place; Malcolm Lowry, Under the Volcano; Doris Lessing, The Golden Notebook; John Updike, The Same Door; Bertrand Mather, Through the Mill; Richard Mason, The Fever Tree)

'I Remember Grossmama', Yorkshire Post, 18 April 1963, p. 4 (review of Niccolò Tucci, Before My Time; Sloan Wilson, Georgie Winthrop; Glendon Swarthout, Welcome to Thebes; Jon Cleary, Forests of the Night)

'Idylls and Ideals', Yorkshire Post, 30 August 1962, p. 4 (review of Phyllis Bottome, The Goal)

'In the H. G. Wells Tradition', Yorkshire Post, 20 April 1961, p. 4 (review of Edward Hyams, All We Possess; Stanley Middleton, A Serious Woman; Pierre Boule, For a Noble Cause; Romain Gary, The Talent Scout; Michael Campbell, Across the Water; J. I. M. Stewart, The Man Who Won the Pools; Max Wilk, Don't Raise the Bridge (Lower the River); Irving Wallace, The Chapman Report)

'Iris Murdoch's Latest', Yorkshire Post, 15 June 1961, p. 4 (review of Iris Murdoch, A Severed Head; Alan Paton, Debbie Go Home; Elizabeth Mavor, The Temple of Flora; James Barlow, Term of Trial; Peter de Vries, Through the Fields of Clover)

'Juice from a Clockwork Orange', Rolling Stone, 8 June 1972, pp. 52–3

'La Noia – And Jealousy', Yorkshire Post, 30 November 1961, p. 6 (review of Alberto Moravia, The Empty Canvas; John Bratby, Breakfast and Elevenses; Herbert Russcol and Margalit Banai, Villa Vardi; Angela Thirkell and C. A. Lejeune, Three Score and Ten; Bertolt Brecht, Tales from the Calendar)

'Light Gravity', Yorkshire Post, 26 July 1962, p. 4 (review of Pamela Hansford Johnson, An Error of Judgement; Hortense Calisher, False Entry; Edgar Mittelholzer, The Wounded and the Worried; Roger Lloyd, The Troubling of the City)

'Lively World of the Dead', Yorkshire Post, 16 November 1961, p. 4

(review of Jerzy Peterkiewicz, *The Quick and the Dead*; Flann O'Brien, *The Hard Life*; Marcel Rouff, *The Passionate Epicure*; Wilder Penfield, *The Torch*; Richard Gordon, *Doctor on Toast*; Roger Falla, *The Sisters of Emergency Ward 10*)

'Love, Shove and the Yobbish Glottal Stop', *Observer*, 17 November 1991, p. 64 (review of George L. Campbell, ed., *Compendium of the World's Languages*)

'The Madhouse and the Couch', *Yorkshire Post*, 10 August 1961, p. 4 (review of Teo Savory, *The Single Secret*; Rosalie Packard, *The Plastic Smile*; Elio Vittorini, *Women on the Road*; John Cheever, *Some People, Places and Things . . .* ; Alexander Fedoroff, *The Side of the Angels*)

'The Magic of Place', *Yorkshire Post*, 16 August 1962, p. 4 (review of Elspeth Huxley, *The Mottled Lizard*; Rupert Croft-Cooke, *The Glittering Pastures*; Mrs Robert Henrey, *Spring in a Soho Street*)

'The Miracle of Mice and Metal Wafers', *Observer*, 21 June 1992, p. 59 (review of *The Oxford English Dictionary on Compact Disc*)

'More Comedians', *Spectator*, 21 April 1967, p. 454 (review of Graham Greene, *May We Borrow Your Husband?*)

'The Muse Steps In', *Yorkshire Post*, 2 November 1961, p. 4 (review of Philip Toynbee, *Pantaloon, or The Valediction*; Eric Linklater, *Roll of Honour*; William Sansom, *The Last Hours of Sandra Lee*; Muriel Spark, *The Prime of Miss Jean Brodie*)

'The Music of Time's Finale', *Yorkshire Post*, 28 June 1962, p. 4 (review of Anthony Powell, *The Kindly Ones*; Joseph Heller, *Catch-22*; Vernon Scannell, *The Dividing Night*; Gusztav Rab, *A Room in Budapest*)

'Nabokov Masquerade', *Yorkshire Post*, 15 November 1962, p. 4 (review of Vladimir Nabokov, *Pale Fire*; Paul Gallico, *Coronation*; Bernard Thompson, *O Tell Me Pretty Maiden*; Marguerite Duras, *Ten-Thirty on a Summer Night*; C. Dawson Butler, *Negative Evidence*; Alexandre Dumas, *The Flight to Varennes*)

'Nasty Middle Ages', *Yorkshire Post*, 24 January 1963, p. 4 (review of Zoë Oldenbourg, *Cities of the Flesh*; Harold Robbins, *The Carpetbaggers*; Barnaby Conrad, *Dangerfield*; Mochtar Lubis, *Twilight in Djakarta*; Norman Thomas, *Ask at the Unicorn*)

'New Fiction', *Listener*, 3 February 1966, p. 181 (review of Graham Greene, *The Comedians*)

'The New Novels: Reviewed by Anthony Burgess', *Yorkshire Post*, 12 January 1961, p. 4 (review of Grace Metalious, *The Tight White Collar*; Mary Ellen Chase, *The Lovely Ambition*; Michel del Castillo, *The Death of Tristan*; Stuart Cloete, *The Fiercest Heart*; Richard Vaughan, *There is a River*; Jonathan Wade, *Back to Life*)

'New Year Signposts', *Yorkshire Post*, 11 January 1962, p. 4 (review of Adrian Mitchell, *If You See Me Comin'*; Errol Braithwaite, *An Affair of Men*; Allan Campbell McLean, *The Islander*)

'New-Type Pagliaccio', *Yorkshire Post*, 10 January 1963, p. 4 (review of Emyr Humphreys, *The Gift*; Antony Trew, *Two Hours to Darkness*; Jim Hunter, *Sally Cray*; Jennifer Dawson, *Fowler's Snare*; Sybille Bedford, *A Favourite of the Gods*)

'The Novelist's Agony', *Yorkshire Post*, 23 November 1961, p. 7 (review of Graham Greene, *In Search of a Character*; Thomas Mann, *The Genesis of a Novel*)

'Off the Path', *Yorkshire Post*, 31 May 1962, p. 4 (review of Paul Ableman, *As Near As I Can Get*; Rosemary Manning, *The Chinese Garden*; Claude Simon, *The Flanders Road*; Stuart Lauder, *Winger's Landfall*; Peter de Vries, *The Blood of the Lamb*)

'Our Universe as Seen from the Desk Top', *Observer*, 7 October 1990, p. 44 (review of David Crystal, ed., *The Cambridge Encyclopedia*; Ian Crofton, ed., *The Guinness Encyclopedia*)

'Poetry for a Tiny Room', *Yorkshire Post*, 16 May 1963, p. 4 (review of Joseph Kell, *Inside Mr Enderby*; Bernard Malamud, *The Natural*; Teo Savory, *A Penny for the Guy*; B. S. Johnson, *Travelling People*; Ralph Dulin, *The Unconquered Sun*; Daphne du Maurier, *The Glass-Blowers*; Evelyn Ames, *Daughter of the House*; Wallace Stegner, *Wolf Willow*)

'Polish and Pin-Stripes', *Yorkshire Post*, 14 June 1962, p. 4 (review of Peter Green, *Habeas Corpus and Other Stories*)

'Politics in the Novels of Graham Greene', *Journal of Contemporary History*, 2 (April 1967), 93–99

'Porridge His Downfall', *Yorkshire Post*, 4 May 1961, p. 4 (review of Roy Bradford, *Excelsior*; Balachandra Rajan, *Too Long in the West*; Storm Jameson, *Last Score*; Frank Rooney, *McGinnis Speaks*;

Agnar Mykle, *The Song of the Red Ruby*; Ann Gardiner, *The Minister's Wife*; H. E. Bates, *Now Sleeps the Crimson*; *The Esquire Reader*; Ronald Firbank, *The Complete Ronald Firbank*)

'Rain in Springtime', *Yorkshire Post*, 5 April 1962, p. 4 (review of Brian Glanville, *Diamond*; Merle Miller, *A Gay and Melancholy Sound*; David Chagall, *The Century God Slept*; Cothburn O'Neal, *The Gods of Our Time*; Bernard Malamud, *A New Life*; Mikhail Zoshchenko, *Scenes from the Bath-House*; Sean O'Faolain, *I Remember! I Remember!*; Arthur Quiller-Couch and Daphne du Maurier, *Castle Dor*)

'The Real Holmes', *Yorkshire Post*, 27 September 1962, p. 4 (review of William S. Baring-Gould, *Sherlock Holmes: A Biography*)

'Religion and the Arts: The Manicheans', *Times Literary Supplement*, 3 March 1966, pp. 153–4

'A Rich Quarry for the Novelist', *Yorkshire Post*, 23 March 1961, p. 4 (review of Nikos Kazantzakis, *The Last Temptation*; Mika Waltair, *The Secret of the Kingdom*; Vladimir Nabokov, *Laughter in the Dark*; Wilfred Sheed, *A Middle Class Education*; Isobel English, *Four Voices*)

'Round the World in Five Novels', *Yorkshire Post*, 23 February 1961, p. 4 (review of William Styron, *Set This House on Fire*; Jim Kirkwood, *There Must Be a Pony!*; William Ash, *The Lotus in the Sky*; Katharine Sim, *The Jungle Ends*; Robert Poole, *London E.1*)

'Samovars From Seattle to Shanghai', *Observer*, 4 March 1990, p. 43 (review of Michael Glenny and Norman Stone, eds, *The Other Russia*)

'A Seeker of Pain', *Daily Telegraph*, 8 April 1989, Weekend section, p. 13 (review of Norman Sherry, *The Life of Graham Greene*, vol. 1)

'A Severed Rose-Head', *Yorkshire Post*, 14 June 1962, p. 4 (review of Iris Murdoch, *An Unofficial Rose*; Roger Vailland, *Turn of the Wheel*; Peter van Greenaway, *The Crucified City*)

'Shattered Dreams', *Yorkshire Post*, 19 April 1962, p. 4 (review of Paul Scott, *The Birds of Paradise*; J. R. Salamanca, *Lilith*; Richard G. Stern, *Europe*; P. H. Newby, *The Barbary Light*; Ronald Marsh, *The Quarry*)

'The Sinner at the Heart of the Matter', *Daily Telegraph*, 4 April 1991, p. 13

'Some Adventures in Hell', *Yorkshire Post*, 22 February 1962, p. 4 (review of Elias Canetti, *Auto-Da-Fé*; Ruth Rehmann, *Saturday to Monday*; Angus Heriot, *Four-Part Fugue*; John and Esther Wagner, *The Gift of Rome*; Kathrin Perutz, *The Garden*; John Williams, *On the Way Out*)

'Spring's Fruits in Autumn', *Yorkshire Post*, 19 October 1961, p. 4 (review of John Dos Passos, *Midcentury*; Anita Loos, *No Mother to Guide Her*; Alan Sillitoe, *The Key to the Door*; V. S. Pritchett, *When My Girl Comes Home*; John Barth, *The Sot-Weed Factor*; Louis Aragon, *Holy Week*; A. J. Cronin, *The Judas Tree*)

'Stone Turned to Flesh and Blood', *Yorkshire Post*, 17 May 1962, p. 4 (review of Olivia Manning, *The Spoilt City*; David Beaty, *The Wind off the Sea*; James Hanley, *Say Nothing*; Louis Battye, *Cornwall Road*)

'Stop the Clock on Violence', *Observer*, 21 March 1993, p. 25 (on *A Clockwork Orange*)

'Talking of Michelangelo', *Yorkshire Post*, 27 July 1961, p. 4 (review of Irving Stone, *The Agony and the Ecstasy*; Maurice Edelman, *The Minister*; Mitchell Wilson, *Meeting at a Far Meridian*; Ernest Raymond, *Mr Olim*; Richard Pape, *And So Ends the World*)

'Tension in Sicily', *Yorkshire Post*, 9 August 1962, p. 4 (review of Federico de Roberto, *The Viceroys*; Carlo Castellaneta, *A Journey with Father*; Nantas Salvalaggio, *The Moustache*; Diana Raymond, *The Climb*)

'Those Voices Again', *Yorkshire Post*, 21 September 1961, p. 4 (review of Ivy Compton-Burnett, *The Mighty and Their Fall*; John Updike, *Rabbit, Run*; James Aldridge, *The Last Exile*; Nevil Shute, *Steven Morris*; Giovanni Arpino, *The Novice*; Ferreira de Castro, *The Mission*)

'Through a Curtain', *Yorkshire Post*, 29 November 1962, p. 4 (review of Slawomir Mrozek, *The Elephant*; Jean Ross, *The Godfathers*; Rachel Trickett, *A Changing Place*; Naomi Jacob, *Great Black Oxen*)

'Time, Space and River', *Yorkshire Post*, 13 December 1962, p. 4 (review of Lawrence Durrell, *The Alexandria Quartet*; Anthony Powell, *A Dance to the Music of Time*; R. H. Mottram, *To Hell with Crabb Robinson*)

'Travels with Graham Greene', *Saturday Review*, January 1981,
  pp. 64–5 (review of Graham Greene, *Ways of Escape*)
'Tribute to a City', *Yorkshire Post*, 6 September 1962, p. 4 (review of
  Harrison E. Salisbury, *The Northern Palmyra Affair*; Friedrich
  Dürrenmatt, *The Quarry*; Diane Giguerre, *Innocence*)
'Twin Problems', *Yorkshire Post*, 12 July 1962, p. 4 (review of Dorothy
  Baker, *Cassandra at the Wedding*; Theodora Keogh, *The Other
  Girl*; Susan Yorke, *The Agency House*; Ronald Hardy, *Act of
  Destruction*; Desmond Meiring, *The Man with No Shadow*)
'Ustinov Portrait of a Nazi', *Yorkshire Post*, 9 March 1961, p. 4 (review
  of Peter Ustinov, *The Loser*; Frederic Prokosch, *A Ballad of Love*;
  Marie-Claire Blais, *Mad Shadows*; Joan O'Donovan, *The Middle
  Tree*; John Hersey, *The Child Buyer*)
'Various Handfuls', *Yorkshire Post*, 14 December 1961, p. 4 (review of
  Peter de Polnay, *No Empty Hands*; Helen Foley, *A Handful of
  Time*; Françoise Sagan, *Wonderful Clouds*; H. E. Bates, *The Day of
  the Tortoise*)
'Wars and Wedded Love', *Yorkshire Post*, 7 September 1961, p. 4
  (review of Jean Larteguy, *The Centurions*; Vernon Scannell, *The
  Face of the Enemy*; David Hughes, *The Horsehair Sofa*; Christine
  Brooke-Rose, *The Middlemen*; Colin Wilson, *Adrift in Soho*)
'The Wearing of the Greene', *Guardian*, 11 November 1966, p. 8
  (review of John Atkins, *Graham Greene: A Biographical and Liter-
  ary Study*)
'Welfare State Satire', *Yorkshire Post*, 1 June 1961, p. 4 (review of Jack
  Lindsay, *All on the Never-Never*; Frederic Raphael, *A Wild Sur-
  mise*; Daphne Fielding, *The Adonis Garden*; Edita Morris, *Echo in
  Asia*; Susan Sherman, *Give Me Myself*; Richard Bissell, *Goodbye
  Ava*; Stan Barstow, *The Desperadoes and Other Stories*)
'Where Dead Men Meet, on Lips of Living Men', *Observer*, 10 Febru-
  ary 1991, p. 55 (review of Peter Raby, *Samuel Butler: A Biography*)
'Works of Protest', *Yorkshire Post*, 9 February 1961, p. 4 (review of
  André Schwerz-Bert, *The Last of the Just*; Witold Gombrowicz,
  Ferdydurke; Mongo Betty Muller, *King Lazarus*; Budd Schulberg,
  What Makes Sammy Run?; John P. Marquand, *Wickford Point*;
  Erskine Caldwell, *Kneel to the Rising Sun*)
'Yankee Giant', *Yorkshire Post*, 18 October 1962, p. 4 (review of

Hiram Haydn, *The Hands of Esau*, Sid Chaplain, *The Watchers and the Watched*; Paul Hyde Bonner, *Ambassador Extraordinary*; Ellen Marsh, *Unarmed in Paradise*)

(4) Interviews, Profiles and Obituaries

Adler, Dick, 'Inside Mr Burgess', *Sunday Times Magazine*, 2 April 1967, pp. 47–50

Anon., 'Anthony Burgess' (obituary), *The Times*, 26 November 1993, p. 23

Anon., 'Anthony Burgess' (obituary), *Daily Telegraph*, 26 November 1993, p. 25

Bradbury, Malcolm, 'Anthony Burgess: A Passion for Words', *Independent on Sunday*, 28 November 1993, p. 3

Churchill, Thomas, 'An Interview with Anthony Burgess', *Malahat Review*, 17 (January 1971), pp. 103–27

Clare, Anthony, 'Unearthly Powers', *Listener*, 28 July 1988, pp. 10–12 (partial transcript of *In the Psychiatrist's Chair* inteview from BBC Radio 4)

Coale, Samuel, 'An Interview with Anthony Burgess', *Modern Fiction Studies*, 27 (1981), pp. 103–27

Coe, Jonathan, 'Any Old Burgess', *Guardian*, 24 February 1989, pp. 29–30

Cullinan, John, 'The Art of Fiction XLVIII: Anthony Burgess', *Paris Review*, 56 (Spring 1973), pp. 118–63; reprinted in *Writers at Work: The Paris Review Interviews: Fourth Series*, ed. by George Plimpton (London: Secker & Warburg, 1976), pp. 323–58

Dix, Carol, 'Anthony Burgess: Interviewed by Carol Dix', *Transatlantic Review*, 42/43 (1972), pp. 183–91

Dix, Carol, 'The Mugging Machine', *Guardian*, 1 January 1972, p. 8

Enright, D. J., 'A Mind Too Riotous for Calculation', *Guardian*, section 2, 26 November 1993, p. 7

Grove, Valerie, 'This Old Man Comes Ranting Home', *The Times*, 6 March 1992, Life and Times section, p. 1

Harthill, Rosemary, 'Anthony Burgess: Unearthly Powers' in *Writers*

Revealed, ed. by Rosemary Harthill (London: BBC Books, 1989), pp. 11–24

Hawtree, Christopher, 'Between Eternities', *Guardian*, 26 November 1993, section 2, pp. 6–7

Hemesath, James B., 'Anthony Burgess: Interviewed by James B. Hemesath', *Transatlantic Review*, nos 55/56 (1976), pp. 96–102

Lewis, Roger, 'Anthony Burgess' (obituary), *Independent*, 26 November 1993, p. 16

Mewshaw, Michael, 'Do I Owe You Something?', *Granta*, no. 75 (Autumn 2001), pp. 29–40

Robinson, Robert, 'On Being a Lancashire Catholic', *Listener*, 30 September 1976, pp. 397–9

Sage, Lorna, 'In Full Spate: The Fertility and Generosity of Anthony Burgess', *Times Literary Supplement*, 17 December 1993, p. 26

Sage, Lorna, 'Still Angry After All These Years', *Observer*, 23 February 1992, p. 51

(5) Books about Anthony Burgess

Aggeler, Geoffrey, *Anthony Burgess: The Artist as Novelist* (Alabama: University of Alabama Press, 1979)

Aggeler, Geoffrey (ed.), *Critical Essays on Anthony Burgess* (Boston, MA: G. K. Hall, 1986)

Bloom, Harold (ed.), *Anthony Burgess*, Modern Critical Views series (New York: Chelsea House, 1987)

Boytinck, Paul, *Anthony Burgess: An Annotated Bibliography and Reference Guide* (New York: Garland, 1985)

Brewer, Jeutone, *Anthony Burgess: A Bibliography* (Metuchen, NJ: Scarecrow Press, 1980)

Coale, Samuel, *Anthony Burgess*, Modern Literature series (New York: Frederick Ungar, 1981)

DeVitis, A. A., *Anthony Burgess*, Twayne's English Authors series (New York: Twayne, 1972)

Dix, Carol M., *Anthony Burgess*, ed. by Ian Scott-Kilvert, Writers and Their Work series (Harlow: Longman, 1971)

Farkas, A. I., *Will's Son and Jake's Peer: Anthony Burgess's Joycean Negotiations* (Budapest: Akadémikiai Kiadó, 2003)

Ghosh-Schellhorn, Martina, *Anthony Burgess: A Study in Character* (Frankfurt am Main: Lang, 1986)

Gregori, Flavio (ed.), *Singin' in the Brain: Il Mondo Distopico di Anthony Burgess* (Turin: Lindau, 2004)

Lewis, Roger, *Anthony Burgess* (London: Faber, 2002)

Mathews, Richard, *The Clockwork Universe of Anthony Burgess*, Popular Writers of Today series (San Bernardino, CA: Borgo Press, 1978)

Morris, Robert K., *The Consolations of Ambiguity: An Essay on the Novels of Anthony Burgess* (Columbia: University of Missouri Press, 1971)

Stinson, John J., *Anthony Burgess Revisited*, Twayne's English Authors series (Boston, MA: Twayne, 1991)

Vernadakis, Emmanuel and Woodroffe, Graham (eds), *Portraits of the Artist in A Clockwork Orange* (Angers: Presses de l'Université d'Angers, 2004)

(6) Journal Articles and Newspaper Reviews

Amis, Kingsley, 'Orwell and Beyond', *Observer*, 1 October 1978, p. 34

Amis, Martin, 'A Stoked-Up 1976', *New York Times Book Review*, 19 November 1978, pp. 3, 60, 62

Bergonzi, Bernard, 'A Poet's Life', *Hudson Review*, vol. 21, no. 4 (Winter 1968–9), pp. 764–8

Bergonzi, Bernard, 'Fiction and Fabulation', *Hudson Review*, vol. 25, no. 2 (Summer 1972), pp. 355–7

Biswell, Andrew, 'Against Utopias', *Times Literary Supplement*, 17 February 1995, p. 21

Biswell, Andrew, 'The Closing Sequence', *Times Literary Supplement*, 29 September 1995, p. 26

Canby, Vincent, '*Orange*: Disorienting But Human Comedy', *New York Times*, 9 January 1972, section 2, p. 1

Cornwell, John, 'The Confessions of Graham Greene', *Observer*, 24 September 1989, pp. 33–4

Daniel, George, 'New Novels', *Spectator*, 26 October 1956, p. 582

Daniels, Don, 'A Clockwork Orange', *Sight and Sound*, vol. 42, no. 1 (Winter 1972–3), pp. 44–6

Grigson, Geoffrey, 'Insatiable Liking?', *Listener*, 7 November 1968, pp. 618–19

Jackson, Kevin, 'Real Horrorshow: A Short Lexicon of Nadsat', *Sight and Sound*, vol. 9, no. 9 (September 1999), pp. 24–7

Kael, Pauline, 'Stanley Strangelove', *New Yorker*, 1 January 1972, pp. 50–53

Kermode, Frank, 'Poetry and Borborygms', *Listener*, 6 June 1968, pp. 735–6

King, Francis, 'Life and Times', *Spectator*, 25 October 1980, p. 22

Kubrick, Stanley, 'Now Kubrick Fights Back', *New York Times*, 27 February 1972, Arts and Leisure section, pp. 1, 11

Laski, Marghanita, 'Morality with Heart', *Saturday Review*, 28 January 1961, p. 17

Lewis, Roger, 'John Wilson Went to Malaya as a Humble Schoolmaster. He Came Back as the Bohemian Novelist Anthony Burgess. So Was It Heat, Lust or Drink That Changed Him?', *Mail on Sunday*, 12 September 1999, pp. 58–9.

McDowell, Malcolm, 'Malcolm McDowell Objects, Too', *New York Times*, 27 February 1972, Arts and Leisure section, p. 11

Richardson, Maurice, 'New Novels', *New Statesman*, 3 December 1960, pp. 888–90

Ricks, Christopher, 'Horror Show', *New York Review of Books*, 6 April 1972, pp. 28–9

Ricks, Christopher, 'Rude Forerunner', *New Statesman*, 24 September 1965, pp. 444–5

Ricks, Christopher, 'The Epicene', *New Statesman*, 5 April 1963, p. 496

Sage, Lorna, 'A Roman Holiday', *Observer*, 6 February 1977, p. 31

Steiner, George, 'Books: Scroll & Keys', *New Yorker*, 13 April 1981, pp. 156–62

Strick, Philip, 'Kubrick's Horrorshow', *Sight and Sound*, vol. 41, no. 1 (Winter 1971–2), pp. 44–6

Strick, Philip and Houston, Penelope, 'Interview with Stanley Kubrick', *Sight and Sound*, vol. 41, no. 2 (Winter 1971–2), pp. 62–6

Tennant, Emma, 'Josephine Wheels', *Listener*, 24 October 1974, p. 552

Treglown, Jeremy, 'The Knowledge of Good and Evil', *Times Literary Supplement*, 24 October 1980, p. 1189

Waugh, Auberon, 'Seat of Pleasure', *Spectator*, 24 May 1968, p. 745

Wheldon, Huw, 'Television and the Arts', *Listener*, 18 February 1965, pp. 257–60

Willett, John, 'Burgess's New Novel', *Listener*, 9 June 1966, p. 849

Wood, Michael, 'A Dream of Clockwork Oranges', *New Society*, 6 June 1968, pp. 842–3

(7) Other Published Sources

Aldgate, Anthony, *Censorship and the Permissive Society: British Cinema and Theatre 1955–1965* (Oxford: Clarendon Press, 1995)

Amis, Kingsley, *The Amis Collection: Selected Non-Fiction 1954–1990*, ed. by John McDermott (London: Hutchinson, 1990)

Amis, Kingsley, *The Letters of Kingsley Amis*, ed. by Zachary Leader (London: HarperCollins, 2000)

Amis, Martin, *Visiting Mrs Nabokov and Other Excursions* (London: Jonathan Cape, 1993)

Amis, Martin, *The War Against Cliché: Essays and Reviews, 1971–2000* (London: Jonathan Cape, 2001)

Barclay, William, *Jesus of Nazareth* (London: Collins, 1977)

Baxter, John, *Stanley Kubrick: A Biography* (London: HarperCollins, 1997)

Bergonzi, Bernard, *Wartime and Aftermath: English Literature and its Background 1939–1960* (Oxford: Oxford University Press, 1993)

Bloom, Harold, *Shakespeare: The Invention of the Human* (London: Fourth Estate, 1999)

Bloom, Harold, *The Western Canon: The Books and School of the Ages* (London: Macmillan, 1995)

Bockris, Victor, *The Life and Death of Andy Warhol* (London: Fourth Estate, 1998)

Bradbury, Malcolm, *No, Not Bloomsbury* (London: André Deutsch, 1987)

Catalogue du fonds Burgess (Angers: Bibliothèque Universitaire d'Angers, 1999)

Ciment, Michel, *Kubrick*, trans. by Gilbert Adair (London: Collins, 1983)

Day-Lewis, Cecil, *Word Over All* (London: Jonathan Cape, 1943)

Duncan, Paul, *Stanley Kubrick: Visual Poet 1928–1999* (London: Taschen, 2003)

Eliot, T. S., *Collected Poems 1909–1962* (London: Faber, 1963)

Enright, D. J., *Man is an Onion: Reviews and Essays* (London: Chatto & Windus, 1972)

Enright, D. J., *A Mania for Sentences* (London: Chatto & Windus, 1983)

Fallowell, Duncan, *Twentieth-Century Characters* (London: Vintage, 1994)

French, Karl (ed.), *Screen Violence* (London: Bloomsbury, 1996)

Greene, Graham, *Ways of Escape* (London: Bodley Head, 1980)

Greene, Graham, *Yours, Etc.: Letters to the Press, 1945–89*, ed. by Christopher Hawtree (London: Reinhardt/Viking, 1989)

Gross, John (ed.), *The Modern Movement: A TLS Companion* (London: Harvill, 1992)

Hare, Steve (ed.), *Penguin Portrait: Allen Lane and the Penguin Editors 1935–1970* (London: Penguin, 1995)

Herr, Michael, *Kubrick* (London: Picador, 2000)

Hewison, Robert, *Culture and Consensus: England, Art and Politics Since 1940* (London: Methuen, 1995)

Jackson, Kevin, *Invisible Forms: A Guide to Literary Curiosities* (London: Picador, 1999)

Jackson, Kevin, *Letters of Introduction* (Manchester: Carcanet, 2004)

Jacobs, Eric, *Kingsley Amis: A Biography* (London: Hodder & Stoughton, 1995)

James, Clive, *The Crystal Bucket: Television Criticism from the Observer 1976–79* (London: Jonathan Cape, 1981)

James, Clive, *The Metropolitan Critic: Non-Fiction 1968–1973*, (2nd edition, London: Jonathan Cape, 1994)

Kagan, Norman, *The Cinema of Stanley Kubrick*, (2nd edition, Oxford: Roundhouse, 1997)

Keneally, Thomas, *Moses the Lawgiver* (London: Collins, 1975)

Kermode, Frank, *Essays on Fiction 1971–82* (London: Routledge & Kegan Paul, 1983)

Kermode, Frank, *Modern Essays* (London: Fontana, 1971)

Kermode, Frank, *Not Entitled: A Memoir* (London: HarperCollins, 1996)

Kubrick, Christiane, *Stanley Kubrick: A Life in Pictures* (London: Little, Brown, 2002)

Larkin, Philip, *Selected Letters of Philip Larkin*, ed. by Anthony Thwaite (London: Faber, 1992)

LoBrutto, Vincent, *Stanley Kubrick: A Biography* (London: Faber, 1998)

Lodge, David, *The Practice of Writing: Essays, Lectures, Reviews and a Diary* (London: Secker & Warburg, 1996)

Lodge, David, *Working With Structuralism: Essays and Reviews on Nineteenth- and Twentieth-Century Literature* (London: Routledge & Kegan Paul, 1981)

McCormack, Thomas, *Afterwords: Novelists on Their Novels* (New York: Harper & Row, 1969)

Maguin, Jean-Marie and Angela, *William Shakespeare* (Paris: Fayard, 1996)

Mitchell, Kirk, *A. D.: Anno Domini* (Rutherford, NJ: Berkley, 1985)

Nelson, Thomas Allen, *Kubrick: Inside a Film Artist's Maze*, (2nd edition, Bloomington: Indiana University Press, 2000)

Nicholl, Charles, *The Reckoning: The Murder of Christopher Marlowe* (London: Jonathan Cape, 1992)

Partridge, Eric (ed.), *A Dictionary of Slang and Unconventional English, Colloquialisms and Catch-Phrases, Solecisms and Catachreses, Nicknames, Vulgarisms and Such Americanisms as Have Been Naturalized*, (4th edition, London: Routledge & Kegan Paul, 1951)

Raphael, Frederick, *Eyes Wide Open: A Memoir of Stanley Kubrick and 'Eyes Wide Shut'* (London: Orion, 1999)

Robinson, Robert, *Skip All That: Memoirs* (London: Century, 1996)

Ricks, Christopher, *Reviewery* (London: Penguin, 2003)

Sanders, Andrew, *The Short Oxford History of English Literature*, (2nd edition, Oxford: Oxford University Press, 2000)

Shell, Alison, *Catholicism, Controversy and the English Literary Imagination, 1558–1660* (Cambridge: Cambridge University Press, 1999)

Shennan, Margaret, *Out in the Midday Sun: The British in Malaya 1880–1960* (London: John Murray, 2000)

Sherry, Norman, *The Life of Graham Greene*, vol. 3 (London: Jonathan Cape, 2004)

Sinfield, Alan, (ed.), *Society and Literature 1945–1970* (London: Methuen, 1983)

St John, John, *William Heinemann: A Century of Publishing 1890–1990* (London: Heinemann, 1990)

Stevenson, Randall, *The Last of England?*, The Oxford English Literary History, vol. 12 (Oxford: Oxford University Press, 2004)

Trevelyan, John, *What the Censor Saw* (London: Michael Joseph, 1973)

Vidal, Gore, *United States: Essays 1952–1992* (London: André Deutsch, 1993)

Walker, Alexander, *Stanley Kubrick, Director* (London: Weidenfeld & Nicolson, 1999)

Walsh, James, *Forty Martyrs of England and Wales* (London: Catholic Truth Society, 1997)

Index

Dulin, Ralph, 274
Dunkeley, Donald ('Lofty'), 158–9, 172
Dunn, John, 211–12
Dunn, Nell, 313
Dunstan, Bernard, 357
Durrell, Lawrence, 307, 389
Dwyer, Agnes, *see* Tollitt
Dwyer, George, 46, 276–7, 332
Dwyer, Madge, 11
Dwyer, Margaret, (Maggie, née Byrne, stepmother), *see* Wilson
Dwyer family, 88, 198

Eagleton, Terry, 295
Edelman, Maurice, 359
Eden, Anthony, 224
Electron, the, 27
Elek, Paul, 312
Eliot, T. S.: Burgess's musical settings, 41, 77; Burgess's reviews of plays, 68–9; Burgess's teaching, 162; Burgess's translation, 163; *The Criterion* magazine, 47; influence on Burgess, 41–2, 60, 113, 124, 142; Memorial Lectures, 41n, 135n; *Murder in the Cathedral*, 69, 120–1; *Poems 1909–1935*, 41; politics, 55; quoted, 284; Riding comparison, 67; *The Sacred Wood*, 50; *Sweeney Agonistes*, 41, 69, 128; *The Waste Land*, 60, 113, 135n, 163
Ellis, A. E., 188
Ellman, Richard, 300
Empson, William, 48, 58
Encyclopædia Britannica, 270
English National Opera, 385
Enright, D. J., 164n, 284, 292
Etchingham: 'Applegarth' house, 229, 231, 281, 330; Burgess's life in, 263–5, 283, 309, 320; village, 229–31, 232–3
Evans, Dwye, 194, 229

Evening Standard, London, 359
Ewart, Gavin, 91

Faber, 314, 317, 318
Face to Face, 77–8, 211
Fenellosa, Ernest, 178
Fennell, J. L. I., 237
Fiedler, Leslie, 283
Fielding, Henry, 372
Fishenden, Margery, 201–2, 213
Fitton, James, 81
Flaubert, Gustave, 60, 385
Flecker, James Elroy, 54
Fleming, Ian, 311
Ford, Ford Madox, 229
Foreman, Harold, 25
Forkner, Ben, 340
France, Anatole, 375
Franco, Francisco, 55, 94, 109
Fraser, George, 91
Frere, Alexander, 270
Freud, Sigmund, 325, 345, 384
Froggatt, Anthony, 116, 139
Fry, Christopher, 127–8

Gallico, Paul, 188
Gant, Roland, 187, 188, 189, 230n, 269
Gardner, Leslie, 390
Garioch, Robert, 367
Garrett, John, 258
Gaunt, Denis Crowther, 51
Gibraltar Chronicle, 99
Gilbert, W. S., 128
Gillon, Diana and Meir, 237, 256, 257, 258, 271, 300
Ginsberg, Allen, 300, 301
Giornale, Il, 387
Girodias, Maurice, 301
G. K.'s Weekly, 93
Godwin, Lance (Walter Blent), 59
Goering, Hermann, 94
Golding, Louis, 20

Mozart and the Wolf Gang, 387; 'Murder to Music', 339; *Napoleon Symphony*, 79, 83–4, 261, 345, 365, 370, 391; *1985*, 375; *Nothing Like the Sun*, 39, 49, 85, 284–93, 306, 345, 391; *Oberon* libretto, 385; *Oedipus the King* translation, 345–6; *One Hand Clapping*, 224–6, 227, 228, 260–1, 272; *One Man's Chorus*, 32n, 340; 'A Pair of Gloves', 322; *The Pianoplayers*, 9, 14, 18–19, 298, 324, 385; preface to Lawrence, 343–4; *The Right to an Answer*, 199–201, 224, 227, 228, 234, 260, 261, 276; 'Samson and Dalila' script, 388; *Schreber* script, 371; *The Sexual Habits of the English Middle Class* script, 371; *Shakespeare*, 295; *Silence, Exile and Cunning* (TV documentary), 32n, 36; 'Somebody's Got to Pay the Rent', 339; *The Spy Who Loved Me* script, 371; 'The Sword', 279; *They Wrote in English*, 196; *Time for a Tiger*, 142, 159, 161, 162, 164, 166, 167–8, 172, 176, 188–9, 305, 338, 391; *Tremor of Intent*, 35n, 39, 42, 74, 114, 233, 261, 304, 306, 311, 337, 375, 391; *Urgent Copy*, 32n, 42, 297, 315–16, 374; *A Vision of Battlements*, 79, 88, 96, 98, 101–7, 115, 132, 147n, 188, 281, 341, 374–5; *The Wanting Seed*, 105, 110, 266–8, 339, 375; *Will!*, 49, 230; *Will and Testament*, 295–6; *The Worm and the Ring*, 132–7, 141, 144–5, 226, 234, 268–71, 375, 391; *You've Had Your Time*, 87, 141n, 239, 246, 260, 304, 321n, 329, 386–7, 392

Wilson, Joseph (b. 1800), 2
Wilson, Joseph (Joe, father): birth, 2; Burgess's portrayal of, 13–14; career,

2–3, 6, 12, 13–14, 18, 22; children, 2, 3–4, 6; death, 5, 64–5, 322, 326–7; death of first wife, 6, 9; health, 41; marriage to Maggie Dwyer, 11–12; piano-playing and interest in music, 3, 13–15, 18; son's career, 40–1; son's education, 14–15, 40, 46
Wilson, Joseph Samuel, 2
Wilson, Liliana (Liana Johnson, née Macellari, second wife, also known as Liana Burgess): affair with Burgess, 308–9; appearance, 308; background, 307; Burgess's death, 390; career, 307, 308, 365; description of, 379; first marriage, 307; first meeting with Burgess, 307–8; life in Malta, 338–9, 342; life in Monaco, 367–8, 378–9; marriage to Burgess, 4, 331–2; move to London, 390; move to Lugano, 387; move to Malta, 333, 335–6; move to Monaco, 365–6; son, 308, 331–3
Wilson, Llewela (Lynne, first wife): affair with Dylan Thomas, 91–2; affairs, 93–4, 108, 117, 118, 159, 167, 212, 216, 374, 386; appearance, 70–1, 202, 277, 281, 327; assaulted by American soldiers, 107–8, 207, 360; birth, 69; Burgess's career, 199, 202; Burgess's illness, 205–6, 210–12, 218; Burgess's music, 278, 283; Burgess's *nom de plume*, 187; Burgess's relationship with Liana, 309; career, 88, 138; death, 4, 327, 329–30; descriptions of, 120, 124, 176, 183, 202, 232, 277–8, 281–3, 338; drinking, 108–9, 124, 176, 184–5, 212, 232, 265–6; education, 70, 71, 72, 76, 87–8, 280; engagement, 76; family background, 69–72, 145, 323; father's death, 306; finances, 145–6, 306–7, 325, 333; first meeting with Burgess, 72–3; funeral,